M000318225

# THE ASCETI

This book is about the ascetic self in the scriptural religions of Christianity, Buddhism and Hinduism. The author claims that asceticism can be understood as the internalisation of tradition, the shaping of the narrative of a life in accordance with the narrative of tradition that might be seen as the performance of the memory of tradition. Such a performance contains an ambiguity or distance between the general intention to eradicate the will, or in some sense to erase the self, and the affirmation of will in ascetic performance such as weakening the body through fasting. Asceticism must therefore be seen in the context of ritual. The book also offers a new paradigm for comparative religion more generally, one that avoids the inadequate choices of examining religions through overarching categories on the one hand and the abandoning of any comparative endeavour that focuses purely on area-specific study on the other.

GAVIN FLOOD is Professor of Religion at the University of Stirling, and the author of *An Introduction to Hinduism* (Cambridge University Press, 1996).

# THE ASCETIC SELF

*Subjectivity, Memory and Tradition*

GAVIN FLOOD

CAMBRIDGE
UNIVERSITY PRESS

PUBLISHED BY THE PRESS SYNDICATE OF THE UNIVERSITY OF CAMBRIDGE
The Pitt Building, Trumpington Street, Cambridge, United Kingdom

CAMBRIDGE UNIVERSITY PRESS
The Edinburgh Building, Cambridge, CB2 2RU, UK
40 West 20th Street, New York, NY 10011–4211, USA
477 Williamstown Road, Port Melbourne, VIC 3207, Australia
Ruiz de Alarcón 13, 28014 Madrid, Spain
Dock House, The Waterfront, Cape Town 8001, South Africa

http://www.cambridge.org



First published 2004

Printed in the United Kingdom at the University Press, Cambridge

*Typeface* Adobe Garamond 11/12.5 pt. *System* LaTeX 2ε [TB]

*A catalogue record for this book is available from the British Library*

*Library of Congress Cataloguing in Publication data*
Flood, Gavin D., 1954–
The ascetic self: subjectivity, memory, and tradition / Gavin Flood.
p. cm.
Includes bibliographical references (p. ) and index.
ISBN 0 521 84338 3 – ISBN 0 521 60401 X (pb.)
1. Asceticism – Comparative studies. 2. Asceticism – Psychology. I. Title.
BL625.F57 2004
204′.47 – dc22 2004045732

ISBN 0 521 84338 3 hardback
ISBN 0 521 60401 X paperback

*For Luke*

Die Welt ist tief,
Und tiefer als der Tag gedacht.

*Nietzsche* Also Sprach Zarathustra *III, 'Das andere Tanzlied', 3.*

# *Contents*

# *Preface*

The question of the ascetic self that this book seeks to address arose from a range of questions about the nature of self and experience, about what is shared and not shared between cultures, and about the nature and possibility of comparative religion in a postmodern world. The renunciation and transformation of desire seem so fundamental to traditions founded on texts (oral and written) that I began to think about the links between text and renunciation, time and renunciation, and the ideals that make men and women live a life of austerity. It seems to me that central to this religious austerity is a textual tradition that claims that through what we might call a reversal of our orientation towards desire and the senses, a higher good and greater happiness can be achieved. Such claims would seem to be instantiated in the histories of the scriptural traditions and so go against the grain of contemporary, Western sensibilities as to be worth exploring. While asceticism has been a central theme of scholarship – one thinks especially of the sociology of Max Weber and his students – rather than simply develop the ramifications of this work, I wanted to explore the subjectivity of the ascetic self and examine subjective meaning rather than objective system.

But the subjective meaning of asceticism can be understood and located within traditions only in so far as the ascetic self is constructed in accordance with their goals and practices. Claiming that constraints within scriptural traditions form the ascetic self is not simply to give an account of a cultural construction but is also to give an account of the discovery or opening out of an interior world. My general claim is that asceticism can be understood as the internalisation of tradition, the shaping of the narrative of a life in accordance with the narrative of tradition that might be seen as the performance of the memory of tradition. Such a performance contains an ambiguity or distance between the general intention to eradicate the will or in some sense to erase the self, and expression, the affirmation of will in ascetic performance such as weakening the body through fasting. I think that this general structure holds true in the three scriptural traditions I examine of Christianity, Hinduism and Buddhism.

There has been quite a degree of interest in the nature of asceticism in recent years, and this book is intended as a contribution to that literature. Of particular importance has been Geoffrey Harpham's *The Ascetic Imperative* and, in a very different way, the edited volume *Asceticism* by Vincent L. Wimbush and Richard Valantasis that has made important inroads into the subject. Valantasis in particular has developed a theory of the social function of asceticism and the place of power in ascetic formation. Many other scholars from a variety of perspectives, especially sociological ones, have added to this growing body of work; the names of Ilana Silbur on sociological comparison and Ariel Glucklich on a physiologically grounded comparison immediately come to mind; in Christianity the work of Peter Brown, Caroline Bynum, Elizabeth Clark, Susan Harvey, Amy Hollywood, Lutz Kaelber, Leif Vaage and many others; in Hinduism Walter Kaelber and Patrick Olivelle; and in Buddhism Steve Collins, Michael Carrithers, Richard Gombrich and Johannes Bronkhorst.

Many, if not all, of these share an assumption that the comparative endeavour is worth-while. I share that assumption and this book is an exercise in comparative religion, expressing a belief that comparisons are not odious but necessary for human understanding. It also expresses a belief that goes against the grain of some contemporary thinking, that there are common features of human being that cut across historical and cultural divides – an insight expressed in earlier centuries as a belief in a common human nature. Perhaps we can encapsulate the issue in the following question. When a teenage boy in the West enjoys Burton Watson's English translation of the poetry of Han Shan, is the Chinese T'ang poet speaking to him or does he simply see his own reflection? I would guess both. When speaking about the self, we are speaking about something highly amorphous (even though selves are always embodied) and while there are semantic equivalents in most, if not all, languages, it is clearly not the case that the identical meaning is conveyed. Cultural histories of the self form complex trajectories, but that Han Shan *can* speak to the teenage boy – even though filtered through translation and recontextualisation – implies that selves can speak, be heard and be received across cultures and histories.

A number of preliminary questions will arise in the reader's mind not only concerning the viability of such a project, but also about the reasons for undertaking it and the author's own situation with regard to it, the place from where I speak. One way of putting the question might be of which community of readers am I, the writer, an index? Because of the particularity of my own narrative, I would place myself at the confluence of a number of intellectual traditions, especially the phenomenological and hermeneutic. While I approach the 'phenomenology of religion' with monitory caution as well as with explicit critique, it does lay claim to be a tradition of thought with its 'canon' of texts that includes the names Van der Leeuw, Wach, Eliade and Smart. We could argue about the boundaries of this 'canon' and which texts could be included or excluded, but the point is that religious studies can claim to be a discipline partly because of the historical density of this literature that claims to be distinct from Christian theology. But although this is the school in which I was formed, I do not inherit it uncritically, and the present text can be seen as an implicit corrective reading to much of the work that has 'compared religions', often in an egregious way.

This corrective reading locates me secondly within a hermeneutic tradition that is open to postcritical developments within the academy. The book might therefore be open to the criticism that it is implicitly theological in taking seriously the writings of ascetics and about asceticism, and in taking seriously the claim about what the ascetic self hopes to become. In the sense that I do intend to take very seriously ascetic claims about the nature of the self and world, then the book is certainly implicitly theological, although it is not theology because it does not stand directly within a theological tradition of discourse. I do not explore the *theological* implications of asceticism, although this is a very rich theme, especially in relation to contemporary concerns about 'the gift'. Could asceticism be understood not only as voluntary discipline but as acceptance of suffering seen as divine gift? (Simone Weil's thought is very close to this.) But I do take seriously ascetic wisdom, and the dialogical interaction of the texts and traditions in the following pages can generate the energy necessary for the further exploration of the truth claims of ascetic traditions.

That religious studies should not go beyond description to explore the conditions for the production of certain kinds of cultural knowledge or even to explore, as David Ford has argued, the truth claims of traditions, is to place an arbitrary boundary around the discipline, although it is not the intention of the book to offer any adjudication on matters of ultimate truth. Religious truth, in the view of this writer, must be understood in tradition-specific ways (although this is not to deny the idea of common constraint), and there is no place outside of tradition from which to judge the broader architechtonics of ascetic truth claims.

The book will be in two sections, 'The Ascetic Self in Text and History' and 'Theorising the Ascetic Self'. It will comprise nine chapters. The first chapter sets the parameters and discusses in more detail the issues raised here. Chapter 2 launches into the account of the ascetic self with a modern example in Simone Weil. From her we look back to examples from the history of South Asia in Chapters 3, 4 and 5. Again looking back from Weil, we next focus on asceticism in Orthodox Christianity and move on to Western Christianity to complete the section. Following the discussion of particular traditions and examples in the first part of the book, 'Theorising the Ascetic Self' comprises Chapters 8 and 9, which locate the ascetic self in ritual and in modernity respectively.

The bibliography comprises abbreviations and references found in the notes. Sanskrit source material is listed in the bibliography. References to ancient and medieval theologians are to the PG and PL and I cite full bibliographical information about translations in the bibliography.

*Christmas, 2003* LITTLE THETFORD

# *Acknowledgements*

First and foremost I should like to thank my colleague and friend Professor Oliver Davies with whom I discussed the book from its early foundations to its final expression. He has encouraged me at times when I doubted the task, guided my reading in Christianity and made many valuable suggestions concerning the text itself. Without our conversations the book would undoubtedly have been so much the poorer. Another source of inspiration has been Professor Peter Ochs of the University of Virginia whom I should like to thank for so carefully going through the manuscript and suggesting ways I could improve it and seek for greater clarity. His semiotic approach to the study of religion and the development of scriptural reasoning (largely down to his efforts) has been a significant influence. Dr Eugene Rogers, also at the University of Virginia, very helpfully suggested bibliographical items and discussed with me some of the issues in the study of Christian asceticism. Dr Emmanouela Grypeou's comments on the text were most helpful, as were discussions with Professor Robert Wicken of UVA. The book has greatly benefited from conversations with Professor John Bowker and Dr Margaret Bowker. I have always come away from their house and great hospitality brimming with ideas and with a deep sense of the seriousness (and, one might add, humour) that the inquiry into religion demands. Our honorary professor, Professor Richard Roberts, and my other colleagues at Stirling University Alison Jasper, Jeremy Carrette and Tim Fitzgerald made useful comments and provided a collegial atmosphere in which to work, graciously putting up with my inadvertent neglect of administrative duties. I should also like to thank Rev. Dr John Jillions for his inspiration and for the way he brings together the life of tradition, thinking and contemporary living. Kevin Taylor at Cambridge University Press encouraged the project all the way (particularly on long runs from Cambridge to Ely) and Kate Brett took up the project in its latter stages. I should also like to thank the anonymous Cambridge University Press readers for their extremely useful reports.

CHAPTER I

# *Setting the parameters*

> The subjective thinker is a dialectician oriented to the existential; he has the intellectual passion to hold firm the qualitative disjunction.
>
> Søren Kierkegaard[1]

> Tradition is the living faith of the dead, traditionalism is the dead faith of the living.
>
> Jaroslav Pelikan[2]

This book is devoted to the possibility of understanding the ascetic self in a time when most of us no longer find a place within ascetic traditions and in which asceticism is treated with suspicion. Ascetic discourse and practice have become alien in a world where religion is de-cosmologised and where the idea of deferring the gratification of desire for some other good is accepted only with hesitation. While there are what seem to be ascetical dimensions to all of our lives, and what appear to be ascetic practices take place by other names in the form of varied bodily regimes, from dietary disciplines for the purposes of health or beauty to physical training for athletic competitions, there is no ideology of repeated abstinence in secular life.[3] The residues of ascetic practice in our culture have become mere technique without the accompaniment of tradition and an articulated idea of transcendence. And while all too many suffer deprivation driven by necessity, this cannot be classed as ascetic pursuit, for asceticism is voluntary. In the cultures of proliferation and excess that mark the modern Western world, in the decentred exuberance of urban life, there is little place for abstinence, self-contraction, containment, and the purification of desire that have been part of the ascetic life of thousands of men and women throughout the centuries. These men and women, in religious orders or practising alone, have all been part of a tradition and linguistic community that legitimated their practice. All have performed the memory of tradition, and it is this memory of tradition that marks asceticism off from mere abstinence or abstinence for a secular pursuit, such as health. Asceticism has normative relevance for religion and some political practice. It is this sense of the ascetic self in relation to tradition and the linguistic community in which she or he is embedded that I wish to explore.

The central contention of the book can be stated quite simply: that the ascetic self is performed. It performs the memory of tradition and it performs the ambiguity of the self. By this I mean that asceticism is always set within, or in some cases in reaction to, a religious tradition, within a shared memory that both looks back to an origin and looks forward to a future goal. But asceticism only flourishes in certain kinds of tradition that might be called 'cosmological'; in traditions where cosmology is lost, asceticism as performance becomes eroded or becomes a purely internalised performance. This will be to defend a fairly robust notion of tradition – and *religious* tradition in particular – and to see asceticism as a quintessentially religious act. There are clearly analogues of asceticism in the contemporary, secularised world, but these are not asceticism, because they do not perform the memory of tradition. Some have tried to explain asceticism in terms of contemporary medical categories, particularly female asceticism in terms of dietary conditions such as anorexia nervosa, but this is to misunderstand the nature of asceticism as acting out the memory of tradition, whether or not these ascetics were actually subject to that condition.

Asceticism within tradition is performed by a self; not a disembodied self, but a historical, language-bearing, gendered person with their own name and story. Asceticism entails subjectivity, it entails a self *who* renounces, but a self that is always expressed through the structures of tradition. Rather than being subjected to individual desire as the person's predominant driving force, asceticism advocates the subjection of oneself to tradition, to a master, in order to undergo a transformation. The ascetic submits her life to a form that transforms it, to a training that changes a person's orientation from the fulfilment of desire to a narrative greater than the self. The ascetic self shapes the narrative of her life to the narrative of tradition. There is a deep ambiguity here. On the one hand, asceticism entails the assertion of the individual will, a kind of purified intentionality, yet on the other it wishes to wholly form itself in the shape of tradition and in terms of the tradition's goals. The goals of ascetic traditions are so often the eradication of subjectivity through the self becoming wholly passive (as in Christianity), through the self realising its non-agency (as in Advaita Vedānta) or through the self understanding its non-essential nature (as in Buddhism). Yet the eradication of subjectivity in ascetic pursuit entails the assertion of subjectivity in voluntary acts of will. Asceticism, then, is the performance of this ambiguity, an ambiguity that is absolutely central to subjectivity. Indeed, we might say that subjectivity comes into view more sharply in the distance between goal and means, between ascetic intention (such as the self's passivity) and expression (such as the weakening of the body through will). In some ways, the ascetic self is an ironic self. This conception of subjectivity as the performance of ambiguity is, of course, rooted in Kierkegaard, but a Kierkegaardian conception fused with tradition. I will say more about this presently.

It is my contention that this fairly simple claim holds up in traditions of asceticism in at least the three religions of Christianity, Buddhism and that amalgam of traditions we call Hinduism. The book therefore makes a claim for some degree of universalism. I am hesitant about the word 'universalism', as it evokes ideas of the grand narrative of Enlightenment reason that has fallen under such criticism in the past thirty years, or of a deeply problematic perennial philosophy that makes claims about a 'universal spiritual truth' and does not give credence to the particularity of tradition and the location of voice. On the other hand, there are equally deep problems about extreme forms of relativism and the implication of closed cultural worlds. Apart from the initial problem that all claims are relative except that claim itself, extreme forms of relativism are not viable. In an obvious sense, we can learn one another's languages, we recognise joy, fear and disgust in all other human beings, and we are all subject to bodily constraint and the need for food, warmth, shelter and company. Above all, we are embodied and are subject to death. This is not to deny, of course, that there is great diversity in the way cultures respond to and deal with human need and the way languages construct our worldviews. Culture, particularly the structures of language, clearly affects the ways we think.[4] But all human beings share fundamental needs and environmental responses.

The book would therefore wish to make a claim about a commonality with regard to the ascetic self, while at the same time wishing not to detract from the richness of tradition and historical depths that have formed events, cultures and people into their particularity. The ascetic self is formed by tradition and internalises tradition and its goals, yet this process is itself shared among traditions. There are methodological implications for this general position that I shall examine presently, but I would wish to claim that this is an attempt to write a kind of comparative religion that is post-foundational or postcritical, and that respects diverse and divergent voices. In what remains of the introduction, I state the general argument about the ascetic self in terms of performance, the memory of tradition, the ambiguity of the self and subjectivity, and conclude with some consideration of the problem of universalism and method.

## ASCETICISM AS PERFORMANCE

What is meant by asceticism? If, as Freud claimed, culture is founded on the renunciation of the instincts, then in one sense all culture is ascetical. In Harpham's excellent study, this is to see the ascetic impulse as pre-ideological.[5] But while this is an important idea, it is too wide a base from which to begin a focussed discussion: we need to delineate a narrower band of cultural practices and ideas to which the term 'asceticism' points. This is not so much a matter of offering arbitrary definitions, but rather a need to develop a strategy of containment within which to discuss a range of cultural meanings. Turning to its Greek roots, the term *askesis* denoted the training of athletes and with early Christianity came to denote the practices of 'spiritual athletes' who trained in morality. In the New Testament *askeo* or 'to do one's best' occurs as referring to the 'voluntary discipline of the self to benefit the soul'.[6] By the early centuries of the Christian era in the ancient world, the term had come to refer to the practice of celibacy and later to more extreme physical disciplines.

To begin, we might say that asceticism is the reversal of the flow of the body, which is also an attempt to reverse the flow of time. Asceticism refers to a range of habits or bodily regimes designed to restrict or reverse the instinctual impulses of the body and to an ideology that maintains that in so doing a greater good or happiness can be achieved. These goals are not simply abstract ideologies or justifications for the power of institutions, they are the future orientations and narrative identities of people: their desire to break through the constraints of time and body, their desire to achieve a goal, the goal of human perfection in this or in some other world. The reversal of the flow of the body is performed in ascetic practice. To reverse the flow of the body is both to perform the memory of tradition and to perform the ambiguity of the self. With few exceptions (although there are some) the ascetic does not intend to die, which would be the closure of the ambiguity, but rather to perform that ambiguity through the reversal of the flow of the body, as we shall see.

Asceticism is a way in which a tradition patterns the body or imposes order upon it, in the sense that the body is subjected to an institutional power by which it is inscribed, but the ascetic self also transcends that institutional power. The ascetic appropriates the tradition to his or her self-narrative for a range of reasons. At one level, this is to achieve a tradition-specific goal of sainthood, liberation, or whatever, through bodily restriction. There will be other reasons too that any one person maps a tradition onto herself and appropriates a cultural meaning, located in the narrative of a particular life and probably in unconscious motivation.

A key feature of the reversal of the body's orientation is the renunciation of food and sexual practice along with the attempted eradication of sexual desire. Not only this: in propounding a life of simplicity and minimal worldly interaction, ascetic cultures often renounce aesthetic pleasures as well, such as music and dancing, although we must not forget the importance of music and beauty in the liturgies of the monastic cultures of Europe. The performance of asceticism can also incorporate mental disciplines, including the cultivation of humility and detachment. Wimbush and Valantasis observe that in a conference on asceticism across cultures, 'familiar patterns of behaviour' began to emerge, such as 'fasting, social withdrawal, [and] continual prayer', along with similar metaphors of 'marriage to divinity, a distrust of body, valuation of the intellect', and correlative theological formulations such as 'ascent to the divine, avoidance of evil, [and] regeneration'.[7] These patterns might themselves be founded on more fundamental imperatives. Collins identifies a cultural logic of asceticism in a South Asian context that connects reproduction with ageing and death and so an escape from ageing and death with a denial of reproduction. He writes:

> . . . from among the many and various responses to physicality, one first connects the body and reproduction to the inevitability of ageing and death. If what is brought into being by physical means is always subject to decay and death, and if it is not possible to imagine and aspire to a kind of well-being which will not decay and die, then that state must be non-physical, or at least even if in some sense physical then asexual, because not physically reproductive.[8]

Although writing about South Asia, this denial of reproduction specified by Collins is a feature common to ascetic ideologies. The denial of reproduction and of sexuality is the reversal of the flow of the body. This reversal describes the central performance of the ascetic self, typically in an ascetic community and always within a tradition. But the reversal of the flow of the body can be performed by those living married lives, generally men, where the ideal of sexual renunciation still remains or is redefined, as in the tantric Hindu context where sexuality is used as a form of asceticism.

The ascetic self performs asceticism through tradition-specific, bodily regimes or habits and in obedience to ascetic discipline. Through an act of will the ascetic self takes on the forms prescribed for it by tradition and generates long-term patterns of behaviour, intended, ironically, to subvert that will. These cultural habits are the hallmarks of asceticism and can be understood as bodily performance. The work of Bourdieu has highlighted the importance of the *habitus* in social formation, where *habitus* refers to dispositions to act and react in certain ways[9] and to submit to collective rhythms.[10] The shaping of the body in a particular way, the conformity to a discipline and conformity of the body to a predetermined, cultural form is conformity to external power structures, such as the power of the state, the church and the tradition. In this sense, power is inscribed upon the body through the *habitus*. The ascetic conforms to the discipline of the tradition, shapes his or her body into particular cultural forms over time, and thereby appropriates the tradition. This appropriation of tradition is a form of remembrance, the memory of tradition performed through the body, and is also the vehicle for change or transformation. Both the male and female body become the re-enactment or performance of the tradition, and through that performance occurs the transformation of the self. The Hindu ascetic holding his arm aloft is conforming to tradition and appropriating a cultural form as an act of will – a will that, in the end, seeks its own destruction.

The bodily disciplines of asceticism not only produce conformity to the power of tradition, they can also express resistance; adapting the body to the form of tradition might be regarded as a means of transcending it. Simone Weil, as we shall see, made her body conform to the regularities of the workplace, not as an act of compliant docility but as an act of freedom. Through accepting the inscription of external power in the form of the work regime, Weil performs an act of asceticism that is simultaneously an act of external conformity and an act of political resistance through inner resistance to the automation of the self. The body and the encoding of tradition and culture upon it become, for her, a means for transcending the body and a reversal of the flow of the body (and so a reversal of time and necessity). Pain, willingly accepted, becomes the method for the body's transcendence. This is a common feature of ascetic traditions. The body is harnessed and controlled, sometimes put into situations of intentional suffering, in order not only to attain an inner transcendence but also to attain a bodily perfection. Through developing ascetic habit, ascetic ideology maintains that the limits of the body can be superseded and a 'new' body created or the body transcended.

Because of the ideology of bodily transcendence or bodily perfection by means of the body, gender is a problematic category through which to view asceticism. Medieval Christian women ascetics, as Hollywood has observed, were concerned with issues about the apostolic life, poverty, work and action, issues that their male counterparts were also concerned with, although hagiographies written by men attempted to see women wholly in terms of the body.[11] Medieval concerns in the West were focussed not so much on the sexualised (and gendered) body, but on the body as the site of corruption and death, in which case there tends to be an equalisation of somatic discourse between men and women.[12] Both men and women shared in the reversal of the body's flow, an attempted reversal of death and corruption. Nevertheless, gender is important in viewing the ascetic self from our perspective in the early twenty-first century. Gender has become an important analytical tool for looking at the histories of asceticism, especially the relationship of the ascetic self to power in terms of conformity and resistance. Indeed, we might claim that *resistance* to power enacted through ascetic performance – including ascetic writing – is mainly female, in contrast to *conformity* to power, which is mainly male. We see this in the life and work of the Beguines and Marguerite Porete, for example, who confronted and resisted Church authority, whereas conformity to domination tends to be male, as men are the wielders of social power.

To reverse the body's flow is to perform asceticism. Asceticism is always performed, which is to say always in the public domain (even when performed in privacy). One of the key features of performance is that it is public and can be observed. Asceticism is therefore performance because the reversal of the flow of the body is enacted within a community and tradition. Ascetic acts performed within the privacy of a cell or forest are nevertheless still public in the sense that they participate in and are given sanction by the wider community and tradition. This is an important point. Ascetic performance is public and only makes sense in the context of community and tradition. Through performing asceticism the ascetic is performing tradition, and the performance of tradition is a public affair. But not only is ascetic performance public, it is also subjective or the subjective appropriation of tradition. To develop the idea of the ascetic self as a kind of performed self is to locate asceticism within the general sphere of ritual understood by Rappaport as the performance of more or less invariant formal actions and utterances (see pp. 15, 214). The ascetic self is formed through ritual, which is the performance of the memory of tradition, but which is intimately connected to subjectivity in the ascetic case. This is to separate subjectivity from modern notions of individuality (see p. 241) and to set subjectivity within the public realm of tradition. Asceticism as the subjective appropriation of tradition is the enactment of a cultural memory. Indeed, the performance of tradition can be seen as the performance of memory: reversing the body's flow is enacting the memory of tradition, a tradition that becomes encoded in the body. This pattern is fundamental to asceticism and can be seen over and over again in ascetic traditions.

## THE MEMORY OF TRADITION

Asceticism entails tradition and is always set within its boundaries. In this sense it is public, and the ascetic subjectivity that performs the memory of tradition is a shared or collective subjectivity. The ascetic self takes on the presuppositions of a particular community, imbibes the ideology of a community's tradition or traditions, and conforms his or her body to the practices determined by it. The nature of tradition is, of course, complex. We might take it simply to mean, as Shils does (echoing Augustine), that which is handed down from the past, a *traditum*,[13] or, as Pelikan does, the 'social glue that brings cohesiveness to a clan or tribe'.[14] Digging deeper, we might distinguish different aspects of tradition, as John Thompson does.[15] But central to the concept of tradition is memory, especially collective memory passed through the generations. The sociologist Hervieu-Léger has described tradition (and religion) as a 'chain of memory' which confers transcendent authority on the past. A tradition 'describes the body of representations, images, theoretical and practical intelligence, behaviour, attitudes and so on that a group or society accepts in the name of the *necessary* continuity between the past and the present'.[16] Tradition is not passively received but actively reconstructed in a shared imagination and reconstituted in the present as memory. It is more than the passive conserving of information, it is the active enlivening of the present through links with the past. Although in one sense tradition is constructed in a shared imagination, this is not to say that tradition is made up and unreal, but rather is in a constant process of (re)construction in the flow of temporal continuity from the past. Although constructed, tradition is also received, in the words of Maximus, 'through succession from those who came before'.[17]

Following Jacques Le Goff, we might take memory to mean 'the capacity for conserving certain information',[18] information deemed important by a community and often with the function of legitimising the power of a particular group. But not only this, memory is also important to ensure the transmission of information and knowledge, important not only for collective identity and the maintenance of power relations but also for individual formation of a life. Ascetic traditions replicate a certain kind of memory of tradition through the generations, a memory that is constantly reconstructed and enlivened but that eventually becomes eroded with changed historical conditions. Memory, as Mary Carruthers has marvellously shown in the medieval monastic world, was central to the transmission of tradition and the process of religious transformation. *Memoria* has a wider connotation than simply repetition or reiteration: it has the sense of creative thought and construction.[19] There are analogues here in the Indian world, as we shall see.

The important point is that ascetic traditions are forms of collective memory enacted in the body through praxis and enacted in language through discourse. Ascetic traditions are set within the wider framework of collective memory, the wider tradition that presents asceticism as central to discourse, and a valued practice. But while representation or imitation, as acts of memory, are central to the transmission of tradition, what is specific to asceticism? Ascetic traditions assume the general background presuppositions of any community, but I think there are three features characteristic of ascetic traditions generally. Firstly, ascetic traditions are always set within or are a part of a *religious* tradition, moreover a *cosmological* religious tradition. Secondly, cosmological traditions interiorise cosmology. That is, there is a tendency in cosmological religions to emphasise interiority, and an interiority that interfaces with the structure of the hierarchical cosmos in a way that goes beyond what might be understood simply as subjectivity. Thirdly, ascetic traditions are the enactment of the memory of tradition, which is also the expression of cosmology, for tradition is understood as an expression of the cosmic structure. Let us look at each of these.

To make claims about religious tradition, that such a concept is even useful, goes against the grain of some recent scholarship that wishes to pull away from any essentialist understanding and sees religion in terms of social construction, culture and power relations.[20] I do not wish to directly engage with this literature here[21] but rather to claim that what distinguishes a tradition as religious is, as I have argued, value-laden narratives and behaviours that bind people to their goals, to their community, and to non-empirical claims and beings.[22] This is to follow Lactantius' sense of *religio* as that which binds, and we might add that people are bound by the memory of tradition. It is also to acknowledge some sense that a *religious* tradition is concerned with 'ultimate concern' for any human being, with meaning, with death and with transcendence.[23] While, of course, the concept of religion is in one sense constructed, developing as an abstract term from the seventeenth and eighteenth centuries in a context that separated it from a 'secular' realm of governance, this does not mean that religion does not refer to provinces of human meaning outside of the West or before that period. A concept can be constructed and at the same time revelatory, opening out a realm of discourse and practice. This is to claim (along with others) that religion is more than simply a matter of local, political concern. Paul Griffiths has very usefully argued that a religious account of the world must be comprehensive, unsurpassable and central to an individual life,[24] and asceticism must be seen in this kind of context. For a man or woman to devote their life to a path and practice that can involve great discomfort and pain is to make a commitment to a goal that has ultimate value for them. It is also to give commitment to a tradition that they regard as giving a comprehensive, unsurpassable and central account of the world. What is distinctive about ascetic traditions is that such an account must also be cosmological.

Asceticism occurs *par excellence* in cosmological religion. By 'cosmological religion', I mean traditions that give an account of the relationship between self and cosmos or, in theistic traditions, self, cosmos and God. Jainism, Śaiva Siddhānta and Orthodox Christianity would be good examples. In such religions, ideas of creation or manifestation will be important and they will have a developed sense of tradition. In Christianity this has meant a strong ecclesiology, in Hinduism a strong sense of tradition itself being part of the flow (*srotas*) from the divine realm. Such traditions are concerned with the order of things, with categories, and with organisms being in their right place. They claim to offer an accurate description of the cosmos and the meaning of human existence within it, from artistic expression to everyday human behaviour. Furthermore, this knowledge is not inconsequential, and knowledge of the spiritual path is also knowledge of the nature of the universe. Cosmological religion provides a map and a route from which individual life-ways can be constructed. They generally have a hierarchical view of the structure of the cosmos, locating pure or advanced beings, such as gods and angels, at the top of the hierarchy and less developed beings, such as plants and insects, at the bottom. The hierarchy is reflected in the institutions of the tradition. This is not necessarily a moral hierarchy, for human beings, although structurally lower, are often regarded as possessing freedom of will (in Christianity) or a quality that allows their liberation (in Buddhism). We can take many examples, and shall do so in coming chapters, from Christianity, Hinduism and Buddhism, but one will suffice here. In a text from one of the traditions of Śiva, the *Mālinitvijayottara-tantra* ('The Supreme Victory of the (Goddess of) the Garland of Letters') composed before or during the tenth century CE, a complex hierarchy is described comprising different worlds in an ordered sequence. This text presents an elaborate system at the end of a long tradition. The hell realms and realms of some other supernatural beings are at the bottom of this sequence, followed by the worlds of plants, insects, and domestic and wild animals, with the human world above these. As we rise up, worlds and deities become more and more refined, along with more refined states of mind.[25] Furthermore, such a cosmology is internalised in two ways: by claiming that the levels of the cosmos are in fact inner states of mind, and by mapping the hierarchy onto the body in a ritual process in such a way that the lower worlds are located in the lower half of the body and the higher in the upper half. The body reflects cosmology, and the enactment of ritual symbolically repeats the emergence and withdrawal of the cosmos.

The tradition from which this example is taken will be elaborated presently, but it illustrates a general point that traditions of asceticism entail cosmologies and that these cosmologies are often mapped onto subjectivity. Subjectivity and interiority recapitulate cosmology. This idea is all-pervasive in the South Asian traditions we shall be examining, but it is also present in the Catholic Christian world from Augustine to Bonaventura[26] and in the Orthodox Christian world from Maximus the Confessor[27] to Silouan the Athonite.[28] A developed sense of cosmology is notably absent from Protestantism, as are developed and institutionalised forms of asceticism. Perhaps one way of saying this is that cosmological religions are premodern. Indeed, with the gradual advent of modernity we see the erosion of cosmological religion in the West and the erosion of the performance of asceticism. Weber has thoroughly documented this shift with the internalisation of asceticism, that is the ceasing of asceticism as performance, and the erosion of religious cosmology with the rise of science and the development of Protestantism.

This line of thinking needs to be developed a stage further in order to understand asceticism as performance, and that is that ascetic practice within the context of cosmological religion is fundamentally concerned with memory. Cosmological religions are focussed on the structure of the cosmos in metaphorical space, but they are also concerned with cosmic time. A cosmological tradition is a way in which cosmic time is related to individual time, and asceticism as the reversal of the flow of the body is also an attempt at the reversal of cosmic time. Through ascetic performance the ascetic self looks back through tradition to an origin, to a source that also becomes a future goal. Ascetic performance becomes the remembrance of tradition and the overcoming of forgetfulness.

As the overcoming of forgetfulness, asceticism is fundamentally opposed to modernity. Le Goff, discussing different understandings of the relation of past to present, makes the general point that in pagan antiquity the valorisation of the past predominated, accompanied by the idea of a decadent present. With the Middle Ages 'the present is trapped between the weight of the past and the hope of an eschatological future'; with the Renaissance the stress is on the present; and from the seventeenth century 'the ideology of progress turns the valorization of time towards the future'.[29] While many historians acknowledge this kind of periodisation to be problematic,[30] the general drift of his argument is surely right, that in premodernity the present is diminished in the tendency to actualise the past and project the future.[31] But while one can see Le Goff's point that with the advent of modernity, time becomes future-oriented, it could be argued that in late modernity time is characterised by a sense of the continuous or extended present. Helga Nowotny has argued that with mechanisation, industrialisation and developments in technology the relation between the future and the present has shifted: '(t)he future is disposed of as if it were in the present, and an extended present is thereby produced'.[32]

If modernity, as Nowotny argues, is characterised by the notion of the extended present, or if modernity is characterised by a future orientation, as Le Goff argues, then either way asceticism goes against the spirit of modernity. In the extended present, the past becomes commodified and perceived to be effectively powerless and forgotten. In contrast, the ascetic inhabits a world that looks both back to the past and to a future that reinstates that past purity, and his or her life is oriented towards reconstituting or recapitulating the past which is also a construction of the future. In the repeated actions of cosmological religion, in the repeated actions of asceticism, forgetfulness is overcome in the body and in discourse. Cosmological religions and ascetical traditions within them are therefore highly liturgical, concerned with the mapping of the year, the mapping of the cosmos and the subjective interiorisation of these processes. This was a general feature of the Middle Ages in the West, as Le Goff observes, and is arguably a feature of premodern cultures in general. We see this in the Orthodox Christian liturgical year and in the tantric rituals of Nambudri Brahmans in temples in Kerala. But we can especially see this in ascetic performance. In asceticism, human time is related to cosmic time by way of tradition and so points back to an origin and forward to an end. The performance of the reversal of the body's flow is the performance of the reversal of time, which is simultaneously an anticipation of the end of time. Indeed, Eliade has repeatedly made the point about premodern conceptions of time,[33] although he has problematically tended to neglect social and power relations and historical particularity.

Asceticism is one form of the memory of tradition. To perform asceticism is to remember the tradition, and the remembrance of tradition is the remembrance of cosmos and of origin. Tradition is the expression of the cosmos and is linked to the structure of the cosmos. In Hindu or Buddhist traditions, that the cosmos is structured in a particular way allows liberation from it. Initiation and consequent practice become a means of escape from time and suffering. In Orthodox Christianity, the Church expresses the possibility and means of transcendence in the world as the expression of God's will. The idea of transformation is central here (and therefore the idea of otherness: that into which the self is transformed). To enact the memory of tradition through ascetic performance is to enact the possibility of transformation. Indeed, any ascetic performance entails the possibility of change. Such an inscribing of the memory of tradition on the body is both an act of will and a consequence of passivity. It is here, of course, that we meet again the ambiguity of the self in ascetic practice.

## THE AMBIGUITY OF THE ASCETIC SELF

The ascetic self acts only through tradition, performing the reversal of the body's flow through the categories and practices of tradition, and thereby subjugating the self to the collectivity of tradition. Yet conversely, the reversal of the flow of the body is an act of will and an assertion of the self. Through an act of will the ascetic self performs the ambiguity of its assertion in ascetic performance (a person needs great determination) and the telos of its eradication (a person intends the eradication of determination). In Christianity, the ultimate religious goal in asceticism is the passivity of the self in which the self's will is replaced by the divine will. (For example, Silouan the Athonite writes: 'It is a great good to give oneself over to the Divine will. Then the Lord alone occupies the soul.'[34]) The self becomes passive and God active. This passivity is indeed seen as a consequence of the activity of the divine, yet that passivity is achieved through the assertion of the will in ascetic action. It is this ambiguity of the self that goes to the heart of ascetic performance and is expressed as praxis in the body and as discourse in language.

The ascetic life is one of order and limitation within tradition in the service of a higher freedom. As John Bowker has observed, the greater the degrees of constraint operating upon an organism, the more complex are the choices available to it. Thus, a single-celled organism has few constraints and is severely limited in its options, whereas more complex organisms with higher degrees of constraint have many more options. The constraints operative within religious traditions allow high degrees of complexity.[35] We can view the ascetic life in a parallel way. To reverse the flow of the body is to place high levels of constraint upon the self – severe restrictions on biological life (*zoe*) – in order to achieve a future state of freedom from biological constraint (even if understood as a transformation of a bodily state). It is almost as though the restriction undergone in asceticism is a necessary condition for the intensification of subjectivity that transcends desire and individualism. This intensification of subjectivity is spoken of in terms of freedom from restriction: freedom from the restriction of sin in a Christian discourse, freedom from the karmic drive whose eventuality is further birth and suffering in a Hindu and Buddhist discourse. The purification of desire, spoken of by Nicholas Lash,[36] as a common theme in asceticism is a synonym for freedom from biological necessity.

In the Christian, Hindu and Buddhist writings that we shall be encountering, the theme of freedom from bodily limitation through bodily limitation is common. At the level of praxis, the flow of the body is reversed by means of the body. Indeed, there is what might be called a shared existential ground that involves the intensification of subjectivity that is simultaneously the transcendence of individuality. The 'I will' of ascetic intention, which ironically seeks to erase itself, creates an interiority that is particular and bound to a specific, historical, temporal frame, to a specific narrative identity, and to location within a specific tradition. Yet while narrative identities are always specific – always the story of *my* life – there are processes that can be abstracted that are non-individual in so far as the *ego* is empty of content. The first person pronoun becomes filled out with different cultural contents, with different stories, implying different power relations. The subject of language (*ego, aham*) is left behind in an interiority that links self and cosmos, inner experience and world.

The claim of this book for a kind of existential commonality of the ascetic self is not an attempt to reconstitute a view of the individualistic subject prior to power relations, but it is to argue that a kind of universality can be established both in terms of praxis and discourse within the range of scriptural traditions here examined. In these traditions the universality of praxis is found in the commonality of temporal, narrative experience, grounded in tradition, in which the body is at the centre. The universality of discourse is found in the languages of subjectivity articulated in the texts. The language of intentionality and the reversal of the flow of the body are fundamental to *askesis* across Christian, Hindu and Buddhist cultures. The existential universality of ascetic discourse therefore entails a structure of language filled out with different contents in diverse cultures of asceticism.

Furthermore, because asceticism entails tradition, we can say that ascetic discourse is inherently dialogical. By this I mean that ascetic discourse, founded on the *volo*, the 'I will', correlatively entails a linguistic content, a community of language users, somebody's story, and so an 'other'. A person's narrative identity, the story of his or her life, comprises a complex of dialogical encounters. Within the dialogical encounter that constitutes language, we have a third presence in the address between the subject of speech and the object of speech. This is, of course, true of all language, which is dialogical by its very nature, but the dialogism of language is particularly brought out in ascetic discourse. Indeed, the third presence in the dialogical encounter of asceticism has been understood as a divine presence: the presence that will replace ascetic volition in the reversal of the body's flow. This is the longing for the end of desire.

The general structure of a dialogical relationship in ascetic utterance, while itself being filled out by different contents, is arguably an existential modality that we repeatedly encounter in the traditions. This structure of language is linked to the particularity of the body through time and to a paying attention to detail in ascetic traditions. Paying attention to the details of everyday living – the monastic rules, the control of the body, the restriction of food – is to enact the memory of tradition. Enacting the memory of tradition reveals a particularity of existence that is subjective yet not individualistic. To practise asceticism is not an act of individuality: it is an act of subjectivity and an intensification of the subjective. The non-individualistic particularity of the ascetic life is reflected in the linguistic structure of the addresser, the addressee and the discourse or third presence. Thus the ascetic's life is linked to the wider community and tradition not only through the body, but also through language. Indeed, ascetic speech is a controlled speech and a controlled discourse that expresses the story of the tradition and recapitulates the memory of tradition. Ascetic selves become indices of tradition. In one sense, the ascetic living alone or in the monastic community becomes just another monk or nun, stripped of cultural signs that mark a person as individual, yet in another sense remains the subject of first person predicates. The narrative of the ascetic becomes an index for the narrative of tradition and the value placed on particularity in ascetic communities at the cost of individuality. It is this particularity, expressed in the body and in the language of asceticism, that articulates the memory of tradition and is what we might call 'existential'.

## SUBJECTIVITY AND INTERIORITY

Given that conceptions of self vary across histories and cultures, could there be a shared notion of the ascetic self in the scriptural traditions? How could such an inquiry even begin, and what are the boundaries or strategies of containment that we need to develop in such a comparative exercise? Various cultures give different accounts of subjectivity and the location of agency; some have externalised conceptions, where agency is located mainly outside of the self,[37] while others have strong accounts of self-determination. Agency of the self implies subjectivity, and in some cultures strong conceptions of subjectivity have developed. My argument about the ascetic self necessitates that the idea of subjectivity has meaning outside of a particular history in the West. In the ascetic cultures of South Asia and Christianity, subjectivity has been thematised both in terms of the self as an essence or substance and in terms of self-experience through time. Moreover, cultures that have thematised subjectivity have also thematised asceticism. Highly reflexive traditions within which asceticism develops have sophisticated accounts of the human subject and highly developed discourses about the self, ways of knowing the self and ways of acting. This can be demonstrated with innumerable examples from the histories of Christianity and Buddhism and from Hindu traditions. These traditions have developed ideas about a disembodied self, have rejected the very notion of a self and have understood the self purely in terms of embodiment, but all have taken the self as a category of understanding.

Such traditions have correlatively and necessarily also thematised in varying degrees the idea of that which is other to the self, namely its transcendence or annihilation. Communities that have invested asceticism with intellectual and material resources have similarly invested in the thematisation of the self and have developed sophisticated accounts of subjectivity. But while such broad generalisations might not be problematic, given the specific historical trajectories of the cultures we are dealing with, we are faced with the problem of the ways in which an account of the self and subjectivity could be developed that, while doing justice to the particularities of history and tradition, also does the work needed for a cross-cultural account.

To develop an account of the ascetic self across cultures we need to focus on subjectivity and to theorise the subjective. I do not believe that this can be done independently of intellectual traditions in the no-man's-land of rational objectivity; instead it must develop organically from within traditions in dialogue with a pre-understanding of subjectivity brought to them. In order to arrive at a cross-cultural theory of the ascetic self we must go by way of tradition-specific understandings. Different cultures have thematised subjectivity in different ways. This is markedly true of Christian Europe and South Asia, where descriptions of the subjective are invested with different values. While I do wish to make claims that cut across the traditions, we must nevertheless tread carefully in our sensitivity to historical and cultural difference. As de Certeau observes, investigators into culture tend to construct a unitary interpretation and 'to think of culture in the singular', which expresses a 'singularity of place',[38] in a situation where cultures are in the plural. This is markedly true *within* the bounded locations of 'Europe' and 'South Asia', with their marked plurality of voices, let alone between them. I propose in this book to proceed in stages, beginning with what for most native English speakers will be the more familiar, and to move from there to the less familiar; to proceed from a modern, Western understanding of a religious subjectivity to an ancient, Indian understanding.

I wish to begin not with the more general term 'the self' that has clear analogues in the languages of Europe and South Asia, but with the more specific notion of subjectivity. The term 'subjectivity' and its close correlates in other European languages (German *Subjecktivität* and French *subjectivité*) has only been in use since the nineteenth century, but its connotations were certainly present in earlier philosophical discourse. The term has developed from the Latin *subiectum*, which translates the Greek *upokeimenon*, a term which designates an underlying foundation.[39] In a general sense, it refers to self-consciousness on the basis of which all knowledge is possible. This sense of subjectivity is closely linked to the idea of interiority or inwardness and, as Charles Taylor has so eloquently shown, the modern notion of the self is constituted by a sense of inwardness – that we are beings with inner depths and inner resources,[40] an idea that has come under sustained critique in postmodernity. The privileging of the self is often traced to Descartes, although a model of depth subjectivity in the West is older and closely related to theological reflection. We must also link subjectivity with the idea that subjective reflection, on the one hand, and experiment, on the other, are the only sure foundations of knowledge once faith and revelation have been rejected. The idea of the self-positing subject has been deeply influential on modern self-understanding. But that the term subjectivity has developed in the more recent history of the West and has been emphasised particularly by German Romanticism, the development of literary criticism and in the development of culture (*Bildung*) raises questions about its universal applicability.[41] Moreover, in late modern times the very notion of subjectivity has come under scrutiny and, as Farrell has observed, there has been a disenchantment of subjectivity that has followed from a disenchantment of nature.[42]

Yet while the term subjectivity and the sense of self that it implies have arisen within a particular historical period in the West, it is not obvious that it does not have reference outside of that history. Indeed, on the contrary, some sense of subjectivity is central to the scriptural traditions. It is apparent, as it was to Friedrich Schlegel, that we find correlates of a sense of subjectivity in the history of Indian religions that, for Schlegel, represented a wisdom not found in European philosophy,[43] and nearer to home a sense of inwardness is certainly present in early thinkers. Augustine, for example, had a developed sense of interiority that the modern reader has little trouble in understanding. In response to the question 'Who are you?' he could respond in terms of an exterior body and an interior soul, and that the 'interior part is better.'[44] Moreover, interiority is strongly linked to cosmology, as Denys Turner has marvellously shown – a theme to which we shall return in the following chapters.[45]

We could develop a claim that subjectivity is central to asceticism through a normative view of the self that is general enough to accommodate the diversity of a variety of cultural concepts. This is certainly possible in a minimal way when understood as the subject of first person predicates. In its barest form, we might take subjectivity to be the abstraction made from the answer to Augustine's question. Castoriadis calls the response to the question 'Who?' 'a mode of subjectivity we call the social individual',[46] making the point that in all human languages it is possible to ask the question '*Who* did this?' and '*Who* said that?' Minimally, subjectivity is indicated simply by the first person pronoun, the subject of first person predicates. But given that subjectivity can become an extremely rich concept when thematised within the histories of civilisations, we need to move far beyond this normative view to a richer formulation. As Ricoeur, beginning with the same question, observes, when we introduce the problematic of the self by the question 'Who?', we open out the many meanings inherent in the question. 'Who is speaking of what? Who does what? About whom and about what does one construct a narrative? Who is morally responsible for what?'[47] This is to introduce the possibility of very wide diversity and opens the discussion to the possibility of significant cultural variation that is yet constrained within the boundaries of the subjective.

Developing this further, my view of the ascetic self as performing the memory of tradition and performing the ambiguity of the self is also influenced by Kierkegaard. Kierkegaard wishes to privilege existence, the particular existence of a lived life, over abstract system and to privilege person over world-historical dialectic. Truth, in his thinking, 'becomes appropriation, inwardness, subjectivity, and the point is to immerse oneself, existing, in subjectivity'.[48] What is important is how I know the world, how I appropriate truth. In this appropriation, truth becomes subjectivity. This emphasis on the existential and the actual is furthermore linked, for Kierkegaard, with repetition, in so far as repetition is a constituent of the self and is teleological in the sense that repetition looks forward while yet maintaining continuity with the past. Through repetition the subject expresses deep investment in his or her particular existence. Linking these Kierkegaardian conceptions of subjectivity with the concept of scriptural tradition, we can develop an existential understanding of the scriptural traditions as the appropriation of tradition and the repetition of the tradition's goals enacted in ritual. This structure is particularly intensified with the ascetic self which develops a tradition-specific inwardness that is ironic in a Kierkegaardian sense, in that the will intends its own destruction, which would, actually, be the perfect appropriation of the truth of tradition. Although this move would no doubt be frowned upon by Kierkegaard himself, it does make sense of the diversity of practices in ascetic traditions and shows their importance for individual persons who have maintained the traditions throughout their long histories. In my view, as I shall argue here, this tradition-specific subjectivity is fundamental to understanding the ascetic self across divergent cultures and histories.

## COMPARATIVE RELIGION IN DIALOGICAL PERSPECTIVE

Two problems of method present themselves at the outset: the problem of comparative religion and the problem of the relation between a macro level of cultural analysis, which deals with wider historical forces through time, and an inquiry into the subjectivities of texts. I would wish to situate these problems in a postfoundational religious studies that intends to present dialogical readings of texts, based on close reading which assumes a philological rigour. To focus on the ascetic self in history is actually to focus on its representation in different textual genres. Our primary model of observation is textual – the reading of text and the reading of cultural practices, of which they are an index, as texts. This inevitable emphasis on textual representation will affect the ways in which the problem of comparative religion and the relation between text and history are approached. Indeed, the book wishes to bring into question modern academia's ideological pre-commitment to individualism and universalism which sees the individual and the universal as norms. The book is in one sense a return to the ideal of phenomenology, of waiting and trying to see what is there in the practices and literatures of the scriptural traditions, although with an awareness of the difficulties involved.

The enterprise of comparing asceticisms is an exercise in comparative religion, yet an exercise that wishes to acknowledge the problematic nature of the enterprise in the first instance and to offer some new ways forward. Comparison is essential to understanding in both the human and the natural sciences. New knowledge depends upon comparison with the old and with other, parallel forms of knowledge. The dialogical comparative enterprise needs, as it were, to inhabit the borderland between languages of subjectivity. Since dialogical relationships are possible between any phenomena articulated through a semiotic medium,[49] there are compelling reasons to think that it is possible to come to an understanding of subjectivity across cultures. Our initial concern must be the ways in which the first person pronoun, as response to the question 'Who?', is filled out with cultural content.

But within the study of religion, comparison has often been done to show the superiority of Christianity to other religions, to show that diverse religions are pointing to a common truth, or to show that Indian traditions are equal to, if not better than, Western ones.[50] This is not the place to develop a history of comparative religion and philosophy,[51] but given the critique of European approaches to other cultures in recent years, especially the critique of Indology and oriental studies from the perspective of post-colonial critique, it is important to address the issue of how a comparative religion is still possible and what can be gained by it.[52] As Ben Ray observes, a political charge of postmodernism is that to compare is to abstract, 'and abstraction is construed as a political act aimed at domination and annihilation; cross-cultural comparison becomes intrinsically imperialistic, obliterating the cultural matrix from which it "lifts" the compared object'.[53] How can a comparative religion be done that avoids a problematic and exclusive essentialism or that does not inevitably bring with it the remnants of a colonial discourse?

Scholars are addressing these questions and revisiting comparative religion in the context of postmodern critique.[54] In a significant volume of papers addressing the issue of comparison edited by Patton and Ray, a theme emerges that a new comparative religion is possible that grows out of cultural specificity and is clear about its purposes in terms of moral and theoretical engagement.[55] A magic still dwells in a postmodern age, but this does not mean that we can, or wish to, go back to a primary naivety. The days of innocence in comparison are gone, and any comparison has to accept the particularity of voice while acknowledging what is common for the theoretical, moral or political task at hand in a specific comparative study.

The difficulty of the comparative task as regards the ascetic self is compounded because different texts address different communities of speakers and for different reasons. How will the texts concerning asceticism encountered in this study speak to us, and how, in the act of comparison, will they speak to each other across historical and geographical divides? Given these problems, I would wish to argue that a kind of comparative religion is yet possible, but a kind that is language- and communication-centred. Any comparison involving the scriptural traditions has to be grounded in the particularity of the texts.[56] As I have argued elsewhere, a dialogical research programme open to the otherness of its 'object' while retaining its 'outsideness' is one way we can responsibly offer a comparative religion.[57] In examining the analogous ways scriptural traditions address the question of the ascetic self, the traditions are drawn into 'dialogue' within my own practice of observation and analysis. By 'dialogical' I mean that knowledge within human communities assumes language and that language not only presupposes the existence of the language system (grammar) but, as Bakhtin observes, the chain of utterances through time (and therefore the community of language users).[58] Language is dialogical in its very nature – every utterance is preceded by another to which it in some sense responds, and is succeeded by a further response. Utterance looks back in responding to other utterances and looks forward in anticipating response; it has the quality of addressivity.[59] The present study assumes that argument and the comparison lies in the close reading of ascetical texts and in their implicit juxtaposition. The dialogism inherent in the chain of utterance entails the notion of time and that utterances form part of a historical sequence. The historical sequence of utterance also entails the idea of text, and it is these two concepts – historicism and text – that we need to examine in relation to comparison.

Why someone should choose particular texts from diverse cultures rather than others as the objects of discourse can be answered in a number of ways. The first is simply that they are present in my field of consciousness as *interest* and so, once the book is read, in the reader's field of consciousness. This is not a trivial response, for the fact that texts are present to my awareness in particular juxtapositions is an index of the Western socialisation and educational processes I have undergone and is an index of the self-representation of traditions. We might also say that the dialogical approach to comparative religion is an analogue of the way in which religions interact in the contemporary world. Traditions find themselves in close proximity – often with dire human consequences – but always in some dialogical relationship. Traditions speak with each other and are united within common fields of awareness.

It is the fact of cultural interaction and proximity and the inevitability of dialogical comparison that gives force to the argument against an extreme cultural relativism, although such a perspective is compatible with some forms of relativism.[60] We can see this in comparative linguistics, for example, where a revival of linguistic relativism has produced fascinating studies in language use, showing how language structures influence cognition and experience in the most basic dimensions of life, such as spatial orientation.[61] Comparison can illuminate difference and can show aspects of a particular form of cultural life that we would not otherwise see. Comparing agrarian societies will tell us something about the nature of agriculture as a mode of production, or a comparison of different societies' material cultures will tell us something about the relationship between human communities and their environments. But comparison is always related to use and context. There will be reasons for comparison and comparison used as a means to justify more general claims – as here, to propose certain features of the ascetic self.

The process of comparison involves a complex interaction between the scholar or scholarly discourse of the one who is 'outside' and the discourses that are being compared. Reading texts in another tradition is already a form of implicit comparison: the reference points of the reader will inevitably be different from that of the text, which, inevitably, will be measured against those reference points. While it is important to establish texts in the narrative context of their occurrence, reading a text from another discourse entails its decontextualising from that place and its recontextualising in the new place of my discourse. The comparative method entails a text being taken out of its original context and reconfigured in a new environment. The mechanism, which Silverstein and Urban have called entextualisation and contextualisation,[62] operative in all cultural transmission, is also operative in the performance of scholarship itself.

This important point is echoed by Ochs's awareness of different communities of readers. The process can become very complex: the act of scholarship I perform in reading texts in a particular way and constructing them in my discourse is further reconfigured by others within that discourse, by readers and other scholars. These reconfigurings of text and placing text in different histories should not be seen as a kind of handicap but form the necessary constraints operative in any reading: a prejudice that allows understanding.[63] The dialogical situation entails a third element, therefore, which is coterminous with the dialogue partners (even when one is a text). Through a 'comparative' reading we can attempt to uncover not only what Ochs calls the 'plain sense' of the text but the deeper sense of a text as a response to questions that might be only implicit within it.[64] We need to offer readings, then, that are sensitive to the primary meanings of the texts and whose interpretative meanings do not disrupt the primary meanings. Interpretative meaning, for our purposes, refers to the translation of primary meanings into the common language and argument of this study: into the language of 'subjectivity', 'interiority' and 'cosmological tradition'. This common language or argument produced is the comparison. Through such reading we can bring into meeting different histories and different subjectivities, set within the framework of the problematic of the ascetic self and tradition. This is an optimistic view of comparison. In the comparative endeavour, as Eivind Kahrs has pointed out in the context of Indian philosophical discourse, we need explanation both in terms of indigenous concepts and thought patterns and in terms of 'concepts and thought patterns that are clearly imposed on it from the outside'.[65] The interplay between indigenous and external concepts is the dialogical enterprise.

But why focus on texts when the whole orientation of asceticism is the reversal of the flow of the body and the embodied memory of tradition? In the light of the turn to the image, to fieldwork and to orality, how do we justify this? The focus on written text in the history of religions, and thereby on the literate, power-wielding and ideology-creating echelons of a society, has often been at the cost of understanding folk cultures, the mass of the population, cultures of resistance and material culture, including the plastic arts and music. In the study of South Asian traditions this occlusion is being addressed in recent work that focuses on oral traditions,[66] along with a turn to the image. In Hinduism, Eck has focussed on the importance of the image;[67] Schopen has argued that through a neglect of the image and a neglect of archaeology a distortion has occurred in our understanding of early and Theravāda Buddhism;[68] Faure has emphasised the role of mediation in Chan Buddhism;[69] and Trainor has focussed on the material culture of Theravāda, showing the centrality of relics.[70] In relation to asceticism, Harpham has written intelligently and at length on

Grünewald's Isenheim Altar, relating readings of it to narrative theory and to wider medieval culture.[71] But it is nevertheless still the case that our historical knowledge of religious traditions and the contents of those traditions is based primarily on texts. Text is arguably the foundation of culture, and while texts can be art objects, not all art objects are texts (because they lack language).[72] Even Grünewald's painting needs narrative to be brought to it, as the painting itself disrupts a unified narrative sequence.[73] Any understanding of religion needs to focus on the texts and narratives embodied in them, while of course taking into account material culture. But text and language remain our primary resource, especially in understanding the subjectivities that produced them.

Finally, a note needs to be added to help frame the study: that although, in the postfoundational approach I adopt here, religions are brought into dialogue within my own study, an important dimension of dialogic analysis is also observing religions in dialogue. Indeed, many postliberal scholars would wish to do this, for example in observing practices of scriptural reasoning. In examining history only the former is possible, i.e. traditions in history can be brought into dialogue only within scholarship; nonetheless, there is great potential in the latter in the contemporary cultural context (although this is not what I do here). That interreligious dialogue as a form of cultural dialogue is important cannot be doubted. According to Dupré, who has written with insight on this matter, what is significant about interreligious dialogue is that it itself is perceived by its practitioners as a religious event.[74]

## MACRO-LEVEL CULTURAL ANALYSIS AND DIALOGICAL READING

If the first methodological difficulty is the idea of comparative religion, the second is the relation between the macro-level of cultural analysis and the study of the text. By 'macro-level' I understand its common use in Sociology, where it refers to large-scale phenomena working through history, such as the rise of modernity or globalisation, in contrast to the micro-level that deals with individual experience, interaction, and subjectivity. We might include here particular texts of a tradition. One of the questions is, therefore, how does a close reading of texts relate to the macro-sociology of culture? On the one hand, asceticism has originated and functioned within a premodern time-frame and must be seen in a wider history that Collins, following Braudel, has called the *longue durée*.[75] How this *longue durée* of ascetic traditions interacts with ascetic subjectivity and the recapitulation of the memory of tradition is one of our tasks. The subjectivities expressed through the text are moulded by the *longue durée* of their history; a text is clearly a product of its age. Yet texts also express the subjectivities of their authors, especially with regard to a topic such as asceticism which is both clearly a product of tradition and is integral to the individual's life-path, to his or her intentions and goals. The *longue durée* of history articulates with the time-frame of the subject in the text. In the cosmological religions we shall be viewing, cosmic time is reflected in subjective time partly through the medium of the text. On the one hand, we enter into the world imagined by the text or its author(s) – into the text's religious *imaginaire*[76] – and, on the other, we see how the text expresses events and power in the 'real' socio-political world. The text is an index both of wider history and of its author(s).

In the following pages, one of the main focuses will be on texts expressing ideas about or experiences of asceticism from different cultural histories. These readings will, I hope, be true to their historical contexts and suggest ways in which subjectivity interacts with history: the ascetic body in the text expresses subjectivity and inwardness in the context of tradition. But the subjectivities of texts can be in conflict. Different voices echo within them,[77] and the subjectivity articulated in a text might be compliant with historical power or resistant to it. While it is vitally important to represent ascetic texts in their own histories, I nevertheless hope to show that the interaction of these texts across history and cultures in the place of my own study will reveal dimensions to the traditions themselves with regard to the ascetic self that would otherwise not become visible.

There are, then, two major tasks in a new comparative religion: the illumination of the horizon of the text or the world internal to the text itself (a descriptive enterprise that might even be called a first-level phenomenology),[78] and the connection between the text and the wider social world. There is an internal coherence to the text that needs to be mapped, but the text is also an index of history and wider social forces operating outside of it. Ochs outlines a 'pragmatic' method of reading that reveals both the horizon of the text and the way the text meets the world. He takes the text to be two kinds of sign: 'an explicit statement (or iconic symbol) about characters that may be attributed to a possible world as envisioned by its author, and an implicit index (or indexical symbol) of events in the actual world from which the statement emerges.'[79]

Even though Ochs is referring here to philosophical texts of a Cartesian-Kantian epistemology, this idea of the world of the text or the world evoked by the text is important for our project. The world envisioned by a text is our prime focus of inquiry. Each text evokes its own *imaginaire*, its possible world or horizon that the reader, receiver or community of receivers learn to inhabit. Learning to inhabit the world of the text, and thereby entering the tradition of practice of which the text is an index,[80] is the first step in the act of reading. To enter the world of the text is to inhabit the subjectivity or subjectivities it articulates. This learning to inhabit the world of the text can also be seen as the embodiment of the text. But we need a sharper understanding of text to complement Ochs. This can be provided by Gracia, who defines texts as 'groups of entities used as signs, that are selected, arranged, and intended by an author in a certain context to convey some specific meaning to an audience'.[81] A text has an intentionality, although an intentionality that might exceed the author's intention, and this intentionality of the text is approached in the initial reading. This initial reading is getting to know what Ochs calls the 'plain sense' of the text, in contrast to the 'interpreted sense'.[82] It is this level that I penetrate through reading and repeated reading, and, unless it is a text of a tradition that I am inside, I can never wholly enter into it. Nor, more importantly, can it enter into me. Indeed, this is a methodological axiom of the dialogical method I wish to promote. Rather than the empathy of phenomenology, in which a text is penetrated from a detached position of epistemic neutrality, a dialogical reading will assume a socially and historically situated position outside of the text. Understanding of the text then occurs not through an objectivism in which the text becomes wholly transparent to the detached, rational reader, but through a stepping into the text while simultaneously retaining outsideness. Bakhtin called this idea 'live-entering' (*vzhivanie*), a concept that is at the basis of Bakhtin's dialogism: going beyond the text itself, 'I' and 'other' are co-constituted in our unique locations within the unrepeatable act of being.[83]

Interpretation, the level of Ochs's pragmatic reading, is close to Silverstein and Urban's processes of textual reception. In engaging in primary and interpretative readings, the scholar is participating in the fate of all texts, to be 'entextualised' and 'contextualised'. But with the texts we are dealing with, my reading will not, of course, be the religious reading of their reception in the traditions of their origin. My scholarly reading is in order to describe these texts in their historical tradition and to bring them into juxtaposition in the sphere of this academic enterprise. This is a historicist understanding of text. In our contemporary situation, the world of the text is entered by a reader or community of readers for purposes other than those envisaged by its composer(s) and earliest receivers. The ascetic texts of Europe and South Asia, which are the object of this study, are read by me and might be read by my readers, all of us having varying degrees of distance from the texts' *imaginaires*. As Ochs says, there will be different communities of readers for whom different readings will be resonant.[84] Different communities of readers will therefore engage with a text at different levels and for different purposes.[85]

If the first task is to understand the text in its own horizon (Ochs's primary sense), then the second task is to understand the text as an implicit index (Ochs's indexical symbol) of the text's context. How does the text relate to wider culture and history? Of which power group or pressure group is it an expression? It is at this level of reading that we see how the subjectivities expressed in a text articulate with macro-cultural history, how the text functions within a specific time-frame and narrative base. For us, the task of reading comes to focus on the way in which a text expresses a discourse about the ascetic self. This different level of reading is to move to Ochs's interpreted sense.

Both tasks of reading are, of course, potentially endless, but both are constrained by our third task of comparative reading that pervades the study. Through reading across traditions, themes, problems and what Ochs, following Peirce, calls 'leading tendencies' can be identified.[86] I will try to show that there are indeed leading tendencies, themes and problems in ascetic texts that emerge in the different social, geographical and historical contexts of Europe and South Asia, namely the relation of the ascetic self to tradition. The leading tendencies of the texts show how the ascetic self is set within a cosmological tradition that runs against contemporary sensibilities. The book therefore wishes not merely to make, in David Ford's terms, third-order statements about the history of asceticism and the discourse about it (which are essentially descriptive), but to make first-order statements about the ascetic self, about the relation between subjectivity and tradition, about the transformation of desire and about the legitimacy of ascetic paths.

## NOTES

1. Søren Kierkegaard, *Concluding Unscientific Postscript to Philosophical Fragments* vol. I, ed. and trs. H. V. and E. H. Hong (Princeton University Press, 1992), p. 350.
2. Jaroslav Pelikan, *The Vindication of Tradition* (New Haven and London: Yale University Press, 1984), p. 65.
3. On the physiology and neurology of asceticism in a comparative context see Ariel Glucklich, *Sacred Pain: Hurting the Body for the Sake of the Soul* (New York: Oxford University Press, 2001), especially pp. 40–62. For an earlier approach from the perspective of the history of medicine see Violet MacDermot, *The Cult of the Seer in the Ancient Middle East: A Contribution to Current Research on*

*Hallucinations Drawn from Coptic and Other Texts* (Berkeley: University of California Press, 1971). For the development of the idea of a biologically grounded, innate and universal human predisposition to asceticism, see the stimulating article by Johannes Bronkhorst 'Asceticism, Religion and Biological Evolution', *Method and Theory in the Study of Religion* vol. 13, no. 4, 2001, pp. 374–417.

4. See John Lucy, *Language Diversity and Thought* (Cambridge University Press, 1992); John J. Gumperz and Stephen C. Levinson (eds.), *Rethinking Linguistic Relativity* (Cambridge University Press, 1992).
5. Geoffrey G. Harpham, *The Ascetic Imperative in Culture and Criticism* (University of Chicago Press, 1987).
6. For references see M. Derrett, 'Primitive Christianity as an Ascetic Movement' in V. C. Wimbush and R. Valantasis (eds.), *Asceticism* (Oxford University Press, 1995), p. 88, notes 4 and 5. See also J. Pinsent, 'Ascetic Moods in Greek and Latin Literature' in Wimbush and Valantasis, *Asceticism*, pp. 211–12.
7. Wimbush and Valantasis, 'Introduction' in *Asceticism*, p. xxxii.
8. Steven Collins, *Nirvana and Other Buddhist Felicities* (Cambridge University Press, 1999), p. 33.
9. John B. Thompson, 'Editor's Introduction' in P. Bourdieu, *Language and Symbolic Power*, trs. Matthew Adamson (Cambridge: Polity Press, 1991), p. 12.
10. P. Bourdieu, *Outline of a Theory of Practice*, trs. Richard Nice (Cambridge University Press, 1977), p. 163.
11. Amy Hollywood, *The Soul as Virgin Wife* (Notre Dame and London: University of Notre Dame Press, 1995) p. 26.
12. Caroline Walker Bynum, 'The Female Body and Religious Practice in the Later Middle Ages' in Michel Feher (ed.), *Fragments for a History of the Human Body* vol. 1 (New York: Zone, 1989), p. 162.
13. Edward Shils, *Tradition* (London: Faber and Faber, 1981), p. 12.
14. Pelikan, *The Vindication of Tradition*, p. 6.
15. John B. Thompson, 'Tradition and Self in a Mediated World' in Paul Heelas, Scott Lash and Paul Morris (eds.), *Detraditionalization* (Oxford: Blackwell, 1996), pp. 91–4. He distinguishes four aspects of tradition: the 'hermeneutic', or a society's background assumptions; the 'normative', or the guides for present action handed down from the past; 'legitimation', or that aspect of tradition that supports authority; and 'identity', or the sense of self and of the collective.
16. D. Hervieu-Léger, *Religion as a Chain of Memory*, trs. Simon Lee (New Brunswick: Rutgers University Press, 2000 (1993)), pp. 86, 87.
17. Quoted by J. Pelikan in 'Maximus in the History of Christian Thought' p. 388, in F. Heinzer and C. Schönborn (eds.), *Maximus Confessor: Actes du Symposium sur Maxime le Confesseur* (Fribourg, Switzerland: Editions Universitaires, 1982), pp. 387–402.
18. J. Le Goff, *History and Memory*, trs. Steven Rendall and Elizabeth Claman (New York: Columbia University Press, 1992), p. 51.

19. Mary Carruthers, *The Craft of Thought: Meditation, Rhetoric, and the Making of Images, 400–1200* (Cambridge University Press, 1998), p. 23. See also Mary Carruthers, *The Book of Memory: A Study of Memory in Medieval Culture* (Cambridge University Press, 1990).
20. For example, Russell T. McCutcheon, *Manufacturing Religion* (Oxford University Press, 1997), especially pp. 127–57; Tim Fitzgerald, *The Ideology of Religious Studies* (Oxford University Press, 1999), e.g. p. 6; Talal Asad, *Genealogies of Religion: Discipline and Reasons of Power in Christianity and Islam* (Baltimore: The Johns Hopkins University Press, 1993), pp. 27–54.
21. I have done so elsewhere. On 'religion' see my *Beyond Phenomenology: Rethinking the Study of Religion* (London and New York: Cassell, 1999), pp. 42–64.
22. Flood, *Beyond Phenomenology*, p. 47.
23. This is not to argue for a *sui generis* concept of religion. 'Religion' is wholly embedded within human histories. On the critique of religion in terms of the 'ultimately real', see McCutcheon, *Manufacturing Religion*, pp. 129–30. However, the term 'religion' and its adjective do distinguish one kind of cultural form from another, but this is not to say that such cultural forms are independent of or are not constrained by politics, social structure or brain structures.
24. Paul Griffiths, *Religious Reading: The Place of Reading in the Practice of Religion* (Oxford University Press, 1999), pp. 6–13.
25. *Mālinitvijayottara-tantra* 2.36–8; 41–6; 49–58; 5.5
26. See Denys Turner, *The Darkness of God: Negativity in Christian Mysticism* (Cambridge University Press, 1995), especially chapters 3 to 5.
27. See Lars Thunburg, *Microcosm and Mediator: The Theological Anthropology of Maximus the Confessor*, Alta Seminarii Neotestamentii Upsaliensis (Lund: Boktryckeri, 1965), pp. 52–99.
28. For example, Archimandrite Sophrony, *St Silouan the Athonite*, trs. Rosemary Edmonds (New York: St Vladimir's Seminary Press, 1999), pp. 171–5.
29. Le Goff, *History and Memory*, p. 11.
30. For example, Michel de Certeau, *The Writing of History*, trs. Tom Conley (New York: Columbia University Press, 1988), pp. 90–91.
31. Le Goff, *History and Memory*, pp. 11–13. See also Le Goff, 'L'histoire nouvelle' in J. Le Goff, R. Chartier and J. Revel (eds.), *La Nouvelle Histoire* (Paris: Retz, 1978), pp. 210–41.
32. Helga Nowotny, *Time: The Modern and Postmodern Experience*, trs. Neville Plaice (Cambridge: Polity Press, 1994), pp. 52–3.
33. For example, M. Eliade, *The Quest* (University of Chicago Press, 1969), pp. 75–7.
34. Sophrony, *Saint Silouan the Athonite*, p. 333.
35. John Bowker, *The Religious Imagination and the Sense of God* (Oxford: Clarendon Press, 1978), pp. 21–2: '. . . once fundamental resources are designated within a religious system as offering a legitimate constraint over the outcomes of any human behaviour or utterance which is to count as appropriate (or which is to come to an ultimately successful outcome, such as salvation or nirvana),

that system will develop mechanisms of transmission and control which will ensure continuity from life to life and from generation to generation'.

36. Nicholas Lash, 'Purification of Desire' in Julius Lipner (ed.), *The Fruits of Our Desiring* (Calgary: Bayeux Publications, 1997), pp. 1–10.
37. See Paul Heelas and Andy Locke (eds.), *Indigenous Psychologies: The Anthropology of the Self* (London: Academic Press, 1981).
38. M. de Certeau, *Culture in the Plural* (Minneapolis, London: University of Minnesota Press, 1997), p. 127.
39. Sylvain Auroux (general ed.), *Encyclopédie Philosophie Universelle: Les Notions Philosophiques Dictionnaire* vol. II (Paris: Presses Universitaires de France, 1990). 'Subjectivité', pp. 2477–80. This article traces its history. The term *subjectivité* first occurs in France in 1801 used by Charles de Villers, describing the philosophy of Kant. The Grimm Brothers' German dictionary of 1842 uses *Subjectivität* as a translation of *subjectivité*. But these concepts have a long history behind them. Plato discusses the idea of a search for an essence of oneself (*auto tanto*) and Aristotle discusses that which is fundamental (*upokeimenon*) to our nature. Augustine, quoted at the end of Husserl's *Cartesian Meditations*, says 'go back to yourself, truth dwells in the inner man' (*in te redi, in interiore homine habitat veritas*), and Ockham distinguishes between subjective being in things and living beings (*esse subiectivum in re* and *esse subiectivum in anima*). The history of the subjective can then be traced in France through Charles de Bovelles (1511), Pierre Ramus, Montaigne (1588), and so to Descartes (1628), who is responsible for the modern conception of the self's stability and identity, and Pascal. In Germany the story can be traced in the eighteenth century to Baumgarten, but particularly Kant, who articulated the idea of the subjective unity of consciousness. This usage can be traced through to phenomenology, from Hegel's self-consciousness to Husserl and Merleau-Ponty, and to existentialism. Kierkegaard, responding to Hegel, must also be identified as a key figure in the development of the concept, and its use can be traced into the twentieth century, where subjectivity and the idea of the subject has been critiqued by Foucault and others.
40. Charles Taylor, *The Sources of the Self: The Making of the Modern Identity* (Cambridge University Press, 1989), part 2.
41. On the romantic self see A. Bowie, *From Romanticism to Critical Theory: The Philosophy of German Literary Theory* (London and New York: Routledge, 1997), pp. 35–42. On Fichte's sense of subjectivity as the self-positing subject see F. Neuhouser, *Fichte's Theory of Subjectivity* (Cambridge University Press, 1990), pp. 117–66.
42. Frank B. Farrell, *Subjectivity, Realism and Postmodernism: The Recovery of the World in Recent Philosophy* (Cambridge University Press, 1994), pp. 1–4.
43. See Wilhelm Halbfass, *India and Europe: An Essay in Understanding* (Albany: SUNY Press, 1988), pp. 77–81.
44. Augustine, *Confessions* 10.6.9, quoted in J. M. Rist, *Augustine* (Cambridge University Press, 1994), p. 147.
45. Denys Turner, *The Darkness of God*, e.g. pp. 102–34 on Bonaventura.

46. C. Castoriadis, *The World in Fragments: Writings on Politics, Society, Psychoanalysis, and the Imagination*, trs. David Ames Curtis (Stanford University Press, 1997), p. 138.
47. P. Ricoeur, *Oneself as Another* (Chicago University Press, 1990), p. 19.
48. Kierkegaard, *Concluding Unscientific Postscript*, p. 192.
49. M. Bakhtin, *Problems of Dostoyevsky's Poetics* (Minneapolis: University of Minnesota Press, 1984), p. 185.
50. Within theology, one of the first and little-remembered theologians to compare Christianity with another religion, in this case Hinduism, was Rowland Williams, who, while being sympathetic to Hindu thought, sought to establish Christianity's superiority (Williams 1856). Other theologians such as Karl Barth claimed that Christianity in essence is not a religion (but rather revelation of the Word) and so is beyond comparison with others, while liberal theologians such as John Hick have on the other hand claimed that all religions are in some sense equal responses to 'the Real', their transcendent referent. In the nineteenth century, secular comparative religion, whose assumptions are implicitly critical of religion, was most famously advocated by Max Müller in his idea of a 'comparative science of religion' that 'he who knows one, knows none' (*Introduction to the Science of Religion: Four Lectures* (1893), Varanasi: Bharata Manishia, 1972, p. 13). Müller, in consonance with his age, sought an objective, truly scientific understanding of religions. Masson-Oursel popularised the idea of comparative philosophy, although, as Halbfass observes in his interesting essay on 'India and the Comparative Method', it was a Bengali scholar, N. N. Seal, who may have first coined the phrase 'comparative philosophy' in his *Comparative Studies in Vaishnavism and Christianity* in 1899 (see W. Halbfass, *India and Europe: An Essay in Understanding*, Albany: SUNY Press 1988, p. 422).
51. See E. Sharpe, *Comparative Religion* (London: Duckworth, 1975); Halbfass, *India and Europe*. For a critique of the enterprise see McCutcheon, *Manufacturing Religion*, e.g. pp. 101–04; Fitzgerald, *The Ideology of Religious Studies*, pp. 33–53. On a discussion of comparative philosophy with reference to Halbfass's work see Eli Franco and Karin Preisendanz (eds.), *Beyond Orientalism: The Work of Wilhelm Halbfass and its Impact on Indian and Cross-Cultural Studies* (Atlanta: Rodopi, 1997). See especially there Francis X. Clooney, 'Wilhelm Halbfass and the Openness of the Comparative Project', pp. 29–47.
52. Among the most important, of course, is E. Said, *Orientalism* (New York: Pantheon, 1978). For a critique of colonial constructions of India and Indian religions see R. Inden, *Imagining India* (Oxford and Cambridge, MA: Blackwell, 1990) and the work of the subaltern studies group, e.g. R. Guha and G. Spivak (eds.), *Selected Subaltern Studies* (Oxford University Press, 1988). For important discussions of the issues see F. Dallmayr, *Beyond Orientalism: Essays on Cross-Cultural Encounter* (Albany: SUNY Press, 1996); Richard King, *Orientalism and Religion: Postcolonial Theory and 'The Mystic East'* (London: Routledge, 1999). On the critique of the category 'Hinduism' see G.-D. Sontheimer and

H. Kulke, *Hinduism Reconsidered* (2nd ed.; Delhi: Manohar, 1997) and Gavin Flood (ed.), *The Blackwell Companion to Hinduism* (Oxford: Blackwell, 2003), pp. 2–4. For a defence of Indology see David Smith, 'Orientalism and Hinduism' in Flood, *The Blackwell Companion to Hinduism*, pp. 45–63.

53. B. C. Ray, 'Introduction', p. 2 in Kimberley C. Patton and Benjamin C. Ray (eds.), *A Magic Still Dwells: Comparative Religion in the Postmodern Age* (Berkeley and Los Angeles: University of California Press, 2000).
54. In relation to asceticism, an interesting volume of papers claims to focus on local specifications, yet in bringing these papers together in a single volume, a more general thesis is already assumed, although not made explicit. K. Ishwaran (ed.), *Ascetic Culture: Renunciation and Worldly Engagement* (Leiden: Brill, 1999).
55. Patton and Ray, *A Magic Still Dwells*, pp. 16–17.
56. This kind of work is being done. Perhaps the most important voice to emerge here in recent years is Frank Clooney, whose project of comparative theology is textually rooted in the Christian and Hindu traditions. He writes: 'I aim simply at some incremental progress in understanding the concerns of Hindu and Christian theologians together, by way of careful consideration of some details of a few particular cases.' Francis X. Clooney, *Hindu God, Christian God: How Reason Helps Break down the Boundaries Between Religions* (Oxford University Press, 2001), p. 15. For a good review of his important work see Matthew N. Schmalz, 'Tradition and Transgression in the Comparative Theology of Francis X. Clooney, S. J.', *Religious Studies Review* vol. 29, no. 2, April 2003, pp. 131–6. For work that considers the theoretical problems of pluralist theology, see Gavin d'Costa *Theology and Religious Pluralism* (Oxford: Blackwell, 1986) and Michael Barnes *Theology and the Dialogue of Religions* (Cambridge University Press, 2002). On comparative monasticism see Austin B. Creel and Vasudha Narayanan (eds.), *Monastic Life in Christian and Hindu Traditions: A Comparative Study* (Lewiston, Queenston, Lampeter: Edwin Mellen Press, 1990).
57. Flood, *Beyond Phenomenology*, p. 214.
58. M. Bakhtin, 'The Problem of Speech Genres' in *Speech Genres and Other Late Essays*, trs. Vern W. McGee (Austin: University of Texas Press, 1986), p. 69.
59. Ibid. pp. 68–9. See Flood, *Beyond Phenomenology*, p. 155.
60. Historicism I take simply to be the idea of historical specificity and unrepeatability. It is related to relativism in that meanings and social events can be understood only in their particular contexts, but is wider. All relativism is historicist, but historicism does not necessarily entail relativism, in that the claim to historical specificity does not exclude comparison, whereas a strong relativism would. For an introduction to the idea of historicism see Paul Hamilton, *Historicism* (London and New York: Routledge, 1996).
61. S. Levinson, 'Relativity in Spatial Conception and Description' in Gumpertz and Levinson (eds.), *Rethinking Linguistic Relativity*, pp. 177–202.
62. M. Silverstein and G. Urban (eds.), *Natural Histories of Discourse* (University of Chicago Press, 1996), pp. 1–4.

63. H. G. Gadamer, *Truth and Method*, trs. Joel Weinsheimer and Donald G. Marshall (London: Sheed and Ward, 1989), p. 267.
64. Peter Ochs, *Peirce, Pragmatism, and the Logic of Scripture* (Cambridge University Press, 1998), p. 170.
65. Eivind Kahrs, *Indian Semantic Analysis: The 'Nirvacana' Tradition* (Cambridge University Press, 1998), p. 8.
66. See for example S. H. Blackburn, *Singing of Birth and Death: Texts in Performance* (Philadelphia: University of Pennsylvania Press, 1988); Alf Hiltebeitel, *The Cult of Draupadi* vols. I and II (University of Chicago Press, 1988, 1991); Philip Lutgendorf, *The Life of a Text: Performing the Ramacaritmanas of Tulsidas* (Berkeley: University of California Press, 1991).
67. Diana L. Eck, *Darshan: Seeing the Divine in India* (Chambersburg: Anima Books, 1985).
68. G. Schopen, *Bones, Stones and Buddhist Monks* (Honolulu: University of Hawaii Press, 1997).
69. B. Faure, *The Rhetoric of Immediacy: A Cultural Critique of Chan/Zen* (Princeton University Press, 1991), pp. 65–6.
70. K. Trainor, *Relics, Ritual, and Representation in Buddhism: Rematerializing the Sri Lankan Theravada Tradition* (Cambridge University Press, 1997).
71. Harpham, *The Ascetic Imperative*, pp. 137–96.
72. Jorge J. E. Gracia, *Texts: Ontological Status, Identity, Author, Audience* (Albany: SUNY Press, 1996), pp. 6–7.
73. Harpham, *The Ascetic Imperative*, p. 175.
74. Wilhelm Dupré, *Patterns in Meaning: Reflections on Meaning and Truth in Cultural Reality, Religious Traditions, and Dialogical Encounters* (Kampen: Pharos, 1994), pp. 258–9. On a very interesting account of dialogue generally see pp. 252–4. Dupré also makes the important point that comparison is possible in religion because human beings share rational thinking (pp. 1–3).
75. Collins, *Nirvana*, pp. 27, 29.
76. My use and understanding of the term is based on Castoriadis, *The World in Fragments*, pp. 5–18. For a discussion of this term and a constructive use of it see Collins *Nirvana*, especially pp. 72–89.
77. For example, M. Bakhtin, 'Discourse in the Novel' in T. Holquist (ed.), *The Dialogic Imagination: Four Essays* (Austin: University of Texas Press, 1981), p. 272; Julia Kristeva, 'Word, Dialogue, and the Novel' in *Desire in Language: A Semiotic Approach to Literature and Art* (Oxford: Blackwell, 1980), p. 66.
78. John Bowker, *God: A Brief History* (London: Dorling Kindersley Publishing, 2002), p. 22.
79. Ochs, *Peirce*, p. 24.
80. Ibid. p. 34.
81. Jorge J. E. Gracia, *Texts*, p. 3.
82. Ochs, *Peirce*, p. 6.
83. M. Bakhtin, *Art and Answerability: Early Essays by M. M. Bakhtin* (Austin: University of Texas Press, 1990), p. 129; *Towards a Philosophy of the Act*, trs. Vadim Liapunov (Austin: University of Texas Press, 1993), pp. 14–16.

84. Ochs, *Peirce*, pp. 246–7. In chapter 8 of his book Ochs takes leave of the 'general reader' and offers readings to particular communities of readers.
85. Griffiths, *Religious Reading*, pp. 40–54; 60–76.
86. Ochs develops a sophisticated reading strategy comprising four stages and three levels of interpretation (*Peirce*, pp. 24–41) which I do not intend to follow here, although I have been influenced by his general approach and some specific suggestions.

PART I

# *The ascetic self in text and history*

CHAPTER 2

# *The asceticism of work: Simone Weil*

> You may be weaker than the whole world but you are always stronger than yourself. Let me send my power against my power.
>
> Gillian Rose[1]

I choose as my starting-point the twentieth-century religious and political philosopher Simone Weil. Why choose to begin with Weil? For three reasons. Firstly, in Weil's work we have a sense of self and subjectivity that speaks directly to us and reflects an existential sense of self and political individualism that resonates with late modernity, even though she advocates a destruction of the ego. Secondly, this subjectivity is linked with ways of thinking, acting and dying that can be characterised as ascetical in so far as she performs the ambiguity of the self and responds to the memory of tradition. Thirdly, Weil can be seen to stand at the end of a tradition of Christian renunciation and asceticism and provides an access point for our understanding of that tradition. Understanding a sense of religious subjectivity with Weil allows us to develop a strong form of the thesis of the ascetic self in relation to tradition. It furthermore provides us with an entry point into the world of South Asian reflection, separated from our twentieth-century example by possibly a thousand years and by different locations and languages. As future chapters unfold, the contrast between the Indian and European accounts will bring into focus the centrality of subjectivity in any description of asceticism.

## THE ASCETIC SELF IN SIMONE WEIL

Simone Weil presents us with a complex and tension-filled response to the question 'Who?' Her thought and life are integrated to an extraordinary degree, and both her life and writings are expressions of her deep convictions about the afflicted nature of the human condition and the reality, for her, of divine grace. Weil is a marvellous example of the performance of the ambiguity of the self. She wishes to eradicate the will, to replace the subjective will with divine will through the reception of grace, yet this is performed through great effort and suffering on her part. In some ways, hers is a pessimistic performance of the ascetic self, in so far as a normative human subjectivity is condemned to egotism and selfishness, although there is always the possibility of transcendence through suffering and grace. Yet in spite of this pessimism, her work is pervaded by a deep sense of subjectivity and inwardness. This subjectivity is closely linked to her sense of affliction – reinforced by the political circumstances into which she was born – alongside a sense of the love of God. A brief sketch of her life is necessary for an appreciation of the force of her thinking.[2]

She was born into a secular Jewish family. She passed out of the Ecole Normale Supérieure as a qualified teacher of philosophy, which she taught at schools in Le Puy, Auxerre and Roanne from 1931 to 1934. She combined her teaching with trade union militancy and, owing to her strong identification with those she perceived to be afflicted, she left teaching to work in an electrical factory making equipment for metro cars in Paris. She worked in two more heavy industry factories, at a stamping press in the Carnault et Forges de Basse Indre works at Billancourt, and as a milling machine operator at the Renault factory at Boulogne-Billancourt, briefly returning to teaching and likewise briefly joining the Republican side in the Spanish Civil War in 1936. Because of an accident in Spain, which McLellan notes probably saved her life,[3] she was forced to return to France. After a spell of sick leave and a long family holiday, she moved with her family following the June 1940 Armistice to the south of France. She had significant religious experiences in 1937 and 1938 that confirmed her Christian orientation: at a popular religious festival in Portugal, in a chapel where St Francis had prayed at Assisi, and at the Benedictine monastery of Solesmes. In the south of France she met the Dominican priest Father Perrin, who introduced her to Gustave Thibon, on whose farm in the Rhône valley she worked. Both became partners in dialogue with her. In 1942 she sailed to New York with her parents to escape occupied France, leaving her notebooks with Thibon, and later that same year sailed to Britain. Here she worked for the Free French organisation in London for a while, contracted tuberculosis, refused food and died at Ashford in Kent aged thirty-four. For some, her death was unnecessary, her condition being exacerbated by a conscious weakening of the body through allowing herself only the food ration of her fellow workers in occupied France. The coroner reported that she died owing to pulmonary tuberculosis and starvation, and that she had killed herself through refusing to eat.

Simone Weil's life and work articulate a very modern, and a very Western, religious subjectivity: very modern, on account of her longing for religious expression coupled with a strong resistance to formalised religion, and very Western, because of her deep engagement with Christianity, her immersion in the language of Western philosophy, especially Plato, and her strong political and ethical individualism. But Weil's asceticism is poignantly ambiguous. She performs ascetic acts, setting these acts within the Christian tradition, yet she strongly resists being placed within tradition by consistently refusing baptism into the Catholic Church to which she was nevertheless deeply drawn.[4] Weil is modern in absorbing a scientific worldview, yet at the same time her asceticism draws on a cosmological Christianity. Simone Weil is a figure with appeal to contemporary Western sensibilities as a dweller on the margins, an inhabiter of the borders, resisting formal commitment yet deeply bound to a religious subjectivity. This subjectivity simultaneously wishes to eradicate the self in order to know transcendence but also wishes to develop the self in its acceptance of necessity: a subjectivity that wishes to willingly embrace suffering, yet wishes to alleviate the suffering of others. Weil's is a subjectivity bound up with time and particularity but which rejects the egotistic development of the personality. As one of her biographers, David McLellan, says, 'Certainly there are few lives which involve as much paradox as hers.'[5] In Weil we have not only a modern example of an articulation of subjectivity but a modern example of asceticism in the service of others.

Her writings are not systematic and do not form a uniform body, but there are certainly recurring themes from her earlier to her later work. The first phase of her work – particularly the text 'Reflections Concerning the Causes of Liberty and Social Oppression' published in *Oppression and Liberty* (see page 40 below) and her early notebooks – reflects a political engagement and identification with ordinary working people which she enacted in becoming a factory worker and then later an agricultural labourer. This identification with the suffering of others was a source of her asceticism and contributed to her eventual demise. The second phase of her work, which includes the letters and essays she wrote for Father Perrin, her later notebooks and *The Need for Roots* written ten years after *Oppression and Liberty*, reveals a keen religious sensibility and a grappling with questions of Christian faith, human meaning and human institutions in a time of great social upheaval. While the later phase of her writing is distinctly religious in character, there is nevertheless continuity with earlier themes, such as the need for work, the nature of work and detachment. In all of her texts is a deep concern with both the social and political nature of being and the nature of the self. I wish here to draw out Weil's sense of self and the distinctly subjective character of her asceticism through focussing on her understanding of work, time and necessity, and waiting. The effect of focussing on these concerns is to produce a fairly consistent reading of Weil's texts, a reading that emphasises the continuities between the earlier and later writings and a reading that places Weil clearly within a Christian tradition of reflection, but a tradition that is in tension with her modernity.

## THE ASCETICISM OF WORK

Throughout her short life, Weil had a strong sense of social justice and a personal need to identify with the oppressed of the world. This is reflected in her involvement with trade unionism, her engagement with Marxism and postcolonialism, and her personal encounters with working life and working people. *Oppression and Liberty* provides a critique of Marx and develops her own political thinking. She agreed with Marxism that 'social existence is determined by the relations between man and nature established by production',[6] and she understood that workers were oppressed with 'brutal force' by falling wages and increasing workloads.[7] The exploitation generated through these relations must be seen in the wider context of power and in terms of the wider concept of oppression. Along with Marx, she thought that nothing takes place other than through material transformation, and that Marx had done more than others to understand the causes and mechanism of oppression. But while Marx analysed oppression in terms of the system of production as a result of historical process, Weil analysed it in terms of a general, pervasive power in which oppressors and oppressed are equally bound.[8] The race for power 'enslaves everybody', and humans throughout history have been the 'plaything of the instruments of domination they themselves have manufactured.'[9] It is not private interest that is the prime motivation in historical relationships, but rather impersonal power which sacrifices human lives, ironically, to achieve a better way of life. She writes:

> Power, by definition, is only a means; or to put it better, to possess a power is simply to possess means of action which exceed the very limited force that a single individual has at his disposal. But power-seeking, owing to its essential incapacity to seize hold of its object, rules out all consideration of an end, and finally comes, through an inevitable reversal, to take the place of all ends. It is this reversal of the relationship between means and end, it is this fundamental folly that accounts for all that is senseless and bloody right through history.[10]

This is essentially a tragic view of history. Human beings desire to improve the conditions of their lot and envisage a utopian future created through the exercise of power, but this future is constantly deferred, and power becomes its own end and humans its victims. Master and slave are both bound up in a power relationship that cannot, it seems, be broken. Although Weil never gave up the idea of improving the human condition, by 1934 she had become disillusioned with the thought that revolutionary change would take place through overt political activity; oppression does not engender revolt but rather submission.[11] Marx is defective for Weil in not addressing the question of how factors of oppression, so bound up with social life, would suddenly disappear with revolution and how workers in factories could be anything other than 'mere cogs'.[12] The state mechanism – enforced through the army, police and bureaucracy – cannot be overthrown by workers' revolution because the workers themselves are so ground down by the master–slave relationship engendered by the industrial process.

Work therefore is an expression of power, and a worker's ability to exercise his or her will upon it is strictly limited. Workers are bound up in relationships with each other and with their overseers, relationships determined by 'technique' and by the production process constraining social interaction. During her time in the factories, Weil experienced at first hand the mechanisms of power operative on the factory floor, an experience that drove home to her the inexorable conditions under which ordinary workers operate and that forged her political and religious ideas. In stressing the species as the location of the process of liberation, Marx, she thought, neglected the individual, the particularity of the one who suffers, whom she encountered every day in her work. She suffered intensely during this period, undergoing great fatigue and violent headaches that accompanied her throughout her life. For example, she writes in her 'Factory Journal' of Wednesday 19 December 1934: 'Very violent headache, finished the work while weeping almost uninterruptedly.' There are frequent references to her debilitating headaches throughout the journal.[13] The effect of exhaustion, she writes in her journal, made her forget the real reason for her working in the factory (to experience work and express solidarity), and she says that she began 'to stop thinking' as a way of alleviating the suffering entailed. Even her feeling of outrage at injustice could become eroded under such circumstances.[14] The worker simply submits to the conditions of oppression and becomes an automaton, subordinating her body to the regimes of institutional, mechanistic power. Force, says Weil, 'turns man into a thing'.[15] A twenty-six-year-old fellow worker, Mimi, observed, 'They take us for machines . . . others are here to think for us . . .', which is precisely, comments Weil, what the engineer Frederick Taylor desired in his system of 'scientific management'.[16] For the industrial, social machine to function, the worker needs to eradicate a sense of self and to become a slave with no rights.[17] Personal will has to be subordinated to institution. Work, along with the human relationships developed around it, is governed by an impersonal power that has ceased to function as a means towards an ideal goal but has become a self-perpetuating end in itself.

Although Weil maintains that work in the service of capitalist production entails exploitation, she has an ambivalent attitude towards it, and her use of the term 'work' contains a certain ambiguity. On the one hand it refers to joyful, meaningful action in the world, action by which we make sense of the world, on the other it refers to paid employment which she thought to be so often degrading and alienating: the physical, dehumanising factory work that places people in a servile relationship to their masters, as she herself experienced. But her linking of work with epistemology accommodates both senses. Work is, as it were, the medium by which we know the world and through which I know myself. Through work, Weil says in the 'Pre-War Notebook', 'man creates a universe around him'.[18] As Moulakis says, 'Work is the linchpin of Simone Weil's thought.'[19] If work is fulfilling, creative and meaningful action, it gives the worker a sense of the complete process of production and the end product as a material expression of himself, as Marx thought work should be. But, on the contrary, work for the industrial, capitalist machine gives the worker a sense of meaninglessness and oppression. Either way, whether work provokes a sense of deep alienation or fulfilment, the objective conditions of the workplace render up knowledge of the world and one's place within it.

Work – the hard, routine, manual work of the proletariat – is oppressive, but can become a means of going beyond the limits imposed by it: work consciously done can become a form of asceticism, a way of reversing the flow of the body and of time. The self can inwardly oppose power and overstep it through detached acceptance, so that work becomes a form of asceticism in that it controls the passions and allows for self-mastery.[20] This is precisely the attitude that Weil took to the factory. Indeed, in her 'Pre-War Notebook', written at about the time she took leave from teaching at Roanne to work in the Paris factory, she speaks of the joy experienced in work, a joy identified with an intensification of a sense of the world's reality.[21] But this does not seem to have been a common experience, and most of the time her work in the factory was drudgery.[22] To avoid being crushed by the mindless, mechanistic machine of the industrial process, she chose to turn work into an ascetic practice as an act of will and to appropriate the bodily discipline the work demanded. Impersonal, sovereign power expressed through work becomes subjectively opposed through its appropriation.

Work must therefore be seen as part of a general theory of action that is related to her understanding of the body – particularly the body in the ascetic process – and the ordering of time in discipline. Her earliest essay that discusses some of these issues is her dissertation for the Ecole Normale, 'Science and Perception in Descartes'. In part two of this essay, Weil attempts her own 'Cartesian' process of attempting to gain apodictic knowledge. Going down the path of radical doubt, the essay follows Descartes in claiming that nothing reveals itself as existing except in so far as I am conscious of it, but unlike Descartes she does not conclude immediately that being follows from thinking. Rather than thinking, it is through the power of thinking – of which the power of doubting is an example – that I know that I am: 'I can act, therefore I am' (*je puis, donc je suis*).[23] She substitutes 'I can (act)' (*je puis*) for 'I think' (*cogito*), with the implication that to think is to act: the ability of decision – the ability to accept and reject – is a kind of action.[24] To know and to exist are part of the ability to act, so 'what I am is defined by what I can do'.[25] In direct response to the question 'Who am I?' Weil can therefore claim that 'I am the being who exercises this power and that apart from the exercise of power I am nothing.' As Peter Winch observes, for Weil the word 'I' simply expresses 'the grammatical subject of the activity-verb; it does not refer to an entity which happens to perform this activity and which might do other things as well.'[26]

Weil's argument therefore radically departs from that of Descartes. Rather than a disembodied *cogito*, a thinking substance experiencing the world through extension in the body, Weil's subject in the Descartes essay is embedded in the world.[27] The nature of being in the world is the ability to act, of which thinking is a particular kind. A more fundamental category than thinking is therefore this power to act (*pouvoir*) or willing, and willing is given expression through action and so through the body. However, this personal power of action is very limited, and the limit of that power is externally imposed. I can act only within the boundaries of contingency or chance (*hasard*). This limit or external constraint on personal power is the existence of an other imposed on the self. The historical power of the industrial machine and the human relationships dictated by it would be an example, but thoughts and fantasies of the imagination that come unbidden are also impositions of other existence. A feature of this imposition through the imagination is that acceptance and rejection, pleasure and displeasure are combined. Only to the extent that I can exert my will over these contingencies in disengaging from them am I free: 'I am free only to the extent that I can disengage myself.'[28] Indeed, liberty is self-control.[29] This other existence, imposed upon me through the imagination, deprives me of sovereignty but leaves me the freedom of resistance to the weight of the world 'which presses on me' as aversion, desire and belief. She writes that 'I do not have sovereign power over my thoughts; I am only their arbiter,' but I do have the power of refusal, which is the power of judgement, and this comprises my freedom.[30] My judgement is the only thing I possess, the power of refusal to assent to a belief or desire, to a refusal of imagination, so as not to become 'the plaything of my impulses'. Weil's understanding of Descartes' doubt is thus to see it as the means whereby one experiences the weight of other existence through resisting it. The power of Descartes' doubt Weil reads as the refusal of the power of other existence over oneself.

Subjectivity for Weil might therefore be said to be of degree. The greater the power of refusal of other existence, the greater the subjectivity; the less we are able to refuse, the more automated we become. We might add that the greater the reversal of the flow of the body, the greater the intensification of subjectivity. Work is therefore the place in which degrees of subjectivity are expressed. Although the action remains the same, the attitude of the worker or the ability to become detached from the work process defines the degree of subjectivity, defines the degree to which we have agency and freedom, and defines the fullness of humanity. Weil notes that a saint and thief appear to walk down the same road, but because of their inner states they walk down different roads. Work is the arena in which subjectivity can therefore be expressed and in which agency is exercised in the refusal of imagination and the refusal of the temptation to become automated. It provides an objective means whereby judgements made on the basis of mere feeling and sensation can be regulated. Weil writes: 'When I respond with work, rather than with feelings of joy or sadness, to the assault of the world that I call sensations, they provide the mind with nothing but an object for work.'[31] Work gives objective contact with the world and allows for knowledge not subject to the vicissitudes of psychological states. Although in her 'Factory Journal' Weil did speak of the joy of work, her point is that joy and sadness need to be transcended through the routine application of the body to the work process.

Although there are elements of a utopianism of work in Weil's writings, the predominant sense is that work, when performed for the relentless industrial machine, creates only alienation. But given mechanistic production in which the worker is virtually a slave to impersonal power, what can be done? Weil's response to this is to work as an act of will and to make the body conform to the processes and the discipline entailed. Work becomes an extension of the body and an expression of subjectivity. The blind man is not simply passive in negotiating the world with his stick, but rather the stick becomes an extension of his body.[32] Similarly, the sailor is aware of his ship 'no less instantly than he senses the messages of his own nerves'.[33] This sense of the extended body is the true sense of work. Indeed, Weil even considers the entire universe to be an extension of the body of the self, 'le *je*' or the *ātman*, as the blind man's stick is an extension of his own body.[34]

With this idea of the extended body, Weil senses a phenomenology – founded on Husserl's distinction between body and lived body – that is significantly later developed by Merleau-Ponty.[35] The body is taken to be, as it were, a field of perception where the immediate environment, such as the workplace, becomes an extension of the body and senses. The regime of work produces in the body a pattern of behaving that, constantly reinforced, becomes habit. The creation of such a habit has positive value for Weil, who observes that the good workman is the opposite of an automaton.[36] Yet she also puts a negative value on this. To labour, she says, is to subject being, body and soul to inert matter and to turn oneself into an instrument. The labourer becomes 'an appendix of the tool which he handles' and the body and attention become 'a function of the requirements of the tool, which itself is adapted to the matter being worked upon'.[37] The body and its adaptation to the work environment are inevitable and necessary but negative in so far as the adaptation to inert matter, to the matter in hand in the labour situation, is akin to death and so is a kind of violence to human nature. This adaptation to work in which the body takes on the form of its object and becomes an extension or appendix of the machine is necessarily temporal. As inert matter is subject to the movement of time, so too is the labourer in the same way. The labourer finds that the 'hours drag' but has no choice other than to carry on, whether he or she feels happy or sad, bursting with energy or tired. Work is 'renewed each morning throughout the entire length of a human existence, day after day, and each day it lasts until the evening, and it starts again on the following day, and this goes on often until death'.[38]

But when approached with an attitude of attention, the mindless repetition of the bodily habit in the work environment can become an ascetic process. Through habit, the body becomes a vehicle to achieve a detachment of the self from the immediate surroundings, a detachment through acceptance of the present condition. The body becomes the means of willing acceptance of work that allows for the individual to transcend the human condition or, more particularly, to transcend the experience of enslavement in depersonalising conditions. This detachment is the reversal of the body's flow. If culture can be defined in terms of embodied practice or structured dispositions to behave in certain ways (Bourdieu's *habitus*[39]), then the dispositions of the workplace set within the body can become dispositions of ascetic transcendence. The degree of subjectivity for Weil that distinguishes the human from the automaton is therefore the degree of the refusal of assent to depersonalisation, even while in the midst of it. As it was for early monks in Egypt,[40] physical labour becomes the 'spiritual core' of a well-ordered social life in so far as it provides the opportunity for transcendence through the individual facing and allowing him- or herself to be subjected to the work regime.

## TIME AND NECESSITY

The discipline of the body entailed in work, the production of a bodily habit, is therefore related by Weil to the acceptance of time and necessity. This is a distinctly non-gendered view of the body. Whatever the body and its social condition, the self is opened through detachment to spiritual perfection. Through this kind of detachment we can overcome the limited viewpoint of the present and pass over to the eternal. The asceticism of work is a means of such a passing over. She writes:

> The spiritual function of physical labour is the contemplation of things, the contemplation of nature.
> Passing over to the eternal is, for the soul, an operation analogous to that by which, in perception, we refrain from putting ourselves at the centre of space although perspective makes us seem to be there.[41]

The contemplation of nature or of 'things' facilitated through physical labour is the attainment of a kind of objective perception. We can see here a strong inclination towards the necessary idea of cosmology: that human action and asceticism must be seen in the context of a wider, cosmic frame. This objective perception is not limited to, and is bereft of, individuality and is characterised by the acceptance of time and the necessity of the way time unfolds. To refrain from putting ourselves at the centre of space is the supremely ascetic act, the act of renunciation that allows us to work in spite of ailing physical conditions and to achieve a kind of non-perspectival perception. There are many instances of this kind of detachment and rejection of particular perspective in the work situation. Her 'Factory Journal' is filled with instances of Weil continuing to work in spite of profound physical distress, particularly crippling headaches, fatigue and even hunger.[42] This perception of the eternal can only occur with the eradication of the passions and attachments, for they obscure discrimination. As we shall see, this idea is very close to certain South Asian models of perception but, as Cockburn discusses, does not involve the eradication of the human. To see things as they really are, without attachment, is to see them 'in a way which involves a cancelling of those concerns which involve a reference to the object's relation to myself',[43] but which nevertheless still remain subjective. With the passage of time modifications occur in us, and if we keep our gaze fixed on a certain thing, then what is illusory and what is real appears. The eternal is not affected by time, and because of this is more easily glimpsed in the past where time is less clouded by attachment. The past becomes the best image of the supernatural reality because we cannot step towards it, but only turn ourselves towards its emanations.[44] The practice of detachment whilst in the midst of activity – in the practice of physical labour – is a turning towards the emanations of the eternal and also an acceptance of necessity in the temporal order.[45] Through subjecting the self to the oppression of the sovereign power of the industrial process, the self can exercise its power of refusal of psychological states. While the necessity of the temporal order is experienced as affliction, through the appropriation of work in the service of asceticism the self can go beyond necessity and affliction to face the eternal. Through the asceticism of work, work is transcended. And, one might add, the body and time are transcended through the body: the flow of the body is reversed.

So far we have seen how, for Weil, the asceticism of physical labour is the way in which the self becomes detached from sovereign power and accepts temporal necessity. This temporal necessity must be seen in the context of Weil's Christian theology. Time keeps us from the eternal and is the consequence, to use Christian mythological language, of original sin. It is from sin that time proceeds as a way in which God alienates himself from himself; it is the creation of infinite distance between the self and God. Miklos Vetö puts this well: 'The originally Kantian sense of the subjectivity of time receives a new meaning. Time is the form of "representations" human beings alone can conceive, but it is precisely the supremely personal act of original sin that "causes" time; time is the limit God imposes on himself through human existence.'[46] Time is the force that drives the world on, which imposes suffering, and which allows the self to fulfil its goals, for action occurs only through the medium of time.

We are tortured by time, says Weil, and attempt to escape from it either by remaining below it – through the flesh – or by passing above it into eternity.[47] To remain with time is to face the affliction of human reality, and to work is to attempt to control it. Work is a way of ordering time, and through the discipline of work we can control time to a limited extent. We are time's slaves, but we do have some power over how it passes.[48]

A complex of related ideas presents itself here that connects the mundane reality of mechanised labour with metaphysical speculation. Work is mechanical and constrained by time. The worker is acutely aware of the passage of time, aware of his or her own time (the beginning and end of shifts), and of the need to produce within a certain time-frame. Linking a Marxist analysis of work with a Christian theology of the fall, Weil sees the passage of time in work as alienating and dehumanising. This dehumanisation is sin, the infinite distance between self and God, but is also necessity. Through necessity, or the inevitability of what actually occurs, the self is afflicted. The concepts of work, time, necessity and affliction are therefore closely linked in Weil's thought. She sees work in the capitalist system of production as the mechanism of affliction, both of the masters and the slaves, and work itself as a structuring of time. Time is furthermore related to necessity, a concept very close to fate. Everything that has happened in the universe is necessity, which (seen from the perspective of the divine) is providence, or God's face turned towards the universe.[49] Paradoxically, this necessity as divine order should be loved simply because its source is God. She writes:

> The order of the world is to be loved because it is pure obedience to God. Whatever this universe accords us or inflicts on us, it does so exclusively out of obedience . . . (A)ll that happens to us throughout the course of our life, having been brought about by total obedience of this universe to God, places us in contact with the absolute good formed by the divine will; in virtue of this, everything, without any exception, joys and sorrows alike, ought to be welcomed with the same inward attitude of love and thankfulness.[50]

This idea is particularly developed in Weil's 1942 essay 'The Love of God and Affliction'. Here she discusses the idea that affliction is a form of existence made present through physical suffering, yet is more than physical suffering and entails social degradation or fear of such degradation. Affliction is an irreducible factor in human life that cannot be adequately explained or described. In deepest affliction there is a total absence of God and 'in this darkness where there is nothing to love, the soul ceases to love'.[51] This is the greatest possible distance, an infinite distance, between the self and God which deprives people of personality and turns them into objects. Space, time and the mechanism that drives matter constitute affliction, which can also be understood as 'the distance put by Love between "God and God"'.[52]

The self afflicted by time and necessity must accept that affliction. There is certainly a paradox here, for the self must also strive to improve conditions in the world as well as strive for detachment from the necessity of affliction. The necessity of affliction is the inevitability of the flow of the body, and striving for detachment is its reversal. This striving, by developing an attitude of detachment in action, is nothing other than becoming receptive to grace. But there is no human effort that can move us towards God: 'we are incapable of progressing vertically', one is no nearer to flying at the top of a mountain than at the bottom.[53] It is God who comes to us, and all we can do is give up our own feelings to allow the soul's passage or the turning in the direction of God. In Weil's startling image, affliction is akin to a nail being hit with a hammer, the point of which contains the shock of the blow. Extreme affliction 'which means physical pain, distress of soul and social degradation' constitutes the nail that is applied to the centre of the soul, the head of which is universal necessity. 'The man to whom such a thing happens has no part in the operation. He struggles like a butterfly which is pinned alive into an album. But through all the horror he can continue to want to love.'[54] In the end, this is all a human can do. Ascetic action is a kind of passivity of the afflicted self, a passivity that is also the love of God and the love of what is ordained. Through this being pinned by affliction and turning the gaze upwards, as it were, to the divine light, the self can become decentred, eliminate self-reference and receive divine grace – an attitude that the Stoics referred to as *amor fati*, the love of the world order.[55]

## WAITING FOR GOD

This passivity of the self waiting for divine grace Weil called 'inactive action'. Finding this idea in the Hindu scripture, the *Bhagavad-gītā*,[56] she speaks of detachment from the fruits of action which is to act 'not *for* an object, but *from* necessity.'[57] That is, action becomes not goal-directed, but is a response to the demands of a situation, accompanied by an attitude of detachment. It is here that Weil's philosophy is fundamentally ethical. Rather than detachment from the fruits of action meaning indifference, on the contrary, passivity means that God is perceived in one's neighbour. Goal-directed activity is self-referential, based on desire and motive, whereas inactive action is not goal-directed but is other-oriented. In not trying to achieve a personal goal, action becomes a response to the demands of a situation, a response which, without the interference of personal desire, is fundamentally ethical. As Cockburn notes, inactive action is a response to external demands: 'I see the beggar's hunger and I give him food. I hear and see the woman's grief on the loss of her child, and I comfort her.'[58]

The basic structure of this theology is that humanity dwells in a fallen state outside of divine light and needs to become a vessel for God's love through self-annihilation. Yet this theology is not articulated in a systematic way but in deeply personal terms. Rather than speaking generally, Weil speaks of herself as one who has been given being by God and whose purpose is to return it to him: 'God allows me to exist outside himself. It is for me to refuse this authorization.'[59] Through a person's refusing the authorisation of being, through the eradication of the self, God, as it were, is reflected back on himself and perceives himself in creation. Quoting the desert fathers, Weil writes in her notebook that '"In the world there is only myself and God" [Even so, it is too many]'.[60] This process of self-annihilation Weil called 'decreation', the process whereby the ego becomes annihilated in God. She writes: 'God creates a finite being who says I, who cannot love God. By the effect of grace, little by little the I disappears, and God loves himself through the creature who becomes empty, who becomes nothing.'[61]

For Weil, the first person pronoun, the 'I', is an index of our ontological distance from the creator, and decreation is the means whereby this distance is crossed. The crossing or eradication of this distance is the elimination of the 'I', and this can only be done by God coming to us. The 'I' confines us within necessity, and by renouncing it we pass 'to the other side' by piercing 'the egg of the world'.[62] Decreation, at the heart of self-knowledge, is the way in which God apprehends himself in love.

While the purpose of an individual life is the annihilation of the self in order for God to be reflected back to himself, this is yet a personal experience for Weil. Indeed, it would seem that personal experience is to be trusted as a source of knowledge when she writes:

> I am absolutely certain that there is a God in the sense that I am absolutely certain that my love is not illusory. I am absolutely certain that there is not a God, in the sense that I am absolutely certain that there is nothing real which bears a resemblance to what I am able to conceive when I pronounce that name, since I am unable to conceive God. But that thing, which I am unable to conceive, is not an illusion. This impossibility is more immediately present to me than is the feeling of my own personal existence.[63]

This higher understanding began to have an existential impact upon her when at the Benedictine monastery of Solesmes. Attending all the church services, she felt the passion of Christ enter her and had further mystical experiences following this, particularly when reciting George Herbert's poem 'Love' as a prayer. She spoke of this moment, when she was in intense physical pain due to one of the severe headaches which plagued her, as a sense of 'a presence more personal, more certain, and more real than that of a human being; it was inaccessible both to sense and to imagination, and it resembles the love that irradiates the tenderest smile of somebody one loves.'[64] These are interesting comments that place Weil clearly within a Christian mystical tradition and the tradition of paradoxical language. Her conception of God is impersonal, yet here we have talk of a person and of love; her claims about the experience of God entail the eradication of the subject of experience, yet here we have a relationality that entails the co-presence of two persons. All this is intensified through and inseparable from the pain that Simone Weil underwent. Indeed, such experience of the divine is inseparable from pain: suffering is a necessary condition for the experience of God and the most extreme suffering in affliction, the point at the foot of the cross farthest from God, is paradoxically where God can be seen. Christ at the extreme of affliction in fear in Gethsemane and in pain on the cross, excluded from the Father ('Why hast thou forsaken me?'), is where Christ is closest to the Father.[65] Going deeper into transcendence requires suffering, yet suffering implies the lack of transcendence because of absorption in present pain. It is here, thinks Weil, that we need to wait for God. It is this state of waiting (*en hypomène*),[66] devoid of attachment, that is a true asceticism, where necessity is accepted and power subjectively appropriated. Waiting for God is the performance of the ascetic self, both the reversal of the flow of the body and the acceptance of necessity.

Although she hardly uses the term, asceticism is at the heart of Weil's thought. It is a peculiarly Christian asceticism, for it is an asceticism of passivity, which can be understood as a turning to receive grace. The sources of Weil's asceticism are mainly Platonic. We see this from her constant evoking of Plato and Greek thought and her resistance to the more body-oriented and vital worldview of Judaism. The god of the Old Testament is close to the Gnostic demiurge for Weil. Indeed, she is strongly influenced by the Cathars, and their persecution by the Catholic Church is one reason for her disdaining to join it. The body is both the friend and enemy of the soul. Echoing Plato she writes that the 'body is a prison . . . the body is a tomb'[67] and that the body is only of use to the spiritual part of the soul, which must 'wall up' the carnal part. Yet the body is also 'the lever of salvation', 'a lever by which the soul acts upon the soul',[68] and Weil evokes stories of monks and hermits showing this. The body is used as the means of transcendence by monks, in manual labour, the solitude of the cell, and through fasting and vigil.[69] The body as the lever to salvation is the abode of waiting, the place where, through acceptance of time and necessity, the self awaits the reception of grace.

## SUBJECTIVITY, COMPASSION, AND RENUNCIATION

Our reading of Weil has highlighted the body in work as an expression of will alongside the development of detachment that allows the body in the world to be understood as a consequence of time and necessity. In the asceticism of work, the self becomes simultaneously detached and aware of affliction. For Weil, both detachment and awareness of affliction are necessary for spiritual development, and both are intimately related. Moulakis comments that there is a discrepancy between the purity of Weil's asceticism and compassion,[70] and although in one sense this is true, for Weil each entails the other. True compassion only arises through detachment and ascetic purity. To become detached is to become aware of affliction both in oneself and in others. Detachment is therefore connected with compassion in that only in detachment, once self-concern is eradicated, can real compassion for the afflicted develop. In her 'New York Notebook' Weil writes:

> It is only unconditional love that can compel the soul to expose itself to moral death, and unconditional love has no other object than unconditioned good, which is God. Therefore it is quite certain that only a soul which has been killed, knowingly or not, by the love of God can really pay attention to the affliction of the afflicted.[71]

Paying attention to the affliction of the afflicted is to see the fullness of the human condition, and seeing affliction entails action to alleviate suffering. But seeing affliction and then acting upon it is not to act from a sense of self, as we have seen, but to simply respond to the demands of the situation from a perspective of inactive action. Only the soul that has been 'killed' by contact with God can truly see affliction and act out of compassion. It is as if both perception of affliction and love of God were one and the same thing, and both are part of the structure of the universe in Weil's theology. Here we are at the heart of the matter. Contact with God through renunciation is necessary in order to transmute human energies that propagate themselves in vegetative life into the love of God. In a late passage in the 'New York Notebook' Weil writes: 'When contact has been made, through total renunciation, with the true God it is then desirable to turn all one's desires without exception towards God in prayer; for this contact burns up all the evil in them and transmutes the energy which sustained them into sustenance for the love of God.'[72]

Weil's thought must be understood on different levels here. From the divine perspective there is no human action, only necessity worked out through time. But from a human perspective, we act as though we possess agency. The self is defined by will and the ability to act, but this action is severely restricted by the unfolding of creation as necessity. Through the practice of detachment, through inactive action developed in situations of action (particularly work), the self can begin a process of decreation and become open to divine grace. This is the performance of the ambiguity of the self, quintessentially performed in asceticism. Becoming open to divine grace is in fact the eradication of the will, the death of the soul, and in its place God loves himself through the creature becoming empty. 'Ask God for spiritual death', she says, in order that a person may no longer live, but God live in him.[73] Through this eradication of the 'I' – for Weil understands the 'soul' as the true subject of first person predicates – affliction in others is perceived and action becomes selfless for the sake of the other.

Affliction is a mixed blessing. To understand God means to renounce the self in order to see God 'at the centre of oneself', but this means 'total renunciation of being anybody and complete consent to being merely a thing'.[74] But becoming a thing, becoming completely objectified, is something characteristic of oppression. Human beings who are worn down by affliction perceive themselves in this way, and the worker in the factory has become merely a thing. But this affliction and objectification has occurred without consent. So although the objective conditions of oppression may be the same for two people, it is the willing acceptance of oppression that characterises the ascetical attitude of the self waiting for God. It is intentional suffering, the acceptance of suffering and affliction as an act of will, that marks off the affliction of the mendicant from that of the worker.

In Weil's work we can see how subjectivity comes into view through suffering, and how the ascetic self suffers intentionally in order to transcend the self. For Weil, the subject is at the mercy of impersonal power expressed in the flow of the body – described as necessity – yet has the power of resistance and can resist this impersonal power through its appropriation and acceptance. Sovereign power is inscribed upon the self, upon the body in the creation of bodily work habits, but the self can resist this power through turning action into renunciation. Renunciation, the reversal of the body's flow, the reversal of necessity, becomes the only real freedom a person has, which is to realise the fullness of humanity and to enable selfless action: through renunciation, the self can act with total compassion for the welfare of others.

## THINKING THE SELF WITH SIMONE WEIL

As we have seen, Weil has a deeply ambiguous attitude towards the self. It is positive in so far as experience happens to someone and she attributes value to human life, and negative in so far as the self is ultimately to be negated and replaced with divine cognition. In so far as human beings have a purpose, it is to become vessels for God's love through self-annihilation. Through an act of will the self accepts affliction, which is what marks off ascetic, intentional suffering from simple suffering, but through this act of will the self desires its own death. Reading Weil, we are left with a sense of strong continuities in her writing and yet also of apparent contradictions and problems. Beneath the prose of her work we need to understand the 'system of exclusions' operating there. There is the problem of the body, namely Weil's ambivalent attitude towards it and her exclusion of the erotic body and the female reproductive body.[75] There is the traditional problem of justification and the grace–effort debate, and there is the problem of Weil's ascetic self intentionally excluded from a contemporary community and tradition. It is the latter problem I wish to focus on here, because the issue of the relation of the self to tradition and the ambiguity of the performance of memory in Weil highlights the problem of agency and power in the ascetic case. I propose to deal with this question by firstly looking at Weil's general problem of the relation of the self to the other, and secondly by looking at the self in relation to tradition and community with specific reference to ritual and power.

### *The self and the other*

Given that Weil's hope for the self is its demise through coming into contact with transcendent love, how is this compatible with the centrality of compassion in her thought and the desire to alleviate human suffering? Weil herself seems to be aware of the tension. In the 'New York Notebook' she states that the 'I' belongs to non-being and that God created the self as a non-being in order that it should emerge from non-being through love.

The subject of first person predicates is an index of nothingness and infinite distance between creation and creator. It follows that other people are also 'illusions of existence for themselves'. She then goes on to say: 'In order to feel compassion for someone in affliction, the soul has to be divided in two. One part absolutely removed from all contamination and danger of contamination. The other part contaminated to the point of identification. This tension is passion, com-passion. The Passion of Christ is this phenomenon in God.'[76]

On the one hand there is complete detachment – the soul removed from any 'contamination' in the world – on the other there is complete identification with the suffering other in the world. The self becomes detached from time and necessity through inner renunciation and acting in the world passively, i.e. through inactive action. This detachment is the desire to become nothing, which is also the replacing of concern for the self with concern for the other. Through becoming empty, the transparency of the 'I' thereby achieved allows the needs of the other to become dominant.

This is central to Christian thinking, and Weil is aware that the tension of which she speaks between the transcendent self and the self wholly identified with the other and emptied into the world parallels the transcendent trinity and the self-emptying of God into Christ. The compassion that the Father feels for the son is the same as the compassion Christ feels for himself, which is the same as the compassion the 'pure soul' feels in affliction and for the affliction of others.[77] Weil is here in line with much modern theology that, responding to Levinas, has emphasised the self in terms of responsibility for the other along with the 'being there for me' of the other.[78] The sense of the ascetic self in Weil's work is clearly developed within a theology of Christian compassion, albeit a somewhat unconventional and unsystematic theology. In Weil's life, this putting the other before the self was expressed in her daily living, in actions such as giving her rations and wages to others, and is intimately connected with her asceticism. In Weil, asceticism is integral to compassion for others, and as a means of personal gain is incoherent.

## *The self, community and tradition*

This concern for the other remains individualistic in Weil's work. In spite of her engagement with Marxism and leftist politics, she is not directly concerned with community and has no strongly developed sense of it. Indeed, this lack of a sense of community is one of the features that marks her out as 'modern', and at first sight she would seem to be a counter-example to the claim that the ascetic self performs the memory of tradition. The central building-blocks of Weil's thought are the self and the self's relation to the other, where the other signifies both the other human being and the divine presence in the world. This is, no doubt, partly due to her existential understanding of the self, but also because the wider community does not sanction her asceticism. By the mid-twentieth century, with the process of desacralisation and secularisation, there are few models of asceticism and sainthood available at a popular level to the wider public. Weil must draw on her own resources for the construction of the ascetic self. Her asceticism is therefore individualistic and her actions – the non-acceptance of food towards the end of her life, for example – are not immediately recognised by those around her. There are few popular cultural models available through which her actions could be recognised, in a way that is not the case with Gandhi, whose fasting was socially legitimated because of popular models of South Asian sainthood.

But we need to tread carefully here, for Weil's writing must itself be seen as an index of a discourse, and while I would wish to place emphasis on agency as crucial to Weil's ascetic subjectivity, this agency operates only in relation to a discourse. Underlying Weil's writing is a strong sense of the Christian tradition and discourse being formed from its Greek philosophical inheritance and an emphasis on the mystical tradition of Christianity. Weil's ascetic self is constructed outside of the Catholic Church, but still within a Christian existentialism and a Christian discourse that is Greek in orientation and sympathetic to the Gnostic desire to free the spirit from the confines of body and matter. Weil was very conscious of tradition and conscious of the ways in which she transgressed it.

Although in Weil there is a deep tension between modernity and tradition, her asceticism still draws on the Christian tradition and can only be made sense of in terms of tradition. Weil's asceticism performs the memory of tradition; she sees her forerunners to be the fathers of the Church and the history of Greek and Christian mysticism, and her asceticism consciously recapitulates what she perceived to be the asceticism of Christ's suffering on the cross. Yet her performance of the memory of tradition must always be curtailed by her lack of community, her developed individualism and her reaction against tradition. In Weil's existential modernity we have asceticism performed in tension with tradition and with only the residues of cosmological, Catholic religion.

This is most evident in her rejection of the Catholic Church as a socio-political institution. Indeed, total adherence to the teachings of the Church she regarded as idolatry. The Church has a bad history for Weil, and she rejected the institution even while accepting what she perceived to be its Christian truths. The mediation of God does not occur through the Church; Christian truth is primarily conveyed individualistically in private illumination from God to the saint in contemplation. Furthermore, this truth is silence.[79] Whether her criticisms are justified is a matter for debate. Father Perrin, her friend and dialogue partner, regarded her understanding on many points, particularly historical accuracy, to be mistaken.[80] She certainly regarded the Church as necessary for the continuation of doctrine and approves of the power of the Church to exclude from the sacraments those who attack it,[81] yet she rejects the Church as the sole arbiter of truth. On the one hand she performs the memory of tradition, on the other she rejects it.

The lack of a developed ecclesiology in Weil and her rejection of baptism draw our attention to the rejection of the memory of tradition and to the personalist nature of her asceticism. Her ascetic acts are performed out of personal conviction and a fusion of her religious motivations with her political and social concerns for the suffering of others. These political concerns themselves come out of a Christian discourse, and her personalist asceticism is itself a part of this discourse, developed particularly within Protestantism and exemplified by Kierkegaard, whose notion of truth as subjectivity is in consonance with Weil's asceticism.[82] Her asceticism does not form part of a discipline ordained by the Church that would clearly link it to a developed cosmology, to ritual and to the inscription of tradition upon the body. Rather, her asceticism is personal in the sense that there are no external constraints other than the political conditions that Weil has chosen to internalise. She does not need to live on half rations, or to drive herself so relentlessly at work, but does so as an act of will, as an act of inner asceticism and as an act of resistance. It is not the Church that provides the ascetic structure of her life through a regime of ritual, fasting and prayer, but the ascetic life is imposed at first through factory work and latterly simply as an act of will. It is these external, political constraints that function, in a sense, in place of tradition, although Weil cannot wholly break free from it. While rejecting the memory of tradition she still needs to draw upon it; it still echoes in her memory and writings.

Although cut off from the community of the Church through her rejection of the sacraments, if Weil feels herself to be anywhere a part of community it is in the factories where, simultaneously, she was most alienated. The regime of the factory is the imposition of external power upon her, which Weil was able to appropriate as an ascetic act, as we have seen. The power of the factory might even be seen in some ways to parallel the power of tradition to impose a regime upon the body. As the religious ascetic in the tradition adopts the form of the tradition and appropriates the tradition as an act of will, so Weil adopts the form of work and appropriates the discipline of work through will as an ascetic act. The performance of the memory of tradition becomes the performance of the memory of modernist industrialisation. Indeed, without the conscious appropriation of the work regime as an act of asceticism, the industrialisation process becomes a process of forgetting. In both the case of ritual and the case of work, the body is moulded to a particular form and pattern which for Weil becomes the moulding of the ascetic self and the means to reverse the body's flow and to realise transcendence.

Thinking the ascetic self with Weil, we can see that her response to the fundamental question about subjectivity, 'Who am I?', is complex. In her essay on Descartes, the self is the subject of first person predicates, but the self is not to be defined as the one who thinks, some non-extended essence, but rather as the one who acts. The self is the reference in the world to whom action-verbs refer in the first person. This is a common denominator and is significant in understanding the ways in which the subject relates to the broader culture. This view is not dissimilar to Bakhtin's philosophy of the act where being is understood in terms of unrepeatable, once-and-for-ever action and performance from a unique and particular place.[83] The subject for both Bakhtin and Weil is the agent of first person predicates, the subject as he or she who responds to the interrogative. For Weil, this subjectivity comes into view in the disjunction between the intention to become the passive receptor of divine grace, for the self to be ultimately destroyed, and the compassion for others; in the denial of the self and the affirmation of the other.

It is here that Weil performs the ambiguity of the self. The self, indicated by the first person pronoun, wills its own eradication through divine grace. This divine grace operates through all-pervasive power as social and political force, through what Weil calls necessity. Yet for the self to become annihilated through grace, it must perform an inner renunciation and thereby assert an act of resistance against power. Through appropriating the work regime and by internalising the harsh conditions of an occupied people in war, Weil performs an act of resistance, an act of will, that is yet intended to eradicate that will and to replace it only with divine will. Power is exercised externally through the regime of work and economic necessity to survive, and internalised both through the acceptance of the regime and through resistance to it as an internal act. Weil's power is all-pervasive and non-subjective, but is made subjective through appropriation and resistance. Her understanding of power is perhaps not dissimilar to that of Foucault, for whom power is an omnipresent force. But whereas for Weil power can be resisted through passivity (which is its acceptance), for Foucault resistance itself is a new form of power. A Foucaultian reading of Weil would see her subjective resistance as itself the product of a Christian discourse that sees power in weakness operating through history as part of the web of power relations. But for Weil this would be to take away the fundamental place of agency and will, albeit an agency which must seek its own eradication. For Weil, her asceticism is a kind of purified intentionality that is certainly historically situated but that can resist the contingencies of history in order to await the intrusion into the self of a higher, non-temporal order through grace.

What, then, can we carry with us from Weil towards a more general formulation of the ascetic self? A more general response to this question will have to wait until we have developed other descriptions of the ascetic self, but for the meantime we can say that the ascetic self is characterised by will, by agency and by resistance, even though the 'I' (*le je*) is an empty sign. This resistance is both to external sovereign power, as in the case of the power of the industrial machine in Weil's life, and to the internal power of the imagination and desire. The ascetic self is the agent who resists.

We can also carry with us from Weil the understanding of the body as the abode of ascetic practice and asceticism as the willed conformity of the body to externally imposed conditions. Although Weil performs the ambiguity of the self, there is yet a rejection of the memory of tradition, while simultaneously, and inevitably, she draws upon tradition. Weil almost attempts to perform the memory of the divine within the body unmediated through tradition, and in so doing inevitably calls on tradition, for there is no tradition-independent language she can use. The ascetic self speaks through silence.

I have tried to draw out aspects of Weil's thought that we can use as a basis for developing an understanding of the ascetic self across cultures. This engagement with Weil has pointed to key features of the ascetic self that will resonate not only with the Christian past but with the traditions of South Asia, although the structures of those traditions are very different from Weil's modern interpretation of Christianity. This engagement with Weil has brought to the fore elements of the ascetic self and an intensification of subjectivity that I wish to claim can be found across traditions of asceticism. To begin to develop a cross-cultural account of the ascetic self we shall now develop some of Weil's ideas in relation to South Asian concepts of subjectivity.

## NOTES

1. Gillian Rose, *Love's Work* (London: Vintage, 1997), pp. 68–9.
2. T. S. Eliot makes the point about the integration of her thought and life. 'Preface' in Simone Weil, *The Need for Roots*, trs. Arthur C. Willis (London and Boston: Routledge and Kegan Paul, 1978 (1952)) and A. Moulakis, *Simone Weil and the Politics of Self-Denial*, trs. Ruth Hein (Columbia and London: University of Missouri Press, 1998), p. 8. The standard biography is Simone Pétremont, *La Vie de Simone Weil*, 2 vols. (Paris: Fayard, 1973), trs. Raymond Rosenthal as *Simone Weil: A Life* (New York: Pantheon, 1976). For a recent, accessible biography see Francine du Plessix Gray, *Simone Weil* (London: Weidenfeld and Nicolson, 2002). Also see Father J. M. Perrin and Gustave Thibon, *Simone Weil as We Knew Her*, trs. Emma Craufurd (London: Routledge and Kegan Paul, 1953). For a biography that places her in a Marxist perspective see David McLellan, *Simone Weil: Utopian Pessimist* (London: Macmillan, 1989); and for a psychoanalytic account see R. Coles, *Simone Weil: A Modern Pilgrimage* (Reading: Addison-Wesley, 1987). The standard bibliography is by J. P. Little, *Simone Weil, Bibliography* (London: Grant and Cutler, 1973).
3. McLellan, *Simone Weil*, p. 123.
4. Simone Weil, 'Hesitations Concerning Baptism' in *Waiting for God*, trs. Emma Craufurd (London: Routledge and Kegan Paul, 1951), pp. 1–7. The complete works (*Oeuvres Complètes*) are being published under the editorship of André A. Devaux and Florence de Lussy. I have mostly used these editions when referring to the *Cahiers*; see Simone Weil, *Oeuvres Complètes*, André A. Devaux and Florence de Lussy (eds.), 6 vols. (Paris: Gallimard, 1994). Otherwise I have used the older editions on which English translations are based.
5. McLellan, *Simone Weil*, p. 1.
6. Simone Weil, *Oppression and Liberty*, trs. Arthur Wills and John Petrie (London: Routledge, 1958), p. 71.
7. Simone Weil, 'La Classe Ouvrière et le Status du Travail', *Oeuvres complètes*, vol. II, iii, p. 264.
8. For an account of Weil's idea of work transformed see Clare B. Fisher, 'Simone Weil and the Civilization of Work' in R. H. Bell (ed.), *Simone Weil's Philosophy of Culture: Readings Towards a Divine Humanity* (Cambridge University Press, 1993).
9. Weil, *Oppression and Liberty*, pp. 68, 69.
10. Ibid. p. 69.
11. Simone Weil, 'Factory Journal', *Formative Writings 1924–1941*, ed. and trs. Dorothy Tuck McFarland and Wilhemina van Hess (London: Routledge and Kegan Paul, 1987), p. 226.
12. Weil, *Oppression and Liberty*, p. 150.
13. Weil, 'Factory Journal', p. 160.
14. Ibid. p. 171.
15. Simone Weil, 'Pre-War Notebook', *First and Last Notebooks*, trs. Richard Rees (Oxford University Press, 1970), p. 14.

16. Weil, 'Factory Journal', p. 196.
17. Once, on the way from a dentist, Weil rode on a tram but had a strong sense that as a slave she had no right to be there, and that anybody would be justified in brutally ordering her to get off. 'Factory Journal', p. 211.
18. Weil, 'Pre-War Notebook', p. 18.
19. Moulakis, *Simone Weil*, p. 94.
20. Ibid. p. 95.
21. Weil, 'Pre-War Notebook', p. 8.
22. Although in her factory journal she records some times of joy. In one entry she describes how, having felt exhausted one lunchtime, she dragged herself back to the factory and resumed work. Fatigue disappeared and was replaced by a sense of gaiety. Weil, 'Factory Journal', p. 173.
23. Simone Weil, 'Science and Perception in Descartes', *Formative Writings*, p. 59. Her thinking here is influenced by her teacher Alain. See Moulakis, *Simone Weil*, p. 85. Weil's idea is later echoed by M. Merleau Ponty: 'Organised signs have their immanent meaning, which does not arise from the "I think" but from the "I am able to",' *Signs*, trs. R. C. McCleary (Evanson: Northwestern University Press, 1964), p. 88.
24. Weil, 'Science and Perception in Descartes', p. 62.
25. Ibid. p. 59.
26. Peter Winch, *Simone Weil: The Just Balance* (Cambridge University Press, 1989), p. 12.
27. Peter Winch provides a good discussion of Weil's reading of Descartes; see his *Simone Weil*, pp. 5–17. Also Moulakis, *Simone Weil*, pp. 85–8.
28. Weil, 'Science and Perception in Descartes', p. 63.
29. Moulakis, *Simone Weil*, p. 85.
30. Weil, 'Science and Perception in Descartes,' pp. 66–7.
31. Ibid. p. 79.
32. Ibid. p. 79; *Cahiers III* in Simone Weil, *Oeuvres Complètes* vol. VI, p. 290.
33. Weil, 'Pre-War Notebook', p. 37; *Cahiers I*, p. 110.
34. Weil, *Cahiers III*, p. 290.
35. E. Husserl, *The Crisis of European Sciences and Transcendental Phenomenology: An Introduction to Phenomenological Philosophy*, trs. D. Carr (Evanson: Northwestern University Press, 1970), pp. 106–08; M. Merleau-Ponty, *The Phenomenology of Perception*, trs. Colin Smith (London: Routledge and Kegan Paul, 1962), pp. 137–47. On the phenomenology of the body see D. M. Levin, *The Body's Recollection of Being* (London: Routledge and Kegan Paul, 1985) and R. Zaner, *The Problem of Embodiment* (The Hague: Nijhof, 1971).
36. Weil, 'Pre-War Notebook', p. 37.
37. Weil, *The Need for Roots*, p. 286.
38. Ibid. p. 287.
39. P. Bourdieu, *Outline of a Theory of Practice*, trs. Richard Nice (Cambridge University Press, 1977), pp. 79–81.
40. Simone Weil, 'New York Notebook', *First and Last Notebooks*, trs. Richard Rees (Oxford University Press, 1970), p. 330.

41. Ibid. p. 84.
42. Weil, 'Factory Notebook', pp. 205–06.
43. David Cockburn, *Other Times* (Cambridge University Press, 1997), p. 327.
44. Simone Weil, *The Notebooks of Simone Weil*, trs. A. Wills (London: Routledge and Kegan Paul, 1956), vol. II, pp. 334–35.
45. For an interesting discussion of Weil's attitude to time see Cockburn, *Other Times*, pp. 324–43.
46. Miklos Vetö, *The Religious Metaphysics of Simone Weil*, trs. Joan Dargan (Albany: SUNY Press, 1994), p. 113.
47. Weil, 'New York Notebook', p. 328.
48. Weil, *The Need for Roots*, p. 301.
49. Vetö, *The Religious Metaphysics of Simone Weil*, p. 15.
50. Weil, *The Need for Roots*, pp. 275–6.
51. Weil, 'The Love of God and Affliction' in *Waiting for God*, p. 66.
52. Ibid. p. 71.
53. Ibid. p. 75; 'New York Notebook', p. 262.
54. Weil, 'The Love of God and Affliction' in *Waiting for God*, p. 77.
55. Weil, *The Need for Roots*, p. 275.
56. *Bhagavad-gītā* 4.18, 20–21; 5.25.
57. Simone Weil, *Gravity and Grace*, trs. Emma Craufurd (London: Routledge and Kegan Paul, 1952), p. 39.
58. Cockburn, *Other Times*, p. 329. Cf. Weil, 'New York Notebook', p. 94: '"Why has it been allowed that he should go hungry?" While one's thought is occupied by this question, one proceeds automatically to find bread for him.'
59. Weil, *Gravity and Grace*, p. 35.
60. Weil, 'New York Notebook', p. 331.
61. Weil, *Notebooks*, pp. 330–31, quoted in Vetö, *The Religious Metaphysics of Simone Weil*, p. 17.
62. Weil, 'New York Notebook', p. 90.
63. Weil, *Notebooks*, p. 127. On the theme of the non-existence of God in Weil see Rowan Williams, 'The Necessary Non-Existence of God' in Bell, *Simone Weil's Philosophy of Culture*, pp. 52–76.
64. Weil, *Selected Letters*, p. 140, quoted in McLellan, *Simone Weil*, p. 137.
65. Weil, 'New York Notebook', p. 328.
66. Weil, 'Spiritual Autobiography', in *Waiting for God*, p. 27.
67. Weil, 'New York Notebook', p. 230.
68. Ibid. pp. 330, 230.
69. Ibid. p. 331.
70. Moulakis, *Simone Weil*, p. 141.
71. Weil, 'New York Notebook', p. 328.
72. Ibid. p. 331.
73. Ibid. p. 265.
74. Ibid. p. 261.
75. Jean Bethke Elsthain, 'The Vexation of Simone Weil' in *Power Trips and Other Journeys: Essays in Feminism as Civil Discourse* (Madison: University of Wisconsin Press, 1990), pp. 13–37.

76. Weil, 'New York Notebook', p. 97.
77. Ibid. p. 94.
78. See David Ford, *Self and Salvation: Being Transformed* (Cambridge University Press, 1999), pp. 66–70; Oliver Davies, *A Theology of Compassion: Metaphysics of Difference and the Renewal of Tradition* (London: SCM, 2001), pp. 155–6.
79. Weil, 'New York Notebook', p. 133.
80. Joseph-Marie Perrin, *Mon Dialogue avec Simone Weil* (Paris: Nouvelle Cité, 1984), pp. 92–3; Perrin and Thibon, *Simone Weil*, p. 55.
81. Weil, 'Spiritual Autobiography', in *Waiting for God*, p. 30.
82. For a discussion of existential Christian discourse see George Pattison, *Anxious Angels: A Retrospective View of Religious Existentialism* (London: Macmillan, 1999).
83. For example, 'I must act from my own unique place, even if I do so inwardly.' M. Bakhtin, *Towards a Philosophy of the Act*, trs. Vadim Liapunov (Austin: University of Texas Press, 1993), p. 42.

CHAPTER 3

# *The asceticism of action: The* Bhagavad-gītā *and* Yoga-sūtras

*tyaktvā lokāṃśca vedāṃśca viṣayāṇīndriyāṇi ca /*
*ātmanyeva sthito yastu sa yāti paramāṃ gatim //*
Abandoning the worlds, scriptures, senses and their objects, he who is established in the self goes to the supreme abode.

*Nāradaparivrājakopaniṣad* 4.1

In the margins of her copy of the *Bhagavad-gītā* Simone Weil pencilled her French translation by a passage, 'I am the doer, the agent . . . and yet I am the changeless one who does not do or act.'[1] Although this is Krishna[2] speaking, for Weil non-acting action (*l'action non-agissante*) is an ideal to be achieved. We act as we must through necessity, as Arjuna must fight in the battle of Kurukshetra, but must remain detached from action and its results if we are to achieve wisdom. So, while the ascetic self at one level is characterised by will, agency and resistance, for Weil a higher understanding is that the self is devoid of agency and the 'I' ('*le je*') is empty, acting only because driven by necessity.[3] In this chapter I shall begin to develop the performance of this ambiguity of passivity and activity in the South Asian context.

Our journey will begin with Brahmanical conceptualisations of the self, showing how the ambiguity of the self is at the heart of this discourse, and moving on to show how the ascetic self performs the memory of tradition, that is, internalises the tradition (and so looks to the past) and its goals (and so looks to the future). We need to understand how this performance is both the expression of tradition and the expression of subjectivity; the ascetic body, as it were, becomes the text. This is not to claim any unified idea of the subject – Hindu and Buddhist discourse is fundamentally divided over metaphysical questions about the nature of the self – but it is to claim that subjectivity and inwardness, always conceptualised within tradition, are fundamental to understanding the ascetic self. Asceticism is the performance of the ambiguity of the self whose goal in general terms is the absence of will through the assertion of will in ascetic performance.

The implication of this claim is that the ascetic self cannot be understood without subjectivity, nor can the ascetic self be understood outside of tradition. The ascetic self in South Asia is not *individual* in the atomic sense usually associated with that term, indeed, quite the opposite, for the ascetic self is always within community and tradition. But this self nevertheless cannot be understood without the concepts of subjectivity and interiority. I intend to treat these themes here through firstly a reading of key texts in the Brahmanical tradition, namely the *Bhagavad-gītā* and *Yoga-sūtras*, and then in terms of social institutions that developed in ancient India.

## THE BRAHMANICAL TRADITION

Within the communities that gave rise to the texts we are using, we have a range of bodily disciplines contingent upon social status and time of life. These include regular daily rituals incumbent upon the high-status social class of Brahmans, occasional life-cycle rituals for householders, yoga practices for hermits and renouncers, and more extreme forms of asceticism for renouncers, such as severe fasting, vowing not to lie or sit, and sleep deprivation. These practices remain throughout the medieval period and up to the present day. In this and the following chapters, I shall focus on the early medieval period, although some of the sources I draw on are much older – sources that provide a template for the self assumed by the later traditions.

By the Brahmanical tradition, I refer to the passing down of ritual and the interpretation of ritual focussed on revelation, the Veda, the earliest layers of which go back to before the first millennium.[4] Beginning as a tradition of elaborate ritual, a Brahmanical discourse developed, focussed on the nature and meaning of ritual and concerned with the nature of language and grammatical categories, with epistemology and with metaphysics. While different schools vied with each other over these philosophical issues, there was a shared terminology and shared procedural assumptions that allowed different Brahmanical schools to dialogue.[5] It is this Brahmanical discourse that is generally associated with the term 'Indian' or even 'Hindu' philosophy, but it is important to remember that the Brahmanical tradition was itself influenced by Buddhism and Jainism and in turn influenced Buddhist and Jain discourse.

In the early centuries BCE, philosophical questions that are easily recognisable in the West developed about the nature of the self, the world and action: who am I? How can I know anything? How should I act? A strong theme developed, articulated in a group of texts called Upaniṣads, that knowledge of the self arises through detachment from action, especially ritual action. Some Brahmans began to question why they performed sacrifice, concluding that the deeper significance of sacrifice is its internalisation, which is the realisation of a higher wisdom. This wisdom frees the self from the bondage of action and repeated action in rebirth. To free the self from bondage, techniques were developed of restricting the body and senses, generally subsumed under the category of yoga, accompanied by a philosophical discussion rooted in texts. Different schools of thinking developed that disagreed over these matters, some rejecting renunciation and asceticism, others embracing it. To understand the ascetic self in Brahmanical discourse we need to focus on Brahmanical notions of inwardness or interiority and the ascetic path. We shall then be in a position to discuss the nature of subjectivity within the social institutions of asceticism in the history of South Asia.

## SELF-KNOWLEDGE AND INTERIORITY: THE *BHAGAVAD-GĪTĀ* AND ITS COMMENTARIES

Two discussions in particular are important for understanding the ascetic self in Brahmanical discourse. One is a primarily philosophical concern about the nature of the self and the nature of agency; the other is a sociological concern about the relation of renunciation to the social order. The two issues are linked in so far as understanding the true nature of the self and agency is generally thought to be the prerogative of the renouncer who has formally stepped outside of normative social transaction and is undertaking a particular discipline. Deep questions arise with the Brahmanical tradition about the values of the householder's and renouncer's lives in relation to each other and about the purposes of human life within the wider cosmological framework. The issue is distilled into the question, as Olivelle points out, posed by Arjuna to Krishna as to which is better, the performance of action or its renunciation?[6] Indeed, this dilemma is at the heart of the text and is behind the opening problem of whether Arjuna should fight in the great battle that sets the scene for the text. The solution presented is that true renunciation is internal, a detachment from the fruits of action rather than its non-performance. Olivelle discusses this solution in relation to the system of the four stages of life or *āśrama* system, which was also concerned with the dilemma and offers a solution to it, as we shall see. But the *Gītā* wishes to show that 'true renunciation does not consist in the physical abstention from activity but in the proper mental attitude toward action. Abandonment of desire for the results of one's actions is true renunciation, which the *Gītā* sees as an inner virtue rather than an external life style.'[7] This tension between the performance of action and its renunciation is at the heart not only of the *Gītā* but arguably of the whole of the epic *Mahābhārata* (of which the *Gītā* is a section) and, as Olivelle points out, the decision to renounce by the hero Yudhishtira reflects Arjuna's initial decision not to fight in the war.[8] This is clearly an issue of asceticism: the expression of action for social good or the restriction of action for a transcendent goal, which the *Gītā* tries to resolve by arguing for their compatibility.

With regard to the primarily philosophical concern about the nature of the self and the nature of agency, two ideas arise again and again in texts from the early centuries BCE: the idea of self-knowledge and the idea of what might be called interiority. Indeed, these are the goals of ascetic practice. In Brahmanical discourse about liberation and the nature of the self, we find a pattern that will be reiterated in other traditions of asceticism: that a component of the goal of practice is the realisation that the will is limited or even illusory. The goal of practice is knowledge of the self and that the self is without agency, a knowledge that is partially attained through asceticism, or rather, asceticism creates the conditions for its realisation. I shall now present a more technical discussion of the terminology in our texts (the *Gītā* and *Yoga-sūtras*) and their commentaries that the non-specialist reader might like to pass over to the more general discussion of the formation of the ascetic self and the social institutions that fostered it (p. 84).

We shall begin our discussion with the question of self-knowledge and agency as articulated in the most famous of Hindu texts. One verse from the *Bhagavad-gītā* that Weil quotes in her notebook is from book 4:

> He who perceives non-action in action,
> And action in non-action,
> Is wise among men.
> He performs all action in a controlled way.[9]

This passage contains key ideas for Indian views of the ascetic self. The passage is concerned with the cultivation of detachment and becoming controlled or disciplined (*yukta*). The term *yukta* is a passive past participle from the root *yuj*, 'to control' or 'to yoke', as Eliade reminds us, from which the term 'yoga' is derived.[10] The controlled or 'yoked' self provides the fundamental model of the ascetic self in South Asia, and asceticism must be understood in the context of this idea. The image of the yoke not only evokes the idea of control but also ability, for a yoke is an enabling device that makes pulling a burden easier. Weil's reading of the text that the wise are detached from action is not dissimilar to traditional views taken by the Brahmanical commentarial tradition. In his commentary on the verse, the non-dualist or Advaita philosopher Śaṅkara in the early eighth century CE presents the following argument for the non-acting nature of the self.

He begins by taking the apparent contradiction (*viruddha*) that inaction (*akarma*) can be seen in action (*karma*) and action in inaction. What this means, Śaṅkara tells us, is that to the dull-visioned (*mūḍhadṛṣṭa*), action appears as inaction and inaction as action. Perhaps sensing that this does not really tell us anything, he goes on to say that this is a basic truth about the way the things are (*yathābhūtadarśanārtha*) told by the Lord and understood by the wise (*buddhimat*).[11] Developing the point, he claims the meaning of the passage to be that action and inaction are confused by the ignorant, as, when viewed from a moving ship, the trees on the shore appear to move although motionless, or as distant bodies appear to be still although actually moving. But here Śaṅkara comes to the crux of his interpretation, namely his metaphysical assumption that the self is without action. As action pertains only to the body and senses, it is really non-existent in the self (*ātmani karmābhāva*), as has been taught in primary and secondary revelation and in logic (*śruti, smṛti* and *nyāya*).[12] Action is falsely attributed to the self, and should anyone think 'I am the agent' (*ahaṃ kartā*) or 'I act' (*ahaṃ karomi*), he or she would be mistaken in attributing qualities to the immutable self that do not belong to it. The person who understands this is a controlled yogi (*yukto yogī*), wise, free, and whose purpose has been achieved. For Śaṅkara, self-knowledge is the wisdom that the self is without agency and that agency is illusory within the realm of nature (*prakṛti*). But the text also says, echoing the final line of the verse, that such a person is the performer of all actions![13] Śaṅkara clarifies this in his commentary on the next verses (4.19–21), that the liberated sage, free from desire and from attachment to the results of action, only performs action either for the sake of worldly people (*lokasaṅgrahārtha*) or for the maintenance of the body. Being without want (*nirāśī*) the sage performs mere bodily action (*śārīraṁ kevalaṁ karma*), with no concern for its results. The ascetic (*yati*) who has realised the non-agency of the self (*ātmanaḥ kartṛtvābhāva*), while appearing to act, knows in his own experience (*svānubhava*) that he does not really act and so is detached from the fruits of action.[14]

A further discussion of the verse places it in the context of ritual obligation and Śaṅkara's critique of the Pūrva Mīmāṁsā school (although not explicitly mentioned), which regarded ritual action as the main purpose enjoined by revelation. If we take the term karma to mean not simply action but ritual action – the daily obligatory rituals of the Brahman (*nityakarma*), then, if their performance produces no effect, it can be considered non-action. Ritual acts are done because of injunction and so are not really to be classed as action, even though the non-performance of such acts leads to bad results, namely a life in hell (*naraka*). Of course, the avoidance of such bad results is not the reason for performing ritual acts in the Mīmāṃsā tradition.

The literal meaning of verse 4.18, according to Śaṅkara, is that both activity (*pravṛtti*) and inactivity (*nivṛtti*) require an agent, but such an agent is illusory, and due to this illusion there is confusion between action and non-action. Liberating knowledge means the realisation that the self is passive. The true self for Śaṅkara is the immutable, passive witness (*sākṣin*)[15] who in reality is untouched by action and ignorance or by the coverings (*upādhi*) that appear to separate the self from true, reflexive knowledge. This undifferentiated self is not individual, but universal consciousness or spirit (*brahman*).[16]

This kind of language is also found in the non-dualist, Śaiva tradition of Kashmir. Rājānaka Rāmakaṇṭha, student of Utpaladeva (ca 925–75 CE),[17] writes in his commentary on verse 4.18 of the *Gītā* that the word 'who' refers to one who knows reality (*tattvavit*), which can be taken to mean one who knows the categories (*tattva*) that comprise the hierarchical cosmos. Such a sage perceives non-action in action as he perceives the 'non-son-ness' of his son, because being a son is due to action performed in the cycle of birth and death (whereas the true self is beyond this relationality). The wise sage regards action as being due to a particular cause that binds a person in the cycle of reincarnation, while liberating knowledge means the destruction of any connection with the passion that keeps a person bound. Although the *Gītā* says that the liberated person is the performer of all action, which Rāmakaṇṭha glosses as meaning someone who has fulfilled the human goals of life (*puruṣārtha*), he is nevertheless beyond action. The liberated person is not an agent because liberation is not caused by action.[18]

Although fundamentally at variance over broader metaphysical claims about the self, the theist Rāmānuja, still within the Advaita tradition, agrees with Śaṅkara about the primacy of self-knowledge. In his commentary on the *Gītā* verse, Rāmānuja claims that by the term 'non-action' (*akarma*) the text actually refers to knowledge of the self (*ātmajñāna*) and that the verse refers to someone who is worthy of liberation (*mokṣārha*), and who can perceive action as a form of knowledge (*jñānākāra*).[19] But unlike Śaṅkara, for Rāmānuja the world of action is not ultimately unreal, although the aspirant has to give up attachment to the fruits of action and turn inwards to the blissful experience or beholding of the self (*ātmāvalokana*).[20] In his commentary on verse 5.24, Rāmānuja says that the renouncer should give up all experience of external objects (*bāhyaviṣayānubhava*) and find contentment within (*antasukha*). The verse reads:

> He who has happiness within, pleasure within,
> And as a consequence, inner radiance,
> This yogin attains extinction in the absolute,
> Absorbed in the absolute.[21]

Inner happiness, pleasure, and radiance in which the yogin is absorbed in contemplation of the spirit are the consequences of renunciation. This inner joy and dissolution in the spirit is, according to Rāmānuja, the joy of experiencing the self (*ātmānubhavasukha*) which is akin to the joy of a pleasure-garden.[22] This inner light is not an experience of outer objects, nor is it experienced through the senses, according to the Advaita commentator Ānandagiri,[23] but is an object (*viṣaya*) internal to consciousness only. For the pure Advaitin, this is the light of the self; for the dualist Madhva, this is the light of the Lord, perceived both without awareness of external objects and when conscious of external objects.[24]

In the long view, for the Advaita tradition the self is devoid of agency or is emptied of will, which understanding constitutes self-knowledge. This wisdom occurs in the self's interiority, for one who is liberated appears, like other people, to perform ordinary actions in the world but only in inner awareness perceives the self to be without action. The metaphor of inwardness or interiority is of central importance in this discourse, and all commentators share this image. True knowledge of the self, or (for Madhva) of the Lord, does not come by means of outer forms or action, but only through inner knowledge and inner renunciation of the fruits of action.

## A READING OF THE *GĪTĀ* COMMENTARIES

All the commentators on the *Gītā* we have so far discussed make claims about the agency of the self. For Śaṅkara the true self is passive and agency is illusory, the agent appearing only within the realm of nature (*prakṛti*). Similarly for Rāmakaṇṭha the limited self does not perform action, although, as we shall see, for the Kashmiri non-dualists Śiva is supreme agent. For Rāmānuja and Madhva the true actor is the Lord who is the inner controller (*antaryāmin*) of the self: the self does not act but only the Lord through the self, although the Lord himself is desireless (unlike the Śaiva Lord). What these models of the self have in common is firstly that knowledge of the self is outside of daily transaction, although someone liberated in life (*jīvanmukta*) still participates in daily activity. For Śaṅkara the self becomes absorbed in its own knowledge. For Rāmānuja and Madhva, this self is in a relationship with the transcendent Lord. Secondly, liberating self-knowledge is the highest human purpose, achieved through renunciation and occurring within the interior of the self's being. The ascetic is the self who practises in order to achieve detachment from outer activity through focussing on the transforming power of interior knowledge.

Yet while the rhetoric of this discourse, the plain sense of our texts, places liberating knowledge within the self's own interiority and outside of cultural forms, it is nevertheless embedded within tradition. Our readings of this plain sense reveal a complexity within these texts concerning the ascetic self. At one level, the discourse itself performs the memory of tradition through the commentarial repetition of argument. Commentary on revealed scripture performs the memory of tradition through the repetition of the text and the rehearsal of inherited meanings. At another level, the commentaries are an index of the ascetic self constructed within tradition. The texts express the memory of tradition that links interiority or subjectivity with temporal duration, or specifically establishes an individual temporality within a cosmic temporality. The cultural form of the tradition mediates between an individual temporality, bound by birth and death, and a cosmic temporality, similarly bound by birth and death but on a much grander scale. These representations show asceticism to be a practice that performs this link between the two temporalities by reversing the body's flow in order to attain the actionless state described. We have here a tradition of discourse and practice that enacts the memory of tradition and expresses the ambiguity of the ascetic self through the assertion of the self, along with the simultaneous negation of its power.

So far I have taken examples from the commentaries on the *Bhagavadgītā*. We have seen how these texts express the ambiguity of the ascetic self, which is both the assertion of will and the undermining of will, and that this process occurs only within the parameters of tradition. It remains now to develop the way in which tradition articulates with subjectivity and interiority, which is the way it links cosmic time to the 'time of the soul'. We need to show how the ascetic performs the memory of tradition, how the ascetic embodies the text, and thereby creates a subjectivity wholly in consonance with tradition. In this way, an agency is established designed to undermine the very notion of agency.

## INTERIORITY, MEMORY AND TRADITION: PATAÑJALI'S *YOGA-SŪTRAS*

Like the *Gītā*, Patañjali's text attained a status that cut across different systems of thought. Composed probably around 300 CE, somewhat later than the *Gītā*, these terse sūtras were commented on by Vyāsa in the late sixth or early seventh century, the text and Vyāsa's commentary (*Yogasūtrabhāṣya*) were in turn commented on by the Advaitin Vācaspati (ca 850), and there is a further sub-commentary (*vivaraṇa*) attributed to Śaṅkara that, if authentic, is earlier.[25] In the eleventh century, the Śaiva King Bhoja wrote a commentary (*Rāja-mārtaṇḍa*), and there is also a commentary (*Yoga-vārttika*) by the sixteenth-century eclectic thinker Vijñānabhikṣu, along with a shorter summary (*Yogasāra-saṁgraha*). In this text we find a close examination of interiority and the way in which the self recapitulates the categories of tradition. At a plain sense level, the text can be read as a manual that maps out inner worlds and, in our interpreted sense, as an explication of the way the ascetic self performs the memory of tradition and the ambiguity of the self.

Although the Patañjali text presupposes the dualist metaphysics of Sāṃkhya philosophy,[26] it is undoubtedly a distinct system in its own right and is quoted in different traditions that assume the general model of the mind it presents. The text is a mapping of interiority. It gives a systematic account of the functioning of consciousness and an account of how to become free from the attachment that keeps the self being reborn in the realm of suffering or cycle of becoming (*bhāva-cakra*). Although the term *tapas*, 'asceticism' or 'austerity', occurs only some four times, the text is fundamentally concerned with asceticism as the withdrawal of consciousness from exteriority and the cultivation of higher states of awareness (*samādhi*) through detachment leading to discriminative wisdom (the discerning of the true self from what is not the self). Patañjali presents us with a kind of phenomenology of the processes of awareness. I intend here to sketch the general shape of this phenomenology in order to demonstrate how the *Yoga-sūtras* are an excellent example of the way in which the ascetic self internalises tradition and recapitulates cosmology in inwardness. Patañjali provides an explanation of the processes of memory whereby this occurs. It will not be possible to offer a full description of the entire Patañjali system or to explicate all of the complex technical terminology,[27] but we need to give an account of the purpose of yoga in Patañjali's terms, the relation between the structure of consciousness and the cosmos, and the form of practice itself. We can then move on to our interpreted reading of the place of memory within this structure and the recapitulation of the tradition within the ascetic self which is also a recapitulation of the goal, thus looking back to the past and anticipating the future.

## *The purpose of yoga*

Classical yoga is a realist system that maintains three eternal realities of matter (*prakṛti*), the self (*puruṣa*) and God (*īśvara*). Its basic metaphysics therefore differs both from the monistic or Advaita Vedānta of Śaṅkara, which maintains their distinction to be mistaken, and from Sāṃkhya, which accepts the duality of self and matter but rejects the idea of God.[28] On metaphysical grounds, the system is akin to theistic traditions such as Śaiva Siddhānta, which similarly accepts the three distinct realities. The ultimate goal of the tradition is the freedom or the isolation (*kaivalya*) of the self from nature or matter (*prakṛti*), although this is not conceived of as union with the Lord, who is simply another, although special and primary, self. This freedom is achieved through detachment and the practice of yoga described in the text.

Patañjali famously defines yoga in the second proposition as 'the cessation of mental fluctuation' (*yogaś-citta-vṛtti-nirodhaḥ*).[29] At one level, the meaning is obvious, that the aim of yoga is to stop consciousness from wandering in order to achieve concentration on a single point (*ekāgratā*).[30] Encapsulated in these few words is the entire yogic way. The path of the yogi leads from the ordinary, scattered sense-experience of the external world to more and more refined states of interiority, which leave behind sense-experience and finally leave behind all mental content as such, to experience a state of pure transcendence. In his commentary Bhoja refers to this cessation as a transformation (*pariṇāma*) of consciousness through one's own agency (*svakāraṇa*): a harnessing into a single point consciousness that is dull and thrown (*kṣipta*) into the world.[31] This apparently simple formulation – that freedom is achieved through the detachment of consciousness from the external world and eventually from all mental content – is expressed in a precise and meticulous terminology, only within which can yogic asceticism be understood. But more than being simply the wandering of the mind, the term *cittavṛtti* has a precise designation. *Citta* is consciousness or mental activity,[32] and *vṛtti*, from the root *vṛt*, 'to turn', refers to five mental functions that restrict consciousness, namely means of knowing (*pramāṇa*), mistaken cognition (*viparyaya*), ideation (*vikalpa*), sleep (*nidrā*) and memory (*smṛti*).[33]

These five constitute the processes of ordinary waking experience. They are the precondition of experiencing the world, although they need to be repressed for the realisation of higher states in yoga. Patañjali simply intends to describe those processes of awareness which are conducive to pleasant (*akliṣṭa*) or painful experience (*kliṣṭa*), whose description I shall follow here. The first fluctuation, the means of knowing or *pramāṇa*, refers to the ways in which we gain knowledge of the world. There are six *pramāṇas* in classical Indian philosophy, but Patañjali recognises only three: perception (*pratyakṣa*), inference (*anumāna*) and verbal testimony (*āgama*). Perception arises through the contact of the mind with the world through the senses; inference is the kind of knowing that comprehends general characteristics of objects and apprehends connections between objects in the same class; and verbal testimony refers to scripture. The second fluctuation, mistaken cognition or misapprehension (*viparyaya*), is false knowledge or the mistaking of something for what it is not. Third, ideation (*vikalpa*) refers to conceptualisation in language that can range from pure imagination to abstract thinking. For a realist ontology that maintains that the world is real and not an appearance, such as Patañjali's, the proposition that language could be a closed system without external reference could not be accepted. The fourth fluctuation, sleep, is a form of cognition, but the cognition of non-being (*abhāva*); and, lastly, memory (*smṛti*) is the cognition of past events or the retention in the mind of some object previously experienced.[34] I shall defer a discussion of memory for now, but simply observe that while it functions to distract the mind from concentration on a single point, it has the positive aspect of enabling the internalisation of tradition and so can facilitate the development of the yogic path.

Yoga as the cessation of mental fluctuation therefore entails the repression of these processes of interaction with the world, indeed, of all that is usually associated with human cognition and experience. The fluctuations function in a mutual relation (*aṅgāṅgibhāva*) and once this is disrupted, consciousness is transformed.[35] The cessation of mental fluctuation is a radical reversal of the usual processes of awareness and a reversal of human time, such that all experience of externality and what is usually associated with subjectivity are transcended. This is pure detachment, in which there is an absence of anything either to be achieved or abandoned,[36] a oneness with the object of contemplation and a state of pure interiority accompanied by a tranquillity of mind.[37]

The goal of yoga is the stilling of the fluctuating mind. Through stilling the mind, the senses are stilled, just as bees follow the queen bee and rest when she rests.[38] With the senses withdrawn, the mind is focussed on an object and absorbed in inwardness, but an inwardness that by gradual stages transcends individuality. The condition that follows from the repression of mental fluctuation is referred to by a number of terms, generally *samādhi*, translated by Eliade as 'enstasis', 'stasis', or 'conjunction',[39] a state of mind in which consciousness is absorbed in its object, and is one-pointed. The mind takes on the qualities of its object, and so contemplation on a pure object will lead to a purified consciousness. Thus, in his commentary Bhoja says that there are two objects of meditation in the development of *samādhi*, either the conscious Lord (*īśvara*) or the unconscious (*ajaḍa*) *tattvas*, the levels or constituents of the cosmos.[40] *Samādhi* itself is divided by Patañjali and the commentators into a number of levels subsumed within two broad categories that he calls *saṃprajñāta-samādhi* and *asaṃprajñāta-samādhi*, that Feuerstein renders as 'cognitive' and 'ultra-cognitive enstasy'.[41] Cognitive enstasy is again subdivided into four levels, as is made clear by the text: 'Cognitive enstasy is accompanied by forms of initial thought, sustained thought, joy, and a sense of I.'[42]

This is a highly technical terminology that needs some explanation. *Vitarka*, akin to the Buddhist *vitakka*, refers to initial concentration, the casting of the mind onto an object, while *vicāra* refers to sustained examination once the mind is fixed, although the semantic fields of the terms include speculation and thinking in the former case, and 'wandering' in the latter. Lance Cousins has shown that there is a continuity of use of this terminology with various Buddhist systems[43] that we shall have cause to return to (see pp. 136–7). Bhoja's commentary says that the level of initial thought (*sa-vitarka*) itself contains all four qualities of initial thought, sustained thought, joy and sense of I,[44] and as consciousness becomes more refined, initial thought falls away to leave only sustained thought, joy and sense of I at the *sa-vicāra* level. Vyāsa's commentary identifies *vitarka* with gross experience (*sthūla ābhoga*) of an object or support of consciousness, while *vicāra* is subtle experience.[45] Sustained thought in turn falls away as consciousness progresses along this path, to leave only joy and the sense of I at the *sānanda* level, and only the sense of I remains at the level called *asmitā-mātra*, 'I-ness only'. We have here the systematisation of a process of refinement in which ordinary mental functioning is gradually transcended in the development of concentration, with even the joy of *samādhi* being left behind until only a sense of subjectivity remains.

To continue the process of refinement and interiority, even this sense of I has to be overcome in the ultra-cognitive or *asaṃprajñāta* condition. Subjectivity or the sense of I (*asmitā*) arises from ignorance through the identification of the true self or 'seer' with the powers of the seen,[46] that is, the identification of the self with what is not the self, namely the manifest cosmos. One sūtra even includes a sense of I (*asmitā*) as one of five afflictions to be overcome.[47] In the sūtra describing *samādhi*, Patañjali defines this 'other' state as being characterised only by the latent residue of mental impressions (*saṃskāras*), the impressions of past actions that can themselves become activated and lead, eventually, out of *samādhi* and into further experience in the world. Liberation is the final eradication of even these latent impressions, so that there will be no more rebirth for the yogin who has attained this state.

What is significant for our purposes about this complex description in the text and commentaries is that subjectivity or the sense of I exists as a purely internal state once there is no awareness of the world and the senses have withdrawn from their spheres of activity (*viṣaya*). Yet this sense of subjectivity is itself transcended through an act of will until only a deeper sense of the true self remains. This is the deeper self (*puruṣa*), contained within itself, the true subject of experience, but beyond the subject of first person predicates.

### *Interiority, self-knowledge and cosmology*

While this structure in Patañjali's text maps out a route for the withdrawal of consciousness from externality to interiority, and so is concerned with psychological processes and self-knowledge, it is also correlated with cosmological structures that are either derived from the philosophical tradition called Sāṃkhya or that the Patañjali yoga tradition has independently inherited. Indeed, this correlation of psychology and cosmology is shared by the Buddhist system of the stages of meditation, the *dhyānas* or *jhānas*,[48] which are earlier and which the yoga tradition has absorbed and adapted, although there is more emphasis on psychological process than cosmology in the Buddhist material, as Cousins observes.[49] This connection between interiority, self-knowledge and the structure of the cosmos is important in these traditions, each idea entailing the others. Inwardness, the journey into the self through privatised yogic practice, leads to self-knowledge or the discrimination of the self from what is not the self, and thereby the discrimination of different elements of the cosmos. Inwardness leads away from exteriority towards knowledge and freedom. This process was central to the *dharma* of the ascetic, as shown by Yādava Prakāśa's compendium of rules for ascetics (*Yatidharmasamuccaya*), which describes Patañjali's eight components of yoga that the ascetic should practise along with understanding the cosmic categories (*tattva*).[50]

The contrast between the inner (*anta-/antara-*) and the outer (*bāhya-*) is ancient in Brahmanical discourse and first appears with philosophical importance in the Upaniṣads and in the *Gītā*. Here 'inner' is combined in a variety of compounds to denote the inner self (*antaḥpuruṣa*,[51] *antarātman*[52]), inner wisdom (*antaḥprajñā*[53]), inner happiness (*antaḥsukha*[54]), inner space (*antārākāśa*[55]) and so on. This interiority can be contrasted with exteriority, by which its purity cannot be touched: the self is like the sun that cannot be defiled by external faults and the inner self cannot be tainted by external suffering in the world,[56] ideas not dissimilar to the early Buddhist, and later Yogācāra idea, of the mind being brightly shining (*pabbasara citta*) and defiled by taints that come from without.[57]

This metaphor of interiority is important for understanding Indian asceticism. The goal of practice is interior and constituted within subjectivity. Self-knowledge entails interiority in Brahmanical discourse, for it is not a kind of knowledge that can be had through worldly interaction, but only through introspection and the cultivation of the ascetic qualities of recollecting the source of being and of concentration. Moreover, interiority is associated with the structure of the cosmos, and to delve into the heart of the self is also to delve into the heart of the universe. While this idea is highly developed in Indian discourse, it is not unique and occurs in other traditions such as medieval Christianity, as we shall see. Indeed, it is probably a feature of cosmological religions before the advent of modernity and is integral to asceticism, where the internalisation of cosmology is endemic.

Refining consciousness, as described by Patañjali, through the levels of *samādhi* is to retrace cosmogony through the levels of emanation described in the Sāṃkhya tradition, until a critical break is reached and the self realises its non-attachment to matter. The spiritual path is therefore both a journey into the self and a journey through the hierarchical cosmos to its unmanifest (*avyakta*) or undifferentiated source (*aliṅga*). More particularly, there are four major cosmological levels listed by Patañjali and described in the commentaries: the particularised, the unparticularised, the differentiate and the undifferentiate.[58] These four levels are the qualities of existence (*guṇa*) that form the universe according to the Sāṃkhya system. They exist in pure, unmanifest potential in an undifferentiated state corresponding to the Sāṃkhya category of unmanifest or potential matter (*avyakta prakṛti*). The differentiate (*liṅga-mātra*) corresponds to the Sāṃkhya higher mind or *buddhi*, the unparticularised (*aviśeṣa*) corresponds to the sense of I and the five subtle elements or potentials that form the manifest universe, and the particularised (*viśeṣa*) corresponds to the mind (*manas*) that interacts with the world or the elements (*bhūtas*) through the senses (*jñānendriyas*) and faculties (*karmendriyas*).[59] Bhoja follows this general pattern, although he associates the unparticularised with the subtle elements and the 'inner instrument' (*antaḥkaraṇa*), by which he presumably means the sense of I along with the 'mind' (*manas*), but excluding the *buddhi* (which is higher).[60]

These levels of the cosmos are levels of experience. The pure sense of I, withdrawn from contact with the world in *saṃprajñāta-samādhi*, corresponds to the *aviśeṣa* level, while *asaṃprajñāta-samādhi* should correspond to the higher levels of the *buddhi* and unmanifest matter, although the commentaries are not clear about this. For example, in his commentary on verse 1.36, that the pacification of the mind occurs when free from sorrow and luminous,[61] Vyāsa says that here the *buddhi* is the object of contemplation experienced in the heart as effulgent light resembling jewels, planets, moon and sun[62] and linked to the absorption of the mind in pure subjectivity or I-ness. Again, Bhoja's commentary reinforces the link with cosmology by referring to the 'world of wisdom' (*prajñaloka*) from which all fluctuations are destroyed.[63]

This somewhat complex formulation of categories and correspondences, while representing a history in which terminologies from different systems are being related to each other, is a good example of the kind of correlation between psychology and cosmology in the Indian systems. The correspondences are not random, but developed in a systematic way that was probably closely linked with practice. The refinement of inner consciousness is thus correlated with an experience of transcending the world of the senses and the apprehension of higher or subtler levels of being. Psychology recapitulates cosmology, and interiority becomes a place where the yogin realises fruits of concentrated practice and detachment. While this certainly involves the cultivation of ethical behaviour as defined within the tradition, above all it means concentration on a single point. Concentration gives access to higher levels of being, and while ethics is important, the emphasis here is on ontology, and progress is linked to cognitive skill rather than to the development of virtue, as it is in the Christian systems.

## *Forms of practice*

Now we come to the crucial role of asceticism as such. The goal of yoga is the cessation of mental fluctuation, which can be stopped through application or practice and dispassion – *abhyāsa* and *vairāgya*.[64] Practice is the application of effort, consistently and over a long time period (*dīrgha-kāla-nairantarya*) to achieve the cessation of mental fluctuation, and detachment is the necessary withdrawal from the realm of the senses. In the application of practice and withdrawal from the senses, asceticism has a central place. Patañjali uses the term *tapas*, 'austerity' (literally, 'heat'), only four times, although the whole orientation of the yoga system is fundamentally concerned with asceticism as the reversal of the body's flow and so the reversal of time. In the first verse of section 2 on the practice of yoga, Patañjali presents his system as the yoga of action (*kriyā yoga*) that comprises the components of austerity (*tapas*), self-study (*svādhyāya*) or the repetition of mantras and devotion to the Lord (*īśvara-praṇidhāna*).[65] This list is also recapitulated in the famous list of the eight limbs (*aṣṭāṅga*) of yoga under discipline (*niyama*).[66] In the commentary Vyāsa describes *tapas* as the ability to bear extremes (*dvandva*) of hunger and thirst, heat and cold, standing and sitting in yoga postures, along with stillness (*kāṣṭa-mauna*) and silence (*ākāra-mauna*). He also includes religious observances (*vrata*) involving fasting and other intentional hardships. Bhoja states that austerity is that which is taught in the texts of tradition (*śāstra*) and goes on to identify it as bodily mortification (*kṛcchra*), and fasting regulated by the moon's course (*cāndrāyaṇa*).[67] Furthermore, through the practice of such austerity the yogin gains perfection of body and senses, that Vyāsa glosses as gaining magical powers (*siddhi*).[68]

We see from these occurrences that *tapas* is an important element in the development of yoga and the cessation of mental fluctuation. Moreover, it creates perfection of the body and faculties (*kāyendriyasiddhi/kāyasaṃpad*), a perfection characterised by beauty, gracefulness, strength and diamond hardness.[69] Rather than weakening the body and making it emaciated, austerity is here thought to make the body strong and perfect it. This perfection is beyond gender, and while the text is arguably implicitly addressed to a male audience, there is no textual exclusion of women. Indeed the perfected body has transcended sexuality and is without desire. The body is perfected in the fire of yoga, and the perfected body becomes an index of liberation. While in the Sāṃkhya system liberation is the retraction of the self from matter, the situation with Patañjali yoga is more complex. Here certainly liberation is the realisation of the isolation of self, but this is achieved in an embodied state, through the body's perfection achieved by austerity. The body is controlled through asceticism. Asceticism constrains the body into a particular form over time and thereby perfects it in terms of the tradition. The body becomes an index of tradition and becomes the place for the inscription of the text. The practice of austerities, the perfection of the body through years of practice, is an expression of the text and of the tradition itself.

## A READING OF MEMORY IN THE *YOGA-SŪTRAS*

To create the perfect body in this way is to become the text and to express the tradition and so to enact the memory of tradition. The memory of tradition is the internalisation of the text and the recapitulation of the goal of tradition in subjective awareness. The perfect body and the states of *samādhi* implied by the body's perfection are the goals of tradition made interior to the yogin through memory and made visible in the form of the body created through practice. The body expresses the tradition and embodies or enacts the memory of tradition through the subjective appropriation of tradition, through remembrance of the goal, which is also a reclaiming of origin. It is to this mechanism that I wish to finally turn.

There is an ambivalent attitude towards memory in the *Yoga-sūtras*. On the one hand it is a *citta-vṛtti* which needs to be suppressed in order to achieve *samādhi*, but on the other it is a condition of *samādhi*. *Smṛti* has a wider semantic field than the English 'memory' and includes not only the recollection of past events but awareness or mindfulness as well. These meanings are within a coherent frame of reference and are furthermore related to the category of scripture or secondary revelation called *smṛti*: the tradition, shared wisdom or collective memory that guides the community. The wider semantic field of *smṛti* is attested in tantric literature too, where the verb in the third person optative (*smaret*) is used interchangeably with other verbs connoting visualisation (*dhyayet, cintayet*).[70]

But let us return to its uses in the *Yoga-sūtras*. As one of the *citta-vṛttis* Vyāsa understands memory to be essentially of two kinds: the memory of things past and the constructed memory of things imagined, the former being associated with the waking state, the latter with dreaming.[71] Both kinds of memory arise out of latent impressions (*saṃskāra*) derived from the fluctuations, that is, derived from the methods of knowing, misapprehension, ideation, sleep or previous memories. Interaction with the world through the senses and usual mental apparatus creates the latent impressions that give rise to memories, and those memories in turn can be the cause of further memories. The arising of *samādhi* follows upon the elimination of the fluctuations, including, or especially, memory. Overcoming the domination of memory in this sense is overcoming the past, overcoming time that keeps the mind distracted.

Yet memory also has a positive role to play, and Vyāsa speaks of it as part of a causal sequence leading to *samādhi*. This is because of the intimate link between memory and latent tendency. Patañjali says that *samādhi* is preceded by faith, energy, mindfulness or memory, concentration and wisdom.[72] Here the mental faculty of memory that usually distracts the mind is used in the repeated recollection of yogic practice and the bringing to mind of previous experience of one-pointed concentration upon an object and how it was achieved. In this sense the use of *smṛti* is directly akin to the use of *sati* in Buddhist meditation, and one is reminded of the story of the Buddha recalling a childhood experience of absorption and so recalling how to enter into it on the eve of his enlightenment.[73] According to Vyāsa, this sequence of faith (*śraddhā*), energy (*vīrya*), recollection (*smṛti*), concentration (*samādhi*) and wisdom (*prajñā*) are causally connected, one leading on to the other. Faith gives the seeker of discriminative wisdom (*vivekārthin*) energy that in turn brings recollection leading to concentration and finally wisdom. Through cultivating discriminative wisdom (*prajñāviveka*), the yogin attains *asaṃprajñāta-samādhi*.[74] Here memory consists of keeping in mind the object of contemplation, the mantra *oṃ* for example, or recollection of the Lord. Thus repetition of mantra is a form of memory, a memory that internalises the tradition, and memory is the recollection and realisation of the tradition's goal and a recapitulation of it in subjective awareness.

The internalisation of the tradition through memory is also the internalisation of the tradition-specific goal. Recollection is integral to the reversal of the flow of the body and so the reversal of individual time that leads to death and repeated birth. This reversal, as we have seen, is linked to the reversal of cosmogony, and the levels of awareness achieved by the yogin are identified with levels of the cosmos. The correspondence between levels of being and levels of subjective awareness is a correspondence between cosmic time and individual time. The rising of the yogin's awareness through these states is a reversal of time, both individual and cosmic: the rise in awareness is a return to a condition before temporal expansion.

## THE FORMATION OF THE ASCETIC SELF

Two final examples will serve to demonstrate this process of forming the ascetic self, the first from the genre of literature prescribing rules for ascetics, Yādava Prakāśa's *Yatidharmasamuccaya*,[75] and the *Gītā*. Yādava Prakāśa's text, edited and translated by Olivelle, is part of a genre of literature dealing with *dharma* called *nibandha*, texts that were original compositions on topics such as criminal law, inheritance, pilgrimage and also the rules for ascetics.[76] This text had become authoritative within the Śrī Vaiṣṇava community by the thirteenth century. What is significant for our purposes is that in Yādava's work we see the ways in which the ascetic body becomes the text, as it were, and expresses the tradition. The ascetic's life is regulated and governed by ritual from dawn to dusk, and his behaviour is self-regulated in accordance with the ascetic's *dharma*. In Yādava's text we see the internalisation of tradition. Each day's conduct is prescribed in accordance with specific rules. Upon rising, the ascetic goes to the toilet, cleans himself in the prescribed manner with soil, sips water and cleans his teeth. He should then bathe, make an offering of water to the rising sun while reciting the Gāyatrī mantra, and undertake silent prayer (*japa*) and yoga. He should then wander to the next village or remain in the same place engaged in controlling the breath, silent prayer, meditation, praising God, and reciting the Epics and Purāṇas that have vedic sanction. His midday duties include worshipping the sun once again with mantras, and he should then go out to beg from house to house, like a bee, collecting food in his bowl. He should eat in a secluded place, recite mantras and sip water once he has finished, wash his bowl with water and a cord of cow's hair, and spend the rest of the day in meditation. In the evening he should perform the twilight worship to the sun and sleep on the ground in an appropriate place such as a cave, deserted house, or temple.[77]

There are clearly continuities here with the Brahman householder's way of life, such as recitation and offering water to the sun at the three junctures of the day. The ascetic's life is entirely ritualised in the text and bodily functions, the flow of the body, closely controlled. Not only behaviour but mental attitude is important, and the ascetic should go about his daily duties with 'speech, mind, eyes, and sex organs under complete control (*sugupta*)'.[78] The ascetic internalises the tradition, subjectively appropriating it and conforming his body, speech and mind to the forms prescribed. He eliminates his individuality, as it were, through a subjective intensification. The ascetic body is inscribed by tradition and becomes the text, in the sense that the ascetic inscribes his body as a text.

Returning to the *Gītā* we find the same ideas. Three kinds of asceticism are mentioned, austerity pertaining to body (*śarīra-tapas*), speech (*vāṅmaya-tapas*) and mind (*mānasa-tapas*).[79] The high caste or 'twice-born' needs to control body, speech and mind in ways defined by Brahmanical tradition. He should revere the gods and teachers of the tradition through the body, by performing acts of worship (*pūjā*), by following rules of purity defined by *dharma*, and developing moral qualities such as sexual continence and non-violence. The commentaries of Śaṅkara and Ānandagiri refer to the austerity of the body as the 'turning back of the body' (*śārīra-nirvartya*),[80] a phrase that indicates the reversal of the body's flow that is a hallmark of asceticism. The Brahman's speech should be controlled, not causing distress, speaking the truth, and reciting sacred texts, and he should practise gentleness, silence, self-restraint and 'purity of being', which we might take to mean the purification of thought.

It is clear from this description that the ideal devotee of Krishna in the *Gītā* constructs himself, his body, speech and mind in ways specified by the tradition. In fact, the qualities listed are the ideals of the orthodox Brahman attested in other literature such as the *Laws of Manu*, where the twice-born householder should perform these very prescriptions: carrying out obligatory actions enjoined by the Veda, being self-controlled, performing sacrifices to the gods and ancestors, constantly reciting the Veda, and guarding his speech and comportment.[81] Austerity of body, speech and mind constructs a self in accordance with the prescriptions of tradition through an act of will, such that the ascetic becomes the embodiment of tradition. Indeed, tranquillity, restraint (*dama*), austerity, purity, patience and virtue (*ārjava*) are the actions of the Brahman expressing his innate qualities (*svabhāvaja*),[82] and a feature of those blessed with a divine destiny (*daivī saṃpad*).[83] There are degrees to which the actualisation of these qualities is successful, and the *Gītā* accounts for this, again in cosmological terms, by claiming that there are three attitudes towards this austerity depending on which quality of existence (*guṇa*) a person is dominated by. Those who practise austerity motivated by highest faith, detached from the results of their action, display the purest or *sāttvika* motivation. Those who practise in a hypocritical way for the sake of worldly honour are said to be *rājasika* or dominated by passion, while those wishing to torture the self or to destroy someone else are driven by darkness (*tamas*).[84] The text has a quite definite idea of what austerity should be, depending on motivation and the way in which it constructs the self.

There are clearly forms of asceticism that the *Gītā* disapproves of, such as extremes of torturing (*karṣayanta*) the body and terrible austerity (*ugra tapas*), not enjoined in scripture (*aśāstra*) and performed by those whose intent is demonic (*āsuraniścaya*).[85] These extremes are not only against tradition but against Krishna himself, for as Krishna dwells within all beings, in torturing the body the ascetic would be torturing him.[86] Asceticism is necessary to realise the self and to create the condition for the reception of Krishna's grace, but only an asceticism whose boundaries are marked by tradition and an asceticism that is, ultimately, an internal detachment rather than external performance. This teaching is predominantly for the householder as the performer of the three acts of sacrifice, giving and austerity, which are ways of constructing the ascetic self in accordance with *dharma* and tradition. Other ways of constructing an ascetic self, through extreme ascetic practices, are outside of vedic injunction and tradition. It is not precisely clear whether the author of the *Gītā* has specific ascetic groups in mind when referring to 'terrible austerity' and 'torturing the body', but such groups did exist and the text is clear that the yogin (for which we might read 'practitioner of the teachings of the *Gītā*') is superior to such ascetics (*tapasvin*).[87]

We have now completed the initial part of our discussion about the nature of the ascetic self and the construction of the ascetic self in Brahmanical discourse. Through examining the *Bhagavad-gītā* and its commentaries we have seen how the ultimate nature of the self is passive, even though asceticism entails action as the assertion of will. The ascetic self performs this ambiguity through tradition that is internalised and we examined the particular internalisation of tradition in the yoga system of Patañjali. The ascetic self is concerned with self-knowledge, with interiority, and developing the path to the goal. Asceticism here, as everywhere, is teleological and the goal is eradication of the everyday self. This erasure of the self is naturally performed by a self, but a self within a community and tradition who constructs him- or herself in a particular way according to the structure of the teachings. Asceticism is a profound way in which the subject appropriates tradition, such that the body becomes the text and itself becomes an index of tradition. Having addressed the primarily philosophical concern about the nature of the ascetic self and the ways in which tradition is appropriated, I wish to turn lastly to the sociological question about the relation of the ascetic self to the social order in the history of Brahmanical discourse, and how the claim to the primacy of subjectivity articulates with wider, sociological concerns.

## SUBJECTIVITY AND SOCIAL INSTITUTION

In the discussion so far, I have given descriptive accounts of the ascetic self in particular texts within Brahmanical philosophical discourse. I have furthermore offered a reading of these texts that shows how any account of asceticism in South Asia needs to take into account the ways in which the tradition is recapitulated in interiority. I have offered readings of the texts that go beyond their plain sense to show that they describe the mechanisms whereby the ascetic self is constructed and how the ascetic self looks back through memory to a past and forwards to a future goal. This is an understanding of subjectivity that cannot be separated from cosmology. Indeed, the relation between subjectivity and cosmos becomes almost a commonplace, but it is nevertheless vital to come back to this principle as it is a defining element of asceticism in these traditions. It now remains to discuss how this understanding relates to sociological or macro-cultural and historical concerns. A discussion of this issue will take us somewhat away from the direct reading of texts and necessitate a move to a different level of discourse.

Given that text is an index of wider social praxis, how does the interiority expressed articulate with social concerns? To address this question we need to look at indigenous social institutions and discourse, particularly the *āśrama* system. And following this question is a second: what is the relation between subjectivity and macro-history in these traditions? I think that there are broadly two approaches that can be taken here. On the one hand we can assert the dominance of macro-history and argue that asceticism in the texts must be understood primarily in sociological terms as the expression of power relations within a cultural history, and the construction of the ascetic self as an internalisation of those power-relations. Here the ascetic self is constructed through power internalised in a hegemonic way. On the other hand, we can assert the primacy of subjectivity and the agency of the self who clearly acts within, but also upon, wider social forces. This is a complex question, and there is truth in both positions. The ascetic self and ascetic practices are clearly given by tradition and the wider culture and internalised by the practitioner. Indeed, this has been a major element in my interpretative reading. But the self is also an agent in ascetic acts, and it is the subject who appropriates the tradition. The self is inscribed by history but operates as a subject within it.

## *The āśrama system*

Let us return to the dilemma posed in the *Bhagavad-gītā* whether virtue lies in the performance of correct, dharmic action or in the renunciation of action. While the *Gītā*'s response has been to claim that both can be done through inner renunciation, one attempted solution to the problem was expressed early in Indian religious institutions in the idea of defined stages on life's way, or the *āśrama* system. In the classical formulation, there are four of these: the celibate student stage, the married householder stage, the hermit stage and renunciation. Olivelle's definitive study has shown that at the time of their original formulation by the end of the fifth century

BCE, they were not simply sequential stages, but distinct styles or lifestyle choices.[88] As expressed in the *dharma-sūtras*, they were 'alternate or parallel vocations open to a young adult male who has undergone vedic initiation and completed the period of study that follows.'[89] Originally, the term *āśrama* did not refer to ascetic practices but rather to the obligations of the Brahman householder, especially the dharmic obligation to perform sacrifice. The term became extended, Olivelle shows, to embrace ascetic styles of living and to legitimate the ascetic lifestyle as being as good as that of the Brahman householder.[90] In time, the *āśramas* as distinct choices after the period of vedic studentship came to be replaced by a sequential formulation by the classical period (which Olivelle takes to be from the first couple of centuries CE to the end of the fifteenth century[91]). There is still an echo, Olivelle reminds us, of the earlier use in the Brahmanical cultural memory, but the increasing tendency of Brahmanical discourse, as exemplified by Manu, is towards the limitation of choice.[92] By the classical and later periods, with which we are mainly concerned, the *āśramas* were a model of sequential development of the Brahman through life. The *āśramas* become an integral feature of Brahmanical ideology along with caste restriction, and the compound *varṇāśrama-dharma* became the standard formulation of Brahmanical orthopraxy.

Although the actual term *āśrama* does not occur in the *Bhagavad-gītā*,[93] the *āśrama* scheme offers a solution to the problem posed by Arjuna, namely whether action or its renunciation is the higher virtue. Indeed, the question is answered by the entire socio-religious structure that claims that virtue (*dharma*) is correct performance with regard to obligations to one's endogamous social group (*varṇa*) and with regard to the stage of life one is at (*āśrama*). The renunciation of action is legitimate, but only at particular points in the journey of life if it is not to disrupt social order. The *āśrama* system attempts to make coherent the apparent contradiction between the vedic injunction to perform action (and the normal human ways of being in the world) and the claim that the renunciation of action (and desire, one might add) leads to liberation and rest. The *Gītā* solution, of course, is more radical and brilliant than this linear development, and posits both the performance of dharmic action and simultaneously the renunciation of action.

An element of asceticism pervades all of the *āśramas*, particularly, of course, the stages of the celibate student, hermit and renouncer. But there were also different kinds of householder, and some householders might remain celibate for periods of time. While the origin of the *āśramas* and their relation to non-vedic renunciation of *śramaṇa* tradition (the terms are cognate) cannot concern us here, it is notable that asceticism is a significant feature of the system. Originally, Olivelle shows, the term referred to a type of Brahman householder, characterised by their matted or braided hair (*jaṭila*), a feature of many later ascetics, and the Pāli equivalent *assama* in Buddhist scriptures refers to the residence of such Brahmans, a meaning it later retains.[94]

When I say that asceticism is a key feature of all the *āśramas* I mean that a marked feature of the system is that they are concerned with the control of sexuality and the intake of food. The householder is enjoined to have sons, but as a householder can legitimately pursue life's pleasures (technically fulfil the human purposes of social obligation, gaining wealth and success, and enjoying sexual and other pleasures). But the student, hermit and renouncer should all practise celibacy (*brahmacarya*), and the law books are quite prescriptive as regards intake of food. Indeed, classifications of ascetics tend to be based on the types of food they can consume, and Olivelle has offered an interesting account of this with particular reference to *dharma* literature.[95] All the ascetics described are in fact non-cultivators, begging and scavenging food, even eating carrion left over by animals in the forest. The *Baudhāyana Dharma Sūtra* gives a classification of ascetics as those who cook food and those who do not, which are further subdivided. Among those who do not cook their food are those who live on water and those who live on air, who, says Olivelle, 'aim at withering their bodies away until death finally overtakes them'.[96] This is certainly not the kind of asceticism approved by the author(s) of the *Gītā*, but a kind of asceticism important in non-Brahmanical traditions such as Jainism.

Although as yet there is no systematic and comprehensive history of asceticism in South Asia, in his extensive publications on the subject Olivelle has moved a long way in the direction of giving a solid, textually instantiated account. It is not intended here to contribute to the textual mapping of this history, but rather to develop the theme of subjectivity as a crucial dimension for understanding asceticism. This literature shows that the ascetic's life was highly ritualised and that ascetics were classified according to food intake, social origin, kind of dwelling, clothing and emblems. All this points in the opposite direction to any notion of individuality and autonomy. Our problem, given these formal classificatory schemes and formalised modes of behaviour, is what is the place of subjectivity here? While the answer to this question has been implicit in the foregoing discussion, we need finally to place this question in the context of Brahmanical social structure.

## *Individual, society and subjectivity*

One of the major discussions in the history of South Asia has been over the question of the relation of the 'individual' to the social order and the importance of 'caste' in the history of South Asia. An extensive literature has arisen around this problem, although mainly in relation to the modern period. Even if the caste system with clearly defined edges grew up only in the wake of the Mughal empire,[97] there was nevertheless by the time of the *Gītā* a formalised system of social stratification with strict rules of endogamy and commensality, and an ideology of *dharma* that linked work, skill and knowledge to hereditary groups. From the third or fourth century CE this ideology came to be expressed in the *varṇāśrama-dharma* formula[98] and in the formula of human goals of life, the *puruṣārthas*.[99] In a famous essay, Louis Dumont has argued that there were two poles of value in the history of India: the values of society and the affirmation of the self as a purely social being, and the values of the individual and the affirmation of the self as a distinct agent. Dumont associated the former 'man-in-the world' with the householder who is embedded within a world of social relations and pursuing the goals of *dharma*, profit and pleasure, while the individual is the renouncer concerned with the goal of liberation (*mokṣa*). For Dumont it is the renouncers who are individuals and from whom all creativity within the Indian tradition comes.[100] By contrast, Veena Das and Burghart argued that there are primarily three sets of values that have controlled caste society, those of the Brahman, king and renouncer, and Bayly has shown the importance of these in the history of caste from the eighteenth century.[101] Heesterman has argued against Dumont that the fault line in the history of Indian society lies between the king and the Brahman, not between the Brahman householder and the renouncer, who are in fact very close.[102] Others have argued that there are no 'individuals' within Indian society, but rather all are subject to change in different contexts. Human beings are 'dividuals' and subject to changes in their 'coded-substance' in different social, transactional circumstances.[103]

The issue is therefore more complex than Dumont's somewhat stark disjunction between 'individual' and 'social actor', where only the former has substance. Clearly, ascetics were not wholly outside of society but embedded within a hierarchical social matrix, often wielding considerable social and political power, as the importance of Shankarite monasteries in the medieval period testifies. There were also continuities between renouncers and martial sectors of society, for both were engaged in controlling and constructing the body through a number of disciplines. Such disciplines and prescribed rules for ascetics eradicated individual markers through taking on the uniform dress, such as the ochre robe, and becoming legally or civilly dead. The renouncer in the fourth stage of life was not a social actor, in the sense that he could not participate in legal transactions and was released from previous contracts: his wife could remarry and he was no longer responsible for his debts.[104] The renouncer was far from an individual in the modern sense of a citizen with legal rites and obligations. And yet Dumont has a point that the renouncer is a very creative figure in the history of South Asia, and the concerns of the ascetic are focussed on individual liberation, the cultivation of particular virtues and the development of higher states of consciousness. We need therefore to distinguish between the ascetic as an individual and the subjectivity of asceticism. Subjectivity, I have argued, is collective or shared in the sense that it is both constructed by tradition and appropriates traditions. It becomes an index of tradition and the ascetic self – both an expression of tradition and a particular realisation of it. Individual, in the sense of a person exercising agency in a legal framework, the ascetic was not, but the cultivator of interiority, the appropriator of tradition in ascetic community, he, and sometimes she, certainly was.

## NOTES

1. Reference from D. McLellan, *Simone Weil: Utopian Pessimist* (London: Macmillan, 1989), p. 215. The reference is to the *Gītā* 4.13. I believe that Weil had Swami Swarupananda's 1933 translation, *Srimad Bhagavadgita with text, word for word translation and English rendering* (Calcutta: Advaita Ashram, 1982), 13th edition.
2. I have used anglicised forms of the names for Krishna and some locations.
3. In her notebooks, Simone Weil extensively quotes the Upaniṣads and the *Bhagavad-gītā*, particularly with reference to detachment. For Weil's discussion of Sanskrit terminology and quotes from texts see in *Cahiers 3*, André A. Devaux and F. de Lussy (eds.) *Oeuvres Complètes* vol. VI (Paris: Gallimard, 1994), pp. 290–91, 314, 324, 326–8, 331, 335, 340–43, 349–51, 358, 361–6, 377.
4. For an overview of this literature, including dates, see M. Witzel, 'Vedas and Upaniṣads' in G. Flood (ed.), *The Blackwell Companion to Hinduism* (Oxford: Blackwell, 2003), pp. 68–101.
5. Eivind Kahrs, *Indian Semantic Analysis: The 'Nirvacana' Tradition* (Cambridge University Press, 1998), p. 7. For an interesting application of Indian discourse (*vāda*), see J. Clayton, 'Thomas Jefferson and the Study of Religion', Inaugural Lecture, University of Lancaster, 1992, pp. 27–32.
6. *Bhagavad-gītā* 5.1. quoted and discussed in P. Olivelle, *The Āśrama System: The History and Hermeneutics of a Religious Institution* (Oxford University Press, 1993), p. 104.

7. Olivelle, *The Āśrama System*, p. 105.
8. Ibid. p. 104.
9. *Bhagavad-gītā* 4.18: *karmaṇyakarma yaḥ paśyed, akarmaṇi ca karma yaḥ, sa buddhimān manuṣyeṣu, sa yuktaḥ kṛtsnakarmakṛt.* (Winthrop Sargeant's translation slightly modified.) For a good account of non-acting action see Simon Brodbeck, *Asakta Karman in the Bhagavadgita* (Ph.D. SOAS, 2002).
10. M. Eliade, *Yoga: Immortality and Freedom*, trs. Willard R. Trask (Princeton University Press, 1970), p. 4. In my opinion, Eliade's is still the best general account of yoga and Indian asceticism available.
11. Śaṅkara's *bhāṣya* on the *Bhagavad-gītā* 4.18, Shastri Gajanana Shambu Sadhale, *The Bhagavadgītā with Eleven Commentaries* vol. I (Bombay: Gujarati Printing Press 1935), 2nd ed., p. 398. I have been greatly assisted in my understanding of this commentary by the extremely clear translation of A. Mahadeva Sastri, *The Bhagavad-Gītā with the Commentary of Sri Sankaracharya* (Mysore: GTA Printing Works, 1901), pp. 113–119.
12. Śaṅkara's *bhāṣya* p. 399. (The references here and below – cf notes 19, 20, 22, 23 and 24 – are to the Sadhale edition.)
13. Ibid. p. 399.
14. Ibid. p. 413. For a clear review of the question concerning the relationship between renunciation of authorship or of the fruits of action see Roger Maracurelle, 'The Basic Types of Renunciation in Hinduism: With Special Reference to Śaṅkara's Gītā-Bhāṣya' in Katherine K. Young (ed.), *Hermeneutical Paths to the Sacred Worlds of India* (Atlanta: Scholars Press, 1996), pp. 104–22.
15. *Bhagavad-gītā* 9.18 and Śaṅkara's *bhāṣya.*
16. For a general account of Śaṅkara's philosophy see Natalia Isayeva, *Śaṅkara and Indian Philosophy* (Albany: SUNY Press, 1993). For a good exposition and parallels with Western thought see Paul Hacker in Wilhelm Halbfass (ed.), *Philology and Confrontation: Paul Hacker on Traditional and Modern Vedanta* (Albany: SUNY Press, 1995); on the self and spirit see pp. 219–23.
17. Rājānaka Rāmakaṇṭha is not to be confused with Rāmakaṇṭha the dualist theologian who wrote commentaries on the *Mataṅgapārameśvsāgama* and the *Kiraṇatantra*. Rājānaka Rāmakaṇṭha is attributed with a commentary on the *Gītā*, the *Sarvatobhadra* cited here, and also a commentary on the *Spandakārikā*. See D. Goodall, *Bhaṭṭa Rāmakaṇṭha's Commentary on the Kiraṇatantra*, vol. I (Pondicherry: Institut Français de Pondichéry, 1998), p. ix.
18. Rājānaka Rāmakaṇṭha, *The Bhagavadgītā with the Commentary Called Sarvatobhadra*, Pandit M. K. Shāstrī (ed.), KSTS 64 (Srinagar: Research Dept. Jammu and Kashmir, 1943), p. 100.
19. Rāmānuja's *bhāṣya* 4.18, p. 402. I have been greatly aided by the English translation of Svāmī Adidevānanda, *Śrī Rāmānuja Gītābhāṣya* (Madras: Sri Ramakrishna Math, 1991), pp. 171–2.
20. Rāmānuja's *bhāṣya* 5.25, p. 408.
21. *Bhagavad-gītā* 5.24: *yo 'ntaḥsukho 'ntarārāmas tathāntarjyotir eva yaḥ / sa yogī brahmanirvāṇaṁ brahmabhūto 'dhigacchati* // My translation loosely follows

W. Sargeant, *The Bhagavad Gītā*, revised ed. (Albany: SUNY Press, 1994) p. 266.

22. Rāmānuja's *bhāṣya* 5.24, p. 406.
23. Ānandagiri *Vyākhyā* 5.24, p. 506: 'So the light is only internal and not (experienced) by means of the senses' (*tathā 'ntareva jyotir na śrotriyadibhiḥ*).
24. Madhva *bhāṣya* 5.24, p. 507.
25. The issue of Śaṅkara's authorship of the commentary is not settled. Paul Hacker has argued on strong grounds that it is the work of Śaṅkara and that, perhaps less convincingly, it represents an earlier stage in his life when he was an adherent of the Yoga school of philosophy. See P. Hacker, 'Śaṅkara the Yogin and Śaṅkara the Advaitin' in Halbfass, *Philology and Confrontation*, pp. 101–34.
26. G. Feuerstein, *The Philosophy of Classical Yoga* (New York: St. Martin's Press, 1980), pp. 109–20.
27. For such a description see Feuerstein, *The Philosophy of Classical Yoga*. I have been strongly influenced by Feuerstein's illuminating reading of the text.
28. On the relation between yoga and Sāṃkhya see F. Edgerton, 'The Meaning of Samkhya and Yoga', *American Journal of Philology* vol. 45, 1924, pp. 1–46.
29. *Yoga-sūtra* 1.2. Hari Nārāyaṇa Āpaṭe (ed.), *Pātañjalayoga-sūtrāṇi* (Benares: Ānandāśrama, 1908). Contains the commentaries of Vyāsa (*Bhāṣya*), Vācaspatimiśra (*Ṭikā*) and Bhojadeva (*Rājamārtaṇḍa*). For the sūtras and Vyāsa commentary I have often based my reading on the edition and translation of the text and commentary by Swāmi Hariharānanda Āraṇya, *Yoga Philosophy of Patañjali*, trs. P. N. Mukerji (Albany: SUNY Press, 1988 (1963)).
30. For a discussion of this see Eliade, *Yoga*, pp. 47–52.
31. Bhojadeva, *Rājamārtaṇḍa*, p. 2.
32. On this term see Feuerstein, *The Philosophy of Classical Yoga*, pp. 58–61.
33. *Yoga-sūtra* 1.6.
34. *Yoga-sūtra* 1.7–11.
35. Bhojadeva, *Rājamārtaṇḍa*, p. 2.
36. *Yoga-sūtra* 1.15.
37. *Yoga-sūtra* 1. 36; 41.
38. *Yoga-sūtra Bhāṣya* 2.54.
39. Eliade, *Yoga*, p. 77.
40. Bhojadeva, *Rājamārtaṇḍa*, p. 6.
41. Feuerstein, *The Philosophy of Classical Yoga*, p. 76.
42. *Yoga-sūtra* 1.17. *vitarka-vicārānandāsmitā-rūpānugamāt saṃprajñātaḥ*. Cousins observes that *rūpa* might here refer to the object of *samādhi*, as in some Buddhist sources. The phrase would then be translated '. . . as result of following a [mental] object with *vitarka* . . .' Lance Cousins, 'Vitakka/Vitarka and Vicāra Stages of samādhi in Buddhism and Yoga', *Indo-Iranian Journal* vol. 35, 1992, p. 156, note 66.
43. Cousins, 'Vitakka/Vitarka and Vicāra', p. 156, note 66.
44. Bhojadeva, *Rājamārtaṇḍa*, 1.17, p. 6.
45. *Yoga-sūtra Bhāṣya* 1.17.

46. *Yoga-sūtra* 2.6.
47. *Yoga-sūtra* 2.3, along with ignorance (*avidyā*), attachment (*rāga*), hate (*dveṣa*) and the will to live (*abhiniveśa*).
48. See R. Gethin, 'Cosmology and Meditation from the Aggañña-sutta to the Mahāyāna', *History of Religions* vol. XXXVI, 1997, pp. 183–217.
49. Cousins, 'Vitakka/Vitarka and Vicāra', p. 149.
50. P. Olivelle, *Rules and Regulations of Brahmanical Asceticism* (Delhi: Sri Satguru, 1997 (1995)), p. 77.
51. For example, *Maitri-upaniṣad* 3.3.
52. For example, *Muṇḍaka-upaniṣad* 2.1.9; *Kaṭha Upaniṣad* 4.1; 6.17; *Śvetāśvatara Upaniṣad* 3.13 in P. Olivelle (trs.), *The Early Upaniṣads: Annotated Text and Translation* (Oxford University Press, 1998); *Bhagavad-gītā* 6.47.
53. *Māṇḍukya-upaniṣad* 4; 7. (The references here and in notes 55–7 are from Olivelle, *The Early Upaniṣads*.)
54. *Bhagavad-gītā* 5.24.
55. *Maitri-upaniṣad* 6.28.
56. *Kaṭha-upaniṣad* 5.12–13.
57. *Anguttara Nikaya* 1.10.
58. *Yoga-sūtra* 2.19. *viśeṣāviśeṣa-liṅgamātrāliṅgāni guṇa-parvāṇi //*
59. Feuerstein, *The Philosophy of Classical Yoga*, pp. 42–50.
60. Bhojadeva, *Rājamārtaṇḍa*, 2.19, p. 22.
61. *Yoga-śūtra* 1.36. *viśokā vā jyotiṣmatī //*
62. This kind of description of inner, yogic perception first occurs in the *Śvetāśvatara Upaniṣad* 2.11, but is also found in the *Yoga Upaniṣads* and later literature. See for example *Advaya-Tāraka-Upaniṣad* 5–8 in G. Feuerstein (ed.), *The Essence of Yoga: Contribution to the Psychohistory of Indian Civilization* (London: Rider, 1974), pp. 208–09. Inner light is also found in the Sant tradition, e.g. Sawan Singh, *Philosophy of the Masters* vol. I (Beas: Radha Soami Satsang, 1963), p. 64.
63. Bhojadeva, *Rājamārtaṇḍa*, 1.36, p. 12.
64. *Yoga-sūtras* 1. 12.
65. *Yoga-sūtras* 2.1. *tapaḥsvādhyāyeśvarapraṇidhānāni kriyāyogaḥ //*
66. *Yoga-sūtra* 2.32. The eight limbs are moral observance (*yama*), self-discipline (*niyama*), posture (*āsana*), breath control (*prāṇāyāma*), withdrawal of the senses (*pratyāhara*), concentration (*dhāraṇā*), meditation (*dhyāna*) and enstasis (*samādhi*).
67. Bhojadeva, *Rājamārtaṇḍa* 2.2, p. 16. *Cāndrāyaṇa* is defined by Manu as diminishing food intake every day in the dark fortnight and increasing it in the bright. *Manu* 6.20.
68. *Yoga-sūtras* 4.1. On the *siddhis* see *Yoga Sūtra Bhāṣya* 3.45, where Vyāsa lists them as ability to become minute (*aṇiman*), levitation (*laghiman*), the power of becoming large (*mahiman*), extension (*prāpti*) – such as 'the power to touch the moon with the fingertips', strong will (*prākāmya*), mastery over the elements (*vaśitva*), lordship over the elements (*īśvaritva*) and resolution (*yatrakāmāvasāyitva*), whereby the yogin can determine the arrangement of the

elements at will. See Eliade, *Yoga*, pp. 85–95; White, *The Alchemical Body: Siddha Traditions in Medieval India* (Chicago and London: University of Chicago Press, 1996), pp. 371–2, notes 14 and 15.

69. *Yoga-sūtras* 2.43; 3.46. *Rūpa-lāvaṇya-bala-vajra-saṃhananatvāni kāya-saṃpat* //. The body becomes muscular and firm like a diamond, adds Bhojadeva, *Rājamārtaṇḍa* 3.46, p. 44.
70. G. Flood, 'The Purification of the Body in Tantric Ritual Representation', *Indo-Iranian Journal* vol. 45, no. 1, 2002, pp. 25–43.
71. *Yoga-sūtra Bhāṣya* 1.11.
72. *Yoga-sūtra* 1.20.
73. *Majjhima Nikaya*, 'Mahāsaccaka Sutta' 36.31. Bhikku Nāṅamoli and Bhikkhu Bodhi (trs.), *The Middle Length Discourses of the Buddha* (London: Pali Text Society, 1995), p. 340.
74. *Yoga-sūtra Bhāṣya* 1.20.
75. Olivelle, *Rules and Regulations.*
76. Olivelle, *Rules and Regulations*, p. 4. For a history of literature on the *dharma* of ascetics see P. Olivelle, *Saṃnyāsa Upaniṣads: Hindu Scriptures on Asceticism and Renunciation* (Oxford University Press, 1992), pp. 11–18; Vāsudevāśrama, *Yatidharmaprakāśa* vol. II (Vienna: University of Vienna Institute for Indology, 1977), pp. 21–26.
77. Olivelle, *Rules and Regulations*, pp. 90–123.
78. Ibid. p. 113.
79. *Bhagavad-gītā* 17. 14–16. 'Reverencing of the gods, the twice-born, teachers, and wise men, purity, virtue, continence and non-violence, is called austerity of body. Words that do not cause distress, truthful, agreeable, and salutary, and practice in the recitation of sacred texts, is austerity of speech. Peace of mind, gentleness, silence, self-restraint, and purity of being, is austerity of mind.' *Devadvijaguruprājña pūjanaṁ śaucam ārjavam / brahmacaryam ahiṃsā ca śarīraṁ tapa ucyate // anudvegakaraṃ vākyaṃ satyaṃ priyahitaṃ ca yat / svādhyāyābhyasanaṃ caiva vāṅmayaṃ tapa ucyate // manaḥprasādaḥ saumyatvaṃ maunam ātmavinigrahaḥ / bhāvasaṁśuddhir ity etat tapo mānasam ucyate //* My translation follows Sargeant's.
80. Śaṅkara *Gītābhāṣya* and Ānandagiri *Vyākhyā* 17.14. Sadhale, *The Bhagavad Gita* vol. III, p. 259.
81. *Manu* 4.1–34.
82. *Bhagavad-gītā* 18.42.
83. *Bhagavad-gītā* 16.3, 5.
84. *Bhagavad-gītā* 17. 17–19.
85. *Bhagavad-gītā* 17. 5–6.
86. *Bhagavad-gītā* 17. 5–6.
87. *Bhagavad-gītā* 6.46. The text simply says that yogins are superior to ascetics, but I am following Madhva's commentary here, which claims that the term 'ascetics' means those whose practice is extreme.
88. Olivelle, *The Āśrama System*, pp. 78–9.
89. Ibid. p. 74.

90. Ibid. pp. 19–20.
91. Ibid. p. 129.
92. Ibid. p. 138.
93. Ibid. pp. 101–03.
94. Ibid. pp. 21–2.
95. Ibid. pp. 164–5.
96. Ibid. p. 164, note 12.
97. S. Bayly, *The New Cambridge History of India*, vol. IV.3 *Caste, Society and Politics in India from the Eighteenth Century to the Modern* Age (Cambridge University Press, 1999), p. 25.
98. The term first appears in the *Yājñvalkya Dharmaśāstra* 1.1. Olivelle, *The Āśrama System*, p. 142.
99. Although Olivelle shows that they are not textually connected, as many scholars have thought. Olivelle, *The Āśrama System*, pp. 216–19.
100. L. Dumont, 'World Renunciation in Indian Religion' in *Homo Hierarchicus: The Caste System and its Implications* (University of Chicago Press, 1980 (1966)), pp. 267–86.
101. For a critical discussion of Dumont see Veena Das, *Critical Events: An Anthropological Perspective on Contemporary India* (Delhi: Oxford University Press, 1995), pp. 34–41; Richard Burghart, 'Renunciation in the Religious Traditions of South Asia', *Man* vol. 18, 1983, pp. 635–53; Susan Bayly, *The New Cambridge History of India* IV.3 *Caste, Society and Politics in India from the Eighteenth Century to the Modern Age* (Cambridge University Press, 1999), pp. 14–16, 19–24.
102. J. Heesterman, *The Inner Conflict of Tradition: Essays on Indian Ritual, Kingship and Society* (University of Chicago Press, 1985).
103. McKim Marriott, 'Hindu Transactions: Diversity without Dualism' in Bruce Kapferer (ed.), *Transaction and Meaning: Directions in the Anthropology of Exchange and Symbolic Behaviour* (Philadelphia: Institute for the Study of Human Issues, 1976), pp. 109–42.
104. Olivelle, *The Āśrama System*, p. 207.

CHAPTER 4

# *The asceticism of action: tantra*

*Ko'haṃ kimātmakaścaiva kimidaṁ duḥkhapañjaram*
Who am I and in what really do I consist? What is this cage of suffering?
*Jayākhyasaṃhitā* 5.7a[1]

In the history of Brahmanical discourse, *dharma* might be seen as the norm of householder practice from which the renouncer, the practitioner of asceticism (*tapasvin*), is formally excluded by the rite of renunciation.[2] The householder is seeking to fulfil the goals of social obligation (*dharma*), profit (*artha*) and pleasure (*kāma*), his legitimate pursuit,[3] in contrast to the renouncer seeking liberation (*mokṣa*) through renunciation and asceticism. For the vedic exegetes, the Mīmāṃsakas, *dharma* is cosmic order expressed in the series of vedic injunctions (*vidhi*) about ritual (*karma*) or sacrifice, and the 'founder' of the school, Jaimini, defines *dharma* as the meaning expressed by vedic utterance (*codana*).[4] This excludes the renouncer, who has technically given up ritual action (even though asceticism is pervaded by ritual). A much later text, Yādava Prakāśa's *Yatidharmasamuccaya* (of which the *terminus ad quem* is the thirteenth century CE), says that the renouncer should give up the vedic ritual of the householder in order to pursue the 'yoga of knowledge' (*jñānayoga*).[5] Although there are ascetic practices common to both householder and renouncer, as we saw in the last chapter (such as the ten points of the *dharma*),[6] the realms of the householder and renouncer are formally distinguished in terms of institution: they are different *āśramas* or stages on life's way and are often separated by the institution of monasticism. In one view, the ascetic is pursuing a higher *dharma* than the householder, and the householder should treat him as superior.[7] Indeed, texts on renunciation clearly set themselves within the genre of dharmic literature, as Olivelle has shown.[8]

Within this context, this chapter will focus on Śaiva tantrism in Kashmir during the early medieval period as represented in the texts of the tantric theologians. Tantric ascetics defined themselves against orthoprax *dharma* and its path of purity by following a path of power through the disruption of Brahmanical inhibition (*śaṅkā*), as Sanderson has demonstrated.[9] Like the orthoprax ascetic, the tantric ascetic questions the values of a householder *dharma* and seeks to transcend that restriction. There is a middle ground between purity and power where the Brahman householder adopted an internalised, tantric path of power described by Sanderson. After some general remarks about the tantric traditions, I shall again present the argument that the ascetic self must be understood both in terms of tradition and in terms of subjectivity. As with our other examples, the tantric ascetic performs the memory of tradition through the reversal of the body's flow. This reversal is traditionally seen in terms of celibacy and fasting, but in the tantric context can involve a sexuality that is transgressive of dharmic values. In this sense esoteric tantric ritual is a form of asceticism. I shall finally return to the theme of *dharma* in considering the problem of gender in our texts.

## THE TANTRIC TRADITIONS

Thanks to the work of a number of scholars such as André Padoux, Alexis Sanderson and his students, our knowledge of the tantric traditions has increased considerably, although scholarship in this field still has a long way to go. Because of our inevitably restricted picture, a thematic presentation on ascetic subjectivity in the tantric traditions is in many ways premature. But we do have sufficient knowledge about these traditions to make some general claims, and tantrism throws up such challenging questions about the nature of asceticism that these traditions cannot be ignored.

This is not the place to describe the development of the tantric traditions and to locate their place within the history of Indic traditions.[10] Suffice it to say that by the tenth century a large body of texts had developed in the different traditions focussed on the great deities Viṣṇu, Śiva and the Goddess. With the development of Śaivism, asceticism becomes a complex phenomenon, being central to Śaiva renouncers, but also being important within a householder setting. There are Śaiva ascetics of the Pāśupata order who do not revere the tantras but whose practices are closely akin to the tantric Śaiva Kāpālikas, the skull-bearing renouncers of the cremation ground, and there are householders who practise forms of asceticism adapted from the renunciate traditions. It is to the largely householder Śaiva Siddhānta and the related non-Saiddhānatika tradition, sometimes referred to as 'Kashmir Śaivism', that we find reference to ascetic practices, not only occurring in ascetic groups on the fringes of society but also absorbed into everyday life and performed in the context of Brahmanical *dharma*. The yearly ritual cycle of the Śaiva initiate into the tantric tradition known as the Trika ('Threefold') involved a high degree of supererogatory ritual and asceticism.[11] In medieval Kashmir, a politics of asceticism developed that saw tantric practices penetrate courtly society in a way that some at the time regarded as a threat to social stability, as Sanderson has lucidly described,[12] and which were articulated in the theology of the Recognition or Pratyabhijñā school. One way of putting this might be that the high-caste, householder's body, inscribed with vedic rites (*saṃskāra*) through initiation, marriage and so on, is further inscribed by the tantric practices. The orthodox body is overcoded with the tantric, ascetic body, which becomes the site of contesting ideologies.

The vast corpus of tantric material presents us with difficult questions. What is the function of these texts? Who composed them, and for whom? What are the procedural difficulties of the uninitiated outsider in approaching these texts? And so on. I cannot go into these questions here, but wish merely to point out that the social reality of which these texts are an index is not precisely clear, although we do have some understanding of the general social hierarchies of South Asian society in which they were composed. Asceticism in the tantras is not thematised in an overt way, as in much *dharma* literature, and yet there are strong continuities with orthoprax, ascetic material and injunctions to ascetic practice. Certainly the tantras were regarded as revelation and treated as words of authority, and certainly they developed in a social context that fostered their dissemination. The tantras, often composed in a simple metre (*śloka*), tend towards objectified description, prescription and instruction, with much use of the third person optative ('one should worship' or 'visualise' or whatever) so characteristic of ritual texts. Wholly lacking in this material and the commentaries is the kind of confessional writing we are used to in the European context, yet these texts are often dealing with deeply personal and intimate themes: with sexuality, with human relationships (such as those between master and disciple), with interiority (in their emphasis on visualisation and recognition of innate divinity), with pain, and with the possibility of transcendence. In their truth claims we have statements about how a person relates to the wider cosmos and society, about the deepest nature of a person's identity, about the possibility of personal transformation, and about social obligation and commitment.

## RENUNCIATION AND TANTRISM

As we have seen, renunciation as a formal institution developed early in the history of India, and while tantrism itself develops much later, there are undoubtedly precursors of tantric practice in earlier renunciate traditions. An important classification of renouncers found in the Law Books, the *dharma-sūtras*, and made famous in the later Advaita tradition, is into four types – the Kuṭīcara, Bahūdaka, Haṃsa and Paramahaṃsa.[13] These were distinguished by the ways they obtained food and by the emblems they carried, particularly the type of staff. Thus, Paramahaṃsas did not carry any staff, while Haṃsas carried a single staff and lower orders a triple staff. Olivelle has discussed at length a controversy over this issue in medieval India: between the Advaita tradition claiming a hierarchy of renouncers indicated by their emblems, and the tradition of Viṣṇu, the Śrī Vaiṣṇavas, claiming that all renouncers should carry the triple staff and wear sacrificial threads.[14] Other classifications added a further type to indicate the transcendence even of the orders of renunciation, the Atyāśramin, one who has transcended the *āśramas*, or one who is 'beyond the fourth' (*turīyātīta*).[15] While the orthoprax renouncers would wish to distance themselves from the tantric, it is here that the tantric sought to distinguish themselves from the vedic. In consonance with the general Indian practice of adding to a list to show the superiority of what had been added, the tantric ascetic regarded himself as being beyond vedic *dharma*. He sought an unrestricted freedom, often living in cremation grounds and courting pollution as a symbol of his transcendence of Brahmanical values.

Precursors of tantric ascetics are found in the systems of Śaivism, the teachings of Śiva (*śivaśāsana*), which was divided into the higher path (*atimarga*) of renunciate ascetics and the path of mantras (*mantramārga*) of renouncers and ordinary householders. The higher path comprised mainly the Pāśupata order, whose observance (*vrata*) is described in the *Pāśupata Sūtras* with a commentary by Kauṇḍinya. These Pāśupatas were Brahmans who claimed to have transcended the four *āśramas* and entered the fifth or perfected life-stage (*siddha-āśrama*)[16] and who practised forms of asceticism culminating in their living in the cremation ground, being uninterruptedly aware of their God, Rudra, eating whatever they can find and waiting for death.[17] But it is the path of mantras that comprises the tantric revelation proper, and within which the tantric paths place themselves. It is to this body of traditions and literature that we must turn.

In the tantric literature of Śaivism we find practices and systems ranging from minimal ritual obligation to supererogatory rites, various kinds of yoga and the famous secret rites of the tantric practitioner, all of which contain ascetic dimensions. Distinct initiatory paths for those desiring liberation (*mumukṣu*) and those desiring power and pleasure in higher, heavenly worlds (*bubhukṣu*) are described. Technically, an adept who followed the path of power and who had undergone a particular kind of consecration was known as a *sādhaka*, and the practice he performed known as *sādhana*. Both terms come from the root *sadh*, 'to succeed'. The term *sādhaka* comes to mean any tantric practitioner in general, but in the conceptual structure of the Śaiva texts it has a distinct meaning. Brunner has described its technical meaning as one who has undergone a particular consecration (the *sādhakābhiṣeka*) after his initiation into the tradition that will ensure his liberation (the *nirvāṇadīkṣā*). The structure of these rites has been well described by Brunner and in other publications,[18] although the extent to which the textual representation reflected social and cultural practice is impossible to determine. All we have are the texts and the representations of practice.

## THE ASCETIC SELF AND TRADITION

The *sādhaka* sought powers prescribed by tradition such as the vanquishing of enemies (*maraṇa*) and the power of subjugation (*vaśikaraṇa*),[19] as well, eventually, as the omnipotence of Śiva. There is an ambiguity about the term 'power'. On the one hand it is used as a scholarly term of analysis, the various meanings of which in relation to Western asceticism have been usefully discussed by Valantasis.[20] On the other, it translates a number of Sanskrit terms used in the sense of political power and sovereignty (*aiśvarya*) and in the sense of personal, supernatural power (*siddhi*) – not that political power is devoid of supernatural connotations, for the power of the king is derived from his place in the hierarchical cosmos, for his power is a consequence of his divinity. The term *śakti* covers both of these senses. Following Valantasis, if we take ascetical power to be the capacity to change and 'a capacity to affect the environment in which change is produced', then the tantric practitioner is clearly intent on producing such change in him- or herself, in the immediate environment of the ritual, and in the wider world.[21] But there is a dimension of asceticism fundamental both to politicised asceticism or asceticism in quest of political power and to asceticism as a quest for personal power, and this is subjectivity. As I have argued, ascetic goals are not simply abstract ideologies or justifications of power, they are the future orientations and narrative identities of people: their desire to break through the constraints of time and body, and their desire to achieve a goal, such as human perfection, in this or in some other world. The tantric Śaiva ascetic performs asceticism in response to the dharmic regularity of the Brahman householder and in response to the call of the higher *dharma* of his tradition. He constructs himself in accordance with tradition, subjectively appropriating its aims.

## THE ŚAIVA ASCETIC GOAL

When the Śaiva initiate practises, he (and it is invariably a he) performs the memory of tradition. The tradition is enacted through performance and recapitulated within the individual practitioner. The recapitulation of tradition is also the recapitulation of the goal and, indeed, the traditions themselves are thought to flow from the divine source which is the *sādhaka*'s eventual purpose.[22] The Śaiva initiate aims to realise his self as co-extensive with the absolute self of Śiva. An important text that deals with the practices of the *sādhaka* is the *Netra-tantra*, a text of the Kashmir valley commented on by the monistic theologian Kṣemarāja (ca 1000–1050 CE, and so predating him). The text is principally about mantra and the supremacy of the Netra ('eye') mantra (namely *OṂ JUṂ SAḤ* in the shorter version), which involves various practices by the *sādhaka* and the visualisation of various forms of Śiva as Mṛtyunjit or Mṛtyunjaya, the conqueror of death. The text describes the qualities and practices of the *sādhaka*, who should possess various virtues as a consequence of his asceticism, as well as describing the goals of practice. This goal is the realisation that the true identity of the ascetic is not the limited subject of first person predicates, but a deeper, transcendental power. This power is a subjectivity that is made absolute. For example, chapter 8 on the subtle visualisation (*sūkṣma-dhyāna*) of Mṛtyunjit or Mṛtyunjaya describes the ultimate goal of the *sādhaka* in the following terms. Here the Lord is addressing the Goddess:

> The supreme, eternal conquest of death is now declared, having attained which there is no (more) turning in the triple cycle of transmigration, O beloved. Śiva, who is omnipresent, all-seeing and omnipotent, shines. I will tell you about it (the conquest of death), since there is no other, attaining which, through becoming identical with it (*tanmayatvena*), one truly transcends old age and death. Speech can never express it, that which is not seen with the eye, not heard with the ears, not smelled by the nose, not tasted by the tongue, and not felt by the skin. It cannot be thought with the mind and is bereft of all form and flavour (yet) proclaimed (to be) with all forms and flavours, immeasurable, and beyond the senses. Having reached that, O Goddess, yogis are truly freed from old age and death. It (is reached)

with extensive practice and with supreme detachment. The immortal, eternal, auspicious, imperishable and supreme (state) is attained due to the abandoning of passion and hate, due to the destruction of greed and delusion, O beloved, due to the abandoning of intoxication and envy, and due to the destruction of the darkness of arrogant opinion.[23]

Here we have statement of the 'object' of the *sādhaka*'s practice and his ultimate goal, and the text lends itself to the monistic interpretation of its commentator Kṣemarāja. The passage describes the goal of practice in generally impersonalist terms, as is seen in the use of the neuter relative pronoun *yat*, which refers to the neuter *mṛtyunjaya*, the name for the form of Śiva visualised here. This impersonal reality which is the object of the yogin's practice is understood within the Pratyabhijñā to be pure consciousness.

This language of attainment in the text – the yogin attains deathlessness through extreme effort – presents us with a model of the practitioner becoming empowered through accessing an immortal, impersonal power within. The text also speaks of this power as the means of its own attainment: this power is achieved through becoming identical with it (*tanmayatvena*), suggesting that the means and the goal are the same. The means to attain Śiva is Śiva himself. Since this state is outside of time and beyond the senses, to reach it is to win freedom from time and the senses and to realise its all-pervasiveness. This is to become cosmologically located as the source of manifestation, the source beyond speech (*vāc*) but manifested through all speech.[24] The goal of ascetic practice is the attainment of this power, an impersonal force that the text identifies with Śiva and which Kṣemarāja identifies with pure consciousness, and which the practitioner appropriates through the realisation that he is already there. The *sādhaka*'s quest is a quest for the self that is located inwardly, and this self, this deepest personal identity and the true subject of all self-narratives, is Śiva or pure consciousness.[25]

According to the monistic Śaiva reading of the text, the realisation of identity is the absolute appropriation of ascetic power. It is the recognition by the yogin of a deeper identity beyond the reach of limited awareness. The language of the *Netra-tantra* and the commentary therefore conveys a particular sense of subjectivity: the subjectivity of transcendent being, to which the first person pronoun 'I' (*aham*) refers, which does not interact through the senses, and yet which is the true self. Abhinavagupta (ca 975–1025 CE) especially develops this idea, and according to him this 'I' is absolute subjectivity, of which the cosmos is an expansion (*ahantā-prathamātmana*).[26] Although bereft of physical organs, this absolute subjectivity sees, hears and smells, and although unacting, composes revelation (*āgama*), tradition (*siddhānta*) and logical treatises (*tarka*).[27] Whenever a person says 'I want', 'I know' or 'I do', ultimately this refers to the wanting, knowing and doing of an absolute subject.[28] The internalisation of tradition is also the internalisation of its source that is absolute subjectivity. The yogin attains true knowledge (*jñāna*) or immersion into supreme consciousness (*saṃvitsamāveśa*) through the tradition (*saṃpradāya*) that flows from the 'mouth of the yoginī' (*yoginīvaktra*), the supreme source and foundation of existence which is that consciousness.[29]

The goal of religious practice is to wake up to the truth of the identity of the limited subject, the apparent subject of first person predicates, with the absolute subject, cultically referred to as Śiva but who transcends all names. The ultimate intention of the elaborate metaphysics and structure of the Śaiva tradition is the existential realisation of the subject of first person predicates, what might be called, following Urban, the indexical 'I' that needs a context to be understood, with the absolute subject, the anaphoric 'I of discourse' in the texts[30] (where 'I' refers to Śiva) – (see pp. 218–19). The limited sense of the first person pronoun is but a contraction of the unlimited, absolute sense.[31] In Abhinavagupta, and in many other texts, there is a shift of reference, and the indexical pronoun 'I' comes to refer not to the limited person but to this absolute subjectivity, the only reality, understanding which has soteriological consequences. Asceticism as subjectivity is highlighted in this material in that the radical intensification of subjectivity is the goal of the whole system.

There is a paradox here. Because all is absolute subjectivity there can be no way of attaining it, for to attain a goal implies a distinction between subject and object, path and goal, but there is no place outside this subjectivity. To distinguish between a path or method (*upāya*) and goal (*upeya*) is an error.[32] If Śiva is the sole truth of the cosmos, there is no condition or place where he is not, and therefore no condition which is impure (*tattvam nāsty aśucis tataḥ*[33]); all states are equal in the light of transcendent subjectivity. Because the individual experient is not clouded by a covering over consciousness, there cannot be the cessation of a covering, and the essence (*svarūpa*) cannot be achieved.[34] There can be no mediation of absolute reality. Yet on the other hand, this is a tradition of textual interpretation and practice, practices which are ascetical in orientation and which imply a distinction between a subject in a state of ignorance and the goal of complete awareness. The texts are aware of this issue and oscillate in their language between statements of pure monistic idealism and statements and prescriptions that imply a distinction between self and transcendent goal and the necessity of tradition, of the teacher (*guru*), and methods to attain this state.

Indeed, this distinction between absolute subjectivity that brooks no distinctions and the necessity of constructing a path to a goal is reflected in the schema of the methods (*upāya*). Abhinavagupta divides these, following the root text of the tradition, the *Mālinīvijayotara Tantra*,[35] into the non-method (*anupāya*) and the method (*upāya*), comprising three paths corresponding to the three faculties of will (*icchā*), cognition (*jñāna*) and action (*karma*),[36] which for Abhinavagupta form a graded hierarchy. The goal of the ascetic self is therefore defined by tradition as the recognition of innate divinity. The ascetic self enacts the memory of tradition in such recognition and in the performance of ascetic actions. In order to recognise this absolute subjectivity, the ascetic must destroy limited subjectivity and a socially constructed, dharmic identity as an act of will through ascetic performance. The tantric ascetic therefore performs the memory of tradition and the ambiguity of the self through the subjective appropriation of tradition and the attempted eradication of the limited self, the indexical I, through will.

## *DHARMA* AND ASCETIC SUBJECTIVITY

Abhinavagupta and the other Śaiva theologians are composing their texts primarily for an educated, Brahmanical, Śaiva audience, familiar with dharmic restrictions. While they would have been predominantly householders, the practices the texts refer to developed in the context of the cremation ground traditions, transgressive of Brahmanical *dharma*, and some of the originary or root texts that Abhinavagupta draws on retain elements of more severe ascetic practice. These texts and practices are, however, contained within the four-fold scheme of the *upāyas* by Abhinavagupta and his student Kṣemarāja, the most severe asceticism occurring within the method associated with the transformation of emotion and extreme sensation, the *śaṃbhāvopaya*. Thus the *Vijñānabhairava-tantra* speaks of the shattering of limiting thought construction through placing oneself in a situation of fear, through sexual desire and through physical pain. For example, the text reads that through piercing any limb with a sharp implement and focussing the mind there, the practitioner goes to the absolute.[37] Or again, one of the key originary texts of the Pratyabhijñā, Vāsugupta's *Verses on Vibration* (*Spanda-kārikā*), speaks of how transcendent subjectivity remains even in the states of violent anger, delight, confusion or physical exertion such as running.[38] There are other examples, a notable one being Abhinavagupta's referring to the energy (*vīrya*) raised within the heart upon seeing a loved one unexpectedly.[39]

A subjectivity is thus conveyed in these tantric texts set within a doctrinal structure intended to transform the practitioner. We can see the creation of a world order to enable liberation from the world through a transcendence of Brahmanical *dharma* or a realisation that the self is deeper than the world of social transaction. This subjectivity is set against the restrictive rules of Brahmanical *dharma* and disrupts them, although not in an overt, public sense. There is an implication here that the realm of political activity and social interaction is transcended by the ascetic self, whose subjectivity the monistic Śaiva regards as the basis of all. The asceticism of the Śaiva householder is not so much an overt public activity as that of the renouncer in the cremation ground, but rather a covert detachment and series of practices inscribed on the body, which in one sense absent the body from the socio-political world. In these practices, we have a recognition of human emotion, such as love and tenderness, of anger, of fear and of desire, which can be turned to the service of a spiritual path. Asceticism becomes integrated into subjectivity and becomes not so much an external discipline imposed from without as an internal one, focussing on the transformation of emotion and the purification of desire.

The inner intention to recognise the unlimited nature of subjectivity is textually instantiated, along with a recognition of the duality entailed in the very process of moving towards a goal. Asceticism becomes the reconfiguring of the personality, a realignment of subjectivity, with a transcendent subjectivity regarded as the source and destiny of all being. Of particular note is the purification of desire and the acute awareness by Abhinavagupta of the importance of sexuality and intimacy in human life, and the potential for its transformation. Yet although the texts might regard this inner transformation as being beyond or deeper than the public realm, it nevertheless does have socio-political consequences in so far as the expansion of subjectivity disrupts Brahmanical *dharma* in transcending any social restriction or inhibition. It is, indeed, the source of what is *dharma* and what is not *dharma*, and both are equal in the light of the infinitely expanded subjectivity. From this perspective there is no difference, says Abhinavagupta, between that which is supported (*dharma*) and that which supports (*dharmin*), for both are forms of energy (*śakti*) of the supreme Lord, who is the pure subject.[40] Through the experiencing of the ordinary, there can be a rupture with it, and a recognition that limited subjectivity, and interaction in the social world, is but a contraction or modality of transcendence.

## ASCETIC SUBJECTIVITY AND TRANSGRESSIVE SEXUALITY

Subjectivity, as we have seen, is thematised in the monistic Śaivism of Kashmir and intensified to the extent of its becoming absolute. The true referent of the first person pronoun is not the limited self but the absolute self of whom the limited self is an appearance (*ābhāsa*). The paths to realisation, the *upāyas*, include as part of the 'individual way' (*āṇāvopāya*) systems of ritual and yoga. There are primarily two ritual systems described by Abhinavagupta, the normative ritual system of the Śaiva householder (*tantra-prakriyā*) and the esoteric ritual (*kula-prakriyā*).[41] The former involves the construction of a trident maṇḍala (*triśulābhjamaṇḍala*) with the deities of the Trika imposed upon it (principally the three goddesses Parā, Parāparā and Aparā). Offerings are made to these deities both in action and in the imagination. The secret *kula* rite adds the use of polluting substances (meat and alcohol) and actions as offerings. Of particular note is the use of sex in a ritual context disruptive of *dharma* and the usual constrictions of caste. Indeed, this is one of the famous features of what later came to be known as 'left-hand' tantra, and a feature which has attracted the attention of the West, almost to the exclusion of all else 'tantric'. But while ritual sex and the promise of lurid tantric texts has fed into late modern religiosity and the pursuit of pleasure in the West, there has been comparatively little serious scholarly attention paid to this material.[42]

While there are undoubtedly ecstatic and orgiastic dimensions in some tantric texts, what is notable about Abhinavagupta's representation is that the *kulaprakriyā* can be seen as a form of asceticism. The sphere of the most intimate subjectivity becomes the field for the transformation of individual subjectivity into transcendent subjectivity. Sex becomes an ascetical act, and a journey from the limited indexical 'I' to the unlimited 'I', freed of particular indexicality. In line with Laidlaw and Humphrey's understanding of ritual as ordinary action performed in a ritualised way,[43] we can see sex here as ordinary action performed in a ritualised way. But what is more significant is that sex in the *kulaprakriyā* becomes a form of asceticism. Abhinavagupta makes it clear that the rite is not for pleasure and the satisfaction of the field of the lower senses, the secondary wheels (*anucakra*), but is a means to the transcendent goal of enlightenment – the recognition of transcendent subjectivity. Through ritualisation or formalisation, the deepest human intimacy becomes not an end in itself, an action for its own sake as it is in *kāma* literature, but a means to an end. Ordinarily sexual activity results in pleasure and children, but in the ritualised context of the *kula* rite it results in liberation and power and so is akin to the renunciation by the orthoprax ascetic.

The esoteric rite is described by Abhinavagupta in chapter 29 of the *Tantrāloka* and must be seen against the background of general mores and attitudes present in early medieval South Asian society. While the pursuit of sexual pleasure (*kāma*) was certainly one of the legitimate purposes of a life, it was nevertheless pursued within the restrictions of caste.[44] Indeed, law books such as the *Manusmṛti* (the *Laws of Manu*) suggest severe punishments for the transgression of caste boundaries,[45] and the extreme ritual restrictions of the Brahman male suggest a somewhat inhibited attitude towards sexuality.

Apart from social attitudes towards sexuality, attitudes to the ascetic are also highly relevant. Within Brahmanical orthopraxy, the renouncer is ideally celibate, one whose semen is 'upturned' (*ūrdhvaretas*), becoming a power contained in his head.[46] Abhinavagupta accepts the legitimacy of this kind of celibate ascetic but extends the meaning of the category, which he refers to as *siddha*, to include the 'hero' (*vīra*) or non-celibate follower of the esoteric path (*kulavartman*). He also uses the term to refer to disembodied *gurus* and their wives who can enter practitioners during the esoteric rite.[47] The ascetic as tantric hero is the concern of Abhinavagupta, for only he has the qualification (*adhikāra*) to perform the secret ritual, and it is he for whom the term 'celibacy' (*brahmacarya*) is redefined to mean the ritual use of the three forbidden substances of wine, meat and sex[48] – a practice that gives gradual perfection (*siddhikrama*) within a month, which would otherwise take thousands of years with floods of mantras.[49] The use of the triple 'm' (*makāratraya* – which became the 'five "ms"' of later Śākta tantrism) is only for the 'hero' who can perform the rite with complete detachment and without desire (*riraṃsā, gardha*), without greed (*lobha*) and without doubt (*vicikitsā*). Qualification (*adhikāra*), moreover, means that the hero has been initiated into the *kula* tradition by a teacher and so has been given the authority and legitimacy to perform the rite. Initiation here means the descent of grace which manifests itself in bodily shaking (*ghurṇi, kampa*) and loss of consciousness (*nidrā*), depending upon its intensity.[50]

During the rite itself, the practitioner or *siddha* undergoes the preliminary purification of bathing and so on, accompanied by the visualisation of the rising of power within his body, the power of the goddess Kuṇḍalinī. He worships pure consciousness, transcendent subjectivity identical to himself, in the form of the goddess Kālasaṃkārśinī. With the arrival of the *siddha*'s female partner, his 'messenger' (*dūtī*) in the rite, meat, wine and sex are offered to the goddess.[51] The substance (*dravya*) or 'emergent form' (*uditarūpa*) which results from their union is passed from mouth to mouth[52] and offered to the *guru* in a pot, according to the commentary. Jayaratha gives a number of citations from texts bearing witness to this practice, which, according to Silburn, also parallels a modern marriage custom in Kashmir of the couple passing food from mouth to mouth.[53] The results of this practice are the experience of the bliss of one's own essence and the attainment of liberation and pleasure in higher worlds (*bhuktimukti*). On the one hand, sexual experience is an analogue of the bliss of liberation, on the other, sex (*maithuna*) is regarded as a ritual substance (*dravya*), along with others, to be offered in *pūjā* ('worship') to deities who demand to be appeased in this way.[54]

Abhinavagupta's text and Jayaratha's commentary are written in a cryptic style and a highly technical vocabulary which link this ritual to the complex ideology of the tradition. The union of the *siddha* with the messenger in the rite is described as 'the worship of the principal wheel by means of the interior organ'.[55] Here the terminology has a complex overlay of meanings and implications. The 'principal wheel' (*mukhyacakra*) is defined by Jayaratha as absolute consciousness (*saṃvit*) or pure subjectivity, but can also be associated with the *yoginīvaktra*, the mouth of the yoginī, with the implication that the goal of practice is achieved through the female practitioner. The term 'interior organ', Silburn observes, refers in its inner meaning to the heart but externally to the sexual organs.[56] This kind of overcoding of terms is pervasive in these texts. The term 'wheel' (*cakra*), for example, has the implication of sphere or realm of perception and knowledge, and so relates to absolute subjectivity where the subject's field of perception is total and non-differentiated: manifestation is non-distinct from its source.

In this exposition of Abhinavagupta's account of the secret *kula* ritual we see how a tantric ideology and practice is overlaid upon Brahmanical *dharma*. While overtly adhering to *dharma*, the Śaiva initiate disrupts *dharma* through expressing his tradition that he regards as going beyond orthoprax prescription. Sexuality in this tradition becomes a form of asceticism and teleological, ritually constructed for the realisation of pure subjectivity. This highly ritualised action shows how tradition is appropriated and can be seen as the performance of the memory of tradition. The tradition is internalised, expressed and realised in the performance of the *kula* rite which is also the performance of the ambiguity of the self, in that desire is eradicated through its expression. This is to eradicate the limited, dharmic self through its ultimate expansion into the limitless subject.

## *DHARMA* AND GENDER

While the process of reading this material presents us with the surface difficulty of inhabiting the world of the text, what Peter Ochs calls the first stage in the reading process, the second stage of arriving at interpreted meanings or reading the text dialogically presents us with considerable difficulty.[57] Our contextualising practices need to be aware of the technical terminology of the Śaiva texts, their overcoding (as, for example, with the *mukhyacakra*), and the text needs to be read in the context of the theme of ascetic subjectivity. It is well to remember that the texts describing sexual rites transgressive of social norms are *textual* representations, and we do not know the precise relationship between text and society in this period. When dealing with tantric ritual we are dealing with textual representations of tantric ritual, and action is pulled back into the realm of text. All we can do is to assume that the text is an implicit index, to use Ochs's phrase, of events in the social world that gave the text life.[58] Looking at this through a Bakhtinian lens, we might say that Abhinavagupta as author stands outside of the 'heroes' of his text and constructs them – namely the *sādhaka* and *dūtī* – in terms of his social and gendered expectations.

Abhinavagupta's text, along with Jayaratha's commentary, is an articulation of a long tradition. The text interfaces with other texts, using them in support of particular practices or doctrinal positions, and describes to a literate audience the structures of liberation. Chapter 29 of the *Tantrāloka* presents a narrative of the ritual sequence. It describes how the practitioner should worship, how he should behave towards his partner in the rite, how in union with her there is their mutual merging into pure consciousness, how they should offer sexual substances followed by offerings to other deities who are located within their own body. This is no ordinary narrative, and the text's *imaginaire* opens out a world between a description of action and an account of subjective states and their cosmological analogues. It is not a philosophical discourse, nor yet a merely prescriptive ritual manual, but rather presents us with an account of subjectivity and subjective processes of perception which are identified with cosmological processes. In this way the text is in consonance with other commentaries that interpret revelation in strongly cosmological terms (for example, Kṣemarāja's commentary on the *Netra-tantra*).

Through subjective desire, transcendent subjectivity is realised, yet subjective desire keeps a person bound in the cycle of reincarnation. The hero of the text is the one who uses desire to overcome desire. So, on the one hand, desire (*riraṃsā*) in the practitioner is an obstacle to realisation which should not be present in the hero;[59] on the other hand, those who have desire (*kāmāḥ*) for realisation may achieve perfection (*siddhi*).[60] Hence, rather than desire itself, it is the object of desire that keeps a being bound. If the object of desire is pure consciousness, the indexical 'I''s true identity, desire becomes purified. Rather than the eradication of desire through ascetic practices, particularly celibacy, desire is used to transcend the lower levels of its operation. In this way the sexual act becomes an ascetic act in the ritual process and the text expresses, albeit in a formalised way, deep human longings and offers the possibility of transformation.

This ascetic subjectivity or the transformation of subjectivity away from concerns with worldly spheres of activity (*laukika, anucakra*) to a transcendental realm (*mukhyacakra*) affects other realms of subjectivity, particularly intimate, intersubjective relationships. Two such relationships are of central importance: the relationship between student and teacher and the relationship between male practitioner (*siddha, vīra*) and female practitioner (*śakti, dūtī*).

## *The representation of women*

Bringing to the text our early-twenty-first-century questions about gender roles, gender rights and the values underlying attitudes to sexuality, we find that the text reveals interesting tensions. On the one hand, the text was written by a Brahman male, Abhinavagupta, in an age in which women were largely written out of public records or are found only in terms of (generally occlusive) male representations. On the other hand, reading these texts reveals a comparatively higher status attributed to women than in orthoprax Brahmanical society. Abhinavagupta, and more so his commentator Jayaratha, represent women as teachers in the tradition and as powerful beings who manifest the power of pure consciousness. There is an ambiguity in the representation of women, and the term *yoginī* refers both to a human being and to a goddess. Jayaratha's commentary says that if the *sādhaka* meditates on his limited individuality as comprising only powers (*śakti*), then, having become a 'sky-goer' (*khecarī*), he can unite with a *yoginī*. The term *yoginī* is ambiguous, implying both a spiritual entity and a physical woman.[61]

Abhinavagupta's text is written for the Brahman male practitioner, probably a married householder, who is undoubtedly understood to be the main actor in the ritual for whom it takes place, and who is the main benefactor of any results that ensue. The lower status of the woman in the rite, his partner, is clear from her title as 'messenger' (*dūtī*), she who mediates between the practitioner and the absolute, and from her identification with Śakti, the power of Śiva, who manifests the cosmos due to his will. The text discusses the type of woman who participates in the rite, and Jayaratha quotes texts describing the *dūtī* in terms reminiscent of Sanskrit poetry, but which objectify her in a way that goes against contemporary, Western sensibilities.[62] Here the female partner is presented as a paragon of beauty with images drawn from standard metaphors in Sanskrit poetic literature. But the text also lists the necessary spiritual qualities, such as possessing an awareness of having destroyed greed and delusion (*lobha-moha-parikṣīṇa-cetasam*), having consciousness as her essence (*cit-svabhāvikām*), with a unique essence, and being someone who experiences the wonder of the oneness of Bhairava (*bhairavaikacamatkāra-carmaṇaika – svarūpiṇīm*).

Yet while Jayaratha quotes extensively from texts of the tradition which elevate the *dūtī* to the status of the goddess, the text nevertheless treats her as instrumental in the attainment of the male *sādhaka*. Indeed, even if the woman is bereft of desirable qualities, perfection or power (*siddhi*) is still attainable for the *sādhaka*, and Jayaratha quotes a text saying that if one cannot obtain a suitable partner, then what is most important is the unwavering concentration of the *sādhaka* in all the ritual action.[63] Abhinavagupta also says that there should be no anticipation (*apekṣaṇa*) of the Śakti's beauty, for the most important quality is that she can become non-distinct (*abheditā*) from the *sādhaka*.[64] There is, then, an inequality in their non-distinction – it is *she* who becomes non-distinct from *him*. Even though generally elevated to a high status at an ideological level, with all the attributes of an enlightened being in the tradition, in Kantian terms the partner in the rite is still a means to an end rather than an end in herself. This is further corroborated by an enigmatic passage in which Abhinavagupta and the commentary seem to restrict the choice of *dūtī* to any female member of the *siddha*'s family, except his wife, in order to ensure that desire does not arise.[65]

We might interpret this to mean that in this ascetic sexuality, the realisation of absolute subjectivity involves the disjunction between intention (the *sādhaka*'s transcending of desire) and expression (the sexual act in a ritual context). Jayaratha quotes various scriptures to this effect that 'he may enjoy the beloved woman steadily, but without any desire',[66] for the aim of the rite is transcendence. Being beyond the community of the worldly (*laukika*) and supra-worldly (*alaukika*) means that the *dūtī* is outside of the categories of usual, or dharmic, human interactions, outside of family relationships and even outside of relationships concerned with the gods and ancestors. If we are to take this passage literally, there is an element of taboo-breaking here, for incest goes against the rules of Brahmanical society. However, as Silburn claims, Jayaratha could be speaking figuratively when referring to the *sādhaka*'s female relatives,[67] although he does cite a passage which indicates that the *dūtī* might be one's wife, sister, mother, daughter or 'beautiful friend'.[68]

Yet our text also contains voices that suggest a different picture from that of the objectified woman as merely the means to the *sādhaka*'s goal of power and perfection. The *dūtī* is Śakti, the goddess and consort of Śiva through whom he manifests the cosmos, and who is furthermore placed at the esoteric heart of the Trika as the deity who transcends all others. In this secret tradition it is she who is identified with pure consciousness and absolute subjectivity and who is iconographically depicted and visualised as dancing on the corpse of her husband Śiva. In the actual *kula* ritual, Abhinavagupta states that the couple (*yugala*), both the *sādhaka* and *dūtī*, penetrate into the supreme realm (*ūrdhvadhāma*) of pure consciousness, which also sets up an agitation of the lower realms of experience, which are then brought into connection with that higher state.[69] Their 'lower wheels' or spheres of the ordinary senses are satisfied in order that they be absorbed into the 'principal wheel' or higher sphere.[70]

Of course, the ideological depiction of women as goddesses does not indicate a higher social status, but it does suggest that gender attitudes are more complex in the medieval tantric world and must be understood in more sophisticated ways than merely seeing women as totally occluded in these traditions. Both the *sādhaka* and *dūtī* in the text experience the bliss of pure consciousness and become absolute subjectivity, and it is highly significant that women are teachers in the tradition. One lineage of teachers, the Ardhatraiyambaka, originated with Traiyamba but was passed on to his daughter, and Abhinavagupta was initiated into the *kula* tradition through Bhagavatī, his teacher Śambhunātha's wife. The *guru* transmits the teaching to the *dūtī*, in Abhinavagupta's case the *guru*'s wife, and she transmits the teaching to men 'by the door in the way described',[71] that is, in the secret *kula* rite. Again, there is a strong element of iconoclasm, in that sleeping with the *guru*'s wife (*gurutalpaga*) was traditionally regarded as a most heinous sin, disrupting the intimate relationship between teacher and student.[72] In this text, however, the relationship is intensified in the ritual setting of initiation, and the ritualised sexual act becomes an ascetic act (also an aesthetic act), performed not for the fulfilment of male desire, nor for procreation, but for the transposition of desire into a higher realm. The sexual act is understood in cosmological terms, and this cosmological sexuality is subjectively appropriated by the practitioners. We can use the plural, for although the social status of the female partner is lower than that of the male, the subjective appropriation of the cosmological structure and, conversely, the identification of an ordinary act with a cosmological structure, is achieved by both.

### *Transgression*

Abhinavagupta's text undoubtedly advocates transgression of normative, Brahmanical *dharma*. In going against the dharmic narrative, it creates its own narrative that sees life in a wider, trans-social context. Even so, the tantric Brahman practitioner must overtly abide by the rules of *dharma*, or be seen to be doing so. While initiation into the *kula* tradition and ritual, described above, eradicates caste, as Sanderson notes, for Abhinavagupta a Śaiva practitioner should be internally a Kaula, externally a Śaiva, but vedic in social practice.[73] While following orthoprax norms, the tantric initiate takes subjective control of them through seeming to follow them, but at their heart subverts them through a sexuality that disrupts caste and family boundaries, and disrupts the usual motivation of desire. The *kula* ritual is therefore ascetical in its disruption of ordinary desire – the practice must be performed with detachment – and discloses a subjectivity at odds with orthoprax prescriptions. The asceticism of the *Tantrāloka* can therefore be read as an assertion of a subjectivity at odds with the construction of the subject by the Brahmanical tradition. It can therefore be read politically as the articulation of a subjectivity that undermines Brahmanical norms and, indeed, consciously seeks to do so through going against Brahmanical prohibition. Through the ritual act, this subjectivity asserts control, a control otherwise not available when subject to orthoprax ritual prescriptions, and the practitioner hopes to align his limited subjectivity with the unlimited, absolute subjectivity of pure consciousness, his true identity, outside of Brahmanical socialisation and control.

Reading the text in the light of what we know about Brahmanical norms and the model of the Brahman found, for example, in *Manu*, as living a highly controlled life hedged about with restriction and prohibition (*śaṅkā*), we can see how Abhinavagupta's text (among others) is transgressive. Indeed, Jayaratha says that those practitioners who do not do what is forbidden due to fear experience a thousand torments in hell.[74]

The body was highly controlled by the orthoprax Brahman, as Sanderson has shown, a body controlled and inscribed in its ritual prescriptions by sovereign power. With the Śaiva tantric Brahman, we find an ascetic body inscribed by orthoprax practices (and so subject to sovereign power) but for whom that sovereign power is undermined by the overcoding of the ascetic body with the tantric rites. The ascetic body is not docile, the passive recipient of codes externally imposed upon it by a conservative and restrictive tradition, but is textually represented as disruptive of such codes. The ascetic body is represented as a tenacious body, through which a subjectivity comes into view involving a narrative identity that relates the subject to the cosmos and in which the subject of first person predicates is identified with an absolute subjectivity. The tantric ascetic is empowered through accessing the impersonal force that affirms his identity with it and disrupts his social identity within Brahmanical society. Through transgression, life is seen in a wider, transnormative context, a context that allows for a particular kind of subjectivity and for the appropriation of a transcendence through the ritual disruption of social norms, expectations and taboos.

The disruption of normative social expectations is great, but because of that the subjectivity revealed is intensified. The ascetic body of the tantric practitioner questions the received values of the Brahmanical tradition and even questions gender roles, although the degree to which this is possible in the context of eleventh-century Kashmir is questionable. While there is little sense of the representation of female subjectivity, we are nevertheless confronted with a strong representation of a Brahman, male subjectivity closely engaged with the ideas and practices of the time and wishing to transcend the limits of any cultural restriction. In the values of the Śaiva householder, an ascetic body is constructed through transgression and resistance to the imposition of a Brahmanical sovereign power: the virtues of control and celibacy are reinterpreted in the light of an absolute subjectivity and the demands of its realisation. Desire is used to transcend desire, and the purification of desire becomes the articulation of ascetic subjectivity.

## *The aesthetics of asceticism*

Lastly, while a reading of this text in terms of social power is central to our understanding and to the construction of an objectified and instrumental view of women, there is nevertheless another reading which takes us in a different direction, a reading in terms of the aesthetics of asceticism. We might even say that one of Abhinavagupta's concerns is aesthetic sensibility and the link between aesthetics and being, located in the spiritual realisation or knowledge of the *sādhaka* in the *kula* rite. The highest aesthetic emotion for Abhinavagupta is the 'flavour of tranquillity' (*śāntarasa*), which is paralleled by the 'innate tranquillity' (*viśrāmam sahajam*[75]) of absolute subjectivity. Abhinavagupta sees the highest achievement of practice in terms of aesthetic experience and the subjective apprehension of beauty. Seen in these terms, the *dūtī* in the *kula* rite becomes not merely a means to the end of the *sādhaka*'s spiritual enlightenment but an object of contemplation as a vision of beauty. The *dūtī* might be seen as a theophany with whom the *sādhaka* becomes one. Here the *sādhaka* eradicates the boundary between the limited and the unlimited, between the indexical 'I' and absolute subjectivity, and between himself as Śiva and his partner as Śakti in the *kula* ritual.

This kind of aesthetic reading moves against a reading wholly in terms of power differentials. The aesthetic view of the ascetic–sexual rite sees both the *sādhaka* and *dūtī* perform the ritual in terms of a dynamic in which the *sādhaka* as Śiva and the *dūtī* as Śakti are polar opposites. Abhinavagupta's text constructs a picture in which distance and opposition are necessary for the effectiveness of the ritual process. On a socio-political reading this structure can, justifiably, be seen in terms of the occlusion of the *dūtī* as an index of the occlusion of women in the wider society. But on an aesthetic reading, the structure can be seen as the necessary conditions for the aesthetic experience of the rite and the identification of the aesthetic experience with the recognition of absolute subjectivity as one's true identity. Perhaps the poignancy of this subjectivity lies in the distance between an absolute subjectivity fleetingly glimpsed and the temporal sequence of the ritual action, in the inner desire and the outer, desireless union, in the affirmation of subjectivity and in the eradication of the boundary between the inner and the outer.

## NOTES

1. *Jayākha Saṃhitā*, Krishnamacharya, E. (ed.) (Baroda: Gaekwad's Oriental Series, 1931, reprint 1967).
2. For example, *Yatidharmasamuccaya* 7.60 on the consequences of relapse. P. Olivelle, *Rules and Regulations of Brahmanical Asceticism* (Delhi: Sri Satguru, 1997 (1995)), p. 131.
3. Kauṭilya, *Arthaśāstra*, 1.7.3 in R. P. Kangle (ed. and trs.), *The Kauṭilya Arthaśāstra in Three Parts* (Bombay: University of Bombay, 1960–65); J. Jolly (ed.), *Mānava Dharma-Śāstra: The Code of Manu* (London: Trübner, 1887), 7.151–2; W. Doniger, *The Laws of Manu* (Harmondsworth: Penguin, 1991), p. 143.
4. Jaimini *Pūrva Mīmāṃsā Sūtra* 1.1.2, trs. G. Jha, vol. I (Baroda: Gaekwad Oriental Series, 66, 1973).
5. *Yatidharmasamuccaya* 1.24. Olivelle, *Rules and Regulations*, p. 37.

6. These are patience, forgiveness, self-control, honesty, purification, mastery of the senses, wisdom, learning, truth and absence of anger. *Mānavadharmaśāstra* 6.91–4; *Yatidharmasamuccaya* 5.17–20. Olivelle, *Rules and Regulations*, p. 74.
7. *Yatidharmasamuccaya* 6.296. Olivelle, *Rules and Regulations*, p. 123.
8. Olivelle, *Rules and Regulations*, pp. 4–5.
9. Alexis Sanderson, 'Purity and Power Among the Brahmans of Kashmir' in M. Carruthers, Steven Collins, and Steven Lukes (eds.), *The Category of the Person* (Cambridge University Press, 1985), pp. 190–216.
10. For example, see Alexis Sanderson, 'Śaivism and the Tantric Traditions' in Stewart Sutherland, Leslie Houlden, Peter Clarke, and Friedhelm Hardy (eds.), *The World's Religions* (London: Routledge, 1988), pp. 660–704; G. Flood, 'The Śaiva Traditions' in G. Flood (ed.), *The Blackwell Companion to Hinduism* (Oxford: Blackwell, 2003), pp. 200–28.
11. See Alexis Sanderson, 'Mandala and Agamic Identity in the Trika of Kashmir' in A. Padoux (ed.), *Mantras et Diagrammes Rituels dans l'Hindouisme* (Paris: CNRS, 1986), pp. 175–207.
12. Sanderson, 'Purity and Power Among the Brahmans of Kashmir,' pp. 202–06.
13. P. Olivelle, *The Āśrama System: The History and Hermeneutics of a Religious Institution* (Oxford University Press, 1993), pp. 165–7.
14. P. Olivelle, *Renunciation in Hinduism: A Medieval Debate*, 2 vols. (Vienna: De Nobili Research Library, 1986 and 1987).
15. Olivelle, *The Āśrama System*, pp. 222–34.
16. Sanderson, 'Śaivism and the Tantric Traditions', p. 664. On the Pāśupata observance see G. Oberhammer, 'The Use of Mantra in Yogic Meditation: The Testimony of the *Pāśupata*' in H. P. Alper (ed.), *Understanding Mantras* (Albany: SUNY Press, 1989), pp. 204–23. Part of their observance entailed acting as if mad and generally anti-socially, behaviour that has its precursors in the Paramahaṃsa described in the *Vaikhānasa Dharma Sūtra*. See Olivelle, *The Āśrama System*, p. 166.
17. Sanderson, 'Śaivism and the Tantric Traditions', p. 665.
18. Hélène Brunner, 'Le Sadaka, Personnage Oublié de l'Inde du Sud', *Journal Asiatique* vol. 263, 1975, pp. 411–43; Richard Davies, *Śiva in an Oscillating Universe* (Princeton University Press, 1991), pp. 89–100.
19. See T. Goudriaan, *Māyā Divine and Human* (Delhi: Motilal, 1978), pp. 310–33, 379–84.
20. R. Valantasis, 'Constructions of Power in Asceticism', *Journal of the American Academy of Religion* vol. 63, 1995, pp. 775–821. On Foucault's understanding of power in relation to religion also see Jeremy Carrette, *Foucault and Religion: Spiritual Corporeality and Political Spirituality* (London and New York: Routledge, 2000), pp. 109–28.
21. Valantasis, 'Constructions of Power in Asceticism', p. 793.
22. On the traditions as streams flowing from a divine source see M. Dyczkowski, *The Canon of the Śaivāgama and the Kubjikā Tantras of the Western Kaula Tradition* (Albany: SUNY Press, 1988), pp. 32, 66–73.

23. V. Dviveda (ed.) *Netra-tantra with udyota by Kṣemarāja* (Delhi: Parimala Publications, 1985), 8.1–8a.
*atha mṛtyuñjayaṃ nityaṃ paraṃ caivādhunocyate / yat prāpya na pravarteta saṃsāre trividhe priye //1// yogī sarvagato bhāti sarvadṛk sarvakṛc chivaḥ / tad ahaṃ kathayiṣyāmi yasmād anyanna vidyate //2// yat prāpya tanmayatvena bhavati hy ajarāmaraḥ / yan na vāg vadate nityam yan na dṛśyeta cakṣuṣā //3// yac ca na śrūyate karṇair nāsā yacca na jighrati / yan nāsvādayate jihvā na spṛśed yat tvagindriyam //4// na cetasā cintanīyaṃ sarvavarṇarasojjhitam / sarvavarṇarasair uktam aprameyam atīndriyam //5// yat prāpya yogino devi bhavanti hy ajarāmarāḥ / tad abhyāsena mahatā vairāgyeṇa pareṇa ca //6// rāgadveṣaparityāgāl lobhamohakṣayāt priye / madamātsaryasaṃtyāgān mānagarvatamaḥkṣayāt //7// labhyate śāśvataṃ nityaṃ śivam avyayam uttamam /*
I have not translated *yogī* in 2a. While it might refer to Śiva, both being in the nominative singular, it more probably refers to the practitioner who is the subject of the optative verb *apnuyāt* at 9a.
24. Kṣemarāja glosses the term 'speech' as the levels of the hierarchical cosmos conceived as sound (*paśyantī, madhyamā* and *vaikharī*). See A. Padoux, *Vāc: The Concept of the Word in Selected Hindu Tantras* (Albany: SUNY Press, 1990), pp. 166–222.
25. This problematic is very close to Augustine's idea of discovering God in his innermost being which is also a discovery of himself. See Denys Turner, *The Darkness of God: Negativity in Christian Mysticism* (Cambridge University Press, 1995), pp. 68–70.
26. Abhinavagupta, *Tantrāloka with the Viveka by Jayaratha*, M. S. Kaul (ed.) (Srinagar: Kashmir Series of Texts and Studies, vol. 1, 1938), 1.125. At 1.132 he writes, echoing the *Bhagavad-gītā*: 'Above all, here the word "I" is the unique term for awareness only. It is also the word for "Protector" and "Lord", declared to be the one who sacrifices and the one sacrificed to.' *sarvātra hyāhaṃśabdo bodhamātraikavācakaḥ / sa bhoktṛprabhuśabdābhyāṃ yājyayaṣṭṭayoditaḥ //*. See L. Silburn and A. Padoux, *Abhinavagupta – La Lumière sur les Tantras, Chapitres 1 à 5 du Tantrāloka* (Paris: Collège de France, Publication de l'Institut de Civilisation Indienne, 1998), p. 103.
27. Abhinavagupta, *Paramārthasāra with the Vivṛti of Yogarāja*, J. C. Chatterjee (ed.) (Srinagar: Kashmir Series of Texts and Studies, vol. 7, 1916), verse 50.
28. Abhinavagupta, *Parātriṃśikalaghuvṛtti*, J. Zadoo (ed.) (Srinagar: Kashmir Series of Texts and Studies, vol. 18, 1947), p. 17.
29. Abhinavagupta, *Tantrāloka* 29.125–25 and commentary.
30. Greg Urban, 'The "I" of Discourse' in Benjamin Lee and Greg Urban (eds.), *Semiotics, Self and Society* (Berlin and New York: Mouton de Gruyter, 1989), pp. 38–9.
31. Kṣemarāja, *Pratyabhijñāhṛdaya*, J. C. Chatterji (ed.) (Srinagar: Kashmir Series of Texts and Studies, vol. 3, 1911), p. 27.
32. Abhinavagupta, *Tantrāloka* 1.145.
33. Kṣemarāja, *Śivasūtravimarśinī*, J. C. Chatterji (ed.) (Srinagar: Kashmir Series of Texts and Studies, vol. 1, 1911), p. 8. Also, for example, the *Vijñānabhairava Tantra* states: 'Wherever the mind goes, whether outside or within, because

of his all-pervasiveness, there is the condition of Śiva. Where (then) will it go?' *Vijñānabhairava with Commentaries of Kṣemarāja and Śivopādhyāya*, M. R. Śāstri (ed.) (Srinagar: Kashmir Series of Texts and Studies, vol. 8, 1918), verse 116: *yatra yatra mano yāti bāhya vābhyantare'pi vā / tatra tatra śivāvasthā vyāpakatvāt kva yāsyati //.*

34. Abhinavagupta, *Tantrasāra*, edited by Mukund Ram Shastri (Srinagar: Kashmir Series of Texts and Studies, vol. 27, 1918).
35. *Mālinīvijayotara Tantra*, M. S. Kaul (ed.) (Srinagar: Kashmir Series of Texts and Studies, vol. 37, 1921), 2.21–3.
36. Abhinavagupta, *Tantrasāra*, p. 6f.
37. *Vijñānabhairava-tantra*, 93.
38. Vāsugupta, *Spanda-kārikā with the Vṛtti by Kallaṭabhaṭṭa*, J. C. Chatterji (ed.) (Srinagar: Kashmir Series of Texts and Studies, vol. 5, 1916), 1.22.
39. Abhinavagupta, *Parātriṃśikāvivaraṇa*, p. 16.
40. Abhinavagupta, *Tantrāloka*, 1.158.
41. Sanderson describes the former in 'Mandala and Agamic Identity in the Trika of Kashmir', pp. 169–207.
42. But with some exceptions – see Sanderson, 'Purity and Power Among the Brahmans of Kashmir', pp. 200–02; J. Masson and M. V. Patwardhan, *Śāntarasa and Abhinavagupta's Philosophy of Aesthetics* (Poona: Deccan College, 1969) pp. 40–42; Lilian Silburn, *Kuṇḍalinī: Energy of the Depths*, trs. Jacques Gontier (Albany: SUNY Press, 1988), pp. 157–204; and D. G. White, *The Kiss of the Yoginī: Tantric Sex in its South Asian Contexts* (University of Chicago Press, 2003).
43. J. Laidlaw, and C. Humphreys, *The Archetypal Actions of Ritual* (Oxford: Clarendon Press, 1994), pp. 12–14.
44. D. Killingley, 'Enjoying the World: Desire (kāma) and the Bhagavadgītā' in Julius Lipner (ed.), *The Fruits of Our Desiring* (Calgary: Bayeux Publications, 1997), pp. 67–79; G. Flood, 'The Meaning and Context of the Purusārthas' in Lipner, *The Fruits of Our Desiring*, pp. 11–27.
45. For example *Manusmṛti* 8.352–78. Doniger, *The Laws of Manu*, pp. 189–92.
46. See J. Laidlaw, *Riches and Renunciation: Religion, Economy and Society Among the Jains* (Oxford: Clarendon Press, 1995), pp. 255–6; M. Eliade, *Yoga: Immortality and Freedom*, trs. Willard R. Trask (Princeton University Press, 1973), p. 134; David White, *The Alchemical Body: Siddha Traditions in Medieval India* (University of Chicago Press, 1996), pp. 233, 240, 248 etc.
47. Abhinavagupta, *Tantrāloka*, 29.41–3 and commentary.
48. Ibid. 29.97–8 and commentary.
49. Ibid. 29.1–3.
50. Ibid. 29.207–08 and commentary.
51. Ibid. 29.97–8.
52. Ibid. 29.128–9: 'Having excited the messenger, desire arises. (The practitioner) should imbibe the mass of substance arising from that (and pass it) from one to the other.' *tato dūtīṃ kṣobhayitvā yasyecchā saṃpravartate / taduttham dravyanicayaṃ prāśayecca parasparam //.*
53. Silburn, *Kuṇḍalinī*, p. 224.

54. Sanderson, 'Purity and Power Among the Brahmans of Kashmir', p. 199. See also D. White, 'Introduction' in D. White (ed.), *Tantra in Practice* (Princeton University Press, 2001), pp. 15–18.
55. Abhinavagupta, *Tantrāloka*, 29.104a: *antaraṅgakrameṇaiva mukhyacakrasya pūjanam.*
56. Silburn, *Kuṇḍalinī*, pp. 213–14.
57. Peter Ochs, *Peirce, Pragmatism, and the Logic of Scripture* (Cambridge University Press, 1998), p. 24.
58. Ochs, *Peirce*, p. 24.
59. Abhinavagupta, *Tantrāloka*, 29.102 and commentary.
60. Ibid. 29.127b.
61. Jayaratha, *Tantrālokavivaraṇa*, 29.64, p. 45.
62. Ibid. 29.100a: Jayaratha quotes the *Tantrarājabhattāraka*: 'Then one should bring the messenger there. Her eyes are rolling with intoxication, she is red-lipped, good-looking, with knitted brows, and beautiful. She is brought like a shining, trembling fawn, smiling sweetly, with a tress of hair tumbling from her head like a quivering swarm of black bees. She has tremulous eyes beneath knitted brows and has the appearance of someone skilled in love. She has the colour and form of molten gold and is not unsteady . . .' *tatastatrānayeddūtīṃ madaghūrṇitalocanām / bimboṣṭhīṃ cāruda(r)śanāṃ sabhrūbhaṅgānanāṃ śubhām // trastabālamṛgābhāsanayanāṃ cāruhāsinīm / sphuradbhramarasaṅgātanibhasatkeśapāśikām // kāmakārmukasaṅkāśabhrūbhaṅgataralekṣaṇām // dravaccāmīkarākārasavarṇāṃ nistaraṅgiṇīm //*
63. Ibid. 29.101a: 'If the messenger should be without qualities for the sādhaka, then he performs all ritual acts with an unwavering, heroic, one-pointed consciousness.' *Yadi lakṣaṇahīn;a syāt dūtī vai sādhakātmanām / vīraikacittā niṣkampā sarvakarmesu gamyate //*
64. Abhinavagupta, *Tantrāloka*, 29.100b–01a.
65. Ibid. 29.101b–02: *laukikālaukikadvyātmasaṅgāttādātmyato 'dhikāt // kāryahetusahotthā sā tridhoktā śāsane guroḥ / sākṣātparamparāyogāttattulyeti tridhā punaḥ //*
66. Jayaratha, *Tantrālokavivaraṇa*, 29.102: *sthityarthaṁ ramayetkāntāṃ na laulyena kadācana //*
67. Silburn, *Kuṇḍalinī*, p. 181.
68. Jayaratha, *Tantrālokavivaraṇa*, 29.102.
69. Abhinavagupta, *Tantrāloka*, 29. 114.
70. Ibid. 29.108.
71. Ibid. 29.123a.
72. For example *Manusmṛti* 9.235–37.
73. Sanderson, 'Purity and Power Among the Brahmans in Kashmir,' p. 205, note 130.
74. Abhinavagupta, *Tantrāloka*, 29.99–100a and commentary p. 357.
75. Jayaratha, *Tantrālokavivaraṇa*, 29.64, p. 45.

## CHAPTER 5

# *The asceticism of the middle way*

*Rāgañca dosañca pahāya mohaṃ sandālayitvān saṃyojanāni /*
*Asantasaṃ jivitasañkhyamhi eko care khaggavisāṇakappo ti //*
Leaving behind passion, hatred, and delusion, having torn the fetters apart, not trembling at (the time of) the complete destruction of life, one should wander solitary as a rhinoceros horn.

*Sutta-nipāta* 'The Rhinoceros Horn', 74[1]

The early Buddhist sources tell us that Siddhārtha Gautama, the Buddha to be, practised extreme forms of asceticism in his search for enlightenment but abandoned this course of action and found the middle way between extremes of mortification and indulgence. The Buddha is said to have rejected severe asceticism as profitless, in that it did not lead to enlightenment. This story is so familiar that it hardly needs to be restated. But in spite of this apparent abandoning of asceticism, the Buddha did allow harsher practices, the *dhūtāṅgas,* and the middle way of the monastic tradition is nevertheless very ascetic by modern, Western standards. This chapter will continue our theme and we shall discover that again, while the goal of the tradition is different, along with the methods to attain it, the process of the ascetic self internalising the tradition remains the same as in the Hindu traditions we have examined. This chapter will focus on only the Theravāda tradition articulated in Pāli sources, where we find an ascetic self constructed in a tradition-specific way and following a path leading to a tradition-specified goal. The experience of this path is rooted in the body which, through effort and will, conforms to the shape of tradition not only in the bodily *habitus*, but also in processes of awareness. Indeed, in many ways the psychological analysis of the ascetic self or phenomenology of consciousness is more sophisticated in the Buddhist texts than in any of the other scriptural traditions we are examining. It is here that we find a close attention to the details of the processes of awareness, a close attention to subjectivity, yet with the concomitant claim that subjectivity is a construction. What is particularly significant about the Buddhist case is that asceticism is seen as integral to the development of virtue, without which there can be no enlightenment. Rather than a mechanical method for eradicating impurity, asceticism becomes a moral endeavour that leads the ascetic self, after long struggle, to see 'things as they are' (*yathābhūta*).

## IS BUDDHISM REALLY ASCETIC?

That the Buddha disparaged extremes of mortification is clear from the Pāli sources, although he had himself practised extreme mortification before his enlightenment. Indeed, these ascetic practices – wandering naked or in rags, barely alive through starvation, living in wild places in all seasons – became part of the narrative of his life and the path to awakening.[2] This distancing from extreme asceticism must be located in the contemporary practice and traditions that formed his context. The Buddha is reacting to both Brahmanical ideas of purity – that purification occurs through ritual bathing for example – and to renouncer groups. At the time of the Buddha, who died around 400 BCE, groups of wandering renouncers (*śramaṇa/samaṇa*) comprised a number of traditions, the most important of which that survives into the modern world is Jainism. The Jains maintained that all action, both bad and good, keeps a being bound in the cycle of reincarnation and suffering. The Jains, like the Buddhists, adhere to the general idea that an action results in an appropriate effect at a later date. For the Jains, action (*karman*) is a substance that adheres to the moist and sticky soul and liberation is the expunging (*nijjarā*) of this substance by means of asceticism, thereby allowing the soul, freed from the weight of its actions, to ascend to liberation at the top of the universe.[3] The Jains wished to eradicate former actions through asceticism and not perform new actions. Ascetic behaviour brings the results of action to fruition and, by not creating new karma through minimising interaction with the world, liberation is finally attained. This ideal of non-action for Jain renouncers could culminate in a voluntary, ritual starvation to death (*sallekhanā*).[4] The Buddha rejected this understanding, as Richard Gombrich has shown, turning karma into a purely ethical idea that the moral quality of an action lies in its intention (*cetanā*).[5] As Gombrich observes, once karma is ethicised in this way by the Buddha's identifying it with intention, 'the whole universe becomes an ethical arena, because everywhere all beings are placed according to their deserts.'[6] The distinction emphasised by some scholars between an arena of religion concerned with gaining merit (kammatic Buddhism in Spiro's terms) and a concern with soteriology (nibbanic Buddhism) should not be overemphasised. Virtuous action is preferable to immoral action and virtuous action results from skilful (*kusala*) rather than unskilful (*akusala*) states of mind. While, of course, ultimately all karma is transcended in nirvana, karma that arises from non-greed, non-hatred and non-delusion is preferable and contributes to a person's spiritual development.[7]

This is a very different orientation from the Jain insistence on intentional suffering as the remover of karmic substance. Indeed, as Gombrich convincingly argues, the Buddha opens up a world of moral obligation and duty, shifting the emphasis from ritual to ethics. In a parallel way, Buddhist ascetic actions must be seen in the context of morality. Rather than asceticism as ritual purification – in the Jain case the almost physical removal of karma from the soul – asceticism becomes integrated into the development of virtue necessary for higher insight. In various discourses in the Pāli canon the Buddha addresses groups of Jain monks, arguing against their position and trying to show the superiority of the Buddhist teaching (*dhamma*). For example, Gombrich cites a sutta where the Buddha is in conversation with a group of Jains. The Buddha asks the Jains why they torture themselves through the asceticism of not sitting (or lying down). They reply that in the teachings of their master, who is omniscient, they must expunge formerly done evil deeds through asceticism (*tapas*) and prevent further influxes into the soul through not acting. Through eradicating karma in this way they will eradicate suffering. The Buddha responds by contrasting the suffering of the Jains with the contentment of the Buddha who has nevertheless expurgated karma.[8]

Rather than embrace intentional suffering and misery, the Buddha dwells in peace through developing three kinds of purification (*visuddhiya*) or expungings (*nijjarā*) that direct a person towards the cessation of suffering and destruction of the 'inflows' (*āsava*). The term *āsava* was taken over by Buddhism from the Jain notion of karma flowing into the soul. Enlightenment is the 'destruction of the inflows', which are listed as three – sensual desire (*kāma*), desire for further existence (*bhāva*) and ignorance (*avijjā*). In some lists a fourth is added, wrong view (*diṭṭhi*).[9] But whereas for the Jain the *āsavas* must be eradicated through severe mortification to wipe the soul clean, for the Buddha they are eradicated through liberating insight resulting from following the middle way rediscovered by the Buddha. Rather than cultivating intentional suffering, the Buddhist must train in virtue, the four states of meditation (*jhāna*) and wearing out the inflows. As Richard Gombrich remarks, these three are in fact the standard division of the Buddhist path into virtue (*sīla*), meditation (*samādhi*) and wisdom (*paññā*)[10] and are what distinguish the Buddhist *dhamma* from other teachings.

So when the Buddha rejects extreme mortification, we must examine what he is rejecting and the context of that rejection. The context is Jain ascetic theory and practice, and the Buddha wants to reformulate the doctrine of karma into a mainly ethical one rather than a ritual one, as Gombrich has shown. Nevertheless, the Buddha is not advocating an easy life but, on the contrary, an alert and disciplined life directed towards the control of the senses and the development of an ascetic self. It is not that Jain asceticism is wrong, rather it is ineffective in the Buddha's view in bringing about enlightenment. Indeed, there is even a place for more extreme asceticism on the Buddha's path (the *dhūtāṅgas*) and, as we shall see, some later writers (namely Buddhaghosa and the author of the *Questions of King Milinda*) considered it to be an integral constituent of the middle way. When the Buddha rejects extreme mortification as being ineffective in bringing about enlightenment he is also rejecting a particular Jain view of karma as a material substance adhering to the soul. It is not through a physical cleansing process but through detachment and the development of higher or skilful states of consciousness that the road to liberation lies.

But in developing detachment and higher states of awareness an ascetic way of life is indispensable. Even the more extreme forms of mortification – such as not lying down – which were criticised by the Buddha have some place in this development; but they are not an end in themselves. The Buddhist path is clearly ascetic in our sense of developing a disciplined life as an act of will, with the ultimate goal of awakening to the awareness that karma is destroyed and there is no further rebirth. The Buddhist ascetic, while desisting from the extremes of the Jains, still performs to reverse the flow of the body, still performs to disrupt the socially conditioned *habitus* and still performs to curb sensory desire.

## A MODERN EXAMPLE

The ideal of the Buddhist saint attested in our sources is not simply articulated in ancient texts but is very much a part of the living Theravāda tradition in contemporary Sri Lanka and South-East Asia.[11] I wish to begin by briefly describing a modern example before going on to examine more closely some of the sources of the tradition and the ideal of the ascetic self exemplified there.[12] Tambiah recounts the life of the Thai ascetic monk Phra Acharn Mun (1870–1949), revered as a great teacher and by many considered to have been an enlightened person or *arhant*. Tambiah points out that his biography, published in 1976 by one of his disciples, is not regarded as something bizarre but represents a saint highly revered by the establishment.[13] This fascinating document recounts the life of Acharn Mun as an ascetic monk (*dhūtāṅga bhikkhu*). As a youth he had a prophetic dream which involved his being taken by a white horse over a vast plain (the plain of repeated births and deaths), at the end of which was a glass case containing the Buddhist scriptures, the Pāli canon (Tipiṭaka). Taking this as an assurance that he would achieve the goal of enlightenment, he undertook rigorous meditation and the standard, Buddhist ascetic practices, the *dhūtāṅgas* (see below). These included wearing only robes made from rags, refusing robes offered by a donor, begging for alms except on fast days, eating only food deposited in his almsbowl, eating only one meal a day, eating only from his almsbowl, possessing only three robes, and dwelling only in wild places such as forests.[14] Along with the ascetic practices he cultivated the concomitant attitudes, such as meditating upon the repulsiveness of food in his almsbowl and, while eating, cultivating 'continual mindfulness of its repulsiveness'.[15] He sought out a teacher (*kalyāṇamitta*) who taught him meditation but who could not help him beyond a certain point and encouraged him to continue the path through his own efforts alone. Acharn Mun practised meditation at various monasteries and wandered alone, dwelling particularly in a distant cave in North-East Thailand where he achieved the condition of the non-returner, a state prior to full enlightenment in which the monk is assured that at death there will not be a return to this world but he will await full liberation from a higher plane.

On a second visit to the North-East, Acharn Mun finally achieved full enlightenment and became an *arhant*, a fully enlightened saint.[16] Tambiah gives the following description of Acharn Mun's lifestyle:

> After the morning almsround, followed by the day's only meal, he would begin his walking meditation, which would last till noon. After a brief rest, he would begin his sitting meditation, which would continue for one and a half hours. Then he would resume his walking meditation. At four o'clock, he would sleep and tidy up the area around the place he was staying (whether it be monastic residence or a jungle platform). Then he would bathe and practice walking meditation until about 8 or 9 o'clock in the evening, when he would resume his sitting meditation. Generally, he went to sleep at 11 o'clock and rose at 3 a.m. to resume meditation until the almsround. If sermons had to be given to celestial or other supernatural beings late at night, he would adjust his sleeping hours to accommodate them.[17]

Following this regime, in due course he attained full enlightenment in which he understood the Buddhist doctrine of dependent-origination, that everything arises and passes away through a process of causation. He also exhibited the complete range of powers described in the Buddhist tradition such as telepathy and clairaudience or hearing discussions from a great distance.[18] Other miracles are thought to have been performed by the monk, such as eradicating smallpox from a village in Laos through the power of his lovingkindness (*metta*).[19]

Nyanasampanno's biography presents many stories of Phra Acharn Mun and his disciplines, all of which illustrate the way in which the practitioner internalises the tradition, and strives for and achieves tradition-specific goals, and likewise the way in which these achievements are acknowledged by the community. The ascetic practice of Acharn Mun is a specifically Buddhist ascetic practice of the *dhūtāṅgas*, and his realisation is the realisation of the Buddhist doctrines of the cessation of suffering, the impermanence of all things, and that the self is constructed through causes and conditions. There is intersubjective agreement by the Buddhist community that Acharn Mun is an ascetic saint and by many that he achieved the enlightenment taught by the Buddha. His life is one of conformity to the paradigm of the saint within the Theravāda tradition, and he follows the example of the Buddha himself in his solitary quest for freedom from suffering. The life of Acharn Mun also shows complete conformity to Buddhist cosmology. Indeed, he follows the prescription of the Pali canon outlined above that to attain enlightenment a person must train in virtue, the four states of meditation (*jhāna*) and wearing out the karmic inflows. Acharn Mun develops Buddhist virtue through following the monastic rules and ascetic practices; he develops meditation through his hours of constant practice; and he eradicates the inflows through Buddhist insight into the nature of things.

Moreover, Acharn Mun illustrates the integration of the highest Buddhist ideals with popular cosmological ideas. Through his mastery of different levels of meditation the monk is able to converse with supernatural beings who inhabit those corresponding levels of the cosmos, preaching to them and subduing demons. On this latter point, the cave where Acharn Mun first went to meditate was, says the biography, inhabited by a demon that had caused the death of other bhikkhus who went there. But through the power of his meditation he was able to resist the demon. In a pattern familiar from the discourses of the Buddha in the Pāli canon, the monk reasons with the demon (communicating telepathically) that although he has power, he does not have power beyond karma and *dharma*, which govern the human world. The Buddha's teaching, however, leads to the complete cessation of suffering and so transcends the demon's local power. As a consequence of the admonition the demon becomes a protector of the monk and thereby a protector of the *dhamma*.[20] Following the paradigm of the Buddha, the ascetic monk convinces by example, by the power resulting from his meditation, and by the reasoning of his preaching. Acharn Mun exemplifies a continuous tradition of forest asceticism that we find in early Pāli sources through to the modern world and exemplifies a particularly Buddhist kind of sainthood. To those sources we must turn for a deeper understanding of the Buddhist saint.

## ASCETICISM AND THE MONASTIC LIFE IN BUDDHISM

The origins of Buddhism lie in the ascetic, renunciate traditions of India, but it quickly becomes demarcated from those other traditions in its doctrines, practices and style. While the 'southern' school of Buddhism, the Theravāda, contains very old traditions in its scriptures, the Pāli canon, there are also ancient sources preserved in Chinese and Tibetan. The Pāli commentarial literature preserves a traditional exegesis that goes back many centuries and may contain traditions as old as the canon itself that reach back to the Buddha and are the common inheritance of all Buddhist schools.[21] In these sources we see that asceticism becomes ethicised by the Buddha in the sense that ascetic acts are practised for the development of virtue, which in turn allows for the development of meditation and insight that culminate in the Buddhist goal: the eradication of desire and volition. That is, asceticism becomes integrated into a pattern of monasticism and becomes an important part of the ideal saint. No longer are ascetic acts merely ritual; now they are identified with intention and so with virtue.

By the time of the Buddha's death or supreme enlightenment (*parinirvāṇa*) around 400 BCE,[22] it is likely that a settled pattern of monastic life had been established, with monks living in permanent residences (*vihāra*), although there is disagreement among scholars about this.[23] But if we are to trust the Pāli sources, the community first accepted the donation of lodgings for the monks at Rājagaha from a wealthy merchant, and later a seven-storied monastery was established at Savatthi and another at Kosambi paid for by a banker.[24] The monastic pattern had certainly been established by the early centuries CE, as is attested both by the Pāli commentaries and by the Chinese Buddhist pilgrims Fa hsien, (399–415), Hsuan tang (630–43) and I-tsing (671–95). From these sources we see that by this time monks lived in permanent residences (*vihāra*) that contained a recitation hall (*posadha*) for fortnightly recitations of rules, a memorial for relics (*thūpa*), a bodhi tree and a shrine hall.[25] Although monks themselves were not permitted to handle money, many of the larger monasteries became wealthy through farming their lands, which was facilitated by employing lay workers. A pattern begins to develop of a settled monastic community in a reciprocal relationship with the laity and the state. Tambiah has outlined a triadic relationship between *saṅgha* ('monastic community') and state that has persisted from early times to the formation of Buddhism in Thailand and into modern Thai history. Drawing on early Buddhist ideas of the ideal, universal monarch (*cakkavatti*), the ruler in a Buddhist country such as Sri Lanka supported the *saṅgha* and was in turn supported and legitimated by the monastic community. The monastic community itself comprised village- or town-dwelling along with forest-dwelling monks and nuns. The latters' relationship with the laity and state was minimised, and they pursued ascetic ideals which were – and are up to the present in Buddhist countries such as Thailand – supported by the official ideology of the state.[26] It is the forest-dwelling monks and nuns who have historically practised – and still do practise – the more severe asceticism permitted by tradition.

The monastic life was not open to all. A monk had to possess the requisite qualities which excluded many (if not most) of the population, including small children, those with various diseases, those who had been subjected to systems of justice (and bore the scars resulting from it), people suffering various disabilities and even 'the very ugly'.[27] Buddhist monasticism clearly advocated a kind of liminality but was averse to accepting those who inhabited other forms of social marginalisation – the sick, the disabled, runaway slaves and those on the margins of the social order. The Buddha was not a social reformer.[28] The Buddha's doctrine of renunciation seems to have appealed mostly to the urban middle class and the prosperous, attracting young men used to the good life (*bhaddavagiya*) and wealthy courtesans such as Ambapāli.[29] With the permission of his parents, a young man from a respectable family could become a monk through the two stages of the minor (*pabbajjā*) and major ordination (*upasampadā*).[30] According to some sources he would possess only eight items: three robes, an almsbowl, a razor, needle, belt and water strainer. Others list only four: offered food, robes made from rags, lodging and medicine.[31] The Buddha encouraged the young rather than the old to join the community, those with the ability to learn and to take up his path of transcending desire. With shaved head and wearing an ochre robe, the novice would take the three refuges in the Buddha, the teachings (*dhamma*) and community (*saṅgha*), along with ten moral precepts and thereby become a monk (*bhikkhu*). Women were allowed into the community, and the *bhikkunī saṅgha* is attested in the Sri Lankan chronicles,[32] but, as Faure notes, women remain passive in Buddhist history,[33] and we could say that the nun must in some way become masculine in order to subject herself to the process of textualisation required to develop the ascetic self (see pp. 248–9). Kawanami has argued along these lines in the case of Burmese nuns, that by removing womanhood a nun is free to pursue her inner spirituality.[34] The nun must conform to the established pattern of male renunciation.

From an early date – almost certainly within the Buddha's lifetime – a settled pattern of monastic living had developed that involved the monks and nuns remaining in a single place during the rainy season. In time this extended to all-year-round settlement, while at the same time allowing for a more itinerant life for monastics so inclined. Monastic practice in the sense of a settled, regulated life of communal renunciation seems to have originated with Buddhism in South Asia, although the *āśrama* system of renouncers living apart from society is obviously close (see pp. 85–7). The genius of Buddhism – which becomes the first religion to spread globally – is its ability to adapt to local conditions and cultures and its ability to absorb and transform earlier cultural practices and make them its own. We can see this absorption happening within the Buddha's lifetime – and indeed within the narrative of the Buddha's life itself – in the appropriation of the renouncer ideal, in the appropriation of ascetic practices and in the appropriation of meditation which is transformed into a distinctly Buddhist practice. While the monastic institution routinised the monk's day, the ideal of the solitary, wandering ascetic seeking his own liberation was still a strong cultural trope in the community and, indeed, a social reality in the forest-dwelling monks. Despite the fact that the tradition developed monasticism as an institution, it never loses the ideal of the Buddhist path as solitary. Although living in community, each follows the path alone; although eradicating individual choice and individuality markers, each asserts the will to follow the path.

The ideal monk has renounced the world and family ties, renounced a settled life in a home and wanders in order to seek his own liberation in the course of time. This ideal is frequently upheld in the Pāli sources. The *Suttanipāta*, for example, compares the solitary ascetic wanderer to a rhinoceros horn. Going forth to an open-air life, the wanderer avoids the constriction and pollution of a house and avoids evil deeds performed with the body.[35] He seeks his own liberation and, although relying on alms, is psychologically self-contained and reliant not on other people but only on the teachings. The Buddhist path is the path of the one (*ekayanna*). It is a path travelled alone 'with a mind secluded from the objects of the senses', that is found in the single place of the Buddha's teachings and leads to the one place of *nibbāna*.[36] It is in this context and in memory of the solitary, wandering ascetic that the tradition allowed for more extreme ascetic practices which were codified into the thirteen *dhūtāṅgas* and presented an analysis of the path both as description and prescription. We must locate the ascetic self in a terminological matrix that emphasises the development of particular forms of awareness – which the tradition calls skilful states of consciousness – and in the classification of types of person and goal. Let us begin with the ideal of the ascetic self as hero (*viriya*), an idea that will be not unfamiliar from the much later Hindu sources we examined in the last chapter, who through an act of will (*chanda*) develops the practice and code of the Buddhist path (*dhamma vinaya*). Buddhaghosa's *Path of Purity* is a text for the solitary 'heroic' renouncer, treading the path to *nibbāna*.

## THE ASCETIC PRACTICES

Within this commentarial literature, Buddhaghosa's *Path of Purity* (*Visuddhimagga*) is a text that codifies and systematises earlier sources and can be read as an inner map for the individual practitioner who is regarded as solitary, even if living in a community.[37] That the text is seen as being the articulation of tradition is clear from the story of Buddhaghosa's coming to Sri Lanka. In order to test his Theravāda orthodoxy, the Sinhalese elders gave him only two verses of the Pāli canon upon which to comment. Basing his work on these verses he composed the *Path of Purity*, which summarised the Buddha's teachings along with the teachings of the commentarial tradition. The legend has it that, to further test his orthodoxy, the god Sakka stole the finished text, thereby making Buddhaghosa compose it again. The new version turned out to be identical to the first. Sakka then stole that version too, and Buddhaghosa composed a third, again identical to the original! This story illustrates the Theravāda emphasis on maintaining what it perceived to be the unchanged teachings of the Buddha and the continuity of tradition that hands down the teachings through the generations.[38] In his book Buddhaghosa sets out the stages of the Buddhist path, provides an analysis of mundane and higher mental states and gives an account of ascetic practices integrated into the monk's development. It is a manual for the cultivation of a distinctly Buddhist meditative experience and for the construction of a distinctly Buddhist ascetic self.

Buddhaghosa's text systematically exposits a threefold division of the Buddha's eightfold path into the development of virtue (*sīla*), concentration (*samādhi*) and wisdom (*paññā*).[39] Under wisdom it discusses insight (*vipassanā*) into the nature of existence and discernment of right and wrong paths. Under concentration it discusses various states of meditation that can be achieved, along with supernormal powers thereby attained, and under virtue it discusses moral precepts, along with the more severe ascetic practices, the *dhūtāṅgas*. The hero (*viriya*) cultivates virtue (*sīla*) through asceticism. Practise the *dhūtāṅgas*, Buddhaghosa says, to purify virtue. Virtue is purified (*parisuddha*) and impurity (*mala*) washed clean (*vikkhālita*) through developing the qualities of fewness of wishes (*appichatā*), contentment (*santuṭṭhitā*), severe austerity (*sallekha*), solitude (*paviveka*), diminution of worldliness (*apacaya*), strenuous energy (*viriyārambha*), being easily supported (*subharata*) and fulfilment of vows (*vata*).[40]

This is an interesting list of qualities that combines behaviours, such as solitude, relying on the minimum of alms and severe austerity, with the effects of those behaviours, namely strenuous energy, the minimising of desires and contentment. Yet Buddhaghosa regards them all as 'ascetic states' (*dhutadhamma*), fewness of wishes and contentment falling under non-greed (*alobha*) and austerity and solitude under non-greed and non-delusion (*amoha*).[41] Asceticism is not merely a set of practices but an inner attitude of detachment, an intention (*cetanā*) or act of will that, like all other intentions, results in action that bears fruits. The fruits of asceticism are purification and detachment, and finally the complete detachment of *nibbāna*. The term *sallekha* in this list is familiar from Jainism, where, Richard Gombrich observes, it may have originally meant the 'scraping away' of old karma.[42] But in the Buddhist context it refers to ascetic behaviour that is part of developing virtue rather than the more mechanistic Jain meaning.

The ideal of the ascetic self is minimum interaction with the world and an inner detachment cultivated through asceticism. In the *Anguttara Nikaya* of the Pāli canon, another list of qualities to be cultivated by the monastic includes virtue (*sīla*), religious observance (*vata*), austerity (*tapas*) and celibacy (*brahmacariya*), although they should not be cultivated in order to become a deity (*deva*).[43] This list clearly indicates the ideal of the ascetic lifestyle and that for Buddhist ethical values to have effect they must be rooted in the body. The term *vata* is familiar from its Sanskrit form, *vrata*, 'vow' or 'observance', and in the Pāli canon it also refers to non-Buddhist ascetics who performed various kinds of practice involving the imitation of animals which the Buddha wished to distance himself from. For example, a naked ascetic called Kora behaves like a dog, as does the ascetic Seniya, while Puṇṇa behaves like a cow.[44] When Puṇṇa asks the Buddha about the benefits of Seniya's canine practice, the Buddha predicts that he will be reborn among dogs! The occurrence of the term *vata* to denote this kind of observance is very close to its much later use in the context of the Pāśupata ascetics whose observance (*vrata*) included the imitation of animals, particularly dogs (see p. 98).

Similarly *tapas* and *brahmacariya* are familiar from the Hindu context, as we have seen. Of particular note is celibacy and the control of sexual desire. Sexual intercourse is strictly prohibited to the monk, an offence for which he or she could be excluded from the *Saṅgha*.[45] As Faure observes, arguably the main problem confronting the monastic community is desire, which includes the paradoxical desire for enlightenment.[46] The regular, twice-monthly recitation of the two hundred and fifty or so monastic rules served to remind the community of these prohibitions, and there is clearly the idea present that desire is to be transmuted into meditative experience.[47] This is common to other forms of asceticism, and the Pāli sources must be seen within the broad spectrum of the history of South Asian asceticism.

But while the Pāli canon bears witness to a broader, ascetic context, the list of thirteen *dhūtāṅgas* is uniquely Buddhist. The list occurs in the *Vinaya* section of the Pāli canon[48] and is more extensively discussed in two texts, the *Visuddhimagga* and the *Questions of King Milinda* (*Milindapañha*, chapter 6). While there are passages in the canon that partly condemn these ascetic behaviours[49] and, as we have seen, the Buddha disagreed with the extremes of Jain ascetics' intentional suffering, that these key texts should discuss them at such length and consider them integral to the development of virtue is significant. For Buddhaghosa the development of asceticism is fundamentally linked to the development of Buddhist virtue as a means for controlling desire and the senses. Not only are the higher stages of the path built upon virtue, they can also be strengthened by the ascetic practices. The implication of the name *dhūtāṅga* is one who has shaken off (*dhuta*) evil dispositions or obstacles to spiritual progress.[50]

Buddhaghosa himself is aware of this etymology and describes them as practices (*aṅgāni*) of monks for shaking off defilement (*kilesa*) achieved through an act of will (*cetanā*). This is made clear by Buddhaghosa who quotes the following commentary: 'It is the person who undertakes [asceticism]. He undertakes it through the states of mind and mental properties. The ascetic practices [are brought about] through the will of taking them upon oneself. It is the basis that is rejected.'[51] The verb *samādiyati*, 'he undertakes', implies the taking of something upon oneself. That is, the ascetic (*dhuta*) takes on the ascetic practices as an act of will through the appropriate disposition or mental states (*dhamma*), and thereby rejects the usual basis of the unsteady mind. It is strength of will that allows a person to undertake asceticism and to appropriate the ascetic practices.

Most importantly, these practices are set within tradition. Buddhaghosa describes how the *dhūtāṅgas* were practised at the time of the Buddha under his direction, after his death under the direction of the chief disciple and in his absence under descending grades of monk from those of high spiritual achievement to scholars of the scriptures. In the absence of any teacher at all they may be practised alone but as though under the direction of a supreme Buddha.[52] Even the solitary ascetic is part of the family of the tradition, and ascetic acts are to be practised within the constraint of tradition, within the continuity of the lineage of teachers from the Buddha and within the Buddhist monastic rules. Again, we see that through an act of will (*cetanā*) the ascetic internalises the tradition and performs austerity only within it. Indeed, Buddhaghosa quotes a source that identifies the will with ascetic practice: 'They say that which is will is ascetic practice.'[53] We might link this quotation with the one briefly discussed earlier where the Buddha identified will or intention with action. As it is the intention behind the action that matters, so here it is the will that drives ascetic acts, which themselves are designed to contribute to the eradication of karma. Again we see that the essential dimension of asceticism is the assertion of will, yet through the assertion of will, the will is finally eradicated in *nibbāna*, which is defined as the eradication of all volition.

Buddhaghosa therefore has a very positive attitude towards the ascetic practices. He regards them as integral to the Buddhist path and fully integrated into the monk's life within the general spectrum of behaviour and attitude expected. While not being requirements for all, the ascetic practices develop and strengthen virtue, upon which wisdom and concentration are built. This pattern is attested throughout the tradition as Phra Acharn Mun, who practised them all, attests.[54] The actual thirteen practices listed by Buddhaghosa, and which occur elsewhere in the canon, are as follows:

1. The refuse-man's practice – making robes from old rags found in places such as a cremation ground or in the street.
2. The three-rober's practice – the wearing of three robes, inner clothing, an upper garment, and a cloak of rags.
3. The almsman's practice – the consuming of lumps (*piṅda*) of food offered.
4. The house-to-house-goer's practice – begging from houses without distinguishing between them.
5. The one-sessioner's practice – the consumption of a single meal in a day.
6. The bowl-fooder's practice – the consumption of food mixed together in a single bowl.

7. The afterfood-refuser's practice – the refusal of further offerings of food.
8. The forester's practice – dwelling in a forest.
9. The tree-rootman's practice – dwelling at the foot of a tree.
10. The open-spacer's practice – dwelling in the open air.
11. The cremation-ground-dweller's practice – living in a cremation ground.
12. The any-bed-user's practice – sleeping in any place allotted.
13. The sitting-man's practice – not lying down and sleeping only in a sitting position.

A number of things are of note in this list. All are focussed on attire, eating and dwelling or sleeping. Dressing in rags disrupts attachment to fine clothes and disrupts any notion of conventional style and conformist identity-markers fundamental to culture. The restriction of eating again goes against cultural norms and attempts to control the bodily urge to eat through allowing only a single, meagre meal a day. All monastics were allowed one meal a day according to Vinaya rules, but this ascetic ruling excludes the light refreshment or 'medicine' permitted in the afternoon. These practices also advocate dwelling alone, outside of community, in wild places and without the security of a regular abode. The sitting-man's practice further illustrates the disruption of the body and its cultural *habitus* through an act of will in order to develop transworldly qualities. Buddhaghosa himself says of the list that three are most important: the practices of the house-to-house-goer, the one-sessioner and the open-spacer. He rhetorically asks what need there is of the tree-rootman's or any-bed-user's practice for him who keeps the open-spacer's practice.[55] That is, the general monastic behaviour of begging from house to house, only eating one meal and not dwelling in a building are the foundation of the others and of all Buddhist monastic practice in general designed to develop non-clinging to food or lodging.

Of particular interest is the practice of dwelling in the cremation ground, 'an open and public display of asceticism',[56] as this locates Buddhist practice within the cremation-ground asceticism of the Indian traditions and shows the importance of the contemplation of death in achieving the Buddhist goal. Indeed, there is evidence in the Pāli canon of cremation-ground ascetics visualising Kālī in a way not dissimilar to later tantric tradition.[57] The practice of the monk in the burning ground (*sosānika*) is weighty (*garuka*) according to Buddhaghosa and should be practised according to the grade one is able to adopt. There is the extreme practice of dwelling where there is continual burning and the constant smell of bodies, accompanied by weeping of relatives; the moderate practice is where only one of these phenomena is present; and the mild practice is to dwell in a place that minimally fulfils the requirements of the burning ground. The ascetic who lives in this way, meditating on death constantly, attains awareness of death, dispels lust, overcomes fear, gets to understand the intrinsic nature of the body as impermanent and cultivates a heart with a leaning towards ultimate release (*nibbānaninnahadaya*).[58] Thus, although other ascetics dwell in cremation grounds, the Buddhist ascetic seeks a Buddhist goal and his practice is within the constraints of the Buddhist tradition, sanctioned by a monastic elder. The practice of the cremation-ground ascetic clearly has connections with the mindfulness of death or the meditation on death that comprises contemplating different stages of a corpse's decomposition. Such meditation can also be accomplished purely in the imagination, as is attested by Phra Acharn Mun, who visualised stages of death and a skeleton falling apart, a vision he would then apply to his own body.[59]

## THE ASCETIC BODY AND THE MEMORY OF TRADITION

But while the ascetic practices are advocated by Buddhaghosa and there is a strong forest tradition from the time of the formation of the canon through to the present, there is nevertheless a question mark over more extreme asceticism within the tradition. Again, the emphasis is away from the mechanistic action of purging the self of impurity towards an ethical view of asceticism as a necessary part of virtue. In the *Questions of King Milinda*, upon seeing forest monks 'ascetic in quality' (*dhute guṇe*) the king asks the monk Nāgasena to explain what the point of asceticism is. If even householders can attain enlightenment and 'awaken in Dhamma', why practise asceticism?[60] In typical fashion for these texts, Nāgasena responds to the king by listing twenty-eight special qualities of ascetic practices that have made them 'desired by all the Buddhas' and that emphasise their ethical importance. These qualities include that the ascetic way of life is a pure means of livelihood; it does not bring anguish to others; it is conducive to mental development; it eradicates attachment and aversion, destroys pride and cuts out wrong thought. This is high praise indeed, as eradicating pride and cutting out wrong thought are qualities of *nibbāna*. The monk then presents another list to the king of eighteen qualities of the ascetic. These include pure behaviour, well-guarded speech and body, mental purity, the dispelling of false views about the self (*attānudiṭṭhi*), lovingkindness (*metta*) and skill in meditation or 'abiding where there is comfort'.[61] These practices are a necessary stage on the path to enlightenment. All the enlightened householders that the King refers to are reaping the results of their actions in previous lives, for they could not achieve liberation without first going through the ascetic practices. Using a rich range of similes, the text illustrates the centrality of asceticism in attaining liberation. Only through ascetic training with a teacher, a good friend, is liberation possible, in the same way that a skilled archer makes his students practise in varying degrees of difficulty before they achieve the necessary skill and its reward.[62] Asceticism is like a leader of a caravan reaching the city of *nibbāna* or like a mirror showing the practitioner the formation of karma (*sankhāra*) and allowing for the development of skilful states of awareness.[63] As seeds need to be sprinkled with water to grow, so a person cannot understand *dhamma* without purification through asceticism. Asceticism is like a boat that takes a person to the further shore and gives confidence to those fearful of ageing and dying.

In a passage detailing the thirteen practices, the author of the *Milinda* clearly locates them within the general teachings of the Buddha's path:

> Thirteen are these ascetic practices, sire, purified by which [a man] having entered the great sea of Nibbāna shall bathe in the pleasure of its manifold qualities. He shall attain the eight meditative absorptions in the fine-material and immaterial spheres, and achieve the forms of psychic power (*iddhi*), divine ear (*dibbasotañāna*), knowledge of others' minds (*cetopariyañāna*), recollection of previous lives (*pubbenivasanussatiñāna*), divine eye (*dibbacakkhuñāna*), and knowledge of the destruction of the inflows (*āsavakkhayañāna*).[64]

Here the ascetic practices allow a person to bathe or 'play' (*abhikīḷati*) in *nibbāna*. (I have taken *bahuvidhadhammakīḷam*, the object of *abhikīḷati*, to refer to the manifold pleasures of 'bathing' in *nibbāna*.) They are the basis of all Buddhist attainment, providing the foundation for the development of the eight absorptions or *jhānas* and the six superknowledges (*abhiññas*). On one view, the development of meditation in higher, or what the tradition calls skilful, states of consciousness is essential for the attainment of *nibbāna*. The *jhānas* are probably preBuddhist and were taught to the Buddha by his own meditation masters. Through the practice of calmness meditation (*samatha*) the hindrances that keep the mind restricted and tend towards the senses (namely sense-desire, ill-will, sloth and torpor, restlessness and worry, and doubt) are repressed through effort. In their place the monk develops the *jhāna* factors (initial thought, sustained thought, joy, happiness, and one-pointedness) that lead from this world into the first level of meditation.[65] These are refined until at the fourth *jhāna* further 'formless' levels of greater refinement can be achieved. From the fourth *jhāna* the six superknowledges listed in the above passage are developed.

There is a question in the tradition about whether it is necessary to develop these refined states of meditation to attain liberation. According to tradition the Buddha experienced these states but discovered the higher levels did not lead to *nibbāna*, although he himself attained *nibbāna* from the fourth *jhāna*. What he had to do was apply insight (*vipassanā*) into the nature of life as being characterised by suffering, impermanence and having no substantial, unchanging essence. It is insight meditation that is new with the Buddha, and this appears to have led to some tension in the community between those who practised insight and those who practised calming meditation. If insight leads to freedom, why practise calming? Buddhaghosa's commentary on a sutta of the Aṅguttara-nikāya (II 155–6) speaks of a person who reaches the goal being 'dry-visioned' (*sukkha-vipassaka*), liberated by insight only, without developing the *jhānas*. This is a commentary on a passage that distinguishes those who reach the final goal with effort (*sa-saṅkhāraparinibbāyī*) and those who reach it with ease (*asaṅkhāra*).[66] Only those who reach it with ease develop the *jhānas*. The Pali canon itself attests to monks who, although being *arhants*, did not possess magical powers because they had not developed the *jhānas* but only insight. Susīma, a non-Buddhist renunciate who does in the end convert, asks the group of monks who claim to be enlightened whether they have the first five superknowledges, to which they reply in the negative, that they are enlightened by insight only.[67]

This distinction between calm and insight is also related to a distinction between types of release, those liberated through mind (*cetovimutti*) by developing the *jhānas* and then insight, and those liberated through wisdom (*paññavimutti*) by developing only insight (and so becoming 'dry-visioned'). Another term for *cetovimutti* seems to be 'liberated both ways' (*ubhatobhagavimutti*), through both calm and insight.[68] The Buddha himself was liberated in this sense by first developing the *jhānas* and then applying insight that led to final release in the fourth *jhāna*. Others too are liberated in this way, although it takes practice to make this state permanent. The *Middle Length Sayings* describe a group of monks who became emaciated and weak in the hot, dry season and fell away from their liberation by mind, going back to the material things of the world.[69] There is also the story of Godhika, who achieved liberation through mind but fell away from that state six times. He then killed himself with a knife in order to remain there permanently – and this apparently with the Buddha's approval, for with this act he had 'passed utterly away'.[70] Leaving aside ethical problems in this case, the story clearly illustrates the passing away into nirvana to be the highest value and the most difficult achievement.

## THE PATH AS TRADITION

Returning to the list of achievements cited in the *Milinda*, we must remark on the six superknowledges (*abhiññā*). The list in the text is a standard formula found in the canon that is divided into three 'worldly' (*lokiya*) and three 'otherworldly' (*lokuttara*) categories. The three worldly superknowledges comprise a list of eight psychic powers (*iddhi*) that are also found later in the *Yoga-sūtras* (see p. 79), along with the power of the divine ear or the ability to hear conversations at a distance, and the ability to know the minds of others or communicate telepathically. These powers are illustrated even in the modern era in the life of Phra Acharn Mun and are frequently attested in the Pāli canon itself.[71] But it is the last three, the otherworldly or transcendent superknowledges possessed by the Buddha[72] that are especially significant in giving direct understanding of Buddhist doctrines, an important point made by Jayatilleke.[73] Recollection of previous lives – a power possessed by the Buddha who could, so it is claimed, cast his mind back to a particular time and place and recall details of that birth – gives direct knowledge of the doctrine of no-self (*anatta*). That is, through casting his mind back over innumerable, previous lifetimes the Buddha is able to verify in his own experience that there is no unchanging self, constantly being incarnated into different bodies. Rather there is a constant process of change and chain of causation.[74] Divine eye refers to the ability to perceive the changing states of others dependent upon their karma and so gives understanding of impermanence. Knowledge of the destruction of the inflows gives the final, saving knowledge that there will be no future birth and that all karma that will come to fruition in a future life has been eliminated.

There is, of course, the question about how those enlightened by insight only could have the three superknowledges, given that they can only be acquired from the fourth *jhāna*. In strictly doctrinal terms they could not have these knowledges, which suggests that the *samatha-vipassanā* path is superior to the *vipassanā* path that does not develop the *jhānas*. But while some of these technical debates are somewhat arcane, the important general point is that the Buddhist ascetic self sets out on a path with clearly demarcated points of achievement and arrives at a goal which, along with the claim of ineffability, is a Buddhist goal with content defined in terms of Buddhist doctrine.

The highly technical discussion found in the Theravāda texts, particularly as developed by Buddhaghosa with great clarity, illustrates in precise detail how the ascetic self is to develop levels of awareness that came to be refined and defined by tradition in particular ways. Of course there are practices and terms that cut across traditions – which is part of the argument of this book – but practices and terms are developed within particular historical trajectories. There are parallels between Jain and Buddhist asceticism, but they are distinct in their aspirations and, as we have seen, in the reasoning behind the practices. The Buddhist ascetic seeks a Buddhist goal and develops forms of calm and insight that are articulated in a way particular to the tradition. The Buddhist ascetic passes through defined stages on the path to enlightenment, becoming what the tradition calls a stream-enterer, a once-returner and a non-returner. There are undoubtedly parallels between, say, Buddhist meditation and the *Yoga-sūtras* in the use of terminology and process, and we can draw general conclusions about process – we can develop a metalanguage – but the particularity of a tradition's terminology inevitably remains unique and resists reduction to any over-arching paradigm.

We can see this very clearly with the Buddhist tradition. The ascetic recapitulates the tradition within her- or himself and, through an act of will, makes the body conform to the shape of tradition. The Buddhist ascetic body enacts the memory of the Buddhist tradition. The tradition is inscribed upon the body and the body made to conform through will: through the practice of asceticism Buddhist ethical values become rooted in the body. The noble body is controlled and indeed is noble because it has developed the ethical code and moral habit of the monastic. The ascetic lives at the root of a tree, as the *dhūtāṅgas* advocate, being aware of the body through mindfulness and forming the body into a particular posture that allows for its control and the control of thought and feeling. Steadfast, and with calm clarity, the monastic seeks the eradication of regressive habits, changing the orientation of the body away from the gratification of the senses to the realisation of the Buddhist path. The inner tranquillity of the body is reflected in the body's composure and the ascetic habit developed makes the monastic reflect tradition. The monastic's body becomes an index of the eradication of individuality, along with an intensification of subjectivity and an index of the tradition itself.

The experience of the body is therefore rooted in tradition, and the Theravāda monastic order is oriented towards constructing a particular kind of experience of the body. The ascetic body, as we have seen, was developed by other traditions in their own way, particularly in Jainism, but with Buddhism the ascetic body becomes uniquely ethicised and linked into the development of virtue. As Richard Gombrich has shown with the notion of action, in a similar way ascetic practice becomes redefined not as the almost physical removal of karma but as integral to moral development. The ascetic body becomes a virtuous body, controlled, and oriented to what the tradition calls skilful states and away from unskilful ones that produce bad actions (*pāpa*).

A central concept here is mindfulness (*sati;* Sanskrit *smṛti*). Rupert Gethin has shown that there are a number of related concepts encapsulated by the term *sati. Sati* is remembering or the slightly wider concept of not losing what is before the mind. It is 'presence of mind', guarding the mind through being aware of what is beneficial and what is not. It 'calls to mind', which means that it is able to relate things to each other and so understand a wider perspective, and thus is related to wisdom, seeing things as they really are (the Buddha's goal).[75] In the *Questions of King Milinda* Nāgasena defines mindfulness as calling to mind and taking hold. *Sati* calls to mind thoughts (*dhammas*) that are both skilful and unskilful, thereby allowing a person to resort to skilful *dhammas* and avoid unskilful ones.[76] This calling to mind is crucial in the development of the ascetic self and is a crucial means whereby the ascetic body is formed. Through mindfulness the ascetic becomes aware of the body and learns to control and regulate the body in its habitual behaviour in conformity with tradition. Rather than being subject to desire or cultural expectations, the monastic learns to be aware of the senses and their fields, gradually learns to control awareness in the body–mind complex, and in so doing recapitulates the tradition.

The four foundations of mindfulness (*satipaṭṭhāna*), namely mindfulness of body, feelings, mind and *dhamma*, establish the monk on the Buddhist path. They represent a gradation or a gradually expanding awareness from the body, beginning with the in and out breathing, to positive, negative or indifferent reactions to the world, to awareness of the contents of consciousness, and to understanding the teachings.[77] Through mindfulness the ascetic self monitors inner processes of body and awareness. In this concentration on interiority and subjective processes, he becomes aware of breathing, not only in meditation but in daily movement; he becomes aware of inner feelings arising and passing away owing to causes and conditions; and he becomes aware of the contents of consciousness. Lastly he becomes mindful of *dhamma*, which can be taken at a number of levels because the semantic range of *dhamma* varies from referring to thoughts, to the teachings of the Buddha, to *nibbāna*.[78] What is significant is that the ascetic self focuses on the body and from there extends attention to the teachings themselves and to the goal. Through an act of will and constant practice the body conforms to the prescriptions of the texts and brings to mind the teachings and the reason for the practice; tradition becomes expressed through the body. These acts must have meaning for the practitioner who undertakes the practice voluntarily, although within the constraints of social expectation. The continued application of oneself to the daily schedule of discipline leads in due course to the expurgation of the defilements and the realisation of the different stages of the path. Through constant vigilance the monastic intends to create himself in conformity to the prescriptions of the teachings and, ultimately, the Buddha.

When examining the Buddhist material we are dealing with a tradition that has developed a sophisticated terminology and clearly defined stages and goals. These goals, above all the ultimate goal of the cessation of suffering in *nibbāna*, are regarded as highly desirable goods by the communities who adhere to them. We have seen here how the Theravāda tradition articulates its goals and that these are internalised by the practitioner. With Buddhism the practice of asceticism, which was of course preBuddhist, becomes closely linked to ethics. To develop virtue along the Buddhist path, the monastic must have developed the particular ascetic practices at some point. Virtue is dependent upon the control of the senses, and without virtue there cannot be the development of meditation to further strengthen the ascetic hero and insight to allow the wisdom to see things 'as they are' and achieve the goal. Some of these patterns will be recognisable in the very different world of the Christian West, to which we now turn.

## NOTES

1. Norman, K. R. (trs.) *The Group of Discourses* (with alternative translations by I. B. Horner and Walpola Rahula) (London: Pāli Text Society, 1984), pp. 7–11.
2. *Majjhima Nikāya* 1.77–80. I. B. Horner (trs.), *The Middle Length Sayings* vol. I (London: Pāli Text Society, 1967), pp. 103–07.
3. P. Dundas, *The Jains* (London: Routledge, 1992). J. Bronkhorst, *The Two Traditions of Meditation in Ancient India* (Delhi: Motilal, 1993), chapters 1 and 2 on Jain practice and the Buddhist criticism.
4. On this see S. Settar, *Inviting Death: Indian Attitudes Towards the Ritual Death* (Leiden: Brill, 1997); J. Laidlaw, *Riches and Renunciation: Religion, Economy and Society Among the Jains* (Oxford: Clarendon Press, 1995), particularly his moving account of the modern Jain saint who performed this, Sri Armarcand ji Nahar, pp. 230–34.
5. R. Gombrich, *Theravada Buddhism: A Social History from Ancient Benares to Modern Columbo* (London and New York: Routledge and Kegan Paul, 1988), pp. 66–9. See also R. Gombrich, *How Buddhism Began: The Conditioned Genesis of the Early Teachings* (London: Athlone Press, 1996), pp. 48–57.
6. Gombrich, *Theravada Buddhism*, p. 69.
7. Gombrich, *How Buddhism Began*, p. 53.

8. R. Gombrich, 'The Buddha and the Jains: A Reply to Professor Bronkhorst', *Etudes Asiatiques* vol. 48, 1994, pp. 1069–96. The text discussed is the *Cūla Dukkha-kkhandha Sutta* (MN 1.91–5).
9. Gombrich, 'The Buddha and the Jains', pp. 1085–6.
10. Gombrich, 'The Buddha and the Jains', p. 1091.
11. The historical continuity of the forest tradition since ancient times is, however, problematic. It could be that the tradition was revived in the nineteenth century, particularly in Thailand in 1898 by Subodhananda. See M. Carrithers, *The Forest Monks of Sri Lanka: An Anthropological and Historical Study* (Delhi: Oxford University Press, 1983), p. 104.
12. For interesting accounts of the recent forest tradition see Carrithers, *The Forest Monks of Sri Lanka*; Kamala Tiyavanich, *Forest Recollections: Wandering Monks in Twentieth-Century Thailand* (Honolulu: University of Hawaii Press, 1997).
13. S. Tambiah, *The Buddhist Saints of the Forest and the Cult of Amulets: A Study of Charisma, Hagiography, Sectarianism, and Millennial Buddhism* (Cambridge University Press, 1984), pp. 81–2.
14. Nyanasampanno, Phra Acharn Maha Boowa. *The Venerable Phra Acharn Mun Bhuridatta Thera,* trs. Siri Buddhasukh (Wat Pa Barn Tard: private printing, 1982), pp. 2–4.
15. Nyanasampanno, *The Venerable Phra Acharn Mun*, p. 9.
16. Ibid. p. 115.
17. Tambiah, *The Buddhist Saints of the Forest*, pp. 91–2.
18. Ibid. p. 100.
19. Nyanasampanno, *The Venerable Phra Acharn Mun*, pp. 62–3; Tambiah, *The Buddhist Saints of the Forest*, p. 94.
20. Nyanasampanno, *The Venerable Phra Acharn Mun*, pp. 20–21.
21. R. Gethin, *The Buddhist Path to Awakening: A Study of the Bodhipakkhyaddhamma* (Leiden: Brill, 1992), p. 14. See Gethin's note 60 for references.
22. I am assuming the more recent dating of the Buddha to be correct. See Heinz Bechert 'The Date of the Buddha Reconsidered', *Indologica Taurinensia* vol. 10, 1982, pp. 26–36; 'A Remark on the Problem of the Date of Mahavira', *Indologica Taurinensia* vol. 11, 1983, pp. 287–90; 'Remarks on the Date of the Historical Buddha', *Buddhist Studies* vol. 17, 1988, pp. 97–117; Richard Gombrich, 'The Date of the Buddha: A Red Herring Revealed' in Heinz Bechert (ed.), *The Dating of the Historical Buddha Part 2* (Göttingen: Vandenhoeck and Ruprecht 1992), pp. 237–59.
23. See R. Gethin, *Foundations of Buddhism* (Oxford University Press, 1996), p. 96.
24. Mohan Wijayaratna, *Buddhist Monastic Life According to the Texts of the Theravāda Tradition* (Cambridge University Press, 1990), pp. 22–3.
25. Gethin, *Foundations*, p. 97.
26. Tambiah, *The Buddhist Saints of the Forest*, pp. 72–7.
27. Wijayaratna, *Buddhist Monastic Life*, pp. 120–21.
28. Gombrich, *Theravada Buddhism*, p. 30.
29. Wijayaratna, *Buddhist Monastic Life*, pp. 4–6.
30. Ibid. pp. 117–21.

31. Gethin, *Foundations*, p. 88.
32. Tessa Batholomeuz, 'The Female Mendicant in Buddhist Sri Lanka' in J. I. Cabezon (ed.), *Buddhism, Sexuality, and Gender* (Albany: SUNY Press, 1992), pp. 37–61.
33. B. Faure, *The Red Thread: Buddhist Approaches to Sexuality* (Princeton University Press, 1998), p. 11. I do not systematically deal with the question of gender in this chapter, as my focus is on the textual construction of the ascetic self. In principle the same processes that occur in the male ascetic of controlling the body–mind complex and seeking the transcendent goal of nirvana are identical in both communities.
34. H. Kawanami, 'Can Women be Celibate? Sexuality and Abstention in Theravada Buddhism' in Elisa J. Sobo and Sandra Bell (eds.), *Celibacy, Culture and Society: The Anthropology of Sexual Abstinence* (Madison: University of Wisconsin Press, 2001), pp. 137–56.
35. *Sutta-nipāta* 1.3. K. R. Norman (trs.), *The Group of Discourses* (with alternative translations by I. B. Horner and Walpola Rahula) (London: Pāli Text Society, 1984), pp. 7–11.
36. For a full discussion of this term see Gethin, *The Buddhist Path to Awakening*, pp. 59–66.
37. Buddhaghosa, *The Path of Purity*, trs. Pe Maung Tin (London: Pāli Text Society, 1975); Henry Clarke Warren (ed.), *The Visuddhimagga of Buddhaghosacariya* (Cambridge, MA.: Harvard University Press, 1950). For good descriptions of the contents of the text see Tambiah, *The Buddhist Saints of the Forest*, pp. 28–52; Carrithers, *The Forest Monks of Sri Lanka*, chapter 3; D. Goleman, 'The Buddha on Meditation and Higher States of Consciousness', *The Wheel Publication*, nos. 189/190 (Kandy: Buddhist Publication Society, 1973), pp. 1–60.
38. The story is recounted by Tambiah, *The Buddhist Saints of the Forest*, pp. 28–9.
39. The three divisions relate to the eightfold path in the following way: wisdom refers to the first two categories, right view and right intention; virtue refers to the next three, right speech, right action and right livelihood; and concentration refers to right effort, right mindfulness and right concentration. See Gethin, *Foundations*, p. 81.
40. *Vissudhimagga* 2.1. Pe Maung Tin, *The Path of Purity*, p. 66. *Evam hi 'ssa appichatā-santuṭṭhitā-sallekha-pavivekāpacaya-viriyārambha-subharatādiguṇa-salila-vikkhālitamalam sīlañ c'eva suparisuddham bhavissati.*
41. *Vissudhimagga* 2.84
42. Gombrich, 'The Buddha and the Jains', p. 1086, note 32.
43. A. iv. 461. E. M. Hare (trs.), *The Book of Gradual Sayings* vol. IV(Oxford: Pāli Text Society, 1995), p. 303.
44. MN vol. 2. 1.387–92. I. B. Horner (trs.), 'Discourse on the Canine Ascetic' (*Kukkuravatika-sutta*) in *The Middle Length Sayings* vol. II, pp. 54–9; Gombrich, *How Buddhism Began*, pp. 143–4.
45. For example V 1.60; 74. I. B. Horner (trs.), *The Book of Discipline* (London: Pali Text Society, 1951), pp. 108, 124; Faure, *The Red Thread*, p. 74. On the rules see C. S. Prebish, *Monastic Discipline: The Sanskrit Prātimokṣa Sūtras of*

*the Mahāsāṁgikas and Mūlasarvāstivādins* (Philadelphia: University of Pennsylvania Press, 1975).

46. Faure, *The Red Thread*, pp. 7, 18.
47. On the link between sexuality and meditation see M. Spiro, *Buddhism and Society: The Great Tradition and its Burmese Vicissitudes* (London: George Allen and Unwin, 1971), p. 56.
48. Hermann Oldenberg (ed.), *Vinaya Pitaka* vol. V (London: Pāli Text Society, 1964), p. 193.
49. For example S 4.4. J. F. L. Woodward (trs.), *The Book of Kindred Sayings* part IV, vol. V (London: Pāli Text Society, 1972), pp. 241–2.
50. T. W. Rhys Davids, and William Stede (eds.), *The Pāli Text Society's Pāli–English Dictionary* (London, Henley and Boston: The Pāli Text Society, 1921–1925), 342.
51. *Visuddhimagga* 2. 12: *yo samādiyati, so puggalo. Yena samādiyati, cittacetasikā ete dhammā. Yā samādānacetanā, taṇ dhūtāṅgaṇ.* Pe Maung Tin, *The Path of Purity*, p. 69. I have modified the translation.
52. *Visuddhimagga* 2.13.
53. Ibid. 2.89: *yā cetanā, taṇ dhutangan ti vadanti.*
54. Nyanasampanno, *The Venerable Phra Acharn Mun*, pp. 34–6.
55. *Visuddhimagga* 2.87. Pe Maung Tin, *The Path of Purity*, p. 93.
56. Carrithers, *The Forest Monks of Sri Lanka*, p. 120.
57. Gombrich, *How Buddhism Began*, pp. 158–9.
58. *Visuddhimagga* 2.67–8.
59. Nyanasampanno, *The Venerable Phra Acharn Mun*, p. 312; also p. 43.
60. I. B. Horner (trs.), *Milinda's Questions* vol. II (London: Pāli Text Society, 1964), p. 201.
61. Horner, *Milinda's Questions*, vol. II, pp. 208–09.
62. Ibid. vol. II, pp. 210–11.
63. Ibid. vol. II, p. 214.
64. Ibid. vol. II, p. 221. V. Trenckner (ed.), *The Milindapañho: Being Dialogues Between King Milinda and the Buddhist Sage Nāgasena* (London: Pāli Text Society, 1962), p. 359. *Tenas 'me maharāja dhutangāni yehi suddhikato nibbānamahāsamuddhaṃ pavisitva bahuvidhadhammakiḷam abhikiḷati, rūpārūpa-aṭṭasamāpattiyo vaḷañjeti, iddhividhan dibbasotadhātuṁ paracittavijānanaṃ pubbenivāsānussatiṁ dibbacakkhuṃ sabbāsanakkhayayañ – ca pāpuṇāti.* (Some change to the translation.)
65. The standard formula is that the meditator focuses on an image or sign (*nimitta*) arising in the mind's eye, throwing the mind onto the object with initial thought (*vitaka*) and keeping it there with sustained thought (*vicāra*). As meditation is refined these factors fall away – first, initial and sustained thought, leaving only joy, contentment and one-pointedness in the second *jhāna*. These in turn gradually fall away until only one-pointedness remains in the fourth. See Lance Cousins, 'Buddhist *jhāna*: Its Nature and Attainment According to the Pāli Sources', *Religion* vol. 3 (1973), pp. 115–31. See also his 'Samatha-yāna and Vipassanā-yāna' in G. Dhammapala et al. (eds.), *Buddhist Studies in Honour*

*of Hammalava Saddhatissa* (Nugegoda: University of Jayewardenepura, 1984), pp. 56–68.

66. Reference from Lance Cousins, 'Samatha-yāna and Vipassanā-yāna', p. 63. Cousins notes that the term *sukkha-vipassaka* only later became understood as 'dry-visioned', the original meaning simply being 'just insight'.
67. S xii. 7.70. Caroline A. Rhys Davids, *The Book of Kindred Sayings* part II (London: Pali Text Society, 1972), pp. 86–8. See Gombrich, *How Buddhism Began*, pp. 124–5.
68. For an interesting discussion on these types of release and types of person in the Pali sources see Gombrich, *How Buddhism Began*, chapter 4. Gombrich argues that originally *cetovimutti* and *paññavimutti* were synonymous. *Paññavimutti* came to refer to enlightenment without meditation later, but enlightenment without meditation was never envisaged by the Buddha (p. 131).
69. M. I. 156. Horner, *The Middle Length Sayings* vol. I, p. 100.
70. S I. 120. Rhys Davids, *The Book of Kindred Sayings*, part I, vol. I, pp. 150–52.
71. For example at S IV 290 (Woodward, *Kindred Sayings*, part IV, vol. V, pp. 197–8). Mahā Moggalāna reads the mind of Anuruddha (*Kindred Sayings*, part IV, vol. V, p. 263) and the deva Kakudha (A.iii. 122 Hare, *Gradual Sayings* vol. III, p. 96). In A. iv. 84 the Buddha magically appears before Moggalāna to reprimand him for nodding off to sleep.
72. For example he demonstrates them in the 'Lion's Roar Sutta', M 1.75–77. I. B. Horner, *The Middle Length Sayings*, pp. 100–03.
73. K. N. Jayatilleke, *Early Buddhist Theory of Knowledge* (London: George Allen and Unwin, 1963), p. 446. See also N. Katz, *Buddhist Images of Human Perfection* (Delhi: MLBD, 1982), pp. 99, 104–06.
74. For a lucid exposition of the doctrine, placing it in the context of contemporary, Brahmanical understandings of the self see S. Collins, *Selfless Persons: Imagery and Thought in Theravada Buddhism* (Cambridge University Press, 1982).
75. Gethin, *The Buddhist Path to Awakening*, p. 44.
76. *Milinda* 37–8. In Gethin, *The Buddhist Path to Awakening*, p. 37.
77. For a thorough account see Gethin, *The Buddhist Path to Awakening*, chapter 1.
78. See Gethin, *The Buddhist Path to Awakening*, pp. 147–8.

CHAPTER 6

# *The asceticism of the desert*

Ὅταν γὰρ ἀσθενῶ τότε δυνατός εἰμί
When I am weak, then am I strong.[1]

In Dostoyevsky's *The Brothers Karamazov* the body of the ascetic, the elder Zossima, is prepared for burial and placed in his coffin in the room where he once gave audience. But towards the end of the day while the Gospel is read over him, a distinct odour of corruption exudes from the coffin.[2] Of course, this should not happen to an ascetic saint whose body, according to the Orthodox tradition, should remain pure even in death. Alyosha's puzzlement over this event and Rakitin's cynicism reflect a deep concern not simply about the sanctity of this particular holy man, but about the very notion of sanctification itself. Dostoyevsky expresses in this image a rampant, rationalist modernity at odds with tradition, and with the death of Zossima we can see the modernist death of faith in the old cosmology, a death that itself is presaged by the holy man's own 'modernism' in apparently denying the existence of devils. Zossima should emit no scent of corruption in a cosmological structure that identifies corruption with unredeemed matter and the sanctification of matter with the saint. The ordered universe of the monastery is challenged by the wind of modernity that had been blowing for several hundred years by the time Dostoyevsky enlivened his characters. With the loss of an Orthodox Christian cosmology we have the erosion of the justification for asceticism, and Zossima's whole life is brought into question with the sign of decay.

While it is too simplistic to see the tide of modernity as sweeping religion before it, as Dostoyevsky subtly acknowledges, it is nevertheless the case that the ascetic self entails cosmological religion. As we have already seen with Simone Weil, the erosion of traditions that understand themselves in cosmological terms entails the erosion of asceticism and the consequent reconfiguring of asceticism in other terms. Weil performed her asceticism in a comparative and self-imposed isolation from community and church that in previous Christian centuries had sustained ascetics in their practice and provided a discourse from which to justify that practice. With Dostoyevsky, in contrast to Weil, we have an author born into a cosmological Christianity, and he may have modelled Zossima on a particular Russian saint or *starets*, Ambrose, and he was certainly familiar with the famous Russian monastery at Optimo.[3] It is to this tradition of Orthodox monasticism to which we must now turn, but first we need to locate this tradition within the broad context of Christian asceticism.

## ASCETICISM IN CHRISTIANITY

Asceticism has had a central place within Christianity, not only in monastic communities and as part of the practice of the laity but in its theology and anthropology. The concern with asceticism has been accompanied by an ambivalent attitude towards the body, which on the one hand has been evaluated in positive terms as part of creation and on the other negatively as the locus of the passions, the locus of sin that keeps us away from God. This negative attitude towards the body has been associated with a dualism inherited from the Greek world that associates matter and body with impurity and constraint. Indeed, Origen (184–254 CE) interpreted his Christian faith through the lens of Platonic philosophy, and a strong tradition of fusing Greek with Christian thinking followed. Although many monks in the Egyptian desert tended towards dualism, seeing the body as an evil that prevents the soul from ascending to God,[4] a clear mind/soul and body dualism is too simple a model by which to understand Christian asceticism. The fault lines in the tradition are different. Rather we have a distinction between a sanctified and non-sanctified or, in the cosmological terms developed by Origen, between a pre-fall and post-fall state. The ultimate goal of Christian asceticism has been the reconstitution of the pre-fall state through withdrawal (*anachoresis*) and self-mastery (*enkrateia*).

A Christian anthropology has always been concerned with will and with hope, and central to this concern has been the body. While the body is the locus of the passions, it is also formed in the likeness of God and it is this divine nature of the body, its true nature, which has to be realised in asceticism. By the late fourth century, as Bynum has shown, the doctrine of bodily resurrection can be linked to the cult of relics, which points to 'stasis over decay'.[5] Through the control of the passions and through repentance and penance the self can aid in the restoration or reconciliation achieved through Christ. As the divine became human, so the human can become divine, although theologians have been keen to understand this in quite a specifically Christian way and have set this alongside an apophatic language that God is unknowable in human terms. In Orthodox Christianity the goal of divinisation or *theosis* is the becoming one with Christ, although the Orthodox Church was careful to avoid a Neo-Platonic identification of the self with the One.[6] While there is undoubtedly a strong Platonic influence in the ascetic life as a life of beauty and the saint as a walking icon, *theosis* is not a 'pagan' union with divinity. In the Latin West the idea of *theosis* generally drops away, although the aim of ascetic practice is still the restoration of the link between human and divine, but understood more in terms of virtue than of cosmology, as we shall see. The important point is that asceticism is closely bound up with the doctrines of the Church and integrated with the liturgical or sacramental life of the Church,[7] or more specifically, the non-Protestant Churches: Protestantism has generally repudiated overt asceticism. The liturgical pattern in the Orthodox and Catholic Churches has pervaded Christian asceticism and, conversely, there are marked elements of asceticism in the liturgical life of the laity. Actual ascetic performance has varied in Christianity from celibacy, fasting and sleep deprivation from at least the second century to more extreme practices such as the wearing of irons by Egyptian monks, and the later notorious flagellation and wearing of the hair shirt. Often asceticism is only temporary, linked to the liturgical year or to a particular penance, while for some monks – as for the stylite ascetics – it was a life-long observance.

This is not the place to describe at length the origins of Christian asceticism, but suffice it to say that there are precursors in the *New Testament* where Jesus calls his disciples to renounce material goods. In his important work in this area, Richard Valantasis has shown how there are clearly ascetical dimensions to texts such as the non-canonical *Gospel of Thomas* if we understand asceticism in such positive terms as the refashioning of the self rather than mere renunciation,[8] although many scholars are diffident about the application of the term itself to the gospels.[9] Mary Tolbert makes an important point that asceticism in the sense of self-chosen suffering, which develops in the later tradition, is not present in the earliest Christian tradition as expressed in Mark's gospel. Persecution was a feature of this early community and suffering comes directly from outside, imposed on the community by those in power. But once Christianity triumphs politically with Constantine I (306–337) and the persecution of Christian communities comes to an end, then suffering for the faith has to be self-chosen. The world of the earliest monastic communities is very different from the world of Mark's gospel.[10] Martyrdom is replaced by asceticism, which becomes its transformation. What the martyrs achieved through torture and destruction, Ephrem the Syrian (before the fourth century) observes, the monks achieve through mortification.[11] Ephrem writes, 'Hunger that eats up your flesh offers you the bliss of Eden; thirst that drinks your veins supplies you the source of life; fasting that dries up your person illuminates the countenance and pacifies you.'[12] Thus martyrdom comes to be replaced by the bloodless or white martyrdom of the monastics.

Asceticism in a Christian context cannot be discussed without the institution of monasticism in its broadest sense as a communal life of prayer, poverty, obedience and labour. There were forms of asceticism that predated formally monastic communities,[13] and there were solitary ascetics still within a tradition and part of a community. The most famous of these is Symeon the Stylite (ca 386–459), who lived for over forty years at the top of a high pillar and attracted a community around him near Antioch.[14] Originating in the third and fourth centuries, monasticism developed in Asia Minor and in Egypt, although there were monastic communities in the Middle East as well, in Syria and Mesopotamia.[15] Elm has shown how in Asia Minor communities of men and women grew up that were referred to as a communal household (*synoika*), brotherhood (*adelphotes*), community (*koinonion*) and, later, 'community of solitaries' (*monasterion*).[16] Women were crucial to this development, transforming the model of the family into the ascetic community, dedicating their lives to the service of God as a 'virgin' (*parthenos*) and following a specific daily regime.[17] *Parthenos* was not a term of physical description but referred to someone who had made a public proclamation to remain celibate. Thus these early communities could include widows and mothers who had undertaken a resolve to 'become virgins'. Indeed, a feature of ascetics is that they are *aeiparthenos*, 'perpetually virgin'.[18] This ideal of virginity became central to monasticism, and texts from Syria, for example, show that sex was regarded as an obstacle to eternal life.[19]

At first, men and women lived together 'as brother and sister', mutually supporting each other,[20] but with changing political circumstances in the early Church, the sexes were segregated and a double monasticism developed of men and women following the same rule under one superior but living separately.[21] The Cappadocian Fathers, especially Basil of Caesarea (ca 330–379), reformed monastic arrangements in such a way that the developments where men and women did not live in community together were heralded as the tradition and the older forms of communal living 'found themselves branded as heretical innovations'.[22] There was some debate in the early centuries of Christianity whether the hermitic or coenobitic life was preferable. With the notable exception of some theologians such as Basil, many believed the hermitic life of the monks of Nitria, the desert of Scete and the marshes of the Nile delta to be superior to the more overtly communal life of religious communities.[23] Cassian, for example, regarded the communal life to be an apprenticeship for the hermitic life of solitude exemplified by the monks of the Egyptian desert.

## THE EVAGRIAN TRADITION

Ascetic communities developed in Asia Minor and Egypt. Men and women retreated from the towns and villages to the 'desert' to realise ideals of ascetic perfection, as Elm says, living 'extraordinary lives shaped by their extraordinary surroundings'.[24] Palladius estimated five thousand monks to be living on the Mount of Nitria, congregating at weekends in the great church and spending their days in silence, prayer and the memorisation of scripture.[25] A genre of literature, the *Apophthegmata Patrum*, the *Sayings of the Desert Fathers*, records the lives and sayings of these extraordinary men and women,[26] among whom St. Anthony has been made famous through Athanasius of Alexandria's *Life of St. Anthony.*[27] These texts became widely disseminated and influenced thinkers such as Jerome and Augustine. The *Sayings of the Desert Fathers* contain many stories of monks in the Egyptian desert and within these narratives the *Sayings of the Desert Mothers* bear witness to a thriving community of female ascetics. This strong tradition of ascetic withdrawal in Egypt and Asia Minor and intense theological interest in the works of the founding fathers of the tradition, such as Basil of Caesarea, provided rich resources for the development of a theology of Christian asceticism in later centuries. A key figure and contemporary of Basil was Evagrius Ponticus (ca 345–99), who articulated a theology of the desert fathers within the framework of the theologians of the Alexandrian school, particularly Clement of Alexandria (150–215) and Origen (184–254). Evagrius also speaks of the importance of his master Macarius the Great (ca 300–ca 390) and his personal experience with him.[28] In later years, after the Fifth General Council of Constantinople in 553, Evagrius' writings were condemned as heretical for espousing the views of Origen,[29] but he remains a crucial figure in the transmission of Christian ascetic theology, especially in Syria and Egypt, and the development of monasticism through his disciples, among whom were John Cassian (ca 360–after 430) and Palladius (ca 364–420/30).

Cassian was the link from eastern to western monasticism, although he bemoans the quality of the monks in comparison to the 'pure' Egyptians,[30] founding two monasteries in Marseilles and writing important works: the *Institutes*, which lays down rules for the monastic life, the *Conferences*, which records the teachings he received in the East, and *De Incarnatione*, a condemnation of Nestorius' Christology that Christ was two persons, divine and human.[31] It is Cassian who introduces the term *apatheia* into the Latin tradition,[32] and with Cassian the cosmological doctrine of Evagrius becomes linked more closely to virtue. Palladius wrote the *Lausiac History*, a text intended to drive away the excitement of world conceit and to cure forgetfulness of piety.[33] Another important influence on the formation of Orthodox asceticism was the Greek text, the *Macarian Homilies*, attributed to Macarius, although composed by an unknown writer in Mesopotamia during the fourth or fifth centuries. It is this Evagrian tradition that we need to pay attention to and whose expression finds clear articulation in the writings of two theologians, Maximus the Confessor (ca 580–662), and John the Ladder or Climacus (ca 579–649), who wrote the highly influential *Ladder of Divine Ascent*.[34] The tradition grows and settles with ascetic theologians such as Simeon the New Theologian (949–1022), developing ideas of contemplation (*theoria*), practice (*praxis*) and purity of heart (*hesychia*).[35] These thinkers, particularly Maximus, illustrate the subjection of the self-narrative to the narrative of tradition and the ascetic transformation of the self through performing the memory of tradition. Above all, they illustrate the way in which asceticism is integrated into a Christian cosmology.

## COSMOLOGY IN THE EVAGRIAN TRADITION

One of the most important theological controversies of the fourth century concerned the cosmological doctrines of Origen, which were rejected by many Christian writers and especially by Epiphanius of Salamis, Jerome and Methodius of Olympus, and which were later condemned by the Fifth General Council of Constantinople in 553.[36] The source of this condemnation was the adoption by Origen of Platonic philosophy, which he saw as being compatible with the truths of the Gospels.[37] More specifically, the accusations concerned Origen's alleged subordination of the Son to the Father, the pre-existence of souls and an alleged denigration of matter in the doctrine of two creations. Epiphanius and Methodius, for example, accuse Origen of being the father of Arianism and also of having a pagan conception of the body in which the soul is entombed.[38] Origen, however, is arguably more subtle than this and Evagrius, schooled in Origenist teachings, adopted an Origenist cosmology, making it integral to his Christian eschatology. Origen's teachings, filtered through Evagrius, in turn deeply influenced the ascetic theology of Maximus.

In a letter to Melanie the Ancient, a remarkable Roman woman who had adopted a life of asceticism in Jerusalem, where she founded a monastery on the Mount of Olives, Evagrius clearly lays out his ideas.[39] He was evidently deeply influenced by Melanie and read Origen with her and his friend Rufin with great enthusiasm.[40] In his letter he sets out his cosmological vision which, with the *Kephalaia Gnostica*,[41] gives us a general narrative of creation and restoration. Evagrius adopts the central Origenist claims about the pre-existence of souls and the two-fold nature of creation. Both of these doctrines are intimately linked. In the narrative, God initially created beings with reason, pure intellects or *logikoi*, who turned away from the contemplation of God and thereby necessitated a second creation of matter. Torn by sin from their sublime state, they produced a movement (*kinesin*) and became 'souls' (*psuchai*). A 'soul' is an intellect that, through its negligence, has fallen from a state of unity and has descended to the level of secondary, worldly contemplation or *praktike* and so is embodied in the second creation. On this account, the second creation has been necessitated by the fall of the intelligible beings, that is, by sin. Intellects in the first creation were created in perfect nakedness, but because they sinned and chose to turn away from unity, God clothed their nakedness with a body. But the body must not be identified wholly with sin, for it is the vehicle of the soul's restoration and contains within it an imprint of our original nature as pure intellect. Our bodies bear a trace of the beings we once were, the *logikoi*, and Christ traces the wisdom of the *logikoi* in our bodily nature, says Evagrius, as children trace letters on their tablets.[42] This is an important idea, as we shall see with Maximus, for in saying that Christ traces the wisdom of the *logikoi* on our bodily nature, Evagrius is saying that the body bears the memory of this wisdom always mediated through the Church. The ascetic body bears the memory of tradition and, more deeply, the memory of our former, pre-embodied condition. Indeed the body is a sign and instrument of the soul's progress towards knowledge of God.[43]

In a way not dissimilar to the Indian material we have described, the body for Evagrius must be located within a cosmological structure. The body and the world of its experience are integral to each other, and the kind of world experienced is contingent upon the kind of body that a being possesses. Animated by the soul, the human body is characterised by mutually exclusive features such as waking and sleeping, hunger and satisfaction, anger and peace, sadness and joy.[44] The body/soul moves from one state to another and desires the higher nourishment of the virtues by which it is transformed.[45] There is, then, a range of bodies or ordered sequence of bodies and worlds depending on the degree of a being's fall: the worlds of angels, humans and demons. Both angels and demons were originally pure intellects, but because of the fall they have become differentiated and have received different names corresponding to their states and, for the angels, to their functions in the cosmic hierarchy. Thus the bodies of demons are characterised by their extreme coldness, while the bodies of angels are characterised by fire. Indeed, the kind of body a being has depends upon the combination of four elements that exist within it. It is the variable proportion of elements that distinguishes bodies from each other, so 'there is with the angels a predominance of intellect (*nous*) and fire, with men a predominance of concupiscence (*epithumia*) and earth, and with the demons a predominance of anger (*thumos*) and air.'[46] These three qualities make angelic bodies light and demonic bodies dark and heavy.[47] From the condition of embodiment in the second creation, there must be a return to the pure state of contemplation if beings are to be saved. From this fallen condition of diversity in the material world souls must return to a state of unity and knowledge of the one who is also the trinity. The return to the one is an end to imprisonment in the body, which can be seen as punishment for the movement away from pure contemplation, a goal (*telos*) which is the attaining of the kingdom of heaven and, in a different terminology, the purity of heart.

This account by Evagrius is a curious combination of a mythical narrative of the fall alongside a philosophical account of the movement from being to becoming, from unity to multiplicity, and an account of human psychology in which the ascetic moves from the practice of virtue, to detachment, and so to love. The hierarchy of states is also a hierarchy of bodies, associated with the qualities of intellect, concupiscence and irascibility, which in turn are associated with angels and demons: the angels are driven by intellect, humans by desire and demons by anger. We have here a precursor of an idea developed by Maximus where a human psychology derived from the Platonic tradition can be understood as the internalisation of the cosmic hierarchy: as the demons and angels are associated with subjective powers, so these forces within the self are associated with demons and angels. We have seen this kind of thinking before in the Indian traditions. But it seems clear that Evagrius is not speaking analogically or simply metaphorically when describing cosmology and the fall. He intends this to be a historical narrative as well as an account of the place of the body in relation to the soul.

In giving such an account Evagrius does not wish to present a simple dualism between soul and body or between a pure creation of intellects and a second creation of evil matter; this is no Manichean vision, which Evagrius is careful to avoid. Even though there is a strong element of Platonism in which the body is identified with the tomb of the soul, Evagrius is generally favourable towards the body, for 'nothing created by God is bad'.[48] Through the body in the second creation the soul can attain sanctity and rise to the spiritual gnosis from which it had fallen. Evagrius uses a striking, though complex, New Testament image of an ear of corn that contains a grain which in turn becomes another ear and so on.[49] This implies a chain of bodies: the soul, becoming free from one, then moves into a further form, until it is restored as in the first creation. This image makes clear that Evagrius does not hold to any sharp dualism of body and soul but rather presents a fluid model in which the embodied soul (for it is a soul only by virtue of its embodiment) is constantly transformed. In Psalm 141.8 there is the phrase 'make to leave my soul from the prison', which Epiphanius accuses Origen of using to express the idea of the body as a prison. But this very sentence is used by Evagrius to support his claim that the body should not be denigrated.[50] The body is not a prison for those who can become detached from the passions, but a vehicle for the elevation of the soul back to a state of the pure contemplation of God and part of a chain of being, a chain of bodies, although he does not hold to a physical resurrection. It is here that we see Evagrius' cosmology being integral to his asceticism, for through the ascetic control of the body, the body is transformed and the soul comes to realise itself as a pure intellect. The development of soul and body are inseparable: the transformation of the body in asceticism is the transformation of the soul, and to develop the soul's virtues is to transform the body, for a soul is soul only by virtue of embodiment.

This is not a vision that was to be condoned by orthodoxy, as it denies the resurrection of the fleshly body, a view not uncommon at the time. Epiphanius, writing in 374 in his *Ancoratus*, condemned Egyptian, Origenist monks for denying that the resurrected body was the body of flesh, and Methodius defends the idea of paradise as a physical place.[51] Evagrius' transformative view of the body makes the nature of the body dependent upon the balance of elements within it, which are in turn contingent upon the moral qualities of the soul. The resurrection of the body at the time of judgement is a transformation of the body from an inferior to a superior quality, which for Evagrius means that the person becomes an angel or a demon.[52] There are some indications of the changed status of the body in the terminology of the texts. Guillaumont notes that the terms for 'body' used in the Syriac texts of Evagrius are *pagrâ* and *gušmâ*, both of which translate the single Greek term *soma*, but which are generally used to indicate the body of flesh in the former case and the body of angels or demons, i.e. a spiritual body, in the latter.[53] This quality of the body at the time of the eschaton, whether an angel or a demon, is contingent upon the degree or intensity of contemplation. A psychological state, or more specifically an act of will in contemplation, determines the form in the cosmological scheme.

It is here that we see the importance of the ascetic life and the centrality of the body for Evagrius. What is achieved through ascetic striving at the level of worldly contemplation or *praktike* will have consequence for regaining gnosis and contemplation of God. Whatever is accomplished in *praktike*, 'on the sixth day' as it were, will be reflected in the resurrection body on the seventh.[54] Human souls will produce new angels and new demons.[55] But eventually an 'eighth day' will dawn, when there will be a dissolution of the body and those who have been united to a body will of necessity be liberated from it. Christ will be the victor, with his enemies, the demons, under his feet. The demons will submit to him and Christ will rule over them.[56]

This is a very ecumenical vision and presents a universal soteriology in the sense that the cosmos will be redeemed at the end of time when even the demons submit to Christ's power and the intellects return to their disembodied state of pure contemplation. Although the doctrines of Evagrius were anathematised in 543 and 553,[57] the idea that the final goal is anticipated in the ascetic life is in consonance with the Church's general teachings. It is this Evagrian tradition that becomes the central, ascetic tradition of the Orthodox Church and that produces, in time, that famous defender of ascetic meditation, Gregory Palamas.[58] But it is to the most orthodox of theologians, Maximus the Confessor, that we must turn to see how Evagrius' vision is linked to an orthodox, ascetical theology and to a Church that mediates the cosmological structure.

## MAXIMUS THE CONFESSOR'S COSMOLOGICAL PSYCHOLOGY

Maximus critically inherits the cosmological model of Evagrius along with the apophatic theology of Dionysius the Pseudo-Areopagite (ca 500 – himself influenced by Evagrius) and combines both in a complex theology in which the different elements are held in tension. On the one hand we have deification linked to cosmology and on the other the utter transcendence of God, both doctrines being maintained simultaneously and both being central to a Christian vision of the ascetic self integrated into a theology of Church and liturgy. For Maximus, contemplation of God is a transforming knowledge, a knowledge so transformative that the human being becomes deified, becomes like God. This idea of deification or *theosis* has a long history in the Christian tradition.[59] Maximus derives the term from Pseudo-Dionysius,[60] and like him understands it as being achieved by grace through the Church and sacraments. Deification is the goal of the ascetic life, a goal (and this is an important point) understood wholly within the Christological framework of his tradition and specifically within a Chalcedonian Christology.[61] The human becoming divine is the inverse of the divine becoming human in Christ. God and man (*anthropos*) are in a reciprocal relationship, as Maximus says in his *Difficulties* (*Ambigua*):

> For God and man are paradigms one of another, that as much as God is humanised to man through love for mankind, so much is man able to be deified to God through love, and that as much as man is caught up in God to what is known in his mind, so much does man manifest God, who is invisible by nature, through the virtues.[62]

The hypostatic union in Christ, the union of the divine and human natures, of divine and human wills, provides the structure that allows for human *theosis*. The human person, as Cooper observes, becomes ennobled in a unity of mind (*nous*), reason (*logos*) and sense (*aisthesis*).[63]

In Maximus' Christology, for which he was to suffer persecution and die as a consequence, Christ has two wills linked to his dual nature. In the incarnation, human nature is united to the *logos* and provides the blueprint for human divinisation. The incarnation is a cosmological act that allows the participation of the human in the divine through the 'imitation of the Lord',[64] which is also a spiritual ascent in contemplation, following Christ back to the Father. God 'descends' and becomes human in the incarnation and, conversely, in contemplation the ascetic self 'ascends' to assimilation in the *logos*. This ascending movement is a 'making thin' or a contraction (*sustole*), in contrast to the thickening or cosmic expansion (*diastole*) of the *logos*.[65] The ascent in contemplation or imitation of the Lord is achieved through grace mediated in the structures of tradition and the internalisation of tradition as an act of will.

Yet alongside deification we have the equally strong idea in Maximus that, in God, identity and difference are transcended, along with all language and analogy.[66] God is beyond all knowledge and all predicates; as Maximus says, 'the unsearchable wisdom of the infinite essence does not fall under human knowledge'.[67] This gulf (*chasma*) between human and divine is reflected in the doctrine of *creatio ex nihilo*, that God has brought the visible and invisible creation into existence from nothing, being from non-being,[68] an idea also embodied in the Orthodox liturgy. Because of this utter transcendence, at one level there could never be an equivalence between the human and divine, an idea reflected in a number of terms used by Maximus such as 'difference' (*diaphora*), 'division' (*diairesis*), 'distance' (*diastasis*), 'separation' (*diastema*) and so on.[69] On the one hand we have divinisation and the achieving of a likeness (*homoiotes*) through the hypostatic union in Christ, on the other we have an unbridgeable gap filled, as it were, by a cosmos. Deification, identity with presence, rests alongside infinite distance and awareness of absence. It is here that we see the poignancy of the ascetic struggle and its paradoxical or dialectical nature. Deification is the goal, a goal that cannot be identical with knowledge of God who is necessarily always beyond human grasp, but a goal that is nevertheless realised through the incarnation. We have no power to deify ourselves for Maximus, yet in deification we realise our power in the understanding that we are 'like God'. In turning away from the senses that pull the self downwards towards the passions, through an act of will the self can cultivate the virtues within which the Lord is manifest, and so participate in divinity and become divinised.

We need to distinguish between different levels of discourse here, while bearing in mind that for Maximus these are intimately intertwined. At the level of an ontological discourse we are faced with the dialectic that the being of 'man' can become divine, yet simultaneously there is an infinite distance between self and God who transcends all predicates. At a cosmological level the divine is reflected in varying degrees in a hierarchical sequence of beings, which is furthermore recapitulated within individual psychology. While Maximus adopts, although not uncritically, the cosmological structure of Evagrius and, beyond him, Origen, he integrates this with an account of human psychology and a mapping of the processes that keep a being bound to a lower realm of understanding (and conversely the processes that enable his or her liberation). For Maximus, as for the Indian systems we have examined, psychology recapitulates cosmology and a cosmological discourse is reflected in a psychological one. A human being is a microcosm facing two ways, outwards through the senses and physical body into the sensible world, and inwards towards God and the intelligible world or transphysical universe. The structure of the created self reflects the structure of the cosmos, and a human being contains both a reflection of the divine and a trace of the fall. In particular, Maximus inherits indirectly from Plato through Evagrius a tripartite anthropology that divides a human being into a rational dimension or intellect (*nous*), the irascible (*thumos*) and the concupiscible (*epithumia*).[70] While there are some differences in their use of these terms, and Maximus sometimes refers to *thumos, epithumia* and *logos*, adding *nous* as a fourth element in the soul,[71] the general point is retained, that these are powers (*dunameis*)[72] linked to the cosmological structure. These forces in varying degrees govern the angels and demons, and conversely these forces are associated with demons and angels within a human being. We can in fact see that for Evagrius and Maximus, and for premodern Christianity as a whole, the identification of the demons with the passions, with what were later to become purely psychological forces, is the internalisation of cosmology.[73]

On the one hand Maximus effortlessly identifies mental contents with the work of demons and on the other he presents what we might anachronistically call a 'psychological' interpretation of the forces that keep the ascetic away from contemplation. Using a different kind of language from that of demons and powers, Maximus claims that it is the nature of the mind as wandering that keeps the ascetic from contemplation, and this wandering mind needs to be controlled. In this more psychological perspective, Maximus speaks of the vices, a language derived from Evagrius, developed by John the Ladder[74] and Cassian,[75] that enters the Western tradition, as we shall see, as the seven deadly sins. Evagrius consistently uses the term *logismoi*, 'thoughts', which almost always refers to the vices that keep a soul bound to the lower orders of creation.[76] It is the vices that cause the mind to wander and 'care of the flesh', fornication, uncleanness, passionate thoughts, concupiscence, greed and self-love have to be 'put to death'.[77] To put the vices to death is to become detached from them, to free the mind from their control. In the *Centuries on Charity* (*Capita de Caritate*) Maximus writes in terms reminiscent of the Indian material we have examined, that the mind is like a sparrow tied by the foot. As it tries to fly it is dragged to the earth by the cord, so the mind that does not possess detachment tries to fly to 'knowledge of heavenly things' but is dragged down by the passions.[78] This is an idea present in the earlier fathers, where the mind is described as *aeikinetos*, ever-moving. Evagrius uses this term in the *Centuries* (*Kephalaia Gnostica*), and Cassian draws on the same idea when likening the heart (*kardia*) to a turning mill driven by the pressure of temptation.[79] Yet this kind of description is complemented by a cosmological account that sees the passions as instigated by the demons. In the same text, 'On Charity', Maximus writes that the demons rouse the passions of (male) ascetics through touching their private parts in sleep and through appearing to the mind in the form of a woman to arouse desire.[80] While modern readers might interpret this language metaphorically, for Maximus it is integral to his cosmological vision that the personified powers in the cosmos are also psychological forces within the self.

This account of inner processes is further linked to cosmology in so far as the mind conforms to its objects. The nature of the things we contemplate, says Maximus, enters the mind and teaches it.[81] If the object of the mind is pure, the mind will conform to that state, the purest object of contemplation being God. Maximus writes:

> The mind, in receiving the representations of things, is naturally patterned after each representation; in contemplating them spiritually (*pneumatikos*), it is diversely conformed to each object of contemplation (*theorema*). When it comes to be in God, it is entirely without form and without pattern. For on contemplating Him who is simple, it becomes simple and wholly transfused with light.[82]

In one sense it is this process that allows for divinisation. Through the contemplation of God the mind conforms to that transcendent object. The mind joins to God (*to theo sunaptei*) and so becomes God-like (*theoeides*).[83] Through contemplation of divine light the person becomes filled with divine light. Again, Maximus is not alone in presenting this idea. His precursor is Evagrius, who says that the wandering mind keeps us away from pure prayer (*kathara proseuche*), which lifts the mind up to God and strips the mind naked before him.[84] Prayer is the expulsion of all thoughts.[85] It is this structure that is behind the tradition of light mysticism in the Orthodox tradition. Through purification of the mind in ascetic struggle, the development of the virtues, and grace the self takes on divine qualities such as the virtues of faith, hope and love. But this is not simply a moral development, the eradication of the vices and development of the virtues, but a development of contemplation and a realisation of the way in which the structures of consciousness relate to the structures of the cosmos. The purification of the mind or the elimination of thought, according to these early Christian thinkers, allows us to see the light of God in interiority like a sparkling sapphire[86] (not dissimilar to the sign or *nimitta* of Buddhism), strongly suggesting a particular kind of interiority as constitutive of the ascetic self: an inner perception of light understood as the remembrance of the Trinity, yet which is simultaneously a self-forgetting (*anaesthesia*) or ecstasy (*ekstasis*).[87]

The practice (*praxis*) of morality or development of virtue needs to be accompanied by the contemplation of creation (*phusike theoria*) and scripture (*graphike theoria*), as Paul Blowers observes, to allow for the transition (*diabasis*) to deification.[88] Maximus presents us with an analysis of human drives and a fundamental moral struggle with the passions which is linked to an analysis of the cosmos. The way the mind operates is connected to the way the universe operates, and the work of redemption is keyed in to the cosmic structure. Thus, in spite of the fallen nature of the world, the *logos* is reflected or incarnated not only in Christ himself but also in created beings (*logoi ton onton*) and in scripture.[89] The 'intelligences' or *logoi* that are pre-existent in God are held together, although differentiated, within the *logos* and manifested in the world. These three incarnations, in Christ, in creation and in scripture, are also recapitulated within the ascetic who becomes, as it were, a further site of the incarnation.[90] Contemplation (*theoria*) and practice (*praxis*) are geared towards understanding these ways in which the divine shows itself, and conversely through this encounter a human being can become divine. The contemplation of God and the consequent purification of the mind occur in a subjectivity and interiority that are also an understanding of the cosmic structure: the higher forms are realised in interiority.

From the foregoing discussion we can see that *theosis* as the development of a particular kind of interiority is an enactment of the memory of tradition in so far as only through the mediation of tradition can it occur. For Evagrius and Maximus the experience of pure prayer is the reception of grace by which the self is forgotten and the Lord remembered. Through the liturgical life of the Church, through the ascetic struggle with the passions, and through the internalisation of tradition the self turns desire away from the sensible world towards God. Such a turning away from the world and internalisation of tradition is an act of will supported by the structures of tradition, by which the ascetic intends to eradicate that will. Self-will is replaced by the other-will of God. For Maximus, this eradication of the self's will, this *theosis*, is achieved through the structures of the Church and liturgy, the master and the revealed text.

## COSMOLOGY AND TRANSMISSION: THE CHURCH

Human life, particularly the perfected human life, reflects the cosmos and mediates between it and the transcendent.[91] The Church facilitates this mediation and provides a structure for restoring unity to creation through union with Christ and so, for Maximus, the Church is not simply a human institution but continuous with the cosmos as the body of Christ. Maximus' ecclesiology is therefore closely related to his cosmology, with the Church reflecting the cosmos and being an icon of God.[92] Cosmos and Church are homologous in so far as both can be seen as the body of God and both can be seen as an icon of God. Indeed, the universe is referred to by Maximus in the view of his teacher (probably Sophronius) as *macranthropos*, 'a man enlarged',[93] along with the converse idea of the *microcosmos*, the cosmos made small in the human. As God is reflected in creation, so God is reflected in the Church, which links the human and divine and links the human and cosmic. The teachings of Christ expressed in Scripture are transmitted through the Church, through the tradition of the fathers.[94] The community of all believers, however diverse, finds itself united in the Church and so is part of the body of God. Through the Church, the community is brought into 'sameness',[95] while simultaneously maintaining particular difference. At the heart of the Church is the reciprocity between human and God through the descent of God to the human in Christ and the ascent of the human thereby facilitated as an act of will towards deification. The descent of God in the incarnation is recapitulated in the central structure of the Church, the eucharistic liturgy, which prefigures the final consummation of human with divine and prefigures deification. In this account, the Church is a structure for the transmission of grace, which is cosmological through the incarnation, and so is an icon, if we understand that term as a form that participates in a reality to which it points.

The goal of *theosis* is therefore closely linked to the mediation of the Church, and the ascetic self, in seeking ascent to the realisation of the *logos*, enacts the cosmic structure of manifestation, contraction and redemption in the liturgical act. The liturgy, in von Balthasar's phrase, is a 'cosmic liturgy', the re-enactment of the rite instituted by Christ, and so is an enactment of the memory of tradition. Indeed, for Gregory of Nyssa remembering (*anamnesis*) is a technology for rendering that which is absent, namely the origin and telos of tradition, present.[96] Through the liturgical act, the community looks forward to the telos of redemption, to the last cosmic days,[97] and backwards to the incarnation and to the time before material creation. For the ascetic self, the liturgy is therefore integral to the process of deification and not simply a structure or substitute for contemplation intended for those who cannot achieve the difficult task of *theosis*.

## COSMOLOGY AND TRANSMISSION: THE TEACHER

In this sense of the community of all believers, Christianity is an exoteric tradition and moves against esotericism, especially, of course, Gnosticism. Yet while this is undoubtedly the general case, alongside the idea of transmission through the Church we have the idea of transmission through the teacher and the importance in the ascetic life of direct contact with a teacher or spiritual father (*geron*). The ideal teacher is Christ, and the ascetic life is in imitation of him in his virtue and his suffering. Ephrem the Syrian, for example, places suffering through mortification at the heart of Christian practice in imitation of Christ who, through his suffering, becomes the master and perfect teacher.[98] The monastic teacher is the representative of Christ to his disciple, and the development of virtue comes through submission to this spiritual master and the tradition behind him or her.[99] The term 'teacher' (*didaskalos*) is used by the fathers in a general sense to refer to the apostles, Paul, some fathers of the Church such as John Chrysostom, and even to Christ himself, while the term *abbas*, 'father', is used as a title of respect to denote monks and revered ascetics, although it did not denote an official office in the early period.[100] The term *geron* refers to a respected elder with a more intimate relationship to a monk. While at the monastery of Eukradates in Africa, Maximus was under the tutelage of a spiritual father, Sophronius, who was himself the disciple of the Palestinian monk, John Moschus.[101] It is probably Sophronius who is the elder (*geron*) in Maximus' *The Ascetic Life* (*Liber Asceticus*), a dialogue between teacher and disciple. While the question-and-answer form of the text, which opens with the brother asking the old man about the purpose of the Lord becoming a man, is a literary genre with a history in antiquity and Christian writing,[102] it reflects an important monastic relationship. The importance of this relationship should not be underestimated. While the elder does not have as much significance in the Christian tradition as in the Indian traditions, where divine power is transmitted through the master, he (and sometimes she) nevertheless plays an important role in the transmission of teachings and in being an exemplum of the ascetic life. Palladius says that those without a teacher are plagued by the disease of ignorance.[103]

Of key importance is the dialogical nature of the teacher–student relationship, a relationship adopted from the Greek, Socratic model by teachers such as Origen, who used it to attract young pagans to the study of Christian philosophy. Among them were two brothers, Theodore and Gregory; the latter was later to become the highly venerated saint, Gregory Thaumaturgus. In his *Panegyric* or *Address of Thanks*, Gregory describes the attraction to, and love of, both the 'Holy Word' and the master, 'that divine man'.[104] The Christian teacher is one who combines a life of prayer with a deep knowledge of the scriptures and the ability to convey this to his students in a way that makes them describe the experience as being in 'perpetual sunlight'. Evagrius similarly describes his own teacher Macarius in exalted terms as an embodiment of the virtues.[105] Over two hundred years later Maximus and other writers speak in similarly high tones about their spiritual father, although Maximus does not present a sustained discussion on the nature of the teacher as such.

Other writers offer a fuller account of the spiritual teacher. Cassian (ca 360–after 430) gives endearing examples from his time in the desert and of the centrality of the teacher in the disciple's development. In one example, Cassian speaks of Father Serapion, who told a story about how, when he lived with his own spiritual father, he would steal bread from the table, but upon confessing this, he found that the passion of gluttony and its demonic energy was pulled from his heart into the light.[106] This, and other stories, is used as a teaching device, and Serapion relates his own experience to the biblical tradition, citing passages from *Ecclesiastes* to illustrate the importance of the verbal testimony of confession to cure the 'serpent bite' of sin. The narratives of scripture serve to illustrate how the narrative of the ascetic self should be constructed and, through internalising the tradition, the ascetic forms himself in a particular way: he conforms himself through struggle to the form of tradition conveyed by the teacher. Another example from the *Philokalia* is Neilos of the Holy Mount (d. ca 430), a pseudonym for Evagrius. In his *Ascetic Discourse* (*Logos Asketikos*) he warns about the dangers of the ascetic path. A monk can learn about the outward practices of asceticism – how and when to pray, what to eat, how to dress and so on – but what is important is to master oneself, to refashion the self away from old habit and defilements. The spiritual teacher, in order to advise others, needs to have gained some control over his own passions and to know on the basis of personal experience about the inner warfare.[107] In an interesting passage redolent of the Indian guru, Neilos refers to the teacher as purifying the actions of those who come to him and wiping them clean of their stain through his own defilement. As a basin of water cleaning the hands of those who wash itself receives their dirt, so the teacher in purifying his disciples receives their impurity.[108] This is to accord a very high status to the teacher. Not only does the teacher train the monk in the practice of asceticism and guide the monk in constructing a new self, but, assuming he has the inner purity, is directly instrumental in that transformation. The tradition is conveyed through the teacher and, more than this, the teacher facilitates the purification of the passions. Furthermore, in one reading at least, he takes on or takes responsibility for the disciple's sin as a representative of Christ. The teacher is an analogue of Christ himself and the disciple moulds himself in accordance with tradition to the teacher's will. His own will, through an act of will, is subordinated to the will of the teacher, tradition and so Christ. Cassian says that the disciple should have no will of his own, apart from the orders of the abbot.[109]

## COSMOLOGY AND TRADITION: SCRIPTURE

We have seen that tradition is conveyed through the structure of the Church and through the spiritual master. The Church is the body of Christ and reflects the cosmos as the body of God, and the teacher similarly reflects the cosmic Christ in his or her imitation of Christ the cosmic teacher. Lastly, scripture is central in the conveyance of tradition and its internalisation by the ascetic self. Scripture is enacted in the liturgy (as much as seven times a day according to Cassian!) and is central in conveying Christian teachings from teacher to disciple. The memorisation of scripture was an integral part of the monk's life. It provides answers to the ascetic's questions and reflects the monk's personal struggle (*agon*).[110] In the writings of Maximus and others, the use of scripture is all-pervasive, and Maximus' text *The Ascetic Life* largely comprises scriptural passages linked by his own commentary. This use of text and the tradition of interpretation it implies goes back a long way in Christianity, particularly to Origen, who was influenced by Philo,[111] and Maximus models his own dialogical format on the *Sayings of the Desert Fathers*.[112]

Maximus' *The Ascetic Life* provides a good example of the centrality of the teacher–disciple relationship and of the use of scripture. The master's advice is always supported by scriptural reference and his didactic skill brings the text to life for the brother. Indeed, the dialogical structure is a pedagogical device that Maximus uses to guide the intended reader, a monk in a Christian community, to an understanding of the ascetic life. In the dialogue the disciple is brought to understanding by the elder's responding to his questions largely through scriptural quotation. It is the power of the revealed word that facilitates an effect on the disciple. In more technical terms, the indexicality of the reader locates itself in the indexicality of the text, in the text's 'I of discourse' (see pp. 218–19), and so the text contributes to the construction of the ascetic self. Let us examine this more closely.

The text opens with a central question for Christianity: 'What is the purpose of the Lord's becoming man?' In deceptively simple terms the elder answers, 'For the sake of our salvation.' The text then proceeds to unfold the ascetic path through a series of increasingly more particular questions, such as 'What are the commandments and how can I keep them?' and 'How can I love my neighbour?' The elder gives answers and practical instruction directly relating to the ascetic life. To the brother's inquiry about how to develop soberness, the elder responds that he should develop lack of concern for earthly things, practise meditation on scripture that brings fear of God, and practise devotion to God. The disciple then inquires further about how we can achieve devotion and the elder responds that we can attain this through love (*agape*), self-mastery (*enkrateia*) and prayer (*proseuche*). In this deceptively simple text, we find ourselves in the world of Evagrian cosmological psychology, where love tames anger (*thumos*), self-mastery conquers concupiscence (*epithumia*) and prayer withdraws the mind from the world to God.[113] Through hard work and the development of the virtues of love, self-mastery and prayer, the passions are overcome.[114] Behind the elder's responses is Maximus' phenomenology of consciousness in which the mind can become detached by prayer from objects of sense and mental objects until its content is filled only with desire for God who, in one sense, can never be an object of consciousness, being beyond thought and language, yet who in another sense can fill consciousness with his presence. Through love, self-mastery and prayer the monk is separated from material things[115] and at the summit of prayer, Maximus says in the *Centuries*, the mind dies and leaves all thought of this world.[116] In this state, the mind is undistracted and 'rapt by the divine and infinite light' such that it is no longer conscious of itself or others.[117] This kind of language is very Platonic, and we can see the strong influence of Origen's 'Gnostic' Christianity here. Maximus fully understands the practical difficulties of controlling the passions but has no hesitation in expressing this in the hierarchical, cosmological terms of his tradition. In the terminology we have developed earlier, we can understand Maximus' language as expressing the ambiguity of the self, the ambiguity that the self seeks power over the principalities through weakness and the elimination of the will through its assertion. This is also the imitation of the Lord through tradition.

In his penultimate question, the brother asks the elder why he feels no compunction (*katanuxis*), and the old man answers, 'Because there is no fear of God before our eyes.'[118] He then goes on to illustrate the need for this fear through scriptural quotation, such as Ezechiel saying 'I will pour out my wrath upon thee . . . and then thou shalt know that I am the Lord.'[119] The build-up of these quotations interwoven with a discourse about how we are subject to vice and how we neglect the commandments so that we are become 'instead of a temple of God, a place of business and instead of a house of prayer, a den of thieves'[120] has a deep effect upon the brother. Indeed, he is filled with compunction and in tears his last question is 'What ought I to do?', to which the elder responds that we should go before God with contrition and thanksgiving, for 'with God all things are possible'.[121] The text ends with a plea for the ascetic life. We should 'repent' to become free from the passions (*metanoesomen pathon*) and so achieve forgiveness of sins, we should watch and be sober (*gregoresomen, nephomen*) and imitate the 'holy athletes of the Saviour' (*tous agious athletas tou soteros*), the 'divine Apostle' himself.[122] The first person plural verb 'we should repent' has the implication not only of a mental turnaround or change, but the performance of prostration. Thus the verb *metanoeo* and the noun *metanoia* have the implication not only of repentance but a practice of full prostration as occurs at different times in a vigil, for example.[123] The narrative of the text develops to the point of realisation and awakening of compunction in the brother, achieved through the use of scripture, which also has the implication of bodily performance. While salvation is through Christ and from God, belief alone is not enough, but we must develop the imitation of Christ and the internalisation of tradition as an act of will in order to eradicate that will, which, in other words, is to practise the ascetic life.

## THE ASCETIC BODY

We have seen how Maximus' asceticism cannot be understood in isolation from his theology and anthropology in which the world and human life within it are a reflection or recapitulation (*anakephalaiosis*) of creation as a whole.[124] The structure of creation in which the divine is reflected in the human allows for the realisation of our innate divinity through the imitation (*mimesis*) of the perfect man, namely Christ. Asceticism is not simply the control of the passions but the imitation (*mimesis*) of God and the cultivation of a life of beauty as a reflection of God's being: an imitation or cultivation which is a recapitulation of tradition in interiority and memory. But to interiorise tradition and to imitate Christ, whose life contained both beauty and pain, is to undergo intentional suffering, as suffering and beauty are integral aspects to the Christian ascetic path.

The goal of becoming God-like, of crossing beyond sin, is achieved when tradition and scripture are brought to life in subjectivity. There is a complex of related ideas and terminology in Maximus that express the possibilities of ascetic transformation: imitation, the realisation of passivity (*apatheia*), the cultivation of sobriety, uprooting the passions and understanding the truth of scripture. To perform these tasks is to perform service to the spiritual master and to God, for imitation is imitation of the Master, the great apostle Jesus himself, and the imitation of the elder (*geron*) as the embodiment of tradition. In *The Ascetic Life* Maximus quotes Paul, who commands 'Be ye imitators of me as I also am of Christ,'[125] making the point that access to

Christ is mediated through the tradition, and that to imitate the teacher is to imitate the Lord.

Imitation involves struggle, and for Maximus asceticism is a kind of wrestling, an image which evokes the athlete. We are faced here with a paradoxical contrast between the strength implied in wrestling and the building-up of the body, and the weakness entailed by fasting, although both are held together in the image of the ascetic. In imitating the Lord the ascetic weakens the body and through this expresses power over the demons and ultimately over death – to achieve, in our terms, the reversal of the body's flow. As the incarnation weakens Christ's body and he suffers to attain a conquest of death, so the ascetic weakens his body in imitation to achieve a conquest over the passions that lead to death. In *The Ascetic Life* asceticism is a wrestling with the passions and the demons that try to drag the soul down from contemplation. The cosmological nature of this struggle is made clear through references to Paul's *Letter to the Ephesians* where he writes that their wrestling is not only against flesh and blood but also 'against principalities, against powers'.[126] The ascetic must wrestle with the demons, wrestle with the passions to bring them under control and follow Paul in chastising the body to bring it into subjection.[127] This bringing the body to subjection means weakening the body and reversing its tendency to flow into the world. The demons are driven out through making the body weak by fasting and vigils which thereby empower it. Maximus quotes scripture in *The Ascetic Life*, 'When I am weak, then I am powerful.'[128] This is also the imitation of Christ, for Christ was 'crucified through weakness' and through weakness destroyed death.[129] Once the passions are subdued, the mind is free to soar to the heights of contemplation and to make its way to knowledge of the Holy Trinity.[130] To weaken the body in ascetic practice is to realise the cosmos within the self and to begin to achieve the transition (*diabasis*) from the world of attachment and the passions to the world of divine contemplation and the angels. Through penance and weakness of body, the soul attains forgiveness of sins, emulates the 'holy athletes of the Saviour' and flees the world (*kosmos*) and the 'world's ruler' (*kosmokrator*).[131]

For Maximus, following in the Evagrian tradition, soteriology is integrated with cosmology and, like the liturgy, ascetic action is participation in the cosmic narrative. To participate in the cosmic narrative is to imitate the Lord and to create a habit in which the body is constructed in the image of tradition through an act of will, an act that has as its intention its own eradication. The construction of the ascetic body therefore both looks back to an origin, the pre-fall body of the *logikoi*, and forwards to a telos, the eschaton. Indeed, Cassian even speaks of three renunciations: of the body and its attachments to riches and worldly goods, of our vices and our past, and of the here and now. This latter demonstrates the future orientation of the ascetic self: the goal lies in the future for which we must become detached from the present and contemplate things of the future as represented in scripture.

This process of the entextualisation of the body is sometimes classified into three developmental stages by Maximus, who inherits this from Evagrius, namely the stage of *praktike* or *praxis* identified with asceticism, 'natural contemplation' (*phusike theoria*) or simply *gnosis*, the contemplation of the nature of things or the *logoi* within them, and the third stage of 'mystical contemplation' (*mustike theologia*), becoming divine through direct contemplation of God. This last term Maximus takes from Pseudo-Dionysius, while Evagrius simply uses the term *theologia.*[132] This general structure is presupposed by early Christian writers such as Clement, where Christian gnosis is built upon *askesis* and instruction and so leads to the perfection of salvation.[133] But there is some dispute as to whether these are developmental stages or parallel ways for Maximus. Certainly, for Evagrius they seem to be developmental, but Thunberg argues that Maximus diverges in regarding the practical and contemplative lives as going together, two paths indissolubly united, both rooted in human nature and both leading to the *logos.* This is illustrated in Maximus' interpretation of *Luke* 22.8–12, where Jesus sends Peter and John to prepare the last supper. Peter represents the ascetic or practical path and John the contemplative.[134] Both are necessary, both stand equally together, and both construct the body in conformity with tradition and in conformity with detachment (*apatheia*) and tradition-specific knowledge.

We have seen here how an Orthodox Christian construction of the ascetic self has been closely linked with cosmology and how in Maximus this cosmology is related to an analysis of psychological forces. We have seen that through the structures of tradition the ascetic constructs him- or herself in imitation of God as laid down by tradition and in imitation of the spiritual fathers and mothers. This imitation is the development of the memory of tradition and the development of ascetic habit that becomes inscribed on the body. The inscription of tradition on the ascetic body is also the entextualisation of the body, the creation of the body in the form of the texts of tradition. Indeed, there is no ascetic body outside of text and tradition. Our story continues in the Western tradition, where we see the same basic pattern, although it is in the West that we find the decline of cosmology and its eventual loss and how this is accompanied by the decline of asceticism.

## NOTES

1. II Corinthians 12.10.
2. F. Dostoyevsky, *The Brothers Karamazov*, vol. II, trs. David Magarshack (Harmondsworth: Penguin, 1958), pp. 384–96.
3. S. Bolshakoff, *Russian Mystics* (Kalamazoo: Cistercian Publications, 1976), pp. xxviii, 164–5.
4. H. Chadwick, *John Cassian: A Study in Primitive Monasticism* (Cambridge University Press, 1950), p. 23. He quotes one source that declares, 'My body kills me, I kill it.'
5. Caroline Walker Bynum, *The Resurrection of the Body in Western Christianity* (New York: Columbia University Press, 1995), pp. 108–09. Also see Peter Brown, *The Body and Society: Men, Women and Sexual Renunciation in Early Christianity* (London and Boston: Faber and Faber, 1989), pp. 440–43, and his *The Cult of the Saints: Its Rise and Function in Latin Christianity* (Chicago University Press, 1981), pp. 88–94.
6. See Juan Miguel Garrigues, *Maxime le Confesseur: La Charité Avenir Divin de l'Homme* (Paris: Beauchesne, 1976), pp. 83–112.
7. J. Pelikan, *The Spirit of Eastern Christendom (600–1700)* (University of Chicago Press, 1974), p. 256.
8. R. Valantasis, 'Is the Gospel of Thomas Ascetical? Revisiting an Old Problem with New Theory', *Journal of Early Christian Studies* vol. 7, 1999, pp. 55–81.
9. For example Saldarini, 'Asceticism in the Gospel of Matthew' in Leif E. Vaage and Vincent L. Wimbush (eds.), *Asceticism and the New Testament* (New York and London: Routledge, 1999), pp. 11–27.
10. Mary Tolbert, 'Asceticism and Mark's Gospel', p. 45 in Vaage and Wimbush, *Asceticism and the New Testament*, pp. 29–48.
11. Arthur Vööbus, *History of Asceticism in the Syrian Orient: A Contribution to the History of Culture in the Near East* vol. II *Early Monasticism in Mesopotamia and Syria*. 3 vols. (Louvain: Corpus Scriptorum Christianorum Orientalium, vol. 107, 1960), p. 99. On the relation between asceticism and martyrdom see Edward E. Malone, *The Monk and the Martyr: The Monk as the Successor of the Martyr* (Washington: The Catholic University of America Press, 1950). For a good, brief survey see T. O'Loughlin, 'Martyrs: Western Christian' in William M. Johnston (ed.), *Encyclopedia of Monasticism* vol. II (Chicago and London: Fitzroy Dearborn, 2000), p. 831.
12. Quoted in Vööbus, *History of Asceticism* vol. I, p. 100. For Ephrem, a love for penitence develops the life of prayer. See Sebastian Brock, *The Syriac Fathers on Prayer and the Spiritual Life* (Kalamazoo: Cistercian Publications, 1987), p. 69.

13. R. Rader, 'Christian Pre-Monastic Forms of Asceticism' in W. Skudlarek (ed.), *The Continuing Quest for God, Monastic Spirituality in Tradition and Transition* (Collegeville, MN: Liturgical Press, 1982), pp. 80–87; Susan A. Harvey, *Asceticism and Society in Crisis: John of Ephesus and the Lives of the Eastern Saints* (Berkeley: University of California Press, 1990), pp. 13–27.
14. Harvey, *Asceticism and Society in Crisis*, pp. 15–18.
15. For a comprehensive survey see J. Gobry, *Les Moines en Occident*, 3 vols. (Paris: Fayard, 1985–87); particularly useful is the 'tableau synchronique' at the end of each volume. On the origins of Christian monasticism see especially J. Elm, *'Virgins of God': The Making of Asceticism. in Late Antiquity* (Oxford: Clarendon Press, 1994). On developments in Syria the standard work is still Vööbus, *History of Asceticism.*
16. Elm, *Virgins of God*, p. 14.
17. Ibid., p. 47.
18. Basil Seleucensis, for example, uses the term for Saint Thecla, *se vita ac miraculis Theclae* (1 PG 85.481B). See G. W. H. Lampe (ed.), *A Patristic Greek Lexicon* (Oxford: Clarendon Press, 1961), p. 38 for further references.
19. Vööbus, *History of Asceticism*, vol. I, pp. 70–71.
20. Elm, *Virgins of God*, pp. 48–50. Rosemary Rader, *Breaking Boundaries: Male/Female Friendships in Early Christianity* (New York: Paulist Press, 1983).
21. Daniel F. Stramara, 'Double Monasticism in the Greek East, Fourth through Eighth Centuries', *Journal of Early Christian Studies* vol. 6, no. 2, 1998, pp. 269–312.
22. Elm, *Virgins of God*, p. x.
23. Chadwick, *John Cassian*, pp. 13–26, 49.
24. Elm, *Virgins of God*, p. 255.
25. Palladius, *Historia Lausiaca* 7.2 (C. Butler ed., Texts and Studies Series, vol. II, 1989).
26. PG 65. J. B. Cotélier (ed.), *Apophthegmata Patrum*, pp. 71–440. French trs. J.-C. Buy, *Les Apophtègmes des Pères du Desert, Série Alphabétique* (Textes de Spiritualité Orientale 1: Begrolles, 1968); English trs. Benedicta Ward, *Sayings of the Desert Fathers: The Alphabetical Collection* (Kalamazoo: Cistercian Publications, 1975); Sebastian Brock and Susan Ashbrooke, *Holy Women of the Syrian Orient* (Berkeley: University of California Press, 1998 (1987)).
27. PG 26 *Vita Antonii*, pp. 835–976 with *versio Evagrii*. English trs. R. C. Gregg and introduction by W. Clebsch, *The Life of Anthony and the Letter to Marcellinus*, Classics of Western Spirituality (New York: Paulist Press, 1980).
28. Evagrius, *Les Vertus de Notre Père, le Juste et Grand Abba Macaire* in E. Amélineau (ed.), *Histoire des Monastères de la Basse Egypte, Annales du Musée Guimet*, vol. XXV (Paris, Editions du Cerf 1894), pp. 118–202. See especially the anecdote reported on pp. 157–8, where Evagrius asks his teacher how he should be saved. Reference from Guillaumont, *Les 'Kephalaia Gnostica' d'Evagre le Pontique et l'Histoire de l'Origénisme chez les Grecs et chez les Syriens.* Patristica Sorbonensia 5 (Paris: Editions du Seuil, 1962), p. 54.

29. Guillaumont, *Les 'Kephalaia Gnostica'*, pp. 156–9. Elizabeth Clark, *The Origenist Controversy: The Cultural Construction of an Early Christian Debate* (Princeton University Press, 1992), p. 429.
30. On Cassian see Chadwick, *John Cassian*; Philip Rousseau, *Ascetics, Authority and the Church* (Oxford University Press, 1978), pp. 185–6.
31. PL 49 and 50, *Iohannis Cassiani Opera Omnia.* PL 49, 53–476 contains *De Coenobiorum Institutis.* Also Michael Petschenig (ed.), *Iohannis Cassiani Opera* vols. XIII, XVII (Vindabonae: CSEL, 1886, 1888). For a partial translation see Colm Luibheid (trs.), *John Cassian: Conferences*, Classics of Western Spirituality (New York, Mahwah: Paulist Press, 1985). For a translation of the complete works see E. C. S. Gibson, *The Works of John Cassian*, Nicene and Post-Nicene Fathers Series, vol. XI (Oxford: James Parker and Co., 1894).
32. See Guillaumont, *Les 'Kephalaia Gnostica'*, p. 79.
33. Robert T. Meyer, *Palladius: The Lausiac History* (London: Longmans, Green and Co., 1965), p. 24.
34. PG 88, 631–1164, John the Ladder, *Scala Paradisi.* English trs. Colm Luibheid and Norman Russell, *The Ladder of Divine Ascent*, Classics of Western Spirituality (New York: Paulist Press, 1982).
35. Gregory Collins, 'Simeon the New Theologian: An Ascetical Theology for Middle-Byzantine Monks' in V. C. Wimbush and R. Valantasis (eds.), *Asceticism* (Oxford University Press, 1995), pp. 343–56.
36. See Clark, *The Origenist Controversy*, pp. 85–158; Guillaumont, *Les 'Kephalaia Gnostica'*, pp. 81–119.
37. On the relation of Origen to Greek thought and further references see J. M. Rist, *Eros and Psyche: Studies in Plato, Plotinus, and Origen* (University of Toronto Press, 1964). Also H. Chadwick, *Christianity and the Classical Tradition* (Oxford: Clarendon Press, 1966) and C. Bigg, *The Christian Platonists of Alexandria* (Oxford: Clarendon Press, 1913, 2nd ed.).
38. Guillaumont, *Les 'Kephalaia Gnostica'*, pp. 85–6.
39. The Greek original is lost for the most part, but the text is found in a Syriac version. See Gösta Vitestam, 'Seconde Partie du Traité, Qui Passe sous le Nom "La Grande Lettre d'Evagre le Pontique à Mélanie l'Ancienne". Publiée et Traduite d'après le Manuscrit du British Museum Add. 17 192.' *Scripta Minora* (Lund: Regiae Societatis Humaniorum Litterarum, vol. III, 1963–1964), pp. 3–29. This edition gives the Syriac text edited in 1912 by W. Frankenberg, along with another version of the manuscript and a French translation of both. The Syrian text was retranslated to Greek by W. Frankenberg, *Euagrius Pontikus*, Abhandlungen der Königlichen Gesellschaft der Wissenschaften zu Göttingen, Philologisch-Historische Klasse, Neue Folge, Band XIII, 2 (Berlin, 1912), pp. 612–19. Evagrius stayed with Melanie at her monastery, apparently fleeing from an adulterous love in Constantinople, before going to the Egyptian desert.
40. Guillaumont, *Les 'Kephalaia Gnostica'*, p. 51.
41. PG 40, 1213–86. Guillaumont, *Les Six Centuries des 'Kephalaia Gnostica' d'Evagre le Pontique.* Edition critique de la version syriaque commune et édition

d'une novelle version syriaque, intégrale, avec une double traduction française. Patrologia Orientalis vol. XXVIII, fasc. 1 (Paris: Frimin Didot, 1958). The cosmology is well summarised by Guillaumont, *Les 'Kephalaia Gnostica'*, pp. 37–9, 103–13. I have been generally guided by Guillaumont in my reading of Evagrius' texts. For a recent English translation of Evagrius see Robert E. Sinkewicz, *Evagrius of Pontus: The Greek Ascetic Corpus* (Oxford University Press, 2003). For a good account of Evagrius' texts in Syriac see Vööbus, *History of Asceticism* vol. III, pp. 144–50.

42. Guillaumont, *Les Six Centuries*, 1.57, p. 121.
43. J. Driscoll, 'Spousal Images in Evagrius Ponticus', *Studia Mystica* vol. 38, 1996, pp. 243–56, especially p. 246.
44. Vitestam, 'Seconde Partie', pp. 13–17.
45. Ibid. p. 20.
46. Guillaumont, *Les Six Centuries*, 1.68, p. 49.
47. Ibid. 2.68, p. 87. These qualities are also, of course, within each human being and are susceptible to attack from different demons. The demons who attack the intellect are called birds, those who trouble anger are called animals and those who attack the concupiscence are beasts, 1.53, p. 49.
48. Guillaumont, *Les Six Centuries*, 3.59, p. 121.
49. Ibid. 1.24, p. 26. Guillaumont notes that Paul's text from which the image is drawn (chapter 15 of the *First Letter to the Corinthians*) is used both by those who support the identification of the resurrected body with the physical body, such as Epiphanius, and by those who do not, such as Evagrius.
50. Cited by Guillaumont, *Les 'Kephalaia Gnostica'*, p. 112.
51. Ibid. pp. 84, 109.
52. Guillaumont, *Les Six Centuries*, 5.19, p. 185.
53. Guillaumont, *Les 'Kephalaia Gnostica'*, p. 114, note 149.
54. Guillaumont, *Les Six Centuries*, 2.7, 3.65, 4.38, 6.24, and *Les 'Kephalaia Gnostica'*, p. 115.
55. Guillaumont, *Les Six Centuries*, 5.11, p. 181.
56. Guillaumont, *Les 'Kephalaia Gnostica'*, pp. 115–16, and *Les Six Centuries*, 1.58, p. 45; 6.15.
57. Guillaumont, *Les 'Kephalaia Gnostica'*, pp. 136–51.
58. On the continuity in the theologies of Maximus and Gregory see Lars Thunberg, *Man and Cosmos: The Vision of St Maximus the Confessor* (New York: St Vladimir's Seminary Press, 1985), pp. 137–8. Maximus, for example, anticipates Gregory's distinction between God in essence and energies: Thunberg, *Man and Cosmos*, pp. 37–9.
59. See M. Lot-Borodine, 'La Doctrine de la Déification dans l'Eglise Grecque jusqu'au XIe Siècle', *Revue d'Histoire des Religions* vol. 106, 1932, pp. 524–74, and vol. 107, 1933, pp. 8–35. Thunberg, *Microcosm and Mediator: The Theological Anthropology of Maximus the Confessor*, Alta Seminarii Neotestamentii Upsaliensis (Lund: Boktryckeri, 1965), pp. 454–9. On the place of Maximus in this history see J. Pelikan, 'The Place of Maximus Confessor in the History of Christian Thought' in Heizer F. and C. von Schönborn (eds.), *Maximus*

*Confessor, Actes du Symposium sur Maxime le Confesseur* (Fribourg, Switzerland: Editions Universitaires, 1982), pp. 387–402.

60. See Thunberg, *Microcosm and Mediator*, p. 456, note 2. For the reliance of Maximus on Dionysius (and his critique) see Hans Urs von Balthasar, *Kosmische Liturgie.* French trs. L. Lhaumet, and H.-A. Prentout, *Liturgie Cosmique* (Paris: Aubier, 1947), pp. 71–80; Garrigues, *Maxime le Confesseur*, p. 92.
61. Thunberg, *Microcosm and Mediator*, p. 457. On Maximus and the 'filioque' issue see J.-C. Larchet, *Maxime le Confesseur, Médiateur entre l'Orient et l'Occident* (Paris: Editions du Cerf, 1998), pp. 11–75.
62. PG 91, 113 BC. Maximus, *Ambiguorum Liber de Variis Difficilibus Locis Sanctorum Dionysii Areopagitae et Gregorii Theologi* 10. Trs. by Andrew Louth, *Maximus the Confessor* (London and New York: Routledge, 1996), p. 101. Thunberg, *Microcosm and Mediator*, pp. 31–2.
63. Adam G. Cooper, 'Maximus the Confessor on the Structural Dynamics of Revelation', *Vigilae Christianae: A Review of Early Christian Life and Language* vol. 55, no. 2, 2001, pp. 161–86.
64. Maximus, *The Ascetic Life* vol. III, p. 104; Peter Van Deun (ed.), *Liber Asceticus*, Corpus Christianorum Series Graeca 40 (Leuven University Press, 2000), p. 9: Ὁ τοῦ κυρίου μιμούμενος.
65. PG 91, 1285C. *Ambigua* 33; Thunberg, *Microcosm and Mediator*, pp. 419–20.
66. This transcendence of language by God is articulated in Dionysius the Areopagite, from whom Maximus draws much of his language. See D. Turner, *The Darkness of Dark: Negativity in Christian Mysticism* (Cambridge University Press, 1995), chapter 2. On Maximus and the apophatic tradition see Thunberg, *Microcosm and Mediator*, pp. 436–40.
67. PG 90, p. 1048C. Maximus, *The Four Centuries on Charity* (PG 90, pp. 959–1080), Century 4.3: ὅτι ἡ τῆς απείρου οὐσίας ἀνεξιχνίαστος σοφία, τῇ ἀνθρωπίνῃ ὀυχ ὑποπίπτει γνώσει. Text translated and annotated by Polycarp Sherwood, *St. Maximus the Confessor: The Ascetic Life and the Four Centuries on Charity* (London and Westminster, Maryland: The Newman Press and Longmans, Green and Co., 1955).
68. PG 90, p. 1048. Maximus, *The Four Centuries*, Century 4.3.
69. Thunberg, *Microcosm and Mediator*, pp. 54–67.
70. On the history of this trichotomy and for references see ibid. pp. 187–206.
71. Ibid. p. 185.
72. Ibid. p. 186.
73. Another triad that Maximus discusses is the rational, non-rational and nonsensible souls that correspond to humans, animals and plants, and to vegetative or nutritive function, appetitive and sensible, and rational and intellectual. This triad can be found through into Simone Weil as well. Thunberg, *Microcosm and Mediator*, pp. 184–5.
74. PG 88, p. 948. John the Ladder, *Scala Paradisi*, 22; Luibheid and Russell, *The Ladder of Divine Ascent*, p. 201.
75. John Cassian, 'On the Eight Thoughts', *Praktikos* 6 in Sinkewicz, *Evagrius of Pontus*, pp. 97–103.

76. J. Driscoll, *The Ad Monachos of Evagrius Ponticus: Its Structure and a Select Commentary* (Rome: Studia Anselmiana, 1991), p. 13.
77. PG 90, p. 980. Maximus, *The Four Centuries on Charity*, Century 1.83, 2.8, quoting Colossians 3.5, also Century 2.8, PG 90, p. 985.
78. PG 90, p. 980. Maximus, *The Four Centuries on Charity*, Century 1.85.
79. Evagrius, *Centuries* 3.27 (see note 28 above); Cassian, *Conferences* 1.18 (see note 30 above). For further references see Lampe, *A Patristic Greek Lexicon*, p. 38.
80. PG 90, p. 1012. Maximus, *The Four Centuries on Charity*, Century 2.85, p. 170.
81. PG 90, p. 1045. Maximus, *The Four Centuries on Charity*, Century 3.94.
82. PG 90, p. 1045D. Maximus, *The Four Centuries on Charity*, Century 3.97: Δεχόμενος ὁ νοῦς τὰ τῶν πραγμάτων νοήματα, πρὸς ἕκαστον νόημα μετασχηματίζεσθαι πέφυχε. Θεωρῶν δὲ ταῦτα πνευματικῶς, πρὸς ἕκαστον θεώρημα ποικίλως μεταμορφοῦσθαι. Ἐν δὲ θεῷ γενόμενος, ἄμορφος πάντῃ καὶ ασχημάτιστος γίνεται. Τὸν γὰρ μονοειδῆ θεωρῶν, μονοειδὴς γίνεται καὶ ὅλος φωτοειδής.
83. Maximus, *Liber Asceticus*, p. 49. *The Ascetic Life*, p. 116.
84. Chadwick, *John Cassian*, pp. 84–5.
85. Evagrius, *De Oratione* 70. Reference from Chadwick, *John Cassian*, p. 85.
86. PG 40, p. 1244. Evagrius, *Capita Practica ad Anatolium* 70. Reference from Chadwick, *John Cassian*, p. 85. Evagrius was so concerned about the light perceived in interiority that he visited a holy father to ask about it. The father claimed not to know its source, although the Orthodox view came to be that the light was from God shining upon the *nous*.
87. Evagrius, 'Prayer', Sinkewicz, *Evagrius of Pontus*, p. 194. Chadwick observes that *ecstasis* is seldom used by the fathers, although the term is implied in Cassian's Latin counterpart of *excessus mentis*; Chadwick, *John Cassian*, p. 85.
88. Paul M. Blowers, *Exegesis and Spiritual Pedagogy in Maximus the Confessor: An Investigation of the* Questiones ad Thalassium (Notre Dame: University of Notre Dame Press, 1991), p. 16.
89. PG 91, p. 1031–1418, pp. 1285C–88A. Maximus, *Ambigua* 33; see Polycarp Sherwood, *The Earlier Ambigua of St. Maximus the Confessor* (Rome: Studia Anselmiana, 1955), p. 52; Thunberg, *Microcosm and Mediator*, pp. 80–84, 418–22.
90. Blowers, *Exegesis and Spiritual Pedagogy*, p. 146.
91. On the five forms of mediation in Maximus, between the sexes, between paradise and the world, between heaven and earth, between the sensible and intelligible and between God and creation, see Thunberg, *Microcosm and Mediator*, chapter 6. For a summary see Thunberg, *Man and Cosmos*, pp. 80–91.
92. Maximus develops his ecclesiology in the *Mystagogia*, PG 91, pp. 657–718. See von Balthasar, *Liturgie Cosmique*, pp. 243–9; Thunberg, *Man and Cosmos*, pp. 116–29.
93. Thunberg, *Man and Cosmos*, pp. 73–4.
94. Larchet, *Maxime le Confesseur*, p. 189.
95. Maximus, *Mystagogia* chapter 1, quoted in Thunberg, *Man and Cosmos*, pp. 117–18.

96. Derek Krueger, 'Writing and the Liturgy of Memory in Gregory of Nyssa's *Life of Macrina*', *Journal of Eastern Christian Studies* vol. 8, no. 4, 2000, pp. 483–510.
97. PG 90, p. 1104AB. Century 1.53–54. Maximus, *Theological and Economic Centuries*, quoted in Thunberg, *Man and Cosmos*, p. 63.
98. Vööbus, *History of Asceticism* vol. II, p. 98.
99. In a different context, Stanley Hauerwas expresses this well: 'To become virtuous one must subject oneself to a master, become initiated into the moral life, and undergo a transformation', in S. Hauerwas, *The Hauerwas Reader*, John Berkman and M. Cartwright (eds.) (Durham: Duke University Press, 2001), p. 529.
100. Lampe, *A Patristic Greek Lexicon*, pp. 2, 364–5.
101. Blowers, *Exegesis and Spiritual Pedagogy*, p. 3.
102. See Blowers, *Exegesis and Spiritual Pedagogy*, chapter 1. Hauserr 'Centuries' in *Dictionnaire de Spiritualité* (DDS). An immediate precursor of this dialogic form is Evagrius, who asks his teacher how he may be saved (Amélineau, *Les Vertus de Notre Père*, pp. 118–202). This anecdote is reflected in Maximus' text.
103. Meyer, *Palladius*, p. 21.
104. Quoted in Henri Crouzel, *Origen*, trs. A. S. Worrall (Edinburgh: T & T Clark, 1989), p. 25.
105. Quoted in Crouzel, *Origen*, p. 26.
106. Cassian, *Conferences* 2.11, Luibheid translation pp. 68–70 (see note 74 above). Also in Nikodimus, *The Philokalia* vol. I, ed. and trs. G. E. H. Palmer, Philip Sherrard and Kalistos Ware (London and Boston: Faber and Faber, 1979), pp. 94–108.
107. Neilos, *Ascetic Discourse* in Palmer et al. (eds.), *The Philokalia* vol. I, pp. 215–18.
108. Neilos, *Ascetic Discourse*, p. 220.
109. On obedience in Cassian see Chadwick, *John Cassian*, pp. 60–62.
110. Chadwick, *John Cassian*, p. 151; Blowers, *Exegesis and Spiritual Pedagogy*, p. 71.
111. See the important study by Elizabeth A. Clark, *Reading Renunciation: Asceticism and Scripture in Early Christianity* (Princeton University Press, 1999); Crouzel, *Origen*, chapter 4; J. Daniélou, 'Origène comme Exégète de la Bible', *Studia Patristica* 1, 1957, pp. 280–90; H. de Lubac, *Histoire et Esprit: L'intelligence et l'Ecriture d'après Origène.* (Paris: Aubier, 1950); T. W. Gusie, 'Patristic Hermeneutics and the Meaning of Tradition', *Theological Studies* vol. 32, 1971, pp. 647–58; R. P. C. Hanson, *Allegory and Event: A Study of the Sources and Significance of Origen's Interpretation of Scripture* (London: SCM, 1959); M. Harl, 'Origène et les Interprétations Patristiques Grecques de l'Obscurité Biblique', *Vigiliae Christianae* vol. 36, 1982, pp. 334–71; E. B. Oikonomou, 'Hermeneutical Logotypes: The Basic Elements of Patristic Hermeneutics', *Theologia* vol. 53, 1982, pp. 627–71.
112. Blowers, *Exegesis and Spiritual Pedagogy*, pp. 37–42, 71.
113. Maximus, *Liber Asceticus*, p. 41. *The Ascetic Life*, 19, p. 114.
114. PG 90, p. 989. Maximus, *The Four Centuries on Charity*, Century 2.19, p. 156.

115. PG 90, p. 1001. Maximus, *The Four Centuries on Charity*, Century 2.54, p. 164.
116. PG 90, p. 262. Maximus, *The Four Centuries on Charity*, Century 2.62, p. 165.
117. PG 90, p. 985. Maximus, *The Four Centuries on Charity*, Century 2.6, p. 153.
118. Maximus, *Liber Asceticus*, p. 53. *The Ascetic Life*, 27, p. 118: Ἐπειδὴ οὐκ ἐστὶ φόβος θεοῦ ἀπέναντι τῶν ὀφθαλμῶν ἡμῶν.
119. Maximus, *Liber Asceticus*, p. 55. *The Ascetic Life*, 27, p. 119.
120. Maximus, *Liber Asceticus*, p. 77. *The Ascetic Life*, 34, p. 124: 'For this reason we have become instead of a temple of God, a place of business; and instead of a house of prayer, a den of thieves.' Καὶ διὰ τούτου γεγόναμεν ἀντὶ ναοῦ θεοῦ, οἶκος ἐμπορίου. Καὶ ἀντί οἴκου προσευχῆς, σπήλαιον ληστῶν.
121. Maximus, *Liber Asceticus*, p. 101. *The Ascetic Life*, 40, p. 130.
122. Maximus, *Liber Asceticus*, pp. 120–21. *The Ascetic Life*, 45, p. 135.
123. Lampe, *A Patristic Greek Lexicon*, pp. 855–6.
124. Blowers, *Exegesis and Spiritual Pedagogy*, p. 133.
125. Maximus, *Liber Asceticus*, p. 11. *The Ascetic Life*, 4, p. 105: Μιμηταί μου γίνεσθε, καθὼς κἀγὼ χριστοῦ. The theme of the imitation of Christ was to become particularly important in late medieval Western Christianity. See Giles Constable, *Three Studies in Medieval Religious and Social Thought* (Cambridge University Press, 1995), p. 143–248.
126. Maximus, *Liber Asceticus*, p. 31. *The Ascetic Life*, 14, p. 111: ἀλλὰ πρός τὰς ἀρχάς, πρὸς τὰς ἐζουσίας.
127. Maximus, *Liber Asceticus*, p. 31. *The Ascetic Life*, 14, p. 111.
128. Maximus, *Liber Asceticus*, p. 53. *The Ascetic Life*, 26, p. 117.
129. Maximus, *Liber Asceticus*, p. 31. *The Ascetic Life*, 13, p. 111.
130. PG 90, pp. 980–81. Maximus, *The Four Centuries on Charity*, Century 1.84–88, pp. 149–50.
131. Maximus, *Liber Asceticus*, p. 121. *The Ascetic Life*, 45, p. 135.
132. Thunberg, *Microcosm and Mediator*, pp. 355–6. Another term used for contemplation and vision is *thea*, a term which implies the angels' contemplation according to their capacity or place in the hierarchy, clearly contemplation with a strongly cosmological sense. See Pseudo-Dionysius, *Ecclesiastical Hierarchy* (*de ecclesiastica hierarchia* 4.3.5 M. 3. 480b). For further references see Lampe, *A Patristic Greek Lexicon*, p. 615.
133. John Behr, *Asceticism and Anthropology in Irenaeus and Clement* (Oxford University Press, 2000), pp. 195–6.
134. Thunberg, *Microcosm and Mediator*, pp. 360–61. For the argument with which Thunberg disagrees, that Maximus follows Evagrius, see M. Viller, 'Aux sources de la spiritualité de S. Maxime. Les oeuvres d'Evagre le Pontique', *Revue d'Ascetique et de Mystique* vol. 11, 1930, pp. 156–84; 239–68; 331–6.

CHAPTER 7

# *The asceticism of love and wisdom*

*Come del suo voler li angeli tuoi*
*fan sacrificio a te, cantando osanna,*
*cosi facciano li uomini de' suoi.*
And as your angels make a sacrifice
of their wills unto you, singing hosanna,
so may we men make sacrifice of ours.

Dante *Purgatorio* 11.10–12.[1]

For Lent. No puddings on Sundays. No tea except if to keep me awake and then without sugar.

Gerard Manley Hopkins[2]

In the vibrant and colourful world of medieval Latin Christianity, asceticism takes on a role of great importance within the spectrum of religious practice and in people's devotional lives. Before the eleventh century, fully ordained monastics may have comprised less than half of one per cent of the population,[3] and yet the monasteries became centres of stability in the unstable and conflictual politics of Christendom and central to an ideology that simultaneously gave positive value to this world and looked to the purified world to come. While the laity undertook some forms of asceticism at times of pilgrimage, penance and during the liturgical year, it is with the monastics that it becomes intensified and a defining feature of the self. Patterns of prayer and religious reading develop the inner life of the monastic along with an outer life of adherence to rules and performance of the liturgy. The general aim, as with the Eastern tradition, is the development of the monastic's vision and moral quality whose summit is the Kingdom of God or the indwelling of the kingdom in the ascetic body. But the way this is envisaged is particular to the Western tradition, a tradition formed by the central authority of the Church and a strong intellectual tradition out of which the secular universities were to develop. Again we shall see here how asceticism must be understood in the particularity of the tradition of its occurrence and in positive terms as the gaining of greater meaning subjectively appropriated. The ascetic self is formed through creating a particular kind of inner and outer life in conformity to text and tradition. This is clearly articulated in the work of the ascetic theologian Peter Damian, who understands the centrality of tradition in the formation of the self. Later centuries witnessed the monastic institutions being challenged and questioned by religious movements stemming from a more popular social base and the development of an asceticism that reconfigures the collective memory of tradition in a different way. This can be seen in the Beguines and to some extent the Dominicans, who are within, and wish to remain within, the Church, but whose ascetic vision posed a threat to it. An example here is Margarete Porete, a Beguine whose vision of the ascetic self caused so great a clash that it ended in her death.

## MONASTICISM IN THE WEST

The translation of the ascetic ideal practised in the Egyptian desert to the institution of monasticism in the Latin West is a story of the reconfiguration of that ideal and the development of a complex relationship with feudal society, sovereign power and subjectivity. Egyptian monasticism began to make an impact in the West in the fourth century CE with the founding of a formal ascetic community in Italy by Bishop Eusebius of Vercelli (344–71). By the end of that century there were monasteries for men and women at a number of places in Italy, and by the sixth century there were monasteries throughout the peninsula. By the end of the sixth century there were 220 monasteries in Gaul, and a further 320 by the end of the seventh.[4] A pattern of monasticism develops in the Middle Ages of the establishing of an institution followed by its reform once it is perceived to be lifeless. We see this with the Benedictine order founded in the seventh century, followed by the reform of the Cluny monastery in Burgundy, followed by the Cistercian reform in the twelfth century, followed by the Friars in the twelfth and thirteenth, through to the Reformation.[5] Different emphases in manual work, scriptural study, liturgy and prayer accompany these phases. Manual labour constituted part of monastic training in the early Middle Ages to counteract idleness. This had the effect of developing wealth (the very wealth the movement rejected),[6] but by the eleventh century increased liturgical responsibilities, particularly in the Cluniac order where the daily office took up most of the day, led to a decline in monastic participation in work. Labour functions were taken over by the laity (*familia*) and lay monks (*conversi*).[7] The Cistercian reforms of the twelfth century stressed simplicity, poverty, charity and, again, manual labour.[8]

The Carthusian order founded by St Bruno in Cologne in the late eleventh century re-instituted the eremitical life, but it was the two orders of Friars, the Franciscans and Dominicans, that became the most important monastic and Church reform movements in the thirteenth century. A wide variety of monastic institutions therefore developed with, on the one hand, highly liturgical monasteries focussing on the performance of elaborate liturgies for intercession (notably with the development of the idea of purgatory)[9] and evoking the protection of a saint, and on the other, smaller, ascetic communities, such as those of women in Gaul.[10]

Texts are of key importance in the development of monasticism, notably the *Life of St. Antony* (*Vita Antonii*), St. Benedict of Nursia's written monastic rule and the work of John Cassian, who sets the tone for the future developments of ascetic theology and institutions. Cassian was a Latin speaker who knew Greek and spent time at monasteries in Bethlehem and Egypt, fleeing Egypt around 400 owing to the Origenist controversy to Constantinople and thence to Rome. From there he settled in Marseilles, where he founded two monasteries around 415 and composed two important works, the *Institutes of the Coenobites* (*De coenobiorum institutis*), about the practices of monks living in a community, and the *Conferences* (*Collationes*), discourses and stories of Eastern monks whom he had met.[11] Cassian is suffused with the teachings of his master Evagrius, although careful to avoid any mention of his name or that of Origen in the light of anti-Origenist hostility. His intention was to establish the monastic ethos of the desert and to allow the development of a life of prayer that would culminate in the fullness of time with the monk's realisation of the Kingdom of God. By the Reformation monasticism had undergone such changes as to be wholly different from the earliest, cenobitical communities, but some succeeded in maintaining the spirit of Cassian and through him of Evagrius.

Once out of the desert, monasticism became intimately linked to structures of political power. From what Dunn has called a 'transformative asceticism' characteristic of the Egyptian desert, with its emphasis on transcendence, self-mastery and seeking union with God, asceticism articulated through monasticism became identified with land-owners and the interests of royalty and aristocracy.[12] Monasticism became embedded within a social matrix that reflected a feudal hierarchy while also fostering a transnational identity and intellectual community that could, and sometimes did, critique the social order. But the ideals of transcendence, self-mastery and union are not lost, and even given the alignment of monasticism with the Church, the monasteries must be understood not only as structures to maintain

Church power but primarily as structures to facilitate the development of a transformative, religious interiority. This interiority is particular to the tradition and is formed through private prayer, reading and meditation, along with the overtly liturgical nature of much Western monasticism with its emphasis on monastic rules. Indeed, the development of monastic rules enabled a common pattern of the ascetic life to be established that was theologically acceptable to Western bishops and theologians and provided a structure internalised by the monastic: a way to accomplish the tradition's goal or telos. Indeed, we might view monasticism as a structure or institution to facilitate the collective memory of tradition and to foster an interior transformation. This is not to depoliticise monasticism – the institution was closely connected with the Catholic Church, monasteries embroiled in particular struggles for power and monastic theologians often censured – but it is to recognise the transformative and transcendent intention of the institution. The entire edifice of medieval monasticism can be seen in terms of the cultivation of collective memory, an architecture for thinking which provided cognitive maps for meditation and a graded structure for the realisation of Christian wisdom, for remembering its future goal, as Carruthers has shown.[13]

Monasticism fostered both an inner life comprising silence, prayer, the cultivation of detachment and religious reading, and an outer life comprising the performance of liturgy, work and the development of ethical behaviour that linked the two. The ascetic self is created through the integration of both inner and outer aspects of the ascetic path, fostered over long periods until the self is transformed in tradition-specific ways. The habit inscribes the body with the text and, through an act of will, the ascetic self loses that will in order that the Kingdom of Heaven should become the indwelling truth of the ascetic's being.

## SACRED MEMORY AND THE ASCETIC PATH

Cassian uses the term *scopos* for the goal of ascetic activity, a term lifted from the Greek *skophos*, where it means 'end', 'aim' or 'object'.[14] The *scopos* is the 'destination and goal . . . the proper end'[15] of the ascetic's path, which he describes as eternal life through purity of heart.[16] The ascetic moves along the path to the goal within the institutions of the Church and monasticism. Moving along the ascetic path is a kind of remembrance of the future.[17] Like other walks of life, the ascetic's vocation has a purpose, and Cassian in the character of Abba Moses likens this path to the practice of an art or skill that is similarly teleological. As the farmer suffers inclement weather as he cuts through the earth or clears the ground, says Cassian, and as the trader risks the hazards of the sea without complaint, so the ascetic is not wearied by the hunger of fasting or by the fatigue of vigils. He is not frightened by loneliness and is nourished by reading and endless meditation upon scripture.[18] As those skilled in archery fire their arrows against small, painted shields, so the ascetic aims at a heavenly reward through purity of heart, forgetting 'the sins of the earlier man' and driving himself 'toward the goal of a heavenly reward'.[19]

This analogy of the ascetic path with skill indicates that for Cassian asceticism is a kind of wisdom, a skilful way of behaving and thinking that pulls the ascetic, in Cassian's phrase, towards a 'proper end'. The attraction of the ascetic towards his or her proper end is the wisdom of asceticism: a tradition-specific yet transformational wisdom in which the ascetic path is a kind of meditation. The term *skopos* is used in rhetoric to indicate the goal towards which the mind is drawn via a particular route or *ductus*. The *ductus* is the way in which a composition guides a person to a goal of understanding as, in a parallel way, the ascetic path guides a person to the goal. Carruthers shows how this notion is used by Augustine and others to indicate the process of meditation and an indication of finding a way, of conversion, and moving in a series of linked stages from one to the other.[20] Through a 'conversion' and turning away from a past life, and for Cassian from early memories which distract the ascetic, the ascetic cultivates 'spiritual memory' (*spiritatis memoria*) or 'sacred memory' (*sancta memoria*) by means of the life of prayer, reading and liturgy.[21] The whole orientation of monasticism is towards the cultivation of an interiority as a *ductus* leading to the ascetic goal, and we might see the edifice of the monastic institution – as well as the monastery itself – as a way of cultivating the memory of tradition, of cultivating a 'spiritual memory' that transforms the disorder of the world into the order of the path, the randomness of events into the ordered sequence of liturgical and meditational patterns.

This ascetic path is a way of repetition, namely exercises performed in a repeated sequence over and over again so as to internalise the cultural habit. It is the discipline of mental imagery or visualisation and the repeated recollection of the collective memory, as Carruthers has shown, that became so central to medieval monasticism. Sacred memory is the collective memory of tradition, the internalisation of patterns of thought, speech and action intended to replace the everyday, 'fallen' self. Adopting the model of cognition from Evagrius which we have also found in Maximus, Cassian says that the mind 'veers hither and thither', the prisoner of whatever happens to strike it.[22] It is forever wandering and tossed around as if drunk, but through finding a formula and hanging on to the thought of God, we in time reach perfection.[23] As with Evagrius and Maximus there is an implicitly Aristotelian model implied by the idea that the mind is purified by the purity of its object (pp. 156–7), although this idea was not to reach its greatest articulation until the later Middle Ages with Thomas Aquinas (1225–74), for whom the cognising entity has the form within it of the thing cognised.[24] But the idea that the mind can be purified through repeated practice, through penance, is implicit in the idea of the ascetic path. While *memoria* as the memory of tradition, the internalisation of the virtues, is crucial there is also 'bad' or personal memory encompassed by the term *curiositas*, which has the implication of a crowded, wandering and aimless mind (a tendency that Cassian refers to as *fornicatio*) that runs counter to achieving the ascetic *scopos*.[25] As we shall see presently, Peter Damian regards personal memory as an enemy of the ascetic, used by the devil as a distraction from the path.

The memory of tradition, which is simultaneously the remembrance and imitation of Christ, and which replaces personal memory, is cultivated as an act of will through developing an interiority to overcome the vices and to attain contemplation of God. Cassian is an early example in the West of the need to train the will in obedience to monastic structure to overcome the vices along with the development of a life of prayer. It is Cassian who introduces to the Latin tradition the eight principal vices from Evagrius, along with *apatheia* or detachment, which he renders as 'purity of heart' (*puritas cordis*). These ideas are set within a simplified version of Evagrius' teachings, and in *Conference* 15 they are expressed through the discourse of the Abba Nestorius, who speaks of the monk's path of spiritual knowledge (*de spirituali scientia*) divided into practical and theoretical aspects. By practical knowledge or 'active discipline' (*actualis disciplina*) Cassian means the perfection of morality by rooting out the eight vices of gluttony, lust, avarice, anger, sadness, accidie, vainglory and pride.[26] With Pope Gregory (540–604) these enter Western consciousness as the famous seven deadly sins in his *Morals on Job* (he integrates accidie with 'sadness' (*tristitia*)). The vices, furthermore, become identified with the term 'sin' (*peccatum*) that prevailed after the thirteenth century.

By theoretical knowledge or contemplation (*contemplatio*) Cassian refers to several related things: the contemplation of scripture, the contemplation of God[27] and prayer. These are all related, in that contemplation of scripture is indeed contemplation of God articulated through speech, and prayer is similarly contemplation of God. Cassian records the teachings of the Blessed

Isaac that the whole purpose of the monk is uninterrupted dedication to prayer achieved through unloading of the vices and removal of concern for the body. Gradually the soul rises to contemplation of God.[28] Cassian's chapters on prayer in the *Conferences* make clear its centrality in the monk's life. Prayer becomes internalised, particularly the unceasing repetition of the formula taken from the Psalms (Psalm 69.2) 'Come to my help, O God; Lord hurry to my rescue', and is a device likened to a breastplate for keeping away the onslaught of demons.[29] Evagrius' cosmological doctrine of the transformation of the body through contemplative prayer becomes refocussed in Cassian to emphasise the moral development of the monk and his religious reading.

Religious reading, the internalisation of scripture, is crucial for the performance of the memory of tradition. Through religious reading, which means in the medieval context, as Carruthers has extensively demonstrated, memorisation of scripture and contemplation, rumination on its meaning, the monk appropriates the tradition in subjectivity. Through religious reading, along with other liturgical practices, the body becomes the text. It is to these transformative structures that we must turn, showing how the ascetic self is formed through ascetic practices that internalise the tradition and entextualise the body. Of particular importance here are religious reading and contemplation, prayer, liturgy and more overt ascetic penance constrained by monastic rule. By way of illustration let us examine these themes in that most orthodox of ascetics, Peter Damian.

## THE ASCETIC THEOLOGY OF PETER DAMIAN

Peter Damian (1007–1072) was born in Ravenna to a poor family but became a very talented Latin scholar, poet, administrator and Church reformer. He was a monk at Fonte Avellana, a monastery influenced by St Romuald (ca 950–1027), the founder of Camaldoli and of whom Damian wrote a *Life* (*Vita Romuald*), and he advocated Christianity as a life of solitude and asceticism. His demands were high on the eremitical monks who had to perform long, liturgical observances and heavy fasts. There were twenty hermits at Fonte Avellana, living alone or two in a cell, along with fifteen lay brothers.[30] He endeavoured to equip the monastery with a library, to improve the Church and to generally support the monastic hermits by the work of laity and lay brothers.[31] For Damian the monastery was a gateway to the solitary life of the hermit, although there is a wistful dimension to this aspiration, as his talents meant that he was in demand for his leadership and his administrative and networking skills. In 1043 he was made prior of Fonte Avellana and remained in that position until his death in 1072. From 1057, with great reluctance and under threat of excommunication by the Pope, he was appointed Cardinal Bishop of Ostia, after which he was further sent on diplomatic missions to Milan, Cluny, Frankfurt and other places. He was a prolific writer and composed homilies, sermons and letters explicating his views on asceticism, sexuality (particularly a treatise against homosexuality amongst the clergy), and clerical institutions and appointments.[32] While some of his writing has a quality of severity or austerity, Damian's human qualities come across in his many letters. Here we have a sense of a compassionate man, highly skilled in interpersonal communication, and aware of his own anger and desire.[33] Bernard McGinn observes that along with attacks on clerical vices he was deeply concerned with 'a tenderness of devotional language and a concern for the values of the contemplative order'.[34] Forced to lead an active life in the service of the Church, Peter longed for the solitude of his monastery, to which he would retreat between missions. He died at Faenza, where his body is buried in the cathedral.

Damian left behind a wide range of writings, including 170 letters, 53 sermons, poetry, 7 lives of saints, and treatises,[35] some of which are concerned explicitly with the ascetical life, especially the small works (*opuscula*) 'On the Perfection of Monks' (*De perfectione monachorum.* Opus 13) and 'On the Order of Hermits' (*De ordine eremitarum.* Opus 14).[36] One of his most famous works is *The Book of the 'Lord Be With You' (Liber Dominus Vobiscum.* Opus 11),[37] although *The Book of Gomorrah* (*Liber Gomorrhianus.* Opus 7), an invective against homosexuality, has also been highlighted as an important text,[38] leading some to suspect that Damian was a repressed homosexual;[39] none of the other works, such as the letters, suggest this, however. In his writing Peter drew on a number of sources and, indeed, gathered a library at Fonte Avellana that included Palladius' *Lausiac History*, Sulpicius Severus' *Life of St. Martin of Tours* and Cassian's *Conferences.*[40] The ascetic life Damian advocates is pervaded by scripture, the extensive use of which is a notable feature of his sermons.[41] These texts form an integral part of ascetic practice, and Damian quotes them not just to lend authority and force to his statements but to constantly reinforce an ascetical theology that would be underlined in the day-to-day reading and liturgical use of the texts. Damian is keen to locate his ascetical theology in Church tradition, and in his writing he not only uses scripture (he is a biblical exegete) and the writings of the fathers but also canon law to support his statements, although he only refers to a general *corpus canonum* rather than to specific collections.[42]

Damian's anthropology offers an astute account of the human condition within the framework of his Latin Christianity. He assumes the Christian narrative of human nature being flawed owing to sin and the necessity of restoration to a state of grace and reconciliation with God. Inheriting the Evagrian tradition through Cassian, Damian refers, although inconsistently, to seven cardinal vices – pride (*superbia*), avarice (*avaricia*), vainglory (*vana gloria*), anger (*ira*), envy (*invidia*), lust (*luxuria*) and sadness (*tristicia*)[43] – as the immediate causes of sin (again seven – adultery, murder, theft, perjury, false witness, rape and blasphemy).[44] But it is pride, anger and desire as the main forces driving a human being that need to be overcome in ascetic striving. Our wills are distorted by pride and anger that are so deep within us as to be foundational to human nature. Damian wrote a treatise on anger, and he is here firmly within the tradition of the desert which regarded anger as the fundamental problem to be overcome through ascetic practice.

But for Damian it is sexual desire that is the strongest force to be subdued.[45] Indeed, he saw this as one of the principal problems among the clergy of his day who, he claimed with characteristic vehemence, for a few moments' pleasure would burn in eternity 'in the flames of vengeance' (*comburantur igne vindictae*).[46] His treatise written to Pope Leo IX (1049–54), *The Book of Gomorrah*, against homosexual practices among the clergy, seems to have been in response to an actual problem within his local community. Damian offers a classification of sexual practices that he regards as sins and is highly critical of priests who, having broken the strict rules on sexual behaviour, then confess to each other 'the wickedness' they committed together (*communem nequitiam confitetur*).[47] Damian is critical of canon law that prescribed too lenient a penance and suggests a penance of ten years rather than two for what today might seem mild infringements. The Pope responded, supporting Damian's enthusiasm yet wishing to moderate his suggestion that priests who violate sexual morality should suffer deposition, saying that the Church needed to be more humane (*humaniores*) and making clear that he should not pursue the matter further. Damian's vehemence is perhaps surprising given his clear understanding of the distinction between priestly office and sinful person,[48] that the function of the priest as a vehicle for grace within the Church is not affected by the nature of the human being who performs that role. Clearly, sexual desire was the main biological drive to be overcome for Damian. Whether Damian himself was heterosexual or homosexual is beside the point, but what is important is his astute and honest account of human nature and the overriding conviction that human nature can be overcome through ascetic striving and the constant subjecting oneself to the structures of tradition. Even as an old man he recognised the power of desire in himself and speaks of guarding his eyes from beautiful and attractive faces as he would guard children from fire, ruefully observing that while it is so hard to remember scriptural verses, beauty 'seen but once does not leave the memory'.[49] In many of his writings he advises young monks about the dangers of desire and the virtue of chastity, without which we cannot see God.[50]

While sexual and gendered identity is so central to our sense of subjectivity, for Damian it is an index of fallen human nature. In this he is in accordance with Jerome (331–419), for whom sexuality was an ever-present force even in the desert, resisting all acts of will to drive it out.[51] Behind this antipathy to sexuality is a whole history of Christian asceticism from the early Christian centuries that extolled virginity and an attitude that saw marriage either for procreation or as a buffer against lust and sin.[52] Damian's world of celibate priests, monks and nuns is a direct development of these earlier ideas and practices,[53] but the high standards Damian sought to achieve in personal continence could not be expected of the wider, non-monastic population. Indeed, there is an elitist dimension to Damian's account in the sense that few could achieve the perfection of the eremitical life, but his account is uncompromising in its insistence on monastic virtue and his critique of the clerical practices of his day. In many ways, this is a simple vision that lacks the theological sophistication of the fathers and later mystical theologians. On the one hand there is a life dominated by what he regarded as vice, the common drives of biological nature, and on the other there is a life dominated by virtue, the life instructed by the Church and revealed in scripture. The former is easy and attractive, the latter is a hard, lifelong struggle but with great reward. It is possible to achieve a redeemed subjectivity through ascetic striving.

One way Damian expresses this fundamental division is by a reference to *Deuteronomy* (21.15–17):

> If a man have two wives, one beloved and one hated, and they have borne him children, both the beloved and the hated, and if the first-born son be hers that was hated, then it shall be when he maketh his sons to inherit that which he hath, that he may not make the son of the beloved first-born before the son of the hated which is indeed the first-born: but he shall acknowledge the son of the hated for the first-born, by giving him a double portion of all that he hath; for he is the beginning of his strength; the right of the first-born is his.

Damian interprets this passage to mean that the two wives are respectively virtue (*virtus*) and pleasure (*voluptas*). Virtue is the hated wife who 'causes men to travel a narrow and painful road and always sets before them hard and bitter things', whereas pleasure is the loved wife who allures the husband ('the feeble soul') to seductive delights. The latter pertains to this life, the former leads to everlasting glory.[54] While the androcentric and implicitly misogynistic language offends modern ears, the analogy contains the simple structure of Damian's thought.[55] The path to God is hard but 'the soul may be lifted up by the grace of contemplation to search for the vision of truth' (*per gratiam contemplationis transferatur animus ad indagandam speciem veritatis*). This vision is gained through struggle with the vices that pull the ascetic down. To attain rest and 'enter the king's palace' we must cross the forecourt outside and stretch our sinews 'in many labours and strivings'.[56]

This 'labour and strife' (*labores et certamina*) refers to a hard, ascetical regime undertaken alone as a hermit in a cell with constant self-monitoring against the vices. Damian sees asceticism as a path through mortification to contemplation, although undoubtedly his writings emphasise the former. The monk who renounces the world must 'unlearn' its ways, and Damian exhorts him to:

> love fasting and cherish his lack of the needs of life; let him fly from the sight of men and bind himself by a severe silence; let him withdraw from all outward affairs and keep watch over his lips, so that they do not engage in idle conversation. Let him seek the secret places of his mind where he may strive with all his might to see the face of his Creator; let him long for the grace of tears and entreat his God earnestly for them in daily prayers.[57]

For Damian, mortification must be seen within a spectrum of religious observance and in the context of the narrative of the ascetic's path. This path comprises turning towards God or conversion (*conversio*), in which the soul is at first bathed in the warmth of divine love but which is followed by a life of struggle against temptation, a struggle assisted by adhering to the ten commandments and practising Christian virtue. Confession is also vital in the ongoing struggle against sin and for expiation of past deeds committed by thought, word and action.[58] But it is the life of penance that is the key to holiness and provides atonement for past sins. As Christ suffered for the sins of the world, so the monastic should suffer in imitation. As Christ hung on the cross, so the monastics should 'crucify themselves through the practice of self-denial'.[59] Through penance the monk internalises the suffering of Christ and makes his body conform to the doctrines of the Church. To suffer voluntarily is to participate in the suffering of Christ and to reconstitute the fundamental structures of Christian teaching within the self. Ascetic penance both represses the vices and participates in Christ as the exemplum of Christian virtue.

But ascetic observances are always constrained by the monastic rule. One text that Damian draws on, and which provides the backdrop to all medieval monasticism, is the Rule of St. Benedict (d. ca 547), which became the supreme authority in monastic communities. There were other, earlier rules, notably those by Augustine, Basil and the *Rule of the Four Fathers*, which Benedict knew, but it was Benedict's text that was to provide the template for the monastic life.[60] It opens with the command to listen and obey and a discussion of the merits of different types of monk. For Benedict, cenobites living in community can more easily develop the virtues of obedience to the abbot, silence and humility. Damian's monastery was fundamentally Benedictine but with the additional austerities drawn from the teachings of St Romuald.[61] The more difficult eremitical lifestyle must be based on the cenobitic.[62] Damian is happy with this, although he sees the hermit as the height of monastic achievement. Part of his enthusiasm for austere mortification was no doubt fuelled by what he perceived to be lax and even corrupt practices among some monastics of his day. But for Damian the ideal pattern was for a man (he only occasionally refers to female monastics) to become a monk and then progress to becoming a hermit, although sometimes it is better to miss out the cenobitic stage altogether and avoid what Damian perceived to be corruption in the monastic orders.[63]

Mortification has two effects: the rooting out of desire and penance for sin. Mortification helps the wise man curb the vices:

> with such anxious care (*vehementer intentus*) that he binds with the girdle of perfect mortification his loins and his kidneys, his belly and his flanks. He achieves this when the greedy gullet is kept in check; when the wanton tongue is compelled to be silent; when the ears are shut to scandal-mongering; when the eyes are forbidden to look upon unlawful things.[64]

The ascetic guards the flesh and controls his subjectivity through monitoring and checking hunger, silencing the tongue, closing the ears to scandal, closing the eyes to what is forbidden by monastic law, controlling the limbs and guarding the heart against envy, pride, anger, grief or pleasure.[65] Mortification helps not only in this 'care of the self', this guarding against sin, but more significantly also in reparation for the sin of one's former (premonastic) life. The degree of suffering in this life is related to the joy of the life to come, and conversely a life of pleasure here indicates a life of suffering hereafter: the physician God treats leniently those whom he knows to be worthy of eternal death.[66] Intentional suffering is penance for sin. Sometimes it would be regarded as sufficient penance for former sins if a monk simply followed the monastic rule, but for Damian this is not enough. He recounts how a monk from another monastery once told him of the sins he had committed as a layman, but the lord abbot had imposed upon him no tariff other than the usual monastic practice. In Damian's eyes this is to seriously mislead the brother who had hardly begun to do penance for his past.[67] Indeed, there is a direct correlation between the degree of sin in one's past and the degree of suffering that needs to be undergone. The apostles, for example, experienced different fates according to their former lives. St Paul experienced more suffering than others because of his involvement in the martyrdom of Stephen, whereas John in choosing lifelong virginity died in peace.[68]

## *Mortification*

The most important mortificatory practices for Damian are fasting, flagellation and silence, although he encouraged others, such as prostrations (*metanea*) and blows with the hands on the floor (*palmate*), subject to the zeal of each person.[69] The startling practice of self-flagellation seems to have been a common and popular practice, although not uncontroversial. Pope Stephen IX discouraged it but Damian wrote a tract 'In Praise of Flagellation' (*De laude flagellorum*)[70] justifying it, although he did warn against excess and decreed that the practice be done only during the recitation of forty psalms in any one day and no more.[71] Some monks recited the complete Psalter once or even twice while scourging themselves the whole time, an excess that Damian, though admiring their zeal, thought needed to be limited. What is significant here is that flagellation is not simply self-harm outside of any context but is performed as ritual, integrated into the daily practice of the monks on a voluntary basis, although presumably not in a perfunctory way. Through performing the practice while reciting the Psalter or part of the Psalter it becomes integrated into the liturgical day and part of the formation or shaping of the self in accordance with tradition. This conformity to tradition is the imitation of Christ: as Christ was scourged and suffered, so the ascetic scourges and suffers himself. In flagellation the self sits in judgement 'in its inmost being' on its past actions. In his heart, the monk appoints himself as a judge, in his body he appears as the defendant, and his hands play the role of executioner. The Lord rejoices at the sight of the penitent, and the demons flee while the angels rejoice at the conversion of the sinner. Through this act 'the human body is invisibly joined to that unique sacrifice which was offered on the altar of the cross'.[72] Flagellation or the 'discipline' is thus a more extreme form of other practices recommended by Damian to 'clear the field of weeds,' such as praying with outstretched arms in the form of a cross or making continuous genuflections while reciting the Psalter.[73] All these self-imposed sufferings participate in the action of Christ, and through them the penitent participates in the cosmic work of redemption. It is clear in *De laude flagellorum* that this extreme asceticism is set within the cosmic context of the Christian narrative in overcoming the cunning of the demons (chapter 1) and seeing the wounds of Christ which are imitated in intentional suffering as our remedy (chapter 5). Through the discipline the monk recapitulates the early penitence of Christianity, participates in the mystery of the cross and clears the debt of past sin. It becomes the bodily performance of theology, articulating a relationship of the self to the divine and the cosmos.

Likewise fasting becomes integrated into the ascetic's daily activity. Greed for food was regarded as a stronger drive for those new in the order, and through controlling this 'the fire of lust will as a result be checked' (*flamma libidinis temperetur*).[74] Damian is here drawing on an old anthropology that links greed to lust within the classification of human qualities, as we have seen with Evagrius and Maximus. Both greed and lust are subsumed under *epithumia* in the tripartite scheme of *epithumia, thumos* and *nous* (see pp. 155–6), a connection also made in the Buddhist monastic tradition. The sparse food regime of the monastery was thought to be crucial to the development of the ascetic towards the summit of contemplation. Fasting was integrated into the liturgical year. There were four periods of fasting: from the eighth day after Easter to Pentecost, from Trinity Sunday to the feast of St John the Baptist (24 June), from then until the Exaltation of the Cross (14 September), and the last from mid-September to Easter. Thus during the year there was hardly any time when a monk was not fasting. Damian's regime was strict, and the monks would fast four days of each week on bread, water and salt, taking two meals a day on Sunday, Tuesday and Thursday.[75]

Apart from fast days, the diet in Damian's monastery would be the standard, low-protein monastic fare of bread, wine and oil and seasonable fruit and vegetables. Damian's injunctions are slightly more severe than the usual Benedictine direction in the *Rules* of two cooked dishes at every meal and a third of fruit or vegetables if available. The *Rules* allow for the use of wine and reluctantly, while expressing his disapproval, Damian agreed to allow its use among his monks.[76] Damian forbade meat as part of the ascetic regime except for the sick and does not mention fowls. In a letter to an archdeacon he asks him to send the brothers fish for Christmas, which would enhance the celebration and do good to the archdeacon's deceased parents who would benefit from the monks' prayers! But Damian's strict dietary regime had a positive effect on the monks' life expectancy, which averaged sixty years as opposed to the thirty among the laity in the eleventh century.[77] But Damian urges his monks to go further and to drink muddy water rather than wine and to eat rough, bran bread rather than bread made with fine flour, especially in the early stages of their practice so that reversion to a less strict regime will then seem easy.[78]

Apart from the strong practices of fasting and voluntary flagellation, the monk undertakes other practices of poverty, such as wearing threadbare clothes, bare feet in summer and winter, little sleep, and the more subtle asceticism of unquestioning obedience to the abbot, guarding the senses through, for example, looking at the ground while going about, and silence.[79] To perform this kind of voluntary poverty is to develop humility and to cultivate a subjectivity in which Christ is at the centre of one's being, and Damian speaks of hiding the treasure that is Christ in the chamber (*exedra*) of the heart.[80] Through obedience, the self's will, by an act of will, is subjugated to the will of God expressed through the Church. This subjugation of the will and the internalisation of tradition can be particularly seen in the daily rhythms of the monks' liturgical practice.

## *Liturgy*

The monastic's entire life becomes ritualised once he, or indeed she, has entered the order. For Damian, the crown of the monastic life was the hermitage, where the monk would perform liturgical rites alone, particularly the recitation of the Psalter, although for other monasteries, notably Cluny, collective liturgical practice took up most of the day and religious life revolved around the central Christian rite, the Eucharist.[81] Damian was sent on a visit to Cluny and was impressed by the liturgical regime he found there, although he advised Abbot Hugh the Great (1049–1109) to introduce two additional fast days, a recommendation that was politely rejected.[82] At Cluny, reaching its peak around the time of Damian, liturgy and intercession were at the centre of the daily regime. Two daily Masses were the norm, two litanies, and 210 psalms were recited daily in winter, which meant that the monk spent more time in the liturgy than in his cell. Damian's regime at Fonte Avellana with its eremitical emphasis was liturgically modest and part of a broader monastic move towards a 'new monastic consciousness' in Europe[83] that emphasised moderation and simplicity. Fonte Avellana is thus part of broader monastic reforms that were beginning to take shape in the eleventh century, along with Romuald's Camaldoli, John Gualbert's Vallombrosa, and Robert's Molesme and later Cîteaux.

But Damian sees the eremitical life to be wholly integrated into the Church and its liturgical life. Through the cycles of liturgy the Church orders time and 'governs the changes of time according to her pleasure'.[84] Liturgy and the cycle of the Church year express the mystery of the Church and are more than the sum of its members: it is 'fused into a unity by the fire of the Holy Spirit' (*in unum tamen est sancti spiritus igne conflata*).[85] In *The Book of the 'Lord Be With You'* Damian discusses the phrase recited at a point in the liturgy by the priest to the congregation, 'The Lord be with you.' Some monks at the monastery had objected that in their cells they would simply be speaking to stones were they to recite this, and that when nobody else is present the phrase is superfluous. Damian responds that even though there are no other human beings, the monk is nevertheless participating in the Church through reciting the cycle of monastic prayers and performing the liturgy or parts of it. The whole Church is present, says Damian, even if only one person is performing the rite: 'If, therefore, those who believe in Christ are one, then whenever we find a member according to outward appearances, there, by the mystery of the sacrament, the whole body is present.'[86]

Clearly Damian sees the liturgy, the recitation of the Psalter, as integral aspects of the ascetic path. The hermit does not only perform austerities and inner contemplation, but the pattern of his whole life becomes liturgical. Fasting, the performance of penance while reciting the Psalter or inner prayer performed in silence are all part of the monk's liturgical life. The habit of the monastery becomes wholly internalised and the intensification of subjectivity through the life of solitude is simultaneously a forming of subjectivity in the pattern of tradition. Through extended periods of time and the fast periods in the liturgical year, the monk's rhythms are made to conform to the rhythms of tradition through an act of will which is at the same time a subversion of that will. The body of the Church, the body of tradition, becomes expressed in the ascetic body. The ascetic body in its conformity to the liturgical pattern becomes an expression of the Church and also an expression of the text. The body becomes a text on which the text of tradition is inscribed: fasting, prayer and the recitation of the Psalter while performing flagellation are entextualisations of the body. The ascetic body becomes a sign of the ascetic tradition.

### *Prayer*

Although Damian regards contemplation as the height of the monastic life, he does not systematically deal with prayer. Indeed, as Blum has observed, Damian is weak or theorising,[87] and we are a long way here from the more sophisticated theology of some of Damian's contemporaries or, indeed, the fathers of the desert whose doctrines about the nature of the mind are but a trace or only implicit. Discussion of particular methods of prayer advocated by some of the theologians of the desert, such as simple repetition of a phrase, is generally absent from Damian's work, although he does refer to unceasing prayer. But Damian's importance lies in his integration of asceticism with the liturgical and contemplative life of the Church. His concern is more focussed on the path that leads to contemplation that makes the self conform totally to the tradition in its everyday habits, its thoughts and its reading. While Damian does not present sophisticated theology, he does nevertheless present us with a consistent representation of the ascetic life and a coherent programme for internalising the tradition and realising the goal of Christian perfection. In this way he is in complete accord with his ascetical hero Romuald, who likewise advocated the internalisation of tradition through the eremitical monk's putting behind him the memory of the world and developing the memory of tradition through the inner recitation of the Psalms.[88]

Prayer is integral to the liturgical life, and Damian was a keen advocate of public prayers of the monks in the recitation of the breviary, the Office of the Blessed Virgin, and the Office of the Dead. He explained the process of liturgical prayer in a treatise to a nobleman, *De horis canonicis*, where he outlines the prescribed times for prayers, the 'canonical hours', which he understands primarily as a structure for the overcoming of sin.[89] The monks processing to the church resemble an army, says Damian in his 'On the Perfection of Monks', 'an ordered battle column' on their way to fight the enemy, 'the princes of darkness' who try to distract the minds of the monks with fantastic thoughts.[90]

Not only should the monks perform the public, liturgical prayers of the monastic day, but private prayer in their cells alone or in twos. Although Damian does not deal extensively with private prayer, he recommended one recitation of the Psalter for the living and one for the dead, although prayer also benefits the one who prays. Through prayer the mind begins to rest in the creator and to 'taste the delights of inner sweetness' (*intimae suavitate gustare*) and come before the 'vision of truth' (*speciem veritatis*).[91] Through prayer, the temple of the Holy Spirit grows within a person in the silence that allows the mind not to be distracted but to 'rise to the sublime heights of the spiritual construction' (*sublime fastigium spiritualis structura consurgit*).[92] Again for Damian, prayer is linked to asceticism, and he recommended praying with outstretched arms in the form of a cross,[93] and if tears accompany prayer then so much the better, for they wash away sin.

Prayer and its accompanying asceticism lead to contemplation, which Damian understood to be communion with God, the quietness of intimate sweetness. In his text on the perfection of monks Damian uses a biblical analogy. Jacob desired the younger daughter of Laban, Rachel, but could not 'come to her arms' before he had married the elder sister, Leah. The name 'Leah', says Damian, means 'labouring' and 'Rachel' means 'the word' or the 'vision of the beginning'. Through labour a monk seeking God comes in time to the joy of highest contemplation, which is to rest 'in the embrace of the lovely Rachel', and so through the world to attain the vision of the eternal,[94] although this can only be perfected in the next world.

### *Religious reading*

Closely related to prayer and contemplation is religious reading, the *lectio divina* so important in the development of the monk's spirituality. In spite of a rhetorical anti-intellectualism that inveighs against the liberal arts of his time,[95] Damian himself was well-read, as the library he created at Fonte Avellana testifies, and there is a strong scriptural foundation in his sermons. He warns monks about reading worldly knowledge, which he compares to 'unlawful love of loose women',[96] for the purpose of life is the ascetical path to contemplation, and anything that is not conducive to this is mere distraction. Reading the scriptures and the fathers of the Church should therefore be done as part of the practice of the ascetic life for inspiration and understanding. Indeed, the internalisation of scripture through reading and hearing is important for the monk's progress. As the monk finds food for the body each day in the refectory, so the soul finds food in the daily refectory reading[97] as recommended in Benedict's rule.[98] This is a common trope: reading is to be digested and ruminated as a cow chews the cud or bees make honey.[99]

Apart from readings done during meal times, Damian assumes the institution of religious reading in the Benedictine tradition that comprised the reading of passages from the scriptures and sometimes the Church fathers, and the meditation upon that reading. Reading means memorisation, which would be done subvocally while one reflected upon its meaning.[100] Carruthers has shown that the relationship between *lectio* and *meditatio* is akin to that between reading and reflection, in that meditation is 'the interior reading of the book of one's memory'[101] and that this reading is intimately connected with the formation of moral virtues and the ethical formation of the self.[102] Its purpose is to reveal God, who is behind the words, rather than to understand the authors of the words in a modern sense. As Carruthers puts it, one's first relationship with a text in this world is 'to use it as a source of communally experienced wisdom for one's own life, gained by memorizing from it however much and in whatever fashion one is able or willing to do'.[103] Carruthers quotes the late mystical theologian Hugh of St Victor (early twelfth century) who explains the difference between *lectio* and *meditatio* as study that involves order and method (*ordo et modus*), including the disciplines of grammar and dialectic, in contrast to contemplation of truth where the mind ranges along open ground. Victor describes this in terms of an ark with three storeys, the first being memorisation of scripture, the second the partial appropriation of the virtues of the saints so memorised and the third when knowledge and virtue have become parts of the reader and goodness is completely habitual.[104] Indeed, Hugh's use of the word *habitus* is indicative of the repeated return to the texts and their internalisation as a way for forming the self.[105]

While Hugh is comparatively late, the internalisation of scripture has a long history in Christian monasticism, from Origen (184–254), Ambrose (ca 339–97) and Augustine of Hippo (354–430) to Bede (ca 673–735). McGinn characterises the essential themes of monastic mysticism by the three pairs of *solitudo/silentium, lectio/meditatio* and *oratio/contemplatio.*[106] Founded on silence, a term which indicates attentive concentration,[107] reading and meditation (*lectio/meditatio*) become important in forming the ascetic self. The ascetic learns to inhabit the great edifice of collective memory, the memory of tradition shared by all participants in the community to varying degrees, depending upon levels of skill and application. While this is clearly a subjective activity, it is not private or individual but part of the construction of a subjectivity and interiority that is simultaneously subjective and collective, 'in harmony with the communal prayer of the whole church, the Body of Christ'.[108] This kind of 'religious reading' is in consonance with the liturgical rhythms of the monk and clearly different from the modern experience that Griffiths has called 'consumerist reading', where information is substituted for wisdom.[109] The reading of scripture, the lives of the saints, homilies and so on becomes, along with prayer and liturgy, another way in which the body is entextualised.

Damian himself does not dwell at length in his writings on the practice, but to judge from the library that he installed in Fonte Avellana and from his own writings with their numerous scriptural references it clearly played an important role in the internalisation of the tradition and the journey along the path of Christian asceticism. Through hearing the word of God the monk internalises this, 'chews it over' (*ruminatio*) and so learns to conform his body to the Church. The internalisation of scripture becomes the internalisation of the body of the Church and a conformity to the structures of ecclesiastical authority wherein the path to salvation for the medieval monk lay.

Religious reading is therefore an ascetic practice, integrated into a complete path of transformation, along with other practices as part of the *habitus* of the monastery. The repeated actions of the liturgy, prayer, mortification and religious readings (i.e. memorisation and reflection) serve to replace personal memory with the memory of tradition, to repress the recollection of events in a personal narrative with the collective tropes of the great, transpersonal narrative of the tradition. The internalisation of this 'machine', as Gregory the Great (ca 540–604) calls mnemonic devices of the monastery, is simultaneously intensification of subjectivity and the erosion of the will through the will. My story becomes the story of the tradition and the text.

## LATER DEVELOPMENTS

McGinn locates three strands of late medieval theology: scholastic, monastic and vernacular.[110] By scholastic he means the theology, long recognised, as taught in the great universities (especially Paris and Oxford) by figures such as Aquinas. By monastic he refers to the theology developed within the monasteries themselves by leading figures of monastic movements such as Bernard of Clairvaux, and by vernacular he refers to the theologies that developed in local environments, sometimes outside of a monastic setting, and expressed in vernacular languages rather than Greek or Latin. With Peter Damian we have seen a monastic theology that locates asceticism at the heart of the Church and that advocates an orthodox, monastic theology which wishes to construct subjectivity wholly in accordance with orthodox, Catholic tradition. Subjective transformation occurs through this conformity. Towards the end of the thirteenth century and into the fourteenth new forms of mystical theology developed that creatively responded to monastic practices and were expressed in vernacular languages. This new mysticism attracted women, who had had virtually no voice at all within the Church up to that time and no vehicle for expression, with one or two exceptions such as the influential abbess Hildegard of Bingen. Certainly there were important women monastics at the time of Damian whom he sometimes respectfully refers to, but only in the thirteenth century did an important shift take place, with women taking much more prominent roles as teachers and leaders within the Church,[111] defending Church orthodoxy.[112] This has now been well documented by scholars such as Bynum, Hollywood and McGinn (and is theologically very much a live issue in the Catholic Church, where official policy is that women lack authority to dispense the sacraments or achieve high ecclesiastical office).

The scholastic theologian Henry of Ghent, reported by McGinn, in examining the question around 1290 of whether a woman could be a doctor of theology, said that she could not do so officially because she does not possess the four public marks of doctoral status, namely constancy, efficacy, authority and effect. But he concedes that she could act as a teacher from divine favour if she possessed sound doctrine.[113] The Beguines and their male counterparts the Beghards fell foul of a decree *Ad nostrum* issued by the Council of Vienna in 1311 condemning such heretical beliefs as the belief that it is possible to gain perfection and be incapable of sin.[114] The question of sound doctrine was key here, and some women found that their teachings did not conform to official standards and so were accused of the heresy of the free-spirit.[115] One such case was the Beguine Marguerite Porete. I wish to conclude this chapter with an account of Porete because she presents an ascetic theology at the heart of which is the destruction of the human will (a key feature of asceticism as I have presented it) and yet an ascetic theology that, in complete contrast to Damian's, challenges the teachings of the Church. What is interesting about Porete – and other female mystics of the age – is that while the Church condemns her, she nevertheless illustrates a performance of the memory of tradition, but of a different kind from that condoned by Church tradition. It is not that Porete offers an individualistic vision of mystical transcendence, but rather an alternative reading or instantiation of the collective memory.

The Beguines originated around 1200 in the Low Countries but soon spread to the rest of Europe. Men were part of the movement too, which can be seen as developing from 'the radical wing of the Franciscan Spirituals'.[116] With the revival of the eremitical ideal in the eleventh and twelfth centuries, of which Peter Damian's work is a good example, women began to play a prominent role. McGinn observes that because the wandering life of a hermit was not possible for a woman in medieval society, a rigorous type of enclosure was permitted and female recluses, often widows, developed as a recognised institution.[117] The Beguines were lay women who lead semi-monastic lives in communities with their own rules, although they did not take solemn vows and some, such as Porete, were even mendicants. By the beginning of the fourteenth century they were facing oppression by a Church that feared a women's movement outside of its control,[118] although the movement was never wholly suppressed. In the history of monasticism it is important not only for itself but also for its influence on such monastic reforms as the Cistercians' and Premonstratensians' and for its influence – particularly Porete's – on such important theologians as Meister Eckhart.[119]

## THE NEGATION OF THE WILL

Although she does not refer to herself as a Beguine, Porete can be located within the Beguine tradition. Her book *The Mirror of Simple Souls* or, in a literal translation, *The Mirror of Simple, Annihilated Souls and Who Only Remain in Will and Desire of Love* (*Le Mirouer des Simples Ames Anientes et Qui Seulement Demourent en Vouloir et Desir d'Amour*),[120] is an important text of medieval mysticism. She does not advocate extremes of asceticism, as some earlier women mystics had done, such as Christina of Hane (1269–92);[121] indeed there is very little concerning practice in her strange, yet moving, book. But Marguerite's text expresses an ascetic theology that sets itself within a tradition even though it is outside of any institution: within the tradition of what she calls 'Holy Church the Great', which is nonetheless outside or beyond the Church as an institution, 'Holy Church the Little'. I include her for discussion firstly as an exemplum of a trope in ascetic theology, the annihilation of the will, and secondly because her theology can be read as an alternative reconfiguration of the self, an alternative embodiment of tradition to that accepted by the power of the Church.

Porete did not fulfil the criteria outlined by Henry of Ghent, as she did not possess an authority condoned by the Church and her book was not in accordance with 'sound doctrine'. In 1306 the book was condemned for the first time and publicly burned. On a second occasion, in 1309, it was condemned as heretical by twenty-one masters of theology at a meeting convoked by the Inquisitor of France, Guillaume de Paris. Porete was arrested, tried, refused to respond to the questions of the judges and was burned to death on 1 June 1310.[122] While the motivation behind Porete's trial remains unclear (she was probably condemned more for disseminating the teachings in the vernacular rather than the teachings themselves), the general situation described by McGinn of an increase in competition among religious orders, fear of the proliferation of heresy and a general suspicion of women stepping outside of prescribed controls (she is called *pseudo-mulier*, a 'phoney-woman') were no doubt important factors in her condemnation.[123] External political factors also played a part, with Philip the King of France wishing to display his Catholic, anti-heresy credentials. But within the horizons of her own work Porete did possess authority to disseminate her teachings – an authority that she regarded as having a transcendent source yet still mediated through tradition, a tradition deeper than the institution and comprising the community of the 'simple souls'. It is the form of the mediation as well as the content of the doctrine that the inquisitors took issue with, rejecting her book as divinely inspired and rejecting its claim to authority.

The *Mirror* declares itself to be a product of revelation rather than of Porete's imagination and so claims a transcendent authority.[124] What is striking about the *Mirror* is that in a culture pervaded by the visionary and an emphasis on the image, particularly in women's mystical writings, there is an absence of visionary and ecstatic elements. Indeed, it supports Hollywood's contention that women's mystical writing, rather than being constructed in terms of bodiliness and vision, is concerned with the apostolic life, with poverty, unity, the imitation of Christ, and the relation between action and contemplation.[125] While the text shares in the Cistercian and Beguine milieu of divine love and the mystical eroticism of the Song of Songs, it rejects visionary spirituality and extreme mortification of the kind we have found in Damian and which was present in many Beguines such as Marie of Oignies and others.[126]

The teachings of the *Mirror* in which Love is the central idea are presented in a dialogical form as a conversation between, among others, the soul (*L'Ame*), Lady Love (*Dame Amour*) and Reason (*Raison*). But, as McGinn observes, while 'it is relatively clear *who* is speaking in the dialogues . . . it is often difficult to determine who the speakers represent and what their conversation means'.[127] The book sees itself as a representation of the soul which itself is the image of God, yet a soul whose identity is 'annihilated', leaving only the will of God, a God who is himself beyond full articulation. The soul is not only a participant in the dialogue but also the subject matter of the discourse, and so we are presented with a complex text which reflexively contains different levels of understanding. It draws on genres available at the time, as McGinn and Hollywood show, namely biblical dialogue, philosophical dialogue and French romance literature, making the text 'among the most original of the thirteenth century'.[128] A thorough explication of the text is beyond the scope of this short account and in any case there are excellent discussions by McGinn and Hollywood drawing out some of the implications of the text and explaining Porete's historical context. In what follows I shall therefore simply make the two points stated above, that the text is a fine exemplum of the annihilation of the will that locates itself outside of the accepted formation of the ascetic self. The book reveals paradox at the heart of a subjectivity that simultaneously can be read as an intensification of subjectivity along with its subversion. The passages quoted below demonstrate that Porete should not be read in terms of a mystical individualism fighting against a staid and oppressive institutional Christianity, but rather as drawing on the collective memory in a different way. Like Damian, Porete wishes to subject the self to the form of tradition by which it will be annihilated and the goal, the *scopos*, of the Christian path realised. But unlike Damian this goal is realised beyond the transformational structures of the Church of her time and within a subjectivity that claims itself as a non-subjectivity.

The essential teachings of the *Mirror* can be illustrated by the following two passages:

> Love. Now hear and understand well, you who listen to this book, the true meaning of what it says in so many places, that the soul brought to nothing has no will at all, and cannot want to have any at all, and in this the divine will is perfectly accomplished and the soul does not have its fill of divine love, nor does divine love have its fill of the soul, until the soul is in God and God is in the soul, and when the soul is in such a state of divine rest, from God and through God, then she has all her fill.[129]

And later:

> And now I shall tell you, says Love, how she [the soul] has come to knowledge of her nothingness. It is because she knows that not she or anyone else knows anything of her horrible sins and faults in comparison with what God knows of them. Such a soul, says Love, has not retained any will, but has fallen and come to a state of wishing for nothing, and to a certain knowledge of knowing nothing, and this knowing nothing and this wishing for nothing have excused and freed her. Such a soul, says Love, follows the counsel of the Gospel, where it says 'Let your eye be single, and so you will not sin.'[130]

These passages illustrate that the highest Christian understanding for Porete is that the creature is nothing, is given being by God, and secondly that God can dwell within the self as the self, with the realisation that the self has no will and is nothing. In many ways this is reminiscent of some Hindu conceptions we have looked at, but it is important to see that Porete's annihilation of the self is clearly set within a Christian context and supported by the authority of scripture. The truth of the gospel message is that the self is nothing and, moreover, the limit of the divine Trinity, ineffable and unknowable, is the limit of the soul's nothingness. Porete would clearly seem to be drawing on the apophatic tradition of Christian mystical theology, a tradition within which stands Eckhart, who recognises this in Porete, and whose text he draws on.

Porete's teaching subverts the official Church's view of the ascetic self, for it formulates a self that is free from the constraints of gender and free from the constraints of Church law, structure and discipline. Although Porete locates her teaching within the tradition, she posits this to be a deeper or higher tradition than that of works and effort advocated by the institution of the Church. From the perspective of Love and the soul united with the Trinity, the practice of the virtues is 'nothing but care and labour' (*n'est que soing et travail*) advocated by Reason.[131] While this has a place recognised by Christ himself in his assurance that, through his death, the labour of the soul in the context of the scriptures can be saved, the higher teaching is that the soul is free of all this, and that its end is in the timeless God. But I am in time, according to the soul, 'so that I might obtain from him what is mine; and what is mine is that I be established in my nothingness'.[132] This is pure paradox. The soul wishes to obtain its nothingness, to realise that it is without will through will. While admittedly Porete does give in chapter 118 of her book an ordered account of the seven stages through which the soul must pass, which embrace the usual ascetic practices condoned by the Church,[133] the emphasis on undifferentiated unity between the soul and God undermines the very notion of developmental stages. This is a teaching that internalises the tradition of apophasis and renders the body as a text in a unique way. The body is entextualised in the sense that Porete's readings of scripture are intended to support and substantiate the claims for the soul's nothingness and the body's transcendence. Porete advocates the goal of the ascetic path, the self's elimination of its will, without a path; she asserts the true tradition of going beyond the virtues and the ascetic teachings in an uncompromising act of self-negation and utter transcendence. The intensification of subjectivity that we see in the dialogue of the *Mirror*, in which the interior forces of reason and love are given voice, is further intensified by the very subversion of that subjectivity in its ultimate denial. The *Mirror* can be seen as itself a performance of the ambiguity of the self: the articulation of a subjectivity and a will that seeks its own erasure so that the annihilated soul no longer needs the body and no longer needs the world. In appropriating 'the all', the soul eradicates itself, as two things are made one in a fire or a watercourse enters the sea.[134] Clearly this is a teaching that undermines the position of the Church, undermines the authority of mediation and, in relativising the teachings about virtue, is potentially disruptive and subversive of both ecclesiastical and secular authority.

We have come a long way from the ascetic self of the desert and the rich cosmology of Evagrius and Maximus, but fundamental processes of the ascetic self remain constant. The whole structure of monasticism in the Latin West is oriented towards the subjective appropriation of the collective memory of tradition, the inculcation of a *habitus* to ensure the erosion of the will through an act of will and its replacement with a tradition-specific interiority. Peter Damian advocates a strict regime for the construction of the eremitical self that, while living alone, is wholly conformed to the tradition, a self that constantly remembers the future of the Kingdom of Heaven by inscribing the text of tradition on the body. Although this inscription is completely Catholic and does not step at all outside of orthodox teaching, other forms of ascetic subjectivity developed that drew on tradition in different ways. They wished to stay within tradition but were often rejected by it. This is the case with Marguerite Porete, whose idea of the complete annihilation of the self and eradication of the will so that only the divine Trinity indwells in the ascetic's being, must subordinate all forms of mediation. Hers is an uncompromising vision of the ascetic self that wishes to set itself within tradition and yet claims to be a higher tradition than that of the cultivation of virtues and the usual ascetic practices. From a cosmological vision which the ascetic self places within the body, we have come to an ontological identity between self and God in which the will is eradicated.

We are now in a position to pursue a more explicit comparative agenda in showing how the ascetic self is ritually formed in the scriptural traditions we have discussed. There are great differences between the traditions and figures we have surveyed, yet there are also striking parallels which, I shall argue, are so significant as to allow us to make claims about categories that cross cultures and general claims about the processes that lead to the ascetic self, a self that is not purely an object of historical interest but is of vital and important contemporary relevance.

## NOTES

1. Dante Aleghieri, *Dante Purgatory*, trs. Anthony Esolen (New York: the Modern Library, 2003).
2. Gerard Manley Hopkins, *Poems and Prose*, ed. W. H. Gardner (Harmondsworth: Penguin, 1970), p. 91.
3. Lutz Kaelber, *Schools of Asceticism: Ideology and Organization in Medieval Religious Communities* (Philadelphia: University of Pennsylvania Press, 1998), p. 67.

4. See Marilyn Dunn, *The Emergence of Monasticism: From the Desert Fathers to the Early Middle Ages* (Oxford: Blackwell, 2000), pp. 59, 158, 207–08. I have followed Dunn's account of the translation of monasticism from East to West. On the history of monasticism through monastic literature see A. de Vogüé, *Histoire Littéraire du Mouvement Monastique dans l'Antiquité* part I (Paris: Les Editions du Cerf, 1991). On the medieval context of asceticism see Caroline Walker Bynum, *Holy Feast Holy Fast: Studies in the Spirituality of the Higher Middle Ages* (Berkeley: University of California Press, 1982). She discusses the different logic at work in the symbolism of the male and female bodies of monastics and visionaries.
5. J. Pelikan, *Jesus through the Centuries: His Place in the History of Culture* (New Haven and London: Yale University Press, 1985), p. 117. Along with the institution of monasticism, tropes of asceticism and especially penance pervade medieval literature. See Brian Murdock 'The Origins of Penance: Reflections of Adamic Apocrypha and of the *Vita Adamae* in Western Europe' in *Annals of the Archive of 'Ferran Valls i Taberner's Library'* nos. 9–10, 1991, pp. 205–27.
6. Max Weber 'Religious Rejections of the World and their Directions' in H. H. Gerth and C. Wright Mills, *From Max Weber: Essays in Sociology* (London: Routledge, 1991), p. 332.
7. Kaelber, *Schools of Asceticism*, p. 71.
8. Kaelber, *Schools of Asceticism*, pp. 70–80. Kaelber gives full references for these developments.
9. J. Le Goff, *La Naissance Purgatoire* (Paris: Gallimard, 1981), p. 335.
10. Dunn, *The Emergence of Monasticism*, pp. 92, 98–9.
11. PL 49 and 50, *Iohannis Cassiani Opera Omnia.* PL 49, 53–476 contains *De institutis coenobiorum.* Also Michael Petschenig (ed.), *Iohannis Cassiani Opera* (Vindabonae: CSEL, vols. XIII, XVII, 1886, 1888). For translations see *John Cassian: The Conferences*, trs. Boniface Ramsey (New York: Paulist Press, 1997) and *John Cassian. The Institutes*, trs. Boniface Ramsey (New York: Newman Press, 2000). J. Bertram (trs.), *The Monastic Institutes, Consisting of On the Training of a Monk and The Eight Deadly Sins* (London, 1999). For a translation of the complete works see E. C. S. Gibson, *The Works of John Cassian* Nicene and Post-Nicene Fathers Series, vol. XI (Oxford: James Parker and Co. 1894). On Cassian see Owen Chadwick, *John Cassian* (2nd edn Cambridge University Press, 1968); C. Stewart, *Cassian the Monk* (Oxford University Press. 1998). There are lucid accounts of Cassian in B. McGinn, *The Foundations of Christian Mysticism* (New York: Crossroads, 1995), pp. 218–27 and Dunn, *The Emergence of Monasticism*, pp. 73–8.
12. Dunn, *The Emergence of Monasticism*, pp. 207–08.
13. Even monastic buildings and the plans of monastic buildings were 'meditation machines' whose function was fundamentally visionary and transformative. See Mary Carruthers, *The Craft of Thought: Meditation, Rhetoric, and the Making of Images 400–1200* (Cambridge University Press, 1998). For an example of a building plan as meditation machine see pp. 228–31. Carruthers's excellent

book abounds in convincing examples of the visionary nature of monastic institutions.

14. G. W. H. Lampe, *A Patristic Greek Lexicon* (Oxford: Clarendon Pess, 1961), p. 1241.
15. Cassian, *Conferences* 1.2 (PL 49. p. 483B): *scopon . . . id est, destinationem et telos, hoc est, finem proprium.* Quoted in Lampe, *A Patristic Greek Lexicon*, p. 1241.
16. Cassian, *Conferences*, 1.5 (PL 49. p. 487A): *scopos vero est puritas cordis*, 'The goal truly is purity of heart'. On *scopos* as the goal of the path or *ductus* of remembering scripture see Carruthers, *The Craft of Thought*, p. 79.
17. Ibid. pp. 66–9.
18. Cassian, *Conferences*, 1.2 (PL 49. p. 484A).
19. Ibid. 1.5 (PL 49. p. 487A–B).
20. Carruthers, *The Craft of Thought*, pp. 79–80.
21. Ibid. p. 81.
22. Cassian, *Conferences*, 1.5 (PL 49. p. 487B–C).
23. Ibid. 10.8 (PL 49. p. 829B).
24. Robert Pasnau, *Theories of Cognition in the Later Middle Ages* (Cambridge University Press, 1997), p. 32.
25. Carruthers, *The Craft of Thought*, pp. 82–3.
26. McGinn, *Origins*, p. 219. On the development of the eight vices see Aimé Solignac, 'Péchés Capitaux', DDS, vol. XII part I, pp. 853–62. Solignac traces the use of the term from Evagrius and Cassian through Gregory's new classification. Johannes Climacus hesitates but in the end goes with eight (*Scala* 13, PG 68, 860); Victor of St Hugo (b. 1141) gives seven (*superbia, invidia, ira, tristitia, avaritia, gula, luxuria*) and Aquinas treats the seven briefly (*Summa* 1, 2, q. 84).
27. Cassian, *Conferences*, 14. 1–2 (PL 49). See Dunn, *The Emergence of Monasticism*, p. 77.
28. Cassian, *Conferences*, 9.2–3.
29. Ibid. 10.10.
30. Peter King, *Western Monasticism: A History of the Monastic Movement in the Latin Church.* Cistercian Studies 185 (Kalamazoo: Cistercian Publications, 1999), p. 150.
31. Stephan Freund, *Studien zur literarischen Wirksamkeit des Petrus Damiani* (Hanover: Hahnsche Buchhandlung, 1995), p. 129.
32. For an account of his life, drawing from Damian's disciple and biographer John of Lodi, see Owen J. Blum, *St. Peter Damian: His Teaching on the Spiritual Life* (Washington: The Catholic University of America Press, 1947), pp. 1–36.
33. For example, Letter 80. Owen J. Blum (trs.), *Peter Damian Letters 61–90* (Washington: The Catholic University of America Press, 1992), p. 200.
34. B. McGinn, *The Growth of Mysticism: Gregory the Great through the 12th Century* (New York: Crossroads, 1996), p. 125.
35. *New Catholic Encyclopedia*, 2nd ed. (Washington: Thompson-Gale, 2003), p. 186.

36. PL 145, *Petri Damiani Opera Omnia.* Opuscula. Carmina Sacra et Preces. Opus 13 *De perfectione monachorum*, pp. 291–327. 'On the Perfection of Monks' is translated by Patricia McNulty, *St. Peter Damian: Selected Writings on the Spiritual Life, translated with an Introduction* (London: Faber and Faber, 1959), pp. 82–136.
37. PL 145. Damian, Opus 11 *Liber qui dicitur dominus vobiscum*, pp. 231–51. Trs. McNulty, *St. Peter Damian*, pp. 53–81.
38. PL 145, 172D–174C. Trs. Pierre J. Payer, *Book of Gomorrah: An Eleventh-Century Treatise Against Clerical Homosexual Practices* (Ontario: Wilfred Laurier University Press, 1982).
39. Lester K. Little, 'The Personal Development of Peter Damian', p. 333, in William C. Jordan et al. (eds.), *Order and Innovation in the Middle Ages: Essays in Honour of Joseph R. Strayer* (Princeton University Press, 1976), pp. 317–41.
40. On the contents of his library see Blum, *St. Peter Damian*, pp. 58–64.
41. Ibid. pp. 55–6.
42. J. Joseph Ryan, *Saint Peter Damiani and his Canonical Sources* (Toronto: Pontifical Institute of Mediaeval Studies, 1956), p. 19.
43. PL 145, 223A. Damian, Opus 10 *De horis canonicis*, chapter 1. Reference from Blum, *St. Peter Damian*, p. 82.
44. Ibid. p. 88.
45. Ibid. pp. 81–9.
46. PL 145, 403C. Damian, Opus 18 *Dissertatio 2*. Reference from Blum, *St. Peter Damian*, p. 87.
47. PL 145, p. 167. Damian, *Liber Gomorrhianus*, chapter 7. Payer, *Book of Gomorrah*, p. 49.
48. Ryan, *Saint Peter Damiani*, p. 137.
49. PL 144, p. 458B. Damian, Epistolae 7, 18. Quoted in Blum, *St. Peter Damian*, p. 98.
50. Ibid. pp. 96–7.
51. See Dunn, *The Emergence of Monasticism*, quoting Jerome, pp. 54–5.
52. On these attitudes and the recovery of a more positive Christian orientation to sexuality, see Eugene F. Rogers, *Sexuality and the Christian Body* (Oxford: Blackwell, 1999), pp. 67–85.
53. Peter Brown, *The Body and Society: Men, Women and Sexual Renunciation in Early Christianity* (London and Boston: Faber and Faber, 1989), p. 429.
54. PL 145, pp. 831–38. Damian, Opus 58 *De vera felicitate et sapientia*, chapter 5, p. 835C: *et voluptas quidem ad hanc vitam, virtus ad aeternam pertinet gloriam.* McNulty (trs.), 'Concerning True Happiness', chapter 5, *St. Peter Damian*, p. 143.
55. Although I would not regard Damian as explicitly misogynistic. For example, in Letter 83 he praises a woman ascetic called Bella, who throws herself on the ground. (Blum, *Letters*, p. 244.)
56. Damian, Opus 13 *De perfectione monachorum* (PL 145, chapter 8, p. 303B). McNulty (trs.), 'On the Perfection of Monks', chapter 8, *St. Peter Damian*, p. 99.

57. PL 145, pp. 307D–308A. Damian, *De perfectione monachorum*, chapter 12: *jejunium amet, necessariarum rerum penuriam diligat, aspectus hominum fugiat, sub silentii se censura constringat, ab exteriori se negotio subtrahat, os suum ab otiosa confabulatione custodiat, mentis suae latibulum petat, ubi ad videndam creatoris sui faciem totis nisibus inardescat: ad lacrymas anhelet, lacrymas a deo quotidianis precibus flagitet.* McNulty, *St. Peter Damian*, p. 106.
58. PL 144, p. 519C. Sermo 3: *aut facto, aut verbo, aut cogitatione committimus.* On conversion and confession see Blum, *St. Peter Damian*, pp. 75–81.
59. PL 145, p. 679B. Damian, Opus 43 *De laude flagellorum*, preface. Cited in Blum, *St. Peter Damian*, p. 106. On this important theme of the imitation of Christ see Giles Constable, *Three Studies in Medieval Religious and Social Thought* (Cambridge University Press, 1995), pp. 143–248.
60. Justin McCann (trs.), *The Rules of St Benedict* (London: Sheed and Ward, 1970 [1952]).
61. Blum, *St. Peter Damian*, p. 73.
62. For a good discussion of the rule see Dunn, *The Emergence of Monasticism*, pp. 114–31.
63. Ilana F. Silbur, *Virtuosity, Charisma and Social Order: A Comparative Sociological Study of Monasticism in Theravada Buddhism and Medieval Catholicism* (Cambridge University Press, 1995), p. 168. Silbur observes how Damian was part of political reforms that sought more stringent rules.
64. PL 145, 294B. Damian, *De perfectione monachorum*, chapter 2: *Prudens etenim vir, et ad salutis suae custodiam vehementer intentus, tanta reprimendis vitiis sollicitudine semper invigilat, ut perfectae mortificationis cingulo lumbos suos et renes, ventrem una* [sic] *cum lateribus undique circumstringat.* Trs. McNulty, *St. Peter Damian*, p. 85. (Translation slightly modified.)
65. PL 145, p. 294B-C. Damian, *De perfectione monachorum*, chapter 2. McNulty, *St. Peter Damian*, p. 85.
66. PL 144, p. 474D. Damian, Epistolae. Reference from Blum, *St. Peter Damian*, p. 195.
67. PL 145, p. 301A. Damian, *De perfectione monachorum*, chapter 6. McNulty, *St. Peter Damian*, pp. 95–6.
68. PL 145, p. 299A. Damian, *De perfectione monachorum*, chapter 6. McNulty, *St. Peter Damian*, pp. 92–3.
69. Blum, *St. Peter Damian*, p. 115.
70. PL 145, p. 679C. Damian, Opus 43 *De laude flagellorum: super mactata quippe cadavera descendunt volucres, dum ad rapiendum sacrificium afflictiorum corporum nostrorum, aerae se praecipitant potestates.*
71. PL 144, p. 433B. Damian, *Epistolae* lib. vi. 34, quoted in McNulty, *St. Peter Damian*, p. 39. For the goal of flagellation see F. X. Hecht, 'Geisselung', *Lexikon für Theologie und Kirche*, vol. IV (1932), p. 344. Blum, *St. Peter Damian*, p. 114.
72. PL 145, pp. 679–686. Damian, Opus 43 *De laude flagellorum.* Trs. Blum, *St. Peter Damian*, p. 117.
73. NcNulty, *St. Peter Damian*, p. 39.

74. PL 145, p. 321. Damian, *De perfectione monachorum*, chapter 22. McNulty, *St. Peter Damian*, p. 126.
75. Blum, *St. Peter Damian*, pp. 108–09.
76. Ibid. p. 111.
77. Damian, Letter 78. Blum, *Peter Damian Letters*, pp. 167–8. The observation is Blum's.
78. PL 145, p. 322B. Damian, *De perfectione monachorum*, chapter 22. McNulty, *St. Peter Damian*, p. 127.
79. PL 145, p. 321C. Damian, *De perfectione monachorum*, chapter 22. McNulty, *St. Peter Damian*, p. 126. Also PL 145, p. 334C Opus 14 *De ordine eremitarum.* Reference in Blum, *St. Peter Damian*, p. 92.
80. PL 145, p. 259D. Damian, Opus 12 *De contemptu saeculi*, chapter 8. Trs. Blum, *St. Peter Damian*, p. 93.
81. On the Eucharist in medieval Christianity and the development of the feast of Corpus Christi see Miri Rubin, *Corpus Christi: The Eucharist in Late Medieval Culture* (Cambridge University Press, 1991).
82. Blum, *St. Peter Damian*, pp. 16–17.
83. Dunn, *The Emergence of Monasticism*, p. 208.
84. PL 145, p. 235C. Damian, Opus 11 *Liber qui dicitur dominus vobiscum* chapter 15. Trs. McNulty, *The Book of 'The Lord Be with You'*, *St. Peter Damian*, p. 70. PL 145, p. 244A: *Haec autem idcirco de sacris solemnitatibus juxta compendium dixerim, ut manifeste clarescat, quia sancta Ecclesia non tam constringitur lege temporum, quam ipsas temporum vices ad suum cohibet nutum.*
85. PL 145, p. 236A. Damian, *Dominus vobiscum.* McNulty, *St. Peter Damian*, p. 58.
86. PL 145, 236A. Damian, *Dominus vobiscum.* McNulty, *St. Peter Damian*, p. 59: *Si ergo credentes in christum unum sunt, ubicunque videatur esse per corporalem speciem membrum, ibi etiam per sacramenti mysterium totum est corpus.*
87. Blum, *St. Peter Damian*, p. 146.
88. King, *Western Monasticism*, p. 147.
89. PL 145, pp. 221–31. Damian, Opus 10 *De horis canonicis.* The text is described in Blum, *St. Peter Damian*, pp. 153–4.
90. PL 145, p. 316A. Damian, *De perfectione monachorum*, chapter 17. Trs. McNulty, *St. Peter Damian*, p. 118.
91. PL 145, p. 294D, p. 303B. Damian, *De perfectione monachorum*, chapter 3. Trs. McNulty, *St. Peter Damian*, pp. 86, 99.
92. PL 144, p. 444B. Damian, Epistolae 7, 6. Quoted in Blum, *St. Peter Damian*, p. 122.
93. PL 145, 353C. Damian, *De institutis ordinis eremitarum*, chapter 22.
94. PL 145, pp. 303D–304A. Damian, *De perfectione monachorum*, chapter 8. Trs. McNulty, *St. Peter Damian*, p. 100.
95. Blum, *St. Peter Damian*, pp. 129–34.
96. PL 145, p. 306C. Damian, *De perfectione monachorum*, chapter 11. Trs. McNulty, *St. Peter Damian*, p. 104.

97. PL 145, p. 316D. Damian, *De perfectione monachorum*, chapter 18. McNulty, *St. Peter Damian*, p. 119.
98. PL 66, pp. 601–602. Benedict, *Regula Benedicta*, chapter 38: *mensis fratrum edentium lectio deesse non debet*, 'while the brothers are eating they should not lack in reading' (trs. Mary Carruthers, *The Book of Memory: A Study of Memory in Medieval Culture* (Cambridge University Press, 1990), p. 167).
99. Carruthers, *The Book of Memory*, p. 164. For a discussion of the metaphors of eating and digestion and religious reading generally see pp. 166–72.
100. Carruthers, *The Book of Memory*, p. 164. On *lectio divina* see Kevin W. Irwin, 'Lectio Divina' in W. M. Johnston (ed.), *Encyclopedia of Monasticism* (Chicago and London: Fitzroy Dearborn, 2000), vol. I, pp. 751–52; Jacques Rousse, 'Lectio Divina et Lecture Spirituelle', DDS, 1976 vol. IX, pp. 470–87.
101. Carruthers, *The Craft of Thought*, p. 84.
102. Carruthers, *The Book of Memory*, p. 156.
103. Ibid. p. 162.
104. Ibid. p. 162–3.
105. Ibid. p. 163. See also Paul J. Griffiths, *Religious Reading: The Place of Reading in the Practice of Religion* (Oxford University Press, 1999), pp. 47, 50.
106. McGinn, *Growth*, p. 125.
107. Carruthers, *The Book of Memory*, p. 173.
108. McGinn, *Growth*, p. 132.
109. Griffiths, *Religious Reading*, pp. 42–6.
110. B. McGinn (ed.), *Meister Eckhart and the Beguine Mystics* (New York: Continuum, 1994), Introduction pp. 4–14. I have generally followed McGinn's account of Porete.
111. Amy Hollywood, *The Soul as Virgin Wife: Mechtild of Magdeburg, Marguerite Porete, and Meister Eckhart* (Notre Dame and London: University of Notre Dame Press, 1995); McGinn, *Meister Eckhart and the Beguine Mystics*; McGinn, *The Flowering of Mysticism: Men and Women in the New Mysticism 1200–1350* (New York: Crossroads, 1998).
112. Jo Ann McNamara, 'The Rhetoric of Orthodoxy: Clerical Authority and Female Innovation in the Struggle with Heresy' in Ulrike Wiethaus (ed.), *Maps of Flesh and Light: The Religious Experience of Medieval Women Mystics* (Syracuse University Press, 1993), pp. 9–27.
113. McGinn, 'Introduction', *Meister Eckhart and the Beguine Mystics*, p. 1.
114. See Grace M. Janzen, *Power, Gender and Christian Mysticism* (Cambridge University Press, 1995), pp. 258–64.
115. R. E. Lerner, *The Heresy of the Free Spirit in the Late Middle Ages* (Berkeley: University of California Press, 1972), pp. 45–60, 78–84.
116. McGinn, *The Flowering of Mysticism*, p. 183.
117. Ibid. p. 187.
118. Hollywood, *The Soul as Virgin Wife*, p. 1. There is some debate about whether Porete can be classified as a Beguine, although Church lawyers and chroniclers referred to her as such (p. 207, note 9).

119. Hollywood, *The Soul as Virgin Wife*, pp. 121, 173–6. On the relation of the Beguines to Eckhart, see Oliver Davies, *Meister Eckhart Mystical Theologian* (London: SPCK, 1991), pp. 35–40, 69–79.
120. Marguerite Porete, *Le Mirouer des Simples Ames*, ed. Romana Guarnieri, with Latin text ed. Paul Verdeyen, Corpus Christianorum 69 (Turnholt: Typographi Brepol Editores Pontificii, 1986). I have used the translation by Edmund Colledge, J. C. Marler and Judith Grant: *Margaret Porete, The Mirror of Simple Souls* (Paris: University of Notre Dame Press, 1999).
121. McGinn, *The Flowering of Mysticism*, pp. 282–5.
122. Verdeyen, 'Introduction: l'Auteur et son Traité', *Le Mirouer*, pp. v–vi. P. Dronke, *Women Writers of the Middle Ages* (Cambridge University Press, 1984), p. 217.
123. McGinn, *The Flowering of Mysticism*, p. 245.
124. Hollywood, *The Soul as Virgin Wife*, p. 3.
125. Ibid. p. 26.
126. Ibid. p. 55.
127. McGinn, *The Flowering of Mysticism*, p. 247.
128. Ibid. p. 248.
129. Porete, *The Mirror*, chapter 12, pp. 48–50: *[Amour] Or oyez et entendez bien, auditeurs de ce livre, le vray entendement de ce que ce livre dit en tant de lieux, que l'Ame Adnientie n'a point de voulenté, ne point n'en pent avoir, ne point n'en peut vouloir avoir, et en ce est la voulenté divine parfaictement acomplie; ne jusques ad ce n'a l'ame souffizance de divine Amour, ne Amour divine souffizance de l'ame, jusques ad ce que l'ame soit en Dieu et Dieu en l'Ame de luy par luy en tel estre de divin assise; et donc a l'Ame tout sa souffizance.* Trs. by Colledge et al.
130. Porete, *The Mirror*, chapter 47, p. 142: *Comment l'ame est venue en cognoissance de son nient. On vous diray, dit Amour, comment elle est venue en cognoissance de son nient . . . C'est en ce qu'elle cognoist, que elle ne aultres ne cognosit nient de ses horribles pechez et deffaultes, au regart de ce qui en est ou savoir de Dieu. Telle Ame, dit Amour, m'a retenu nul vouloir, ançoys est venue et cheue a nient vouloir, et en certain savoir de nient savoir, et ce nient savoir et ce nient vouloir l'ont excusee et enfranchie. Telle Ame, dit Amour, tient le conseil de l'Euvangile, qui dit: Ayés l'oeil simple, et ainsi ne pecheras mie.* Trs. Colledge et al.
131. Porete, *The Mirror*, chapters 68, 69. Trs. Colledge et al.
132. Porete, *The Mirror*, chapter 69, p. 124: [Dieu] *qui n'a point de temps – mais je l'ay, pour le myen de luy atteindre; le mien est, que je soie en mon nient plantee.* Trs. Colledge et al.
133. Hollywood, *The Soul as Virgin Wife*, pp. 97–103.
134. Porete, *The Mirror*, chapter 83. Trs. Colledge et al.

# PART II

# *Theorising the ascetic self*

CHAPTER 8

# *The ritual formation of the ascetic self*

> *citrakarma yathā 'nekair raṅgair unmīlyate śanaiḥ /*
> *brāhmaṇyam api tadvat syāt saṃskārair vidhipūrvakam //*
> As a painting gradually develops through (the building up of) many colours, even so priestly status (develops) according to the rules of ritual construction.
>
> Aṅgira *Parāśara* 8.19[1]

Having surveyed the ascetic self with examples drawn from the scriptural traditions of Christianity, Buddhism and Hinduism, we are in a position to develop some general conclusions that cut across different historical trajectories. Important questions arise. Can we generalise about the social conditions that allow for the development of the ascetic self? Even if the ascetic self is apparently similar in different contexts, could it nevertheless be the product of quite distinct historical processes? While this might seem paradoxical, in general terms the response to both these questions is in the affirmative. Different historical trajectories in different continents with varied environmental, economic and political constraints are particular, unrepeatable instances. Yet given the diversity of these historical trajectories – a description of which is far beyond the scope of the present project – that there is a similarity of process in the formation of the ascetic self is precisely the point. We might subsume this process of self-formation under the sign of 'ritual'. The process whereby the self becomes an ascetic self, the shaping of the self in the form of tradition, the entextualisation of the body, is found in all the cultural locations we have examined. More particularly it is found and endorsed as the highest ideal of human being by the scriptural traditions that have come to be known as 'Christianity', 'Hinduism' and 'Buddhism'.

While acknowledging social, political and economic diversity in the histories of the traditions, we might make the general claim that all the examples we have examined in detail (with the exception of Simone Weil) can unequivocally claim to be premodern. The ascetic self is a form of human flourishing that has occurred predominantly in pre-industrial cultures and in forms of religion with highly developed ritual systems which are strongly cosmological. Indeed, as I have argued, where religious cosmology has retreated in the modern West any robust sense of the ascetic self as a cultural form has diminished. Weber has been the most careful theorist to have mapped the shift to modernity, which itself can be seen as the interiorisation of asceticism. We shall return to this theme in the last chapter. But the formation of the ascetic self, while there are modernist analogues, is essentially premodern and to be found in comparatively stable societies with a high degree of hierarchical social coherence and continuity. The ascetic self was formed before the citizen.

Drawing on the traditions we have discussed, the current chapter will bring together diverse elements to construct a general argument that shows how the ascetic self is a formation inseparably linked to both ritual and subjectivity. The appropriation of the tradition through ritual entails an intensification of subjective meaning. To demonstrate this we shall need to develop an account strongly reliant on cultural and linguistic anthropology.

## AN ESQUISSE OF WHAT WE HAVE SEEN

To summarise in very general terms, we might say that the process whereby the self becomes an ascetic self must be understood as the subjective appropriation of tradition. We have seen this over and over again in the examples I have presented: through an act of will the self internalises the tradition and performs the memory of tradition in recalling the tradition and bringing to mind the tradition's telos. This is to perform the ambiguity of the self: the distance between intention and action and the eradication of the will through an act of will. This internalisation of the tradition can also be described as the entextualisation of the body and so is within the general category of ritual. The body becomes the text and is inscribed by the text in the sense that the ascetic writes or inscribes tradition on the body through action. The ascetic *habitus* is defined by the text (by which I do not simply mean a written document – see pp. 24–6), and while the ascetic self performs the memory of tradition and in so doing attempts to become like every other ascetic self in the tradition, this is nevertheless an act of interiorisation. But the development of interiority, a hallmark of the ascetic self, is not the development of individuality. Quite the contrary, it is an erosion of individuality through an act of will that results in ascetic practice, and that is another reason for its disparagement by modernity. However, the intensification of subjectivity in the ascetic self, while being the erosion of individuality, is not thereby a depersonalisation. As Simone Weil claimed, the ascetic self in modernity is the refusal of assent to depersonalisation because of the stress on interiority. As interiority is not linked to individuality in the ascetic case, neither can it be mapped onto the idea of privacy in contrast to public performance. The examples I have discussed clearly show how subjectivity as interiority is developed at the cost of individuality and that this interiority is still performance. (The Buddhist saint Achan Chah, speaking of his teacher, said: 'Outside he was angry, but inside there was nothing. Nobody there.'[2])

When the ascetic sets out on this path he or she is motivated by any number of reasons, perhaps unconscious, particularly the desire for power in some sense. This might include power over desire, power over the self, the power of self-annihilation, supernatural power or simply the power to be heard. Often asceticism weakens the body through a variety of controls and regimes – hunger, sleep deprivation, mortification – in order to gain power. This is where a disjunction between intention and expression lies. There is clearly intentionality (in both the phenomenological and everyday sense) in the self becoming an ascetic self, yet through an internalisation of tradition and the internalisation of the tradition's goal, that intentionality is subverted and eroded. Put in other terms, the ascetic body is not a docile body receiving the imposition of sovereign power but, on the contrary, the weakening of the body through fasting and vigil is the development of a tenacious body and the subjective appropriation of structures of power. Subjectivity as pathos and passion coexist in this disjunction, which is also the paradox of intense desire alongside detachment. We have seen this repeatedly in the examples we have examined, from Simone Weil to the Buddhist saint.

But only elliptically does this kind of subjectivity come into view, notably through ritual. The construction of the ascetic life is a ritual construction in the sense that ascetic patterns are repeated sequentially and the rhythms of the body made to conform to rhythms dictated by tradition: patterns of sleeping and eating are made to conform to patterns determined by tradition. Such repetition of ritual patterns may well, and probably does, have corresponding cognitive structures. Ascetic ritual intensifies the tradition's values, which become rooted in the body: the memory of tradition becomes a somatic memory. This construction of the ascetic self through ritualisation has a double aspect: an aesthetic quality in which the ascetic life might be seen as being akin to a work of art, and an expression of value in which the ascetic life is the paradigmatic human life. In this penultimate chapter I wish to locate the ascetic self in ritual and to develop the idea of this ascetic self in these two directions, the one aesthetic and the other ethical.

## RITUAL AND THE ASCETIC SELF

In the traditions we have examined the construction of the ascetic self is closely related to ritual and the ritual construction of the body. I take ritual minimally to be the patterning of life or the ordering of temporal sequence in conformity with tradition or the received culture. The memory of tradition might well be mapped onto the structure of the brain as cognitivists claim – indeed one would be surprised were this not to be the case – but regardless of mechanism, the important point is that cultures convey often complex rituals embedded in cultural memory through time. The debate about the wider nature of ritual, especially Frits Staal's critique of the identification of ritual with meaning,[3] need not concern us here, as our claim is not about the general nature of ritual but about the ritual construction of the ascetic self. We might say, fairly uncontentiously, that ritual is a form through which culture is recapitulated through the generations and which expresses ethical values, rooting them in the body. Cultural memory is a somatic memory encoded in ritual and in the body. The ascetic self is constructed through ritual and entextualises the body through ritual. Daily repetition and practice eradicates obstacles to the correct expression of ritual procedures, and the body, in time, conforms to ritual patterns.[4] But these rather terse formulations need to be articulated more clearly.

This is not a place to review scholarship about ritual or to discuss the range of definitions now emerging,[5] but Rappaport offers a good starting point when he defines ritual as 'the performance of more or less invariant sequences of formal acts and utterances not entirely encoded by the performers'.[6] This seems to be right. Indeed, the current chapter is strongly influenced by his general views on ritual. The performers of ritual follow patterns established by others over often very long periods of time and make those patterns their own. Of course, no two ritual performances could be identical – each act of being is in one sense unrepeatable, as Bakhtin observed – but two ritual performances could and do follow the same pattern, what Rappaport calls 'adherence to form'.[7] This is not to say that rituals do not change over time – they do, but at a very slow rate, and ritual could be said to be 'more or less invariant'.[8] There is no necessary connection between ritual traditions and their immediate social, political and economic context.[9]

The cultivation of the ascetic self occurs in ritually rich cultures. The kind of human flourishing that asceticism entails is found in traditions that have elaborate formalisations of behaviour, particularly those which punctuate the year through creating a liturgical pattern. The monastic traditions of Eastern and Western Christianity, Buddhist monasticism and Hindu renunciation all organise time in ritual sequences that entail an intensification of particular temporal ranges. The liturgical year in Eastern Christianity follows a pattern that recapitulates the life, death and resurrection of Christ, for example, and early Buddhist monasticism followed a pattern according to the wet and dry seasons, a pattern particularly marked by the recitation of the monastic rules. Furthermore, ritual is closely linked to cosmology in these traditions. The divine liturgy of the Orthodox Church participates in the ongoing cosmic liturgy, and this was also true of the Latin West. Peter Damian, we might remember, regarded even the solitary recitation of the Psalter to be fully participating in the life of the Church (see p. 190). Again, the Śaiva householder recapitulates the emanation and dissolution of the universe within his own body (see p. 100), and although this is a very different world from that of Christianity, it shares an account of the self in which the self participates in a greater whole, a greater being. That degree of participation increases through an act of will in consonance with the decrease of individual, limited will.

Locating asceticism in ritual allows us to sharpen our understanding of the ascetic self and to show how it is a model of the self in the scriptural traditions *par excellence*. Along with other cultural forms such as drama, sport or political debate, ritual is a form of performance, but a performance that entails a particular kind of competence or cultural knowledge that flows through the generations. In all areas of performance asceticism plays an important part. Indeed, the origins of the Greek term lie in athletic training, and Harpham has persuasively argued for asceticism being necessary for all cultural developments (see p. 4). But the prototypical ascetic self is within a tradition that posits a sacred origin and future goal that the ascetic aims to achieve. Asceticism in one sense is clearly required in sport – athletes or body-builders follow strict regimes of diet and training that could conceivably be described as ascetic – but this is not the development of the ascetic self as described here. Again, political protest might entail asceticism in the form of fasting, as could be argued in the case of Gandhi and Simone Weil, but this is not prototypical of the ascetic self, although the case of Weil is more complex, as we have seen. Lastly, medical conditions such as those categorised under the general rubric of anorexia are clearly a cultural performance involving ascetic elements, but they are not the cultivation of the ascetic self. It is surely an error that misses the point of asceticism to read the ascetic self in terms of a modern medical condition.

## ATHLETES ARE NOT ASCETICS

While sport is a form of performance, it is not ritual in Rappaport's sense. Rappaport, following an anthropological tradition set by Lévi-Strauss, distinguishes ritual from games, where games have a disjunctive effect, ending in establishing a difference between players or teams, in contrast to ritual, which has a conjunctive effect between participants or groups. There are intermediate forms between games and ritual, as in Trobriand Island cricket.[10] Sport, particularly athletics, could be seen to be ascetic in the sense that it entails developing a disciplined life, training the body and dietary restriction and is teleological – all features we have highlighted – but it must be distinguished from the formation of the ascetic self within the scriptural traditions. The goal of the scriptural traditions is defined by the tradition, and the ascetic self is constructed in a way particular to that tradition and the orientation towards a transcendent goal. This involves the entextualisation of the body and the eradication of will through an act of will, as we have seen. By contrast, athletic asceticism in the modern world does not entail the entextualisation of the body and the goal is temporally limited: the contest to be won is within a short time-frame and does not involve the eradication of the will.

As there are some games, such as Trobriand cricket, that are between sport and ritual, so there are some bodily regimes that hesitate between the ascetic self and the athlete. The wrestlers in Benares documented by Joe Alter are an example here, who, while not being prototypical, nevertheless create themselves in the form of a Hindu tradition. This might be contrasted with the gay body-builders in the USA described by David Halperin, who are closer to athletic performance than the performance of the ascetic self, although both share this middle ground to some extent.[11] With Halperin's gay body-builders there are undoubtedly elements of an ascetic regime: the body-builders live disciplined lives, controlling diet, cultivating and shaping the body into particular, culturally prescribed forms. Working out becomes an art of existence, 'a strenuous, demanding and transformative daily ritual which often alters the entire shape of one's life'.[12] But in contrast to the Hindu wrestlers, this performance is closer to pure aesthetics and athletics. Although in some ways the gymnasium resembles the monastery, it differs fundamentally because it does not cultivate the ascetic self as the recapitulation of tradition in order to perform the ambiguity of the subversion of the will through its assertion. The gay body-builder, while sharing discipline and control with the ascetic self and while striving to push back the boundaries of what is possible for a self, does not entextualise the body in tradition-specific ways to achieve a transcendent goal as ordained by the scriptural traditions. Indeed, one might say that the ascetic self as the entextualising of the body, the conformity of the narrative of the self to the narrative of the scriptural tradition, excludes secular forms of 'asceticism'. Halperin himself says that modern analogues of asceticism are entirely secularised, with little to do with austerity.[13]

The wrestlers in Varanasi, in contrast to the gay body-builders, cultivate an ascetic self in ways close to those described in this book. They form a particular caste and are devotees of the Hindu monkey god Hanuman, whose shrine is located in every gymnasium. They see their training very much in terms of cultivating a body in conformity to tradition in a 'gymnasium' (*ākhāra*) managed by a master (*guru*) and within the precincts of a temple. The tradition has a sacred text, the thirteenth-century *Malla Purāṇa*. This upholds the ideal of sexual transformation, namely that to achieve bodily and spiritual power semen needs to be redirected upwards within the body to the head, and the wrestler should live a life of disciplined self-control. The wrestler, observes Alter, is super-virile but sexually passive and controlled.[14] All these are typical features of the Hindu ascetic. The wrestler is akin to the renouncer (*sannyāsin*), and wrestlers perceive themselves to be like renouncers in turning their backs on worldly pleasures, in 'cooling down' their bodies, in controlling their bodies and in seeking self-realisation.[15] While wrestlers do not weaken the body through practising severe asceticism such as fasting or self-imposed atrophy of their limbs, they do describe their practice as *tap* or *tapas* ('asceticism' or, literally, 'heat'); they claim to 'wear a necklace of pain' in order to achieve a goal of 'somatic self-perfection'.[16]

It is not possible to give a detailed account of the ethics and vision of the wrestlers so fascinatingly described by Alter, but what is important for us is that these wrestlers, though participating in a performance (wrestling) that can be distinguished from ritual in Rappaport's sense (because it entails contest), are nevertheless concerned with the cultivation of qualities possessed by the Hindu ascetic self. Clearly, the wrestlers are acting out a cultural memory and constructing their bodies through dedicated labour in conformity with tradition, with the aim of achieving a kind of transcendence realised in subjectivity. The wrestlers themselves observe how their practice and the forms their bodies assume contrast markedly with the nearby 'secular' gymnasium which constructs a very different kind of musculature for no other reason than the body's perceived enhancement and strength. But they are also keen to differentiate themselves from the renouncers who live in monastic *ākhāras*: the renouncer 'trains his body to leave the world; the wrestler trains his body to be immune to worldly things but to remain in the world'.[17] The wrestlers of Benares categorise themselves in a middle ground between secular body-building and the ascetic self of Hindu renunciation.

## RITUAL AND TEXT

What is characteristic of the traditions here examined is that they are scriptural traditions and that ritual is inseparably connected to text. The text pervades ritual in these traditions, and the performance of ritual is the performance of text. Of course, this does not necessarily mean a written text and the ritual codification of text can function quite independently of the written word, as Staal has shown with Nambudiri Brahman vedic ritual and recitation.[18] But the traditions of Hinduism, Buddhism and Christianity contain texts at their heart, and the particularity of the ascetic self is constructed in consonance with the textual-ritual tradition. Texts form a chain of transmission and can be seen as icons of a tradition,[19] and ritual articulates and performs this chain of transmission. Through performing ritual, the practitioner is participating in the chain of transmission and ensuring that transmission through making the self conform to its dictates. We might say that ritual as a cultural form demands a response in a particular way or demands a kind of self-formation that is tradition-specific. This self-formation, the way the self becomes that which the ritual structure demands because it is infused with the text, is therefore akin to religious reading, which similarly demands a particular kind of self-formation. This is not to reduce ritual to language, for that would be to miss ritual's irreducible nature, but nevertheless there is a consonance between religious reading and ritual in the scriptural traditions – not in a surface similarity, although that is not insignificant, but in the deeper process of identification. That is, the self, the subject of first person predicates, the one that responds to the question 'Who?', becomes subsumed by both ritual and text. The 'I' becomes subject to a kind of overwhelming, to use David Ford's term,[20] by the processes of ritual and reading.

To understand this relation between the 'I' and ritual on the one hand and the 'I' and text on the other, it is illuminating to draw on work in linguistic anthropology. This relation can be expressed in linguistic terms as the identification of the indexical 'I' with the anaphoric 'I' of the text. In an important paper Greg Urban has argued that this kind of identification is crucial for cultural replication.[21] Firstly, personal pronouns (and most significantly the 'I') are 'empty' signs in that they do not necessarily refer to a specific reality: they do not refer to any class of objects such as a tree or chair but are used only to point to a particular person. The term 'I' is therefore indexical in referring to the utterer of a sentence that contains it. In a text the 'I' can be constructed so that anyone or anything can become a speaker. Secondly, there is a distinction between the indexical, referential pronouns 'I' and 'you' and semantically referential pronouns such as 'she' that do not refer in this indexical way. That is, 'I' and 'you' are context-bound and indexical outside of a text, while 'she' is meaningful but in a non-indexical or anaphoric way within the text. But 'I' can also be used within a text in a non-indexical way, as in the sentence 'Claire said "I am going to the river."' Here the first person pronoun refers to the speaker previously named and not to an indexical, extra-textual referent. This use of the first person pronoun within the text allows for the identification of the indexical-I with the anaphoric-I of the text for, although they are different uses, there is a metaphorical relationship between the two 'I's.

The first person pronoun is of central importance in understanding cultural replication. The indexical-I, my use of the 'I' as an extra-textual being, can become merged with the anaphoric-I through a metaphorical identification. Urban develops this idea and argues that there are degrees of distance between the indexical and anaphoric first person. At a first level the 'I' of the text is anaphoric – as in 'He said "I am going"' – but there are further degrees in a text in which the 'I' becomes more removed from the everyday and first person indexical referent. The 'I' in the text can become 'de-quoted': the quotation marks in which the 'I' occurs can disappear and other structures framing the 'I' take their place. Thus in theatre the 'I' has become de-quoted and the speaker of an utterance, an actor, speaks as the character outside of quotation. The first person pronoun when used by an actor in the context of a theatrical production does not refer to the extra-textual self. It is not indexical outside of the performative context. A further development of this de-quotation is the 'projective I' or the 'I' of trance-states and possession. Here the indexical-I is completely submerged in the projective-I and the self becomes wholly identified with the role or performance.[22]

In sum, the subject of first person predicates, myself, who exists extra-textually and to whom the 'I' refers indexically, can become identified with the 'I' within the text. This 'I' within the text can be clearly anaphoric when in quotation marks and referring to the previous named speaker, but becomes de-quoted in theatre where the 'I' does not refer to the actor but to the character. Further down this route lies possession and madness, in which there is a complete identification of the indexical 'I' with the 'I' of the discourse, with the god or spirit, and there are varying degrees of identification. In Urban's work there is a continuum between text and performance, between text and ritual, in which the first person pronoun functions in different ways but in all cases, simply because of its presence, allows for the identification of the self, the indexical-I, with the text or performance. His own work on the transmission of narratives in South America shows how this ritual transmission is between theatre and possession,[23] and we might cite other examples too, such as the dance possession rites of Kerala described by Rich Freeman.[24] Of course this idea contains the justifiable assumption that all languages contain a first person pronoun or its equivalent function.

The continuity between text and performance in Urban's work is important in highlighting analogous processes of subjective identification between the act of reading and the act of performance, and in some cases there is an overlap between the two. I have argued this with relation to a range of texts in the Sanskrit tantric tradition elsewhere.[25] To summarise the main points, in a particular group of Sanskrit tantric texts concerned with a ritual procedure called the purification of the elements in the body (*bhūtaśuddhi* or *dehaśuddhi*) – and this is generalisable to all ritual texts – there is the frequent use of the third person optative singular ('one should perform' and so on). Here the implied third person pronoun is anaphoric within the text but functions as a substitute for the first person. Indeed, ritual exegesis of the Mīmāṁsā school claimed that ritual injunctions in the third person actually refer to the first person, to 'me'.[26] The third person optative functions as a substitute for the first person in the texts. 'He should perform the purification of the hands' (*hastaśuddhīm kuryāt)* means 'I should perform the purification of the hands.' There can be, therefore, an identification of the indexical-I of the Brahmanical reader with the implied 'I' of the text. This identification is the way the text is replicated through the generations as a meaningful discourse for a community.

These examples and discussion demonstrate that because of the nature of language, especially its indexical features, the self can absorb cultural representations expressed in the text and indeed we might say the self conforms to the structure of the text – subjectivity is constructed in conformity with it. Furthermore, the text makes demands upon the subject to conform to it, and the intentionality of the text (not the author's intention but the intentionality contained in the text itself) makes demands upon the 'reader' to receive it in certain ways. The text elicits a response through both demanding a certain kind of attention and through the reader's response to it. This reception of the text is the construction of meaning in the dialogical relationship between 'addresser' (the text's intentionality) and the addressee (the reader or receiver of the text). Rather than the text being passively received and an original meaning decoded, the text's meaning is constructed between two, between the intentionality of the text and the subjectivity of the reader, and there are varying degrees of conformity of the self to the text, as Urban shows.

In the scriptural traditions this process is extraordinarily important. The text regarded as revelatory or as an index of revelation is an extraordinary kind of text, a text open to constant reconfiguration and different interpretations through the generations. In Bakhtin's terms we might say that the texts of scriptural traditions are polyphonic, containing many voices which are understood in multiple ways.[27] A Buddhist subjectivity constructed in response to the textual tradition is different from a Catholic subjectivity similarly so constructed, but the process of textual demand or constraint, along with the pressure to respond and subjectively appropriate, is a cross-cultural constant in the scriptural traditions.

Extending this idea of subjective identification we might furthermore say that as there can be an identification of the self with the subject of the text, there is a corresponding identification of the self in ritual performance. A scripture is not only set apart from other texts by a community because of its richness or semantic density, but because it is inextricably embedded in ritual. Scriptural traditions perform their texts. As the text (written or oral), particularly a 'scripture', makes demands upon me and so changes me, so ritual injunction makes demands upon me and so changes me. In the technical terminology from pragmatics that I have introduced, the indexical-I conforms to the demands of the 'I' of discourse. The intentionality of the text and the intentionality of the ritual structure elicit a response in subjectivity, a response which itself is not 'private' but an index of the wider community. This is an important point. The self is constructed in terms of text and ritual through the identification of the self with the self therein implied. The Orthodox liturgy, for example, comprises actions along with the performed text. In participating in the liturgy, a person is subsuming the referential or indexical-I to the 'I' of text and performance, and in so doing creates a tradition-specific subjectivity. This subjectivity is not individualistic but is itself a sign of the community and an expression of tradition. So while there is undoubtedly the development of interiority through text and ritual performance, this is not the development of a private self in contrast to a public self. Interiority is not private but developed in a tradition-specific way through the kind of mechanism I have described.

This kind of mechanism is clearly operative with the ascetic self and we are now in a position to sharpen the idea of the ascetic self as being constructed in ritual. Through subsuming the self to the intentionality of tradition the ascetic is performing the memory of tradition, as we have seen, and enacting its telos. The 'I' of the ascetic, through an act of will, conforms to the 'I' of tradition, namely the 'I' of discourse in text and ritual. The indexical-I of the everyday self is eroded by contact with the structure of tradition (text and ritual) and is subsumed by it. The tradition makes demands upon me such that I, were I to follow an ascetic path, would be annihilated in the overarching cosmic structure. The ascetic goal is such that the ascetic paradoxically hopes for the total eradication of the self so that the ascetic expresses only the goal of the tradition. In Maximus the Confessor, for example, we have seen how scripture and the necessity to form the self according to its demands pervade his ascetic theology. Although he does not explicitly comment on the divine liturgy, his emphasis on the discipline of silence, Thunberg observes, indicates 'a respect for this moment in the liturgy'.[28] The subjectivity sought – the silence of the self before the divine presence, the will of the Lord replacing individual will – has a corresponding liturgical form. The self is subsumed by the tradition and an Orthodox subjectivity formed. Even Simone Weil who so strongly (yet ambiguously) rejects tradition uses tradition to form her own ascetic subjectivity. Drawing on a range of texts from the Western philosophical tradition as well as Hindu texts such as the *Bhagavad-gītā*, Weil uses these as models for her own subjectivity, and while together these could not be liturgically expressed in a single tradition, her own ascetic self is constructed through her reading and through the external discipline of secular work.

So far we have established that text and scriptural tradition entail each other, and that scripture is ritually expressed. The self participates in tradition through a somatic identification, through entextualising the body, which entails the linguistic identification of the self with the tradition. The self can appropriate tradition, can internalise tradition in subjectivity, through the merging of the indexical-I with the 'I' of discourse in the texts. Text and tradition make demands upon the self, whose subjectivity is constructed accordingly. In the case of the ascetic self, this subsuming of the self under tradition through ritual is both an intensification of subjectivity and an eradication of the will, a paradoxical structure that we find repeated in the scriptural traditions.

## RITUAL AND SUBJECTIVITY

On the one hand ritual can be seen as the eradication of individuality through conformity to an external form, on the other ritual is effective only because of the kind of subjectivity it cultivates. We can see the way in which ritual interfaces with subjectivity for the ascetic self in the appropriation of tradition and in the concomitant cultivation of semantic density or the intensification of meaning expressed especially in ethics and aesthetics. The appropriation of tradition and the intensification of meaning might at first sight appear to be contradictory, but they are not. The performance of a liturgical order is, as Rappaport shows, an invariant sequence of formal acts and utterances to which it is necessary for the performer to conform. By performing a liturgical order, in Rappaport's words, 'the participants accept, and indicate to themselves and to others that they accept whatever is encoded in the canon of that order'. The participant loses individuality through becoming a part of the liturgical order and thereby becoming both a transmitter and receiver of tradition.[29] This is simultaneously the acceptance and expression of the tradition's values.

Yet this erosion of individuality in the self becoming the transmitter as well as receiver of tradition through the liturgical order, this appropriation of tradition, is at the same time an intensification of meaning. This semantic density corresponds to Rappaport's hierarchy of meaning which is a hierarchy of subjectivity. Rappaport distinguishes 'low-order meaning', by which he means everyday semantics or, in different terms, the differential nature of language, from 'middle-' and 'high-order meaning'. 'Middle-order meaning' refers to 'emotionally charged values', whereas 'high-order meaning' refers to 'the radical identification or unification of the self with the other'.[30] The shift from low to middle to high orders of meaning indicates a move from everyday semantics to the internalisation of a community's values, to the loss of self in participation, 'the *sine qua non* of ritual'.[31] Rappaport characterises each order of meaning as distinction (everyday semantics), similarity (use of metaphor) and identity, which he further identifies with Peirce's tripartite scheme of the symbolic, iconic and indexical (not the same as the indexicality just discussed). These three orders refer to different kinds of relation between signs and what they signify and between signs and those for whom they are meaningful. Thus the symbolic (corresponding to Rappaport's low-order meaning) is characterised by meanings intrinsic to texts or messages which are clearly differentiated from those for whom the messages have meaning. The iconic level of meaning is based on an emotionally charged cognition of similarity in which signs, signifiers and subjects are brought closer together (as in a poem or narrative), and finally at the indexical level all distinctions are reduced 'if not annihilated, as he for whom it is meaningful feels himself uniting with or participating in that which is meaningful to him'.[32] This high-order meaning is a realm where, according to Rappaport, meaning becomes a state of being and is the realm of ritual and ritual identification.

Rappaport's characterisation is useful here in showing the kind of intensification of meaning achieved in ritual. The identification of the self with the forms of ritual entails the reduction of distance between sign, signified and one for whom the sign signifies. This is very close to Urban's idea of the identification of the indexical-I with the 'I' of discourse in which the indexical-I can be wholly subsumed by the 'I' of the text. Ritual identification, in this sense, is therefore an intensification of meaning and the intensification of meaning is 'a hierarchy of subjectivity'. In the case of the ascetic self, this intensification of meaning is through the identification of the self with text and tradition and the encoding of the goals of tradition within the self and body, as we have seen.

This is not an uncontentious claim. There is a strong argument that sees ritual as being essentially 'meaningless', that the way to understand ritual is not in terms of semantics, not in terms of what it *means* (for that changes through history), but in terms of syntax, in terms of its structure. In Frits Staal's terms, ritual must be seen primarily as 'rules without meaning', and the force of Staal's argument as regards vedic Śrauta rituals is very strong – their replication through time clearly demonstrates a pattern or structure replicated through the Nambudiri Brahmans' practice.[33] But that the deeper structure of ritual is relatively invariant does not exclude a semantic overlay or different constructions of meaning at different times. The invariance of ritual structure concerns the competence to perform or a particular kind of cultural knowledge rather than performance itself, although this knowledge is, of course, a necessary condition for performance. In the acceptance of tradition the self conforms to the patterns or structure of ritual handed down through the generations and demonstrates a cultural competence through that acceptance.

Yet performance is not only the expression of ritual structure, it is simultaneously the intensification of meaning, because in accepting the tradition in this way the ascetic intends to approach the goal of tradition and to eradicate the self. If meaning is understood as the location of the self within the larger scheme of tradition and cosmos, in the medieval Christian and Indian worlds everything being in its right place, then ritual is the performance of this ability to locate the self and the context in which this meaning is most clearly demonstrated. Through ritual the ascetic self both eradicates individuality by conformity to the rule and intensifies meaning by locating the self in a larger scheme and eroding the distinction between the sign, the signifier and the interpretant. In the *Tantrāloka*, for example, Abhinavagupta locates the individual being (*aṇu*) at a particular level of the cosmos, enchained in *saṃsāra* but desiring liberation. Through a particular method or series of methods the practitioner attains liberation, which is the absolute reality – or 'supreme meaning' (*paramārtha*) – revealing itself within subjectivity, in the practitioner's intellect (*buddhi*), breath and body.[34] The goal of life and life's ultimate meaning are intensified in the self through tradition and corporeal ritual performance.

In speaking about the construction of the ascetic self through ritual, we are speaking about a particular instance of the production of the cultural body. There is no self without the body and, in appropriating tradition, in conforming the narrative of the self to the narrative of tradition, the ascetic is constructing his or her body in a particular form and, moreover, creating the body as a text. There is a vast literature on the social construction of the body,[35] and this work is arguably so influential that we can simply assume it as a background to discussion, but what the development of the ascetic self shows across the traditions is that it is constructed textually. When speaking about the self we are of course speaking about the body or cultural body (which is the only kind of body in the human case). Bodies are particular to history and culture, and forms of embodiment have been characterised as general habits, techniques of the body or types of *habitus*.[36] The ascetic self forms the body in accordance with tradition and in accordance with the text, as we have seen, and this forming the body or entextualisation of the body is both conforming to a rule and expressing meaning.

Subjectivity entails the culturally or textually constructed body because forms of subjectivity are particular to historical and social circumstance. The ascetic self is both a body and a form of subjectivity (not individuality) constructed in tradition-particular ways through ritualised behaviour and through the internalisation of the text. Peter Damian's monks perform the daily liturgy and in so doing accept the liturgical order, eradicating individuality through becoming Rappaport's transmitters and receivers of tradition, yet also in the internalisation of the text. They make their bodies conform to the dictates of tradition in liturgical performance, fasting, mortification and silence through an act of will. Abhinavagupta's practitioner possesses an intense abundance of energy which is the internalisation of the triad of powers spoken about in the scriptures, namely the goddesses Parā, Aparā, and Parāparā.[37] This performance of the self, the slow construction of the ascetic self on the way to its perfection, is simultaneously the intensification of meaning. The ascetic monks performing the Psalter alone in their cells or the Śaiva initiate meditating upon the co-extension of himself with Śiva thereby make their bodies conform to the tradition and internalise the text: they become both transmitters and receivers. In encoding the text in him- or herself through the kinds of indexical identification we have seen, a practitioner becomes located within a tradition and within a cosmos. Practitioners develop tradition-specific virtue and look to their future life and telos.

For Marguerite Porete the soul brought to nothing, having no will at all, is the conformity of the self to the will of God articulated through the greater tradition (although Porete, as we have seen, rejected the 'lesser' tradition's authority). She wishes to eradicate her will in conformity to the goal (*scopos*) of tradition, that not she but the Lord dwell in her. Porete's body conforms to the dictates of tradition and, in her case, to the dictates of sovereign power, in her being burned at the stake. Yet this conformity is subjectivity located in her ascetic desire to eradicate the will and so achieve what she perceived to be the goal of Christianity. A sharp contrast can be seen here between Damian and Porete. For Damian the ascetic self is formed through the liturgical order and the supererogatory ascetic acts; for Porete the self is formed as an act of will that attempts to receive the ever-present grace of her God. But both are entextualisations of the body in different ways, both attempt to encode the body through liturgical and reading processes, to conform to their perception of Christianity's purpose: the eradication of sin, the development of virtue and the ensuring of salvation.

## THE ASCETIC SELF AS ICON OF BEAUTY

The formation of the ascetic self through ritual, which entails the intensification of meaning subjectively appropriated, can imply an aesthetic dimension and the construction of the self as a work of art. Within the traditions there is a strong sense in which the ascetic self who may become sanctified – that is, rendered a particular status within a tradition – is seen as an icon of beauty. Through years of practice and entextualising the body, the ascetic self reflects a beauty and a truth recognised by the tradition (and indeed outside of it).

The Christian Orthodox tradition maintains that a certain energy pervades being and that this power, eluding words, is concentrated in particular symbols or icons of the tradition. The ascetic self can be such an icon, concentrating this power and becoming not merely a moral exemplum but a figure of beauty and vehicle of transformation. Indeed, beauty and transformation are interlinked in Orthodox theology, and the collections of ascetic writings were themselves called 'love of beauty', *Philokalia*. The walking icon of the ascetic self can be seen as proof of God's existence in so far as the saint has advanced along the way of completing the art of God's work (*theurgia*) in human life. For Russian thinkers such as Pavel Florensky, this is the main task of human life, 'the task of the full transformation of reality by meaning, and the full actualization of meaning in reality'.[38] The ascetic self is believed by tradition to have actualised meaning in this way and to have transformed the self through an act of will but also the reception of grace. Florensky's actualisation of meaning is the development of a semantic density through the linguistic and performative processes we have identified. For Florensky, and for the Orthodox tradition generally, semantic density is linked to beauty: the greater and fuller the meaning realised in subjectivity, the greater the beauty apprehended (the tradition, of course, draws on the Platonic identification of beauty with truth and goodness). Indeed, as we have seen in the cosmologies of Evagrius and Maximus, the human body is a fallen version of the brilliant bodies of angels. This idea, resonating in the works of the Cappadocian fathers as well, itself reflects the archaic Greek view of the body as a dim version of the dazzling bodies of the gods, as Patricia Cox Miller shows.[39]

There are three interconnected areas where the idea of beauty is important. Firstly, beauty is a characteristic of God and is manifested as light. Secondly, beauty is reflected in the incarnation and intensively displayed in the transfiguration, and thirdly this light is reflected through the icon, which refers not only to the objects of veneration but to human beings who reflect God's beauty and even to the Church itself.[40] All of these themes are reflected in the divine liturgy, and through encoding the liturgy in the body, the body comes to reflect the beauty of the incarnation. Specifically, the death and resurrection of Christ are entextualised in the body and realised or fully expressed by the ascetic saint. The Orthodox ascetic becomes a walking icon of tradition, encoding the text of tradition and expressing the telos through his or her body, speech and action.

In a not dissimilar way the Hindu ascetic self reflects transcendent beauty, although articulated in very different terms. As the Orthodox ascetic becomes an icon of tradition, reflecting a *theosis* desired or realised, so the Śaiva ascetic imitating the terrible awe of his deity becomes an icon of tradition. His emaciation reflects his god's transcendence of the lower universe. The physical body becomes a divine body (*divyadeha*) in the twice-daily ritual of the Śaiva initiate, and his experience or 'tasting' of the divine (*brahmāsvāda*) becomes identified with aesthetic experience (*rasāsvāda*) whose goal is tranquillity (*śāntarasa*) in the writings of Abhinavagupta.[41] As the Śaiva ascetic dwells in the cremation ground – a place of awe and terror – he intensifies the experience of living in the universe which is itself a cremation ground, burning with the pyres (*citi*) of consciousness (*citi*), where all bodies are consumed, as Abhinavagupta says in a well-known passage.[42] The realisation and ascetic acceptance of the terror of the universe are partly constitutive of the Śaiva ascetic's wisdom, a wisdom that is an expression of grace. Indeed, the master is one who channels the grace of Śiva through initiation. He is, according to the *Kubjikāmata-tantra*, bereft of bodily imperfections, born in a beautiful place and giving to his disciple out of compassion (*daya*).[43]

The scriptural traditions we have examined have distinct goals and methods of attaining those goals. But what they do share in common are patterns of ritual and patterns of reading in which the ascetic self is formed in tradition-specific ways. This self-construction and move towards tradition-defined perfection is explicitly associated with aesthetics in the Hindu and the Christian Orthodox traditions, where the ascetic self reflects the beauty, sometimes the terrifying beauty, of transcendence. This theme of beauty and the creation of the self as an icon is less explicit in the Buddhist tradition, which rejects all forms of attachment, but it is preserved in Christianity and Śaivism, where desire is not completely eradicated in the sense that desire is a property of the divine recapitulated in the self. The aesthetic quality of ritual and the attempt to form the self in its pattern express desire – not simply the human desire for transcendence but, in Orthodoxy, the desire of a personal God to save humanity through the incarnation and tradition, and, in Śaivism, the desire of Śiva to be revealed to his devotees.

## RITUAL AND VALUE

In one sense ritual is irreducible. Although it expresses text, it is not itself text; although it is pervaded by language, it cannot be expressed in language; and although it embodies ethical values, they cannot be summarised in a list. The aesthetic qualities of ritual in forming the ascetic self in ways particular to tradition simultaneously articulate the tradition's values – the affirmation of a mainstream cultural trajectory or even its disruption. In the shaping of the narrative of the self to the narrative of tradition the ascetic self is engaged not only in an act of self-construction and so an aesthetic act but is also simultaneously involved in appropriating the values of the tradition or community. The identification of the indexical-I with the 'I' of discourse involves an interiorisation of a tradition's values, what is classified as virtue rather than vice, for example, or the values of a transcendent interiority.

The hierarchical cosmos mapped on to the body in Śaiva daily ritual encodes the values of the tradition that sees transcendence of the lower worlds of cosmic emanation as the desired telos. The indexical-I of the ritual participant conforms to the 'I' of discourse in the ritual text and living tradition, which entails the acceptance of the implicit theology of emanation and the ritual enactment of cosmic contraction which is at the same time an opening up of higher worlds. Similarly, participation in the divine liturgy reminds the Orthodox Christian of the resurrection, both the beginning and the end point of the cosmic drama. In both cases we have an intensification of meaning, which is to locate subjectivity in cosmological terms. Meaning is intensified through a ritual self-location that encodes aspiration. The ascetic self is a particularly intensified form of subjectivity in this sense, that through the acceptance of tradition creates a subjectivity or inwardness that both constructs an aesthetic sense of the self and encodes the values of tradition. The body articulates the body of tradition and ascetic inwardness becomes not a matter of private conscience but an interiority which is also performance: the eradication of the private and the inner acceptance of the form of tradition.

This kind of interiority and embodiment of values is set within a hierarchical frame in the traditions we have examined. In the Śaiva case there is a clear hierarchical universe mapped onto the body, and we have come upon a similar idea in the Evagrian tradition where the body aspires to become a body of light and to transcend the heaviness of demonic materiality. Closely related to these epistemological hierarchies are hierarchies of value. The progression away from materiality to more refined levels of the cosmos, which is also a progression to more refined modes of interiority, is a progression to higher levels of value, with the ultimate value of the tradition at the summit of this chain of being. This hierarchy of being that roughly maps onto what Rappaport calls a hierarchy of sanctity[44] might also reflect a hierarchy of social systems. Rappaport argues that values are hierarchically organised to reflect the hierarchical structures of social systems. There is a progression away from material or concrete regulatory values towards increasingly ideological values. Thus practical concerns, such as assumptions about the need to water crops, are concrete and regulatory, whereas ideas about types of market, 'free enterprise' or 'from each what he can give, to each what he needs' are ideological.[45] Divinity is associated with highest-order regulation and the hierarchical dimension of liturgical orders.[46] So, for example, the Śaiva hierarchy of worlds which locates purer beings higher in the structure and impure, demonic beings lower in the structure corresponds to some extent to a social hierarchy.

This is expressed in such texts as the *Īśānaśivagurudevapaddhati*, which contains chapters on possession and exorcism. The text describes the dangers of possession by lower levels of supernatural being classified as two kinds, gentle (*saumya*) and fierce (*agneya*), who respectively desire sexual pleasure (*ratikāma*) or desire to kill (*hantukāma*). These lower beings dwell in liminal places such as cremation grounds, mountains or Buddhist stupas and affect people at the lower end of the social spectrum or those in socially ambiguous situations, particularly the vulnerable. Thus they attack the emotionally excited, those alone in the night, those whose wealth has been lost, the separated, those wishing to die, and women, particularly prostitutes and naked or pregnant women.[47] Conversely, while lower-level beings are associated with the socially marginal and with those at the lower end of the social spectrum, particularly women, the ruler was associated with the highest deity. The fifteenth-century rulers of Vijayanagara were ritually identified with the goddess from whom they derived their power, as Gupta and Gombrich have shown in an important article.[48] In these examples from medieval South Asia we see how the hierarchy of beings is clearly related to a social hierarchy and how the hierarchy of beings reflects a hierarchy of social values.

But the two are not co-extensive, for the hierarchy of being can exist – as embodied in a liturgical order – outside of particular social structures, and the persistence of hierarchical liturgical orders through time in different social circumstances, particularly their intrusion into modernity, demonstrates a more complex relationship between liturgical order and social structure. Indeed, the ascetic self often goes against the prevailing social order while strictly adhering to the hierarchy of being and hierarchy of value embedded within the liturgical order. Abhinavagupta's ascetic 'hero' adheres to a strict hierarchy of beings yet disrupts the hierarchy of Brahmanical values through an appeal to forms of transcendence considered to be demonic by that tradition. Porete disrupts the social hierarchy of the Church through an appeal to what she perceives to be a higher source of value: a God and transcendence that demands our complete annihilation to know him. This transcendence that threatened the Church is, as Janzen has argued, a gendered definition of heresy that reacts with violence against the threat of women becoming divine.[49]

That the hierarchy of values in ritual systems is a gendered hierarchy, reflecting a male control of ideology and resources, is, I would think, generally now uncontested. But the historical picture is complex and nuanced. Thus, medieval women mystics must be understood in terms of contemporary concerns about sinfulness in a way not dissimilar to their male counterparts (see pp. 145, 194), and while we no doubt need to read history in terms of female subjectivity colonised by male power, I have argued that both men and women share the same processes that form the ascetic self. Both men and women have been concerned with developing an interiority that is the eradication of the self and the internalisation of the tradition's goals; both have been concerned with the entextualisation of the body; and both have been concerned with constructing subjectivity through ritual and textual appropriation.

I have tried to focus ideas about how the ascetic self comes to be in the traditions we have examined through focussing on ritual. In the traditions we have surveyed, we can see the centrality of ritual in forming the ascetic self, and I have accounted for this through drawing on work in linguistic anthropology. We have seen how the subjective appropriation of tradition and entextualisation of the body partly come about through mechanisms whereby the self (the indexical-I) becomes identified with the implied subject of the texts (the 'I' of discourse). This construction of the self through ritual can be seen in terms of the aesthetics of the self, the formation of the ascetic self as an object of beauty, an exteriorisation of an ascetic interiority and as the articulation of values embedded in the liturgical order. While ritual cannot be reduced to the values embedded within it, as it transcends the societies that produced it, the values it reflects are inevitably the cultural values of particular historical periods and communities.

In the vast majority of cases such systems of value have been, purely descriptively, produced by men. Even the internalisation of tradition by women has arguably been the internalisation of texts generally produced by men which reflect the values of a gendered hierarchy. Whether these values integral to the ascetic self across cultures are, in fact, the values that we need to adopt or whether it is these very values that need to be subjected to sustained, gendered critique is another question that needs to be addressed in some form. It is partly to this question in the wider context of the secular critique of the ascetic self in modernity to which we must finally turn.

## NOTES

1. R. Pandey, *Hindu Saṃskāras: Socio-Religious Study of the Hindu Sacraments*. 2nd ed. (Delhi: MLBD, 1969), p. 32.
2. Jack Kornfield, 'Questions and Answers with Achaan Chah' (Hemel Hempstead: Amaravati Buddhist Centre, 1986), p. 9.

3. Frits Staal, *Rules Without Meaning: Ritual, Mantra and the Human Sciences* (New York: Peter Lang, 1989).
4. Phillip B. Zarrilli, 'What Does it Mean to "Become the Character": Power, Presence, and Transcendence in Asian In-body Disciplines of Practice' in Richard Schechner and Willa Appel (eds.), *By Means of Performance: Intercultural Studies of Theatre and Ritual* (Cambridge University Press, 1990). His remarks about performance and the body in South Asia are more generally applicable in the ascetic case. He writes: 'daily repetition of physical exercises and/or performance techniques encodes the techniques *in the body*. By daily practice all physical and mental obstacles in the way of correct practice are gradually eliminated. The goal of all such virtuosic systems is reaching a state of "accomplishment" (Skt *siddhi*) in which the doers and done are one. Through such actualised practice comes both control and transcendence of "self"' (p. 131).
5. See C. Bell, *Ritual: Perspectives and Dimensions* (New York: Oxford University Press, 1997, part I: Theories.
6. R. A. Rappaport, *Ritual and Religion in the Making of Humanity* (Cambridge University Press 1999), p. 24.
7. Rappaport, *Ritual and Religion*, p. 33.
8. Ibid. p. 36.
9. R. A. Rappaport, *Ecology, Meaning and Religion* (Berkeley: North Atlantic Books, 1979), p. 207.
10. Rappaport, *Ritual and Religion*, pp. 44–5.
11. David M. Halperin, *Saint Foucault: Towards a Gay Hagiography* (New York and Oxford: Oxford University Press, 1995), pp. 115–19.
12. Halperin, *Saint Foucault*, p. 116.
13. Halperin, *Saint Foucault*, p. 102.
14. J. S. Alter, *The Wrestler's Body: Identity and Ideology in North India* (Berkeley: University of California Press, 1992), p. 151.
15. Alter, *The Wrestler's Body*, pp. 219–20.
16. Ibid. pp. 221–2.
17. Ibid. p. 223.
18. See Frits Staal, 'The Twelve Ritual Chants of the Nambudiri Agniṣṭoma' in J. C. Heesterman et al. (eds.), *Pratidānam Indian, Iranian and Indo-European Studies Presented to Franciscus Bernardus Jacobus Kuiper on his Sixtieth Birthday* (The Hague: Mouton, 1968), pp. 409–29. On the separation of written and aural culture see F. Staal, 'The Independence of Rationality from Literacy', *European Journal of Sociology* vol. 30, 1989, pp. 301–10.
19. Peter Ochs, *Peirce, Pragmatism and the Logic of Scripture* (Cambridge University Press, 1998), p. 34.
20. D. Ford, *Theology: A Very Short Introduction* (Oxford University Press, 1999) pp. 7–11.
21. Greg Urban, 'The "I" of Discourse' in Benjamin Lee and Greg Urban (eds.), *Semiotics, Self and Society* (Berlin, New York: Mouton de Gruyter, 1989), pp. 27–51.

22. Urban, 'The "I" of Discourse', pp. 34–42. For a discussion of this see my *Beyond Phenomenology: Rethinking the Study of Religion* (New York: Cassell, 1999), pp. 180–85.
23. Greg Urban, *A Discourse-Centred Approach to Culture: Native South American Myths and Rituals* (Austin: University of Texas Press, 1991).
24. R. Freeman, 'Formalised Possession among the Tantris and Teyyams of Malabar', *South Asian Research* vol. 18, 1998, pp. 73–98; R. Freeman, 'Dynamics of the Person in the Worship and Sorcery of Malabar' in J. Assayag and G. Tarabout (eds.), *Possession in South Asia: Speech, Body, Territory*, special edition of *Puruṣārtha* (Paris: Ecole des Hautes Etudes en Sciences Sociales, 1999), pp. 149–81.
25. G. Flood, 'The Purification of the Body in Tantric Ritual Representation', *Indo-Iranian Journal*, vol. 45, no. 1, 2002, pp. 25–43.
26. Flood, 'Purification', p. 37.
27. For a discussion of Bakhtin in relation to religion see my *Beyond Phenomenology*, pp. 150–62.
28. Lars Thunberg, *Man and Cosmos: The Vision of St Maximus the Confessor* (New York: St Vladimir's Seminary Press, 1985), p. 152.
29. Rappaport, *Ritual and Religion*, p. 119.
30. Ibid. pp. 70–71.
31. Ibid. p. 72.
32. Ibid. p. 73.
33. Staal, *Rules Without Meaning*, pp. 245–51.
34. Abhinavagupta, *Tantrāloka*, 5.7–8.
35. Beginning arguably with J. Blacking, *The Anthropology of the Body* (New York, London: Academic Press, 1977). But others include P. Mellor and C. Shilling, *Re-Forming the Body: Religion, Community and Modernity* (London: Sage, 1997); C. Shilling, *The Body and Social Theory* (London: Sage, 2003 (2nd ed.)), pp. 62–87 and the important edited works by Maurice Godelier and Michel Panoff (eds.), *La Production du Corps: Approches Anthropologiques et Historiques* (Amsterdam: Editions des Archives Contemporaines, 1998) and their *Le Corps Humain: Supplicié, Possédé, Cannibalisé* (Amsterdam: Editions des Archives Contemporaines, 1998).
36. Mellor and Shilling, *Re-Forming the Body*, p. 4.
37. Abhinavagupta, *Tantrāloka*, 5.23b–25a.
38. V. Bychkov, *The Aesthetic Face of Being: Art in the Theology of Pavel Florensky* (Crestwood: SVS Press, 1993), p. 44.
39. Patricia Cox Miller, 'Dreaming the Body: An Aesthetics of Asceticism' in V. C. Wimbush and R. Valantasis (eds.), *Asceticism* (Oxford University Press, 1995), pp. 281–300; Jean-Pierre Vernant, 'Dim Body, Dazzling Body' in Michel Feher (ed.), *Fragments for a History of the Human Body* (New York: Zone, 1989), vol. I, pp. 18–47.
40. P. Evdokimov, *The Art of the Icon: A Theology of Beauty* (Oakwood: Redondo Beach, 1990 (1972)), p. 300.

41. See G. Larson, 'The Aesthetic (*rasāsvāda*) and the Religious (*brahmasvāda*) in Abhinavagupta's Kashmir Śaivism', *Philosophy East and West*, vol. 26, 1976, pp. 371–87.
42. Abhinavagupta, *Tantrāloka*, 29.183–85b.
43. *Kubjikāmata-tantra*, 3.41–54. Eponymous critical edition by T. Goudriaan and J. A. Schoterman (Leiden: Brill, 1988).
44. Rappaport, *Ritual and Religion*, p. 426.
45. Ibid.
46. Ibid. pp. 263–76.
47. *Īśānaśivagurudevapaddhati*, 42.3–6.
48. R. Gombrich and S. Gupta, 'Kings, Power and the Goddess', *South Asian Research* vol. 6, no. 2, 1986, pp. 123–38.
49. G. Janzen, *Power, Gender and Christian Mysticism* (Cambridge University Press, 1995), pp. 259–64, and *Becoming Divine: Towards a Feminist Philosophy of Religion* (Manchester University Press, 1998), p. 183.

CHAPTER 9

# *The ascetic self and modernity*

> Ecstasy creates its own divine landscape; acedia disfigures the landscape, bleeds sap from nature, poisons life with an ennui which only we, accursed mortals, can still comprehend. Modern acedia is no longer monastic solitude – though our souls are our cloisters – but a void, and the dread of an inefficient, derelict God.
>
> E. M. Cioran *Tears and Saints*[1]

> Forgetfulness is white, – white as a blasted tree,
> And it may stun the sybil into prophecy,
> Or bury the Gods.
> I can remember much forgetfulness.
>
> Hart Crane 'Forgetfulness'[2]

We have discussed the ascetic self in the histories of three scriptural traditions and presented an argument for shared structures in its formation. It remains for our concluding chapter to place the ascetic self in the context of modernity, both in terms of cultural and social developments and in terms of theory. The location and trope of the ascetic self in cosmological, liturgical traditions has, of course, been significantly eroded over several centuries in the West. The general demise of the ascetic self in modernity as both cultural trope and social fact is linked to the demise of traditional cosmologies, to the rise of the human sciences and Enlightenment reason and to the demise of broader religious tradition with the twofold death of 'God' and 'Man'. The idea of progress that goes beyond medieval Christian theology implies that the ascetic self looking back to before creation and forwards to an eschaton is redundant, merely an echo of the past. Weber has shown how Protestantism developed an inner worldly asceticism and how this is linked to the rise of capitalism and modernity, and so to the erosion of the ascetic self as performance in the sense described in this book. Furthermore, Norbert Elias's extensive work has shown how civilisation depends upon inner control rather than outer constraint, and external asceticism has had an important place in this development, only to be replaced by an inner self-control, the superego or conscience.[3] Although the ascetic self has persisted into modernity, and although modern forms of asceticism, especially politicised forms, have arisen (as we have seen with Weil) that repeat the pattern of the ascetic self or attempt to repeat the pattern in a secularised context, undoubtedly the ascetic self as the quintessentially religious self that performs the memory of tradition is a minority pursuit and an idea with little political power in the detraditionalised West.

Secularisation has seen, as Hervieu-Léger documents, the fragmentation of belief and the rupture of the link between society and religion. This fragmentation of individual and collective memory is accompanied by an increasing homogeneity of collective memory.[4] Tradition is in contraction. On the one hand tradition has retreated to the margins of late modern society to become another commodified item in a global marketplace, on the other we see the resurgence of tradition in fundamentalisms that have great political and social consequences, as is evident with the resurgence of political Islam. The problem of modernity is a complex and vast topic whose implications for the ascetic self I intend to approach via three routes. The first route is implicitly a path of the critique of the ascetic self and last two are routes of its defence and future possibility. The first route is to give an account of modernity linked to a sociology that has described the demise of the ascetic self while simultaneously theorising, predicting and promoting this demise. This sociology both provides a descriptive account of the end of the ascetic self with the end of tradition or detraditionalisation and provides a critique of the ascetic self through the critique of tradition and through an account of the modern self in terms of self-assertion. Such an account of self-assertion can be linked to a feminist critique that sees the ascetic self and the formation of ascetic subjectivity in the way I have described as the formation of an exclusively male subjectivity. We have, then, two ways of critiquing the ascetic self: firstly, the critique of the ascetic self is implied by the critique of tradition, and secondly the critique of the ascetic self is made explicit in the development of ideas of self-assertion and autonomy. In response to these critiques, my second route will be a defence of the ascetic self in relation to the account of self-assertion. My third route will be that the postmodern critique of modernity has allowed the re-appropriation of the ascetic self as a legitimate form of subjectivity within the bounds of reconfigured traditions. The idea of the ascetic self marks out a realm of discourse that takes seriously – against the general claims of modernity – the theological legitimacy of pluriform traditions in a quest for transcendence that allows the exploration of the claims to truth of the scriptural traditions. This is also an argument for heteroglossia and the reconfigured discourse of plural theologies within the context of the Kantian aspiration for autonomy.

## MODERNITY AND THE CRITIQUE OF THE ASCETIC SELF

The ascetic self is governed by control, not a Kantian rational control at the expense of desire, but a control governed by tradition and the perceived higher telos that the ascetic self anticipates. This kind of tradition-specific control, the channelling of desire in ways acceptable to tradition, has been the subject of criticism both from the perspective of a Kantian Enlightenment which promotes individualism and autonomy in a rational self-control that resists all forms of heteronomy, and from the Dionysian perspective of a Nietzsche who criticises the ascetic self as weakness, a critique that finds a sophisticated development in the work of Foucault. On the one hand a process of reason can free us from the stifling constraints of tradition and move forward to a pristine future in a progress bereft of superstition, on the other we have the affirmation of the passions, of desire, that can free us from tradition and the repression it entails. It is tempting to relate these three ideals – the tradition-dependent ascetic self, the rational, autonomous self and the desiring self – with three moments in the history of the West, the premodern identified with tradition and repression, the modern identified with rational progress and the postmodern identified with the re-assertion of desire and the critique of reason and progress. But this would be to oversimplify a complex process.

Reflection upon the 'modern age' has been a feature of it since the nineteenth century, and has sought both to critically analyse its origins and to promote certain features, particularly the idea of progress. This reflection has taken the form of philosophical critique (for example by Husserl),[5] psychoanalytic critique (by Freud),[6] but above all a sociological critique (particularly by Marx and Weber). Sociology, as Giddens and Roberts have observed, is deeply implicated in the development of modernity.[7] On the one hand it claims to be descriptive of the nature of human communities, on the other it is prescriptive in its claims to offer solutions to human problems. Sociology, in other words, inherits both an Enlightenment rationality and empiricism that aspires to a scientific analysis of the human, social condition, as well as a deep investment in the idea of human progress. Phenomenological sociology, such as that of Alfred Schutz, which develops via philosophical phenomenology, is in tension with a progressive sociology ultimately stemming from Hegel through Marx to the Frankfurt School and Habermas, which in turn needs to be differentiated from the sociology of Weber and its Nietzschean inheritance.[8] In all three trajectories we have an aspiration towards a complete knowledge – the emergence of which is described by Foucault[9] – and belief in progress, but accompanied (one might say tainted) by a deep scepticism and even nihilism stemming from Nietzsche's death of God to Foucault's death of Man, a nihilism that accompanies the banishing of fundamental human concerns from the social sciences (as Husserl said in the 1930s).[10] Indeed 'modernity', as Simon Critchley observes, is the name for the breakdown of belief in transcendence or God, the 'existential balm' that 'the meaning of human life lies outside of life and outside humanity'. Philosophy begins 'in an experience of disappointment'.[11]

A feature of modernity is the contraction of tradition through the critique of authority, the development of autonomy and an existential self-assertion. The values of the ascetic self rooted in tradition, values that generally seek world transcendence, are brought into question by the values of modernity, by progress and by ideas of universal rationality which themselves have partly come about through the internalisation of asceticism, as Weber has shown. The picture is more complex, however, as these very modernist values are themselves reflexively brought into question in the late or postmodern world.

Implicit – and in some cases explicit – in these developments is a critique of the ascetic self that promotes the idea that humanity moves on beyond restrictive tradition towards 'the roseate light'[12] of universal rationality. There is steady, inevitable progress towards a future through an increase in knowledge and technology almost in spite of human subjectivity. Marx writes about the 'steady forward motion of the mole of real philosophical knowledge from the talkative, exoteric, variously gesticulating phenomenological consciousness of its subject'.[13] This is such a strong trope in Western culture, central to the critique of the ascetic self, that we need to pay attention to it. I intend here to take two examples to illustrate this critique. The first is the implicit critique of Blumenberg, who wishes to assert 'the legitimacy of the modern age'; the second, the explicit critique of Nietzsche, who has had such deep influence on the sociological tradition.

### *Blumenberg's modernity*

Blumenberg's work *The Legitimacy of the Modern Age* is a critique of Karl Löwith's theory that key features of modernity are secularisations of medieval Christian ideas. For Löwith, modern philosophies of history with their idea of progress are a secularisation of eschatology (a position not dissimilar to Milbank's critique of social science), and Blumenberg wishes to defend the idea of progress through arguing, on the contrary, that the future of modernity anticipated by 'progress' is not some transcendent goal but immanent to historical processes. This is not to deny that modernity arises out of what went before – modernity arises out of late medieval theological absolutism for Blumenberg – but that any determined structure, such as a religious cosmology, is overturned by scientific method. The ideal of static perfection is replaced in modernity by movement of a creative spirit of a particular age. Secularisation does not reflect a secularisation of eschatology but a continuity of reflection upon problems inherited from Christianity.[14]

Blumenberg sees one of the most significant themes in the history of the West to be the attempted overcoming by Christianity of Gnosticism, the dualist doctrine – not unconnected with Neo-Platonism – that matter is demonic and traps the spirit (*pneuma*) which has to be delivered back to the realm of light and goodness, the realm of a God who has never been contaminated by matter, but who sent a redeemer to save the lost *pneuma* through knowledge.[15] For Marcion (d. ca 160 CE), the God of love in the New Testament revealed by Jesus must be distinguished from the evil demiurge of the Old Testament who creates matter. Blumenberg's reading of Marcion brings out the problem that God as the omnipotent creator of the world is in conflict with the destruction of the world and the need for salvation as central activities. The God who created man and the world and who behaves 'in the manner of an ill-tempered tyrant' cannot be the same as the 'foreign god' of love who selflessly redeems humankind.[16] In response to the problem of evil, Christianity asserts not that matter is evil, but that badness comes into the world through humankind exercising freedom of will. Augustine, himself a Gnostic before his conversion to Christianity, justifies God at the expense of humankind, a legacy, Blumenberg observes, that stays with Christianity throughout the Middle Ages.[17] Marcion, of course, was declared a heretic in 144 but, according to Blumenberg, Christianity never manages to successfully overcome the Gnostic dualism. Human freedom is transcendent, and a discourse about the right to self-assertion begins long before Descartes. Modernity, for Blumenberg, is a second attempt to overcome Gnosticism, and so modernity is not a return to a pre-Christian pagan past but is a further articulation of problems concerning human freedom, self-assertion and progress inherited from Christianity.

Part of this reflection entails the development of the idea of 'self-assertion'. In Blumenberg's reading of tradition, we have in the late medieval world a re-assertion of the fundamental contradiction between creation and salvation perceived by Marcion. In becoming man for salvation, God performs a pure act of divine will that disempowers humanity, because God could have adopted any species, 'any other nature'. Blumenberg observes 'The incidentalness of man in God's dealings with and for Himself eliminated everything that supported the idea that God's creation of man committed Him, in regard to His Incarnation, to the choice of human nature as the medium of His appearance in the world.'[18] This theological absolutism and objectivisation precipitate a crisis that entails a self-assertion as an act of autonomy that re-asserts human self-interest. Once the theological system of the Middle Ages collapses under the weight of the creation–salvation contradiction and theological absolutism, self-assertion has to come from humanity itself and not from divine providence. While the origins of self-assertion are within Christianity – as can be seen in Augustine long before Descartes – in a world in which a Christian telos has retreated, self-assertion becomes a defining feature of humanity. In Blumenberg's words it 'means an existential program, according to which man posits his existence in an historical situation and indicates to himself how he is going to deal with the reality surrounding him and what use he will make of the possibilities that are open to him'.[19] The contraction of cosmology – an absolute order in conformity to divine will – means that the world becomes, for a time, 'emptied-out'[20] and an expanded sense of subjectivity in self-assertion prevails. The modern situation is one in which self-assertion as an existential feature of human being marks itself out against two kinds of teleology: a theological teleology in which meaning is given from on high that itself is linked to political absolutism, and a biological teleology where self-preservation is the goal.

It might reasonably be argued that Blumenberg is wrong in his claim about a contradiction between creation and salvation, and while it might be argued that he exaggerates the disempowering of humanity in late medieval theology, in so far as human freedom must remain central to Christianity, his description of the emergence of self-assertion is nevertheless compelling. Self-assertion and self-conscious autonomy are key features of modernity, and the focus of modern inquiry moves from a theological absolute to a meaning-creating subjectivity on the one hand and an inquiry into an indifferent, objective order through science on the other. Modernity as such can have no place for the ascetic self, whose telos is transcendence. Stripped of tradition which seeks to impose a transcendent meaning through the structures of text and liturgy, the modern self must fundamentally seek its own self-assertion, a self-assertion that is linked not only to an existential affirmation of self-existence, being-there, but also to the democratisation of the self and the political critique of systems of theological absolutism. On this account the ascetic self falls away with the critique of tradition by philosophies of history and with the development of technologies that question theological patterns of authority and knowledge.

The narrative of the modern self has been a narrative of the development of self-assertion, a self-assertion that becomes articulated in existentialism in the twentieth century through to the primacy of 'self-fulfilment' in late modern Western culture. This narrative does not follow a clearly developmental process, and there are tensions between the ideal of autonomy, along with its corollary in the citizen, and more recent developments that emphasise cultures of therapy that indicate the abdication of autonomy.[21] For our purposes the important point is that self-assertion both as autonomy and fulfilment erodes tradition-dependent ideas of the ascetic self. The ascetic self is neither autonomous, being subject to the rule of tradition, nor self-fulfilled in the modern sense of the satisfaction of experience. The ascetic self has not abdicated will, rather will is placed in the service of tradition, and so the relation of self-assertion to the ascetic self needs to be complexified. Clearly the ascetic self as described here stands against the autonomous and individual self of modernity as well as the fragmented self of postmodernity. But, although in a different sense, the ascetic self is not devoid of self-assertion; indeed, a kind of self-assertion is central to it. As we have seen, the ascetic self in submitting to tradition asserts the self in an act of conformity and ultimately seeks to erase the self through the processes of transforming its own narrative into the narrative of tradition, although this self-assertion is always under the sign of tradition rather than under the sign of an autonomous modernity.

This non-autonomous self-assertion through tradition is not a contradiction but a central feature of the ascetic self, a self always constrained by tradition and a self that seeks through an act of will the eradication of will. The ascetic self is not individual but wholly conforms to the structures of tradition, although this does not entail an externalised self. On the contrary, the ascetic self develops a subjectivity and inwardness that must be distinguished from individuality. The ascetic self desires to form the self in conformity with tradition, which is simultaneously to develop an interiority that provides the self with great semantic density. It might be legitimate to speak of an existential dimension to the ascetic self, but this existential dimension is a tradition-specific subjectivity quite distinct from a modernist existentialism, and a form of interiority that has come under fierce attack along with the critique of modernity itself.

### *Nietzsche's critique of the ascetic self*

Self-assertion becomes a fundamental feature of modernity, developing alongside individuality and a particular kind of interiority that finds its expression in Romanticism, where we become beings with 'inner depths'.[22] In a brilliant book, the *Genealogy of Morality*, Nietzsche argues that the modern self in possession of conscience and agency is not a given but developed through a historical process. This involved a time when a slave revolt against their masters resulted in the replacement of a good/bad distinction with a moralistic distinction of good/evil. In the old morality the good had been associated with the nobles or masters and the bad with the slaves. With the slave revolt (and the emergence of Christianity) the moral order is inverted and furthermore internalised, so that good/evil is not merely a reflection of social standing but becomes a quality of the self. The 'serious illness' of 'bad conscience' has its origin here as the internalisation of morality which prevents the natural discharge of the instincts, which is also the *resentiment* of slaves against their masters. This is 'the internalisation of man' which creates the inner space for what becomes known as his 'soul'.[23] In his third, insightful essay on the ascetic ideal, Nietzsche recognises the teleological nature of asceticism that also looks back to its past. Asceticism is a general feature of human beings throughout history, and in characteristic fashion Nietzsche names the earth as the 'ascetic planet *par excellence*, an outpost of discontented, arrogant and nasty creatures who harboured a deep disgust for themselves, for the world, for all life and hurt themselves as much as possible out of pleasure in hurting'.[24] For the ascetic, life is a bridge to another existence, but for Nietzsche this is a wrong path that 'he has to walk along backwards, till he reaches the point where he starts'.[25] Unlike the ascetic self trying to retrace the journey, the modern self, characterised by self-assertion, begins from where he stands and looks to the future.

Although Nietzsche's account is a mythology, in one sense it is an accurate description in so far as the ascetic self seeks to enact the origin of tradition which is also the goal. Nietzsche's negative moral evaluation of asceticism as being the contradiction of 'life and against life'[26] is connected with modernity's vision that seeks to set humanity free from the constraints of history. Geuss observes that when he refers to 'genealogy' Nietzsche is doing the very opposite of tracing a pedigree. That is, genealogy does not legitimise a current practice but rather reveals a historically diverse number of lines of development that lead to the Christian ascetic ideal and reveals the power struggle and break with the older morality which is based on delusion.[27] For Nietzsche the ascetic self is a deluded self.

The ascetic self as located in tradition is, then, eroded by the self-assertion of modernity that is fundamentally critical of tradition and marked by a disenchantment with it on the one hand and critiqued by Nietzsche's deploration of Christian ascetic values on the other. The Nietzschean critique is in fact deeper than modernity's self-assertion, in that it is pervaded by a nihilism that undermines any metaphysical claims at the foundation of religious doctrines and so undermines any notion of a religious telos. This critique is taken up and developed by one of the most important theorists of asceticism, Michel Foucault.

## *Foucault's genealogy*

Taking up Nietzsche's idea of genealogy, Foucault seeks to give an account of the cultural processes of self-formation, with particular emphasis in his later work on the ascetic self. Through revealing the way in which forms of knowledge (*epistèmes*) have arisen, Foucault wishes to unravel the processes of how the self is formed – in Owen's words, 'to uncover the "rules of formation" which govern particular configurations of knowledge and to highlight the epistemological breaks which mark the movement from one *epistème* to another'.[28] I cannot develop a sustained account of Foucault's important understanding and critique here – this has been done by others[29] – so rather than attempt an inadequate account of a highly nuanced thinker, I shall rather focus on a single text that places him in dialogue with Nietzsche and implicitly raises the problem of the ascetic self, namely the important paper 'Nietzsche, Genealogy, History' which became the introductory chapter in the *Archaeology of Knowledge*.[30]

Foucault's discussion follows roughly the following stages. Firstly he discusses the problem of genealogy and Nietzsche's use of the term *Ursprung* ('origin'), particularly in the *Genealogy of Morality*, distinguishing the term from *Herkunft* ('descent') and *Entstehung* ('emergence'). Genealogy designates the study of numberless beginnings and, in contrast to a quest for origins, the genealogy of values, morality and asceticism 'will cultivate the details and accidents that accompany every beginning'.[31] Thus, in contrast to traditional history that seeks an origin to a particular event or group of events, genealogy does not intend to restore an unbroken continuity but rather to identify different points of emergence. In genealogy the body becomes a focus of inquiry as the 'inscribed surface of events'[32] which shows how it is not only subject to instinctual forces but is socially formed:

> The body is molded by a great many distinct regimes; it is broken down by the rhythms of work, rest, and holidays; it is poisoned by food or values; through eating habits or moral laws it constructs resistances.[33]

Whereas traditional history seeks to account for a particular event by an ideal continuity, 'effective history' (*wirkliche Historie*) is concerned with genealogy and seeks to reveal the unique characteristics of an event, showing how an event is not controlled by historical forces or destiny but by haphazard conflicts. Whereas traditional history is linked to a transcendental subject who contemplates from 'distances and heights' historical periods and abstract ideas, effective history 'shortens its vision to those things nearest to it – the body, the nervous system, nutrition, digestion, and energies'.[34] That is, effective history acknowledges the impossibility of the objectivist overview in affirming that knowledge is perspectival, and so for Foucault, as for Nietzsche, history is linked to 'the historian's history'. Rather than a Platonic form of history, this new sense of history allows for three uses, namely a parody of 'monumental history' in which any stable identity of the historian is put into question; the dissociation of identity that opposes the idea of history as tradition and continuity; and a sacrificial modality or the sacrifice of the subject of knowledge.[35] In the footsteps of Nietzsche, Foucault dispenses with the transcendental subject, with a correspondence theory of truth that historical inquiry can trace descent from an objective perspective, and shows how genealogical analysis is particular and anti-essentialist. Pervading this critique is the idea of power which, as Halperin observes, is not a substance but a relation.[36]

These ideas are by now thoroughly familiar, and Foucault's work has been largely concerned with unfolding the implications of this essay and applying the genealogical analysis to the formation of important human phenomena and institutions, such as madness and sexuality. In the three volumes of the *History of Sexuality* Foucault seeks to uncover by a genealogy the practices 'by which individuals were led to focus their attention on themselves, to decipher, recognise, and acknowledge themselves as subjects of desire'.[37] That is, the genealogical task is to uncover the relationship of the self with the self in the formation of oneself as a subject. Through paying particular attention in volume II to the Greeks, Foucault shows how the ascetic self of Christianity is prefigured in the virtuous hero who turns away from pleasure to an experience of truth and love excluded from sexual activity, an abstention 'that brought them [Greek thinkers] into direct contact with some superior element in human nature and gave them access to the very essence of truth'.[38] Genealogical analysis seeks to show how such conceptions are constructed through historically located practices that express relationships of power within and between subjects. Asceticism, then, is a form or mode of subjectivation (*mode d'assujettissement*) whereby the ethical subject is formed who has mastery over himself and is freed from bondage to the passions, a theme we have seen here in the examples taken from the history of Christianity. Foucault undertakes this genealogy through determining the modes of subjectivation to which the term 'use of pleasure' refers, namely ethical substance or the self's concern with ethical judgement; types of subjection; the forms of 'elaboration of the self' or ways in which the self transforms itself into an ethical subject; and moral teleology, the aim of behaving in a particular way.[39] Through a genealogical analysis of this kind Foucault hopes to show that the cultivation of the self results in particular kinds of subjectivity which are themselves caught up in a web of power implicated in the relationship of the self to the self and to others. That subjectivity is constructed through regimes of knowledge that are regimes of power is also the death of the subject.

In line with his conception of genealogy developed from Nietzsche, Foucault seeks to show how a set of practices, technologies of the self, *techniques de soi*, construct a certain kind of subjectivity and that these practices are historically contingent. Thus the self constituted by them is also contingent.[40] Effective history shows the particularity of such constructions and how they are contingently formed rather than formed through some overarching historical pattern or law. Thus, for the ancient Greeks the 'art of life' or 'art of existence' (*techne tou biou*) comprised sets of practices 'to change themselves in their singular being, and to make their life into a work of art that carries certain aesthetic values and meets certain stylistic criteria'.[41]

Foucault has opened up new and refreshing ways of understanding the history of the self in the West, and in many ways he is sympathetic to the ascetic self and regards the very activity of philosophy as an ascetic, self-forming practice. While bringing into question the self-assertion of modernity and in some ways aligning himself with the ascetic self of tradition, Foucault is nevertheless critical of the self in his analysis of its being wholly historically contingent. His work contains contentious positions and has provoked criticism on historical grounds,[42] criticism of his anti-humanism[43] and criticism that his analysis could only apply to histories with a central state apparatus and so not to the East. But within the confines of the current chapter there are two scepticisms in Foucault's work on the ascetic self that I wish to discuss and, indeed, bring into question, namely, a scepticism towards agency, a scepticism that itself is criticised by feminist discourse, and a scepticism towards tradition. Let us take each of these in turn.

## AGENCY AND FEMINIST DISCOURSE

Foucault's genealogy is not only a critique of autonomous self-assertion but also reflects what Farrell has called a disenchantment with subjectivity, with 'the autonomous, alienated, original, and demiurgic power of subjectivity'.[44] Foucault has presented a strong critique of the Enlightenment subject through the analysis of the conditions that give rise to particular forms of subjectivity in history, yet this critique has itself come under scrutiny, particularly from feminist thinkers, for its neglect of agency. While some have argued that Foucault's earlier work on discipline lacks the concept of subjectivity and reduces people to docile bodies,[45] his later texts have attempted to show how people fashion their own identities within regimes of power. But even here Foucault arguably neglects social relationships and the agency thereby entailed, a point argued by Lois McNay, who claims that Foucault offers 'an overdeterminist view of the subject subsumed by the operations of power upon the body or the solipsistic outlook of an aesthetics of existence'.[46] McNay, by contrast, wishes to develop an understanding of subjectivity that takes agency into account and, drawing on Bourdieu and Ricoeur, emphasises the generative and narrative dimensions of self-formation through time. Agency arises out of the cultural *habitus*, an effect of ritualised practice that is not determinative but allows central place to agency while accepting that agency always operates within the social constraints of power. In the general tension between power and agency both, as it were, are held in balance.

Through the processes of subjectivation, power, for Foucault, is expressed as both domination of the self and as the self's conformity to authority. Subjectivation might also be understood in terms of resistance to authority. Resistance and conformity are closely related for Foucault as two sides of social power. The ascetic self can clearly be seen in these terms as both agent, acting upon the world, and as being subject to forms of authority and domination. Through conformity the ascetic self accedes to the demands of tradition but through resistance rejects those demands, perhaps in the service of an alternative tradition deemed superior. We have seen this throughout the present study where the ascetic seeks his or her own eradication through an act of will. Peter Damian clearly articulates conformity to external power (the power of God mediated through the Church) through asceticism, whereas the asceticism of Weil and the Beguines can be read as resistance to authority, often at the cost of their lives. Within the constraints of tradition and authority, the ascetic self expresses power through abstention and weakening the body in mortification, as either conformity to authority or as resistance to it. Subjectivity is thereby articulated in the disjunction between intention (to resist or to conform) and expression (the weakening of the body through disciplinary regimes). As we have seen, this ascetic agency finds its expression in performance: the internalisation of tradition in a bodily observance, discipline or obedience.

This picture of the ascetic self that emphasises an agency that acts in accord with tradition and implicitly proclaims the validity of those traditional values is at odds with a Nietzschean/Foucaultian evaluation that is fundamentally materialist and cannot allow for the possibility of transcendence. While the metaphysical problem at the heart of the death of the subject is nihilism, the ethical problem is that of justice. Indeed, justice is a fundamental concern of feminist thinkers such as McNay, who resist Foucault's stripping away of subjectivity and thereby of agency. The erosion of subjectivity in a feminist reading is a further erosion of female agency throughout history. Just as feminism begins to articulate a feminist sense of subjectivity, genealogy and effective history claim that there is no subjectivity. The moment subjectivity is gained and justice is seen on the horizon – at great human cost, one might add – genealogy takes subjectivity away. Feminism is therefore resistant to the self-assertion of modernity, which, it can be argued, is a male self-assertion that entails the occlusion of women, and many feminist theorists are resistant to postmodern constructivism that seeks to denude an illusion of subjectivity.

We have, then, three views of subjectivity which are critiqued by some feminist thinkers: the self constrained by tradition which subjugates selves, both male and female, to regimes of unjust authority; modernist self-assertion that seems to privilege agency; and postmodern genealogy that privileges power. There are clearly tensions between these positions and it is not simply a matter of choice which position we adopt, being already implicated as we all are in structures of authority and power. Self-assertion as agency is clearly a key feature of modernity in many ways incompatible with the ascetic self of scriptural tradition, strictly understood as the subjugation of the self to forms of traditional authority. The agency of the ascetic self is constrained by the value system of tradition. This juxtaposition of self-assertion and tradition-constrained, ascetic agency is made more complex by late modern critique of both ideas as being blind to the conditions that allowed the production of these discourses. While both the

Foucaultian and feminist critiques of both tradition and modernity share a common concern with justice, feminism is clearly worried that the emphasis on power takes away agency – a foundation concept for many feminist thinkers.

For feminist theory in general, modern self-assertion and the ascetic agency of scriptural tradition are understood as constructed within a system of signs and practices which have been controlled by patriarchal power. This point has been consistently and rigorously made by feminist scholarship for half a century or more.[47] The self-assertion of an existential modernity along with the critique of that self-assertion in the postmodern disenchantment of subjectivity are both male discourses, politically empowered by the weight of history. The self-assertion that legitimises the modern age described by Blumenberg is an androcentric self-assertion that, in critiquing theological and political absolutism and developing the idea of the citizen, is itself unreflexively blinded by patriarchal power. On this argument, woman is deprived of subjectivity in political action and in discourse when subjectivity is understood as the autonomous, neutral subject and equally when subjectivity is understood as an illusion or mere construct.[48]

## FEMINIST DISCOURSE AND RELIGIOUS TRADITION

If this occlusion is true for the self-assertion of modernity and the undermining of subjectivity in postmodernity, it could be argued that it is even more the case with religion. In this view, male-oriented scriptural traditions have excluded female subjectivity, according to Irigaray, by the very banishment of female divinity that can define female subjectivity (at least in the Abrahamic traditions).[49] The argument might run that if sexual difference defined by male power is latent within all scriptural religions, the ascetic self is a male self and the processes of subjectivity and inwardness that I have described must exclude women.

This is a complex issue. On the one hand we are undoubtedly dealing with historically situated and socially constructed senses of the self. On the other we are talking about fundamental forms of human subjectivity that, in my view, are irreducible to power and to purely sociological, historical or gendered explanation. One way of approaching the problem is to posit the question of how a narrative self-understanding which is intimately connected to gender relates to the meta-narrative (or ideology) of tradition. Indeed, this book has been a response to that question in showing how the narrative of the self is formed in terms of the narrative of tradition in the three scriptural traditions of Buddhism, Christianity and Hinduism. But within the confines of the present discussion focussed on the relation of gender to subjectivity, I think there are two responses we need to consider. The first is that the ascetic self is historically and ideologically not exclusive of women. In this book I have tried to show how the ascetic self conforms to the narrative of tradition and internalises the tradition's telos, which is simultaneously an enactment of an origin, the performance of the memory of tradition that involves the erosion of the will through its assertion. This performance or enactment of the memory of tradition can itself be understood in terms of political protest, as in the case of Porete and Weil, but more significantly as a gender-transcending quest that erodes sexual difference in the aspiration to a transformation beyond sexual difference. This is a point that must be rejected by a Foucaultian position that accepts the death of metaphysics and any notion of transcendence, that hope lies outside of the human condition, but it is not incompatible with feminist discourse. We can legitimately read the ascetic self in terms of resistance to structures of male dominance – as can be seen in very different ways in Porete and Weil – but protest does not exhaust the semantic density of tradition (or life) either for women or for men.

The second response is that in looking at modernist self-assertion we are looking at narrative identities in which the very notion of narrative implies self-construction. Agency and self-construction are not incompatible in so far as a constructed cultural world clearly opens out or reveals something real. The ascetic self, I have argued, is constructed in conformity with tradition, which is simultaneously the operation of agency and the opening out of levels of semantic density. Something constructed opens out a reality, and that construction, it could be argued, is well-winnowed over generations and is effective. The self-construction in conformity with tradition is arguably a legitimate pursuit for both men and women, where 'legitimacy' refers to their ability to act in accordance with historically constrained processes of reason. Women have expressed their agency in severely limiting circumstances throughout history, and arguably monastic institutions in the medieval West as well as in ancient India are structures that allowed such expression – an expression that was almost wholly to disappear in the centuries following the demise of the monastic orders and the rise of self-assertion. We might say that the ascetic self is voluntaristically self-oppressive in the desire to internalise the transcendent goals of tradition, but this internalisation (and performance) contains the potential for the political resistance to injustice and contains the metaphysical resources for opening out a world previously closed.

Indeed, the self-assertion of modernity might be seen to be gender-exclusive in a way that a tradition-based ascetic self is not. A modernist, male-defined subjectivity described by Kristeva and Irigaray is determined by a symbolic order, the order of language, that *ipso facto* excludes women. Conversely, while the structures of tradition have been androcentric this does not mean that they have necessarily been non-transformative for women or that women have been excluded from them in a way that, it might be argued, they have from a modernist symbolic order. I raise this as a question rather than a proposition. The ascetic self as the performance of tradition might have some future in feminist discourse and practice in a way that a purely modernist self-assertion could never have, and clearly there are women strongly situated within scriptural traditions who think this might be so.

But rather than examining contemporary feminist developments within scriptural traditions – a task way beyond the remit of this project and my ability – I wish to conclude this section by pointing in two directions that have implications for the ascetic self. What might be called a 'religious' dimension of feminist discourse can be located not only in the development of feminist theology but in the future-oriented, nature-transcending vision of Donna Haraway on the one hand and in a nature-affirming, pagan spirituality on the other, routes that have been fascinatingly mapped by Richard Roberts.[50]

In rejecting certain forms of male, modernist, subjectivity, Haraway wishes to advocate what she calls 'cyborg feminism', which we might see as a form of the ascetic self. Haraway's argument in her early work claims that the self can be – and needs to be – dismantled both conceptually and through biotechnology and recreated in egalitarian social relationships beyond gendered identities. Furthermore, such a recreation, encapsulated in the image of the cyborg, indicates a transcendence of nature, a new ability to go beyond the constraints of biology, although this vision is still within a materialist paradigm.[51] Clearly the ascetic self has potential here, but an ascetic self that is so reconfigured as to be almost unrecognisable in any traditional sense. The construction of the self in terms of the cyborg feminist narrative is a vision that is grounded in technology but remains as fragile as that technology. The transforming potential of such a vision certainly inherits values of transcendent gnosis found in different scriptural traditions and might possibly be seen in Blumenbergian terms as the reassertion of Gnosticism, but it is a vision that is fundamentally earth-bound and material. Indeed, in the materiality of the vision and the unarticulated idea of the 'spiritualisation' of matter, cyborg feminism could be seen as an extension of Christianity rather than a resurrection of the Gnostic myth or a return to paganism. But the apparent ascetic transcendence of Haraway's cyborg is just that, merely an appearance of transcendence, for in reality the vision must be grounded in materiality and relations of production that give rise to her enabling technology.

Richard Roberts has contrasted this technologically enhanced Gnosticism (or, arguably, transformed Christianity) with a chthonic feminism in the work of Monica Sjoo, for example, whose assertion of pagan values sees a sacramental relation to nature as fundamental to human survival.[52] We need to recognise the fundamental constraint on our existence as being grounded in nature, a vision that empowers women and erodes patriarchy. These Gnostic and chthonic aspects of non-secularised feminism do not exhaust feminist possibilities, especially an even more politically driven, materialist feminism, but they may present possibilities for developing the ascetic self in a consciously non-androcentric context. There are a number of reservations we must note here, for while these developments might seem to hold promise for the future of the ascetic self, in some ways they undermine it. Haraway's transcendence of nature through technology is not the transformation of the ascetic path, the minimising of transaction with the world and the cultivation of detachment. Nor could the ascetic self be part of a return to nature in an ecstatic spontaneity or instinctual eruption, which, while certainly entailing a loss of self, is not the loss of self as the telos of a structured path, and loses the tension between ascetic intention and goal.

But the ascetic self is not necessarily set exclusively within a male discourse. Firstly the ascetic path has historically attracted many women across cultures – the Beguines and the women who wrote the poems of the *Therigata* come immediately to mind – and has itself been a vehicle for female theological and political expression. Female renouncers in India and anchorites in the West have been empowered through asceticism and renunciation. Secondly, the critique of modernity and the disenchantment of subjectivity, part of which is a feminist critique, have allowed the emergence of multiple possibilities for self-construction in the contemporary West. The ascetic self still has potential in late modernity as a possible narrative construction of the self. This does not mean that the self can be constructed in any way at all, for there are, of course, constraints on the possible ways identity may be changed,[53] but it does mean that if narrative is fundamental to a coherent sense of self – as argued by Oliver Davies, for example[54] – then the ascetic self is an option in the construction of narrative coherence. Such narrative coherence of the ascetic self, we have argued here, is given through the tradition, which provides the context and legitimacy for a life, whether male or female, and through that construction opens up a world possibly infinitely rich.[55]

The critique of scriptural tradition by modernity has inevitably eroded the ascetic self. We have seen this in terms of the conflict between modernist self-assertion and tradition. Modernity has criticised scriptural tradition both on metaphysical grounds for advocating what is perceived to be the illusion of world transcendence and on political grounds for advocating authoritarian, oppressive structures of authority and power that doctrines of the ascetic self support. While from the vantage point of late modernity many such claims are historically accurate, this does not entail that the values of the ascetic self have *de facto* been overtaken. There is yet a legitimacy to the ascetic self in terms of an existential self-assertion that is still constrained by scriptural tradition, distinct from a modernist self-assertion, and distinct from a postmodern fragmentation of the self. To this possible justification for the continuing and persistent trope of the ascetic self we must finally turn.

## THE LEGITIMACY OF SCRIPTURAL TRADITION IN LATE MODERNITY

I wish to conclude this somewhat complex material by considering the question of the legitimacy of the ascetic self in late modernity as a question about the legitimacy of the scriptural traditions. As I have argued throughout this book, the ascetic self is inextricably associated with the scriptural traditions as a product of those traditions and any question about contemporary asceticism must be linked to the question of their place in contemporary discourse. Leaving aside the sociological question about the extent of detraditionalisation and the erosion of religion in the modern West,[56] it would nevertheless appear to be the case that scriptural traditions retain an importance for community, political identity as well as for articulating positions about the nature of the world and the human. We only have to listen to the news to appreciate this point.

One response to the Nietzschean critique of tradition might be to argue for a distinction between legitimacy and claims to truth: that there is a legitimacy to the ascetic self rendered through the scriptural traditions in their response to modernity. Given the rupture with modernity and the questioning of overarching rationality from perspectives that Nietzsche himself was very influential in developing – perspectivism and the critical theory of religion – we can argue that scriptural traditions have a legitimacy and importance in the contemporary world context. The importance of religion and its imbrication with politics can be seen in the often violent eruption of fundamentalisms that are clearly one response to the perceived injustices of modernity. Yet tradition does not necessarily respond to secularised modernity in this way, and we can accept both humanistic reasoning and the authority of tradition as a given for a particular community: enlightenment autonomy can be reconciled with the heteronomy of tradition, although of course the product will be tradition transformed.

While a detailed development of this theme is outside the scope of the present study, its contemporary relevance to the ideal of the ascetic self needs to be articulated if only to indicate the persistence of that ideal into late modernity. Scriptural reasoning as envisaged by Peter Ochs in the context of Jewish philosophy[57] and later in a Christian context by David Ford, Dan Hardy[58] and Oliver Davies claims that there are dimensions of scripture that become meaningful only through hermeneutical practices of particular religious communities – communities for which those texts are indeed 'scripture'. This is not so much to protect scripture from the hermeneutics of suspicion of a modernist, philological tradition, but rather, while recognising the necessity of historical scholarship, to maintain that there are dimensions of meaning to a text – a semantic density – that are accessible only to a particular community. Following the semiotics of Peirce, Ochs observes that such reading practices involve a three-part hermeneutic, that 'the text (the first part) has its meaning (the second) for a normative community (the third), rather than identifying the meaning of the text with some historical or cognitive "sense" that is available to any educated reader'.[59] There are ways of reading rich texts that address particular problems for particular communities of readers.

The relevance of this for the ascetic self is simply that bringing together modern text-critical approaches grounded in humanistic reasoning with tradition-particular ways of reading provides a way in which a discourse of the ascetic self may be articulated in the context of modernity.[60] The ascetic self is a legitimate goal and ideal within the scriptural traditions and within practices of reading that nevertheless accept much of the critique of religion and accept the processes of secular reasoning. Such contemporary scriptural readings might, for example, legitimise a path of Christian asceticism for some person or group and support the justification of a Christian ascetic path (inevitably a minority pursuit) in the face of overwhelming conformity to a commodified culture of unchallenging ease.

On this view the ascetic self is not simply consigned to history or a residue left-over in the post-traditional world after the death of religion but remains an important, continuing presence – largely outside the West – that may yet have great (or devastating) historical consequences. We have witnessed a highly politicised ascetic self emerging in Islam where 'martyrdom' might be seen as a form of asceticism (as, conversely, asceticism was called 'white martyrdom' in early Christianity), and within the West retraditionalised forms of religion are tracing routes to an ascetic past. This points to the centrality of subjectivity and the desire for transcendence as a persistent trope in culture, arguably fundamental to human nature. Theology as contemporary discourse in the secular universities needs arguably to re-assert the ascetic self as a paradigm or model of interpretation that avoids the fundamentalist repudiation of modernity on the one hand and also avoids an absorption into secular, sociological discourse on the other.[61] There can be tradition-based discourse that promotes the virtues of ascetic selves while at the same time accepting critical reason. Inevitably discourses of the ascetic self will change along with the icon of the ascetic self, but it still has a compelling power over people in proclaiming that the values of tradition are less eroded than Nietzsche would have thought or hoped.

## NOTES

1. E. M. Cioran, *Tears and Saints* (University of Chicago Press, 1998), p. 86.
2. Hart Crane, *The Complete Poems and Selected Letters and Prose of Hart Crane*, ed. Brom Weber (London: Oxford University Press, (1968)), p. 137.
3. N. Elias, *The Civilizing Process: The History of Manners and State Formation and Civilization* (Oxford: Blackwell, 1994 (1939)), p. 451.
4. D. Hervieu-Léger, *Religion as a Chain of Memory*, trs. Simon Lee (New Brunswick: Rutgers University Press, 2000 (1993)), pp. 29, 129.
5. E. Husserl, *The Crisis of the European Sciences and Transcendental Phenomenology*, trs. David Carr (Evanston: Northwestern University Press, 1970).
6. For example S. Freud, *Civilization and its Discontents*, trs. J. Strachey (New York: Norton, 1961).
7. A. Giddens, *The Consequences of Modernity* (Cambridge: Polity Press, 1990); R. Roberts, *Religion, Theology and the Human Sciences* (Cambridge University Press, 2002), p. 208.
8. This is an inevitably oversimplified account. For a good overview see D. Levine, *Visions of the Sociological Tradition* (University of Chicago Press, 1995).
9. M. Foucault, *The Order of Things: An Archaeology of the Human Sciences* (New York: Pantheon, 1970), p. 384.
10. On this see Roberts, *Religion*, pp. 211–12.
11. S. Critchley, *Very Little, Almost Nothing: Death, Philosophy and Literature* (London and New York: Routledge, 1997), p. 2.

12. Schiller, 'Es freue sich,/ Wer da atmet im rosigten Licht' ('Let him rejoice who breathes up there in the roseate light!' 'Der Taucher' cited in S. Freud, *The Future of an Illusion*, trs. J. Strachey (New York: Norton, 1961), p. 260.
13. Quoted by H. Blumenberg, *The Legitimacy of the Modern Age*, trs. R. M. Wallace (Massachusetts Institute of Technology, 1983 (1966)), p. 142.
14. For a good summary of Blumenberg's position see R. M. Wallace, 'Translator's introduction' to Blumenberg, *Legitimacy*, pp. xvii–xxx.
15. Blumenberg, *Legitimacy*, p. 128.
16. Ibid. pp. 129–30.
17. Ibid. p. 133.
18. Ibid. p. 176.
19. Ibid. p. 138.
20. Frank B. Farrell, *Subjectivity, Realism, and Postmodernism: The Recovery of the World in Recent Philosophy* (Cambridge University Press, 1994), p. 155.
21. Charles Taylor, *The Sources of the Self: The Making of the Modern Identity* (Cambridge University Press, 1989), p. 508.
22. Ibid. p. 185.
23. F. Nietzsche, *The Genealogy of Morality*, trs. Carol Diethe (Cambridge University Press, 1994), p. 61.
24. Ibid. p. 90.
25. Ibid. p. 90.
26. Ibid. p. 93.
27. R. Geuss, *Morality, Culture and History: Essays on German Philosophy* (Cambridge University Press, 1999), pp. 3–5.
28. David Owen, *Maturity and Modernity: Nietzsche, Weber, Foucault and the Ambivalence of Reason* (London and New York: Routledge, 1994), p. 144.
29. I have particularly benefited from Geoffrey Harpham's reading of Foucault, *The Ascetic Imperative in Culture and Criticism* (University of Chicago Press, 1987), pp. 220–35 and from David Halperin's *Saint Foucault: Towards a Gay Hagiography* (Oxford University Press, 1995). For a discussion of Foucault on asceticism and religion more generally see Jeremy Carrette (ed.), *Religion and Culture by Michel Foucault* (Manchester University Press, 1999); *Foucault and Religion: Spiritual Corporality and Political Spirituality* (London and New York: Routledge, 2000), pp. 118–20; J. Behr, 'Shifting Sands: Foucault, Brown and the Framework of Christian Asceticism', *The Heythrop Journal* vol. 34, 1993, pp. 1–21.
30. Foucault, 'Nietzsche, Genealogy, History' in Paul Rabinow (ed.), *The Foucault Reader* (Harmondsworth: Penguin, 1984), pp. 76–100.
31. Ibid. p. 80.
32. Ibid. p. 83.
33. Ibid. p. 87.
34. Ibid. p. 89.
35. Ibid. pp. 93–7.
36. Halperin, *Saint Foucault*, p. 16.

37. Foucault, *The History of Sexuality vol II: The Use of Pleasure*, trs. Robert Hurley (London: Penguin, 1992 (1984)), p. 5.
38. Foucault, *The Use of Pleasure*, p. 20.
39. Ibid. p. 32. See Arnold I. Davidson, 'Ethics as Ascetics: Foucault, the History of Ethics, and Ancient Thought' p. 118, in Gary Gutting (ed.), *The Cambridge Companion to Foucault* (Cambridge University Press, 1994), pp. 115–40.
40. Farrell develops this point: Farrell, *Subjectivity, Realism and Postmodernism*, p. 276.
41. Foucault, *The Use of Pleasure*, pp. 10–11.
42. For example, P. Hadot, 'Un Dialogue Interrompu avec Michel Foucault: Convergences et Divergences' in *Exercices Spirituels et Philosophie Antique* (Paris: Etudes Augustiniennes, 1987), pp. 229–33.
43. Farrell, *Subjectivity, Realism and Postmodernism*, pp. 276–8.
44. Ibid. p. 30.
45. Lois McNay, *Gender and Agency: Reconfiguring the Subject in Feminist and Social Theory* (Cambridge: Polity Press, 2000), p. 9.
46. McNay, *Gender and Agency*, p. 9.
47. For example, on feminism in the history of philosophy see the interesting essay by Genevieve Lloyd, 'Feminism in the History of Philosophy: Appropriating the Past' in Miranda Fricker and Jennifer Hornsby (eds.), *The Cambridge Companion to Feminism in Philosophy* (Cambridge University Press, 2000), pp. 245–63.
48. For example, on the perceived exclusion of women from male philosophical discourse see Joanna Hodge, 'Subject, Body and the Exclusion of Women from Philosophy' in Morwenna Griffiths and Margaret Whitford (eds.), *Feminist Perspectives in Philosophy* (London: Macmillan, 1988), pp. 152–68.
49. Luce Irigaray, *Amante Marine de Friedrich Nietzsche* (Paris: Les Editions de Minuit, 1980), pp. 83–127. *Je, Tu, Nous: Pour une Culture de la Différence* (Paris: Bernard Grasset, 1990), pp. 19–22, 25–31.
50. Roberts, *Religion*, pp. 282–91.
51. Donna J. Haraway, 'The Cyborg Manifesto', *Simians, Cyborgs, and Women: the Reinvention of Nature* (London: Free Association Books, 1991), pp. 149–81.
52. Roberts, *Religion*, pp. 288–9.
53. See McNay, *Gender and Agency*, p. 80.
54. Oliver Davies, *A Theology of Compassion: Metaphysics of Difference and the Renewal of Tradition* (London: SCM, 2001), pp. 20, 37–41.
55. On narrative coherence in religion see G. Flood, *Beyond Phenomenology: Rethinking the Study of Religion* (London and New York: Cassell, 1999), pp. 118–23. On the implications of sainthood and its moral possibilities in a postmodern world see Edith Wyschogrod, *Saints and Postmodernism: Revisioning Moral Philosophy* (University of Chicago Press, 1990). This is a particularly important work with regard to saintly narrative and hagiography as resources for moral theory.
56. For example, Bruce argues that religion is a mere residue in Western culture that will probably not survive (*God is Dead: Secularization in the West*, Oxford:

Blackwell, 1992), while others argue that religious conversions are increasing – see Jorge J. E. Gracia, *Can We Know What God Means? The Interpretation of Revelation* (New York and Basingstoke: Palgrave, 2001).

57. P. Ochs (ed.), *The Return to Scripture in Judaism and Christianity* (New York, Mahwah: Paulist Press, 1993).
58. D. W. Hardy, Peter Ochs, David F. Ford with Basit Koshul (eds.), 'The Tent of Meeting' (unpublished, version 4, 2003).
59. Ochs, *The Return to Scripture*, p. 4.
60. On religious reading there is an article which is a model of clarity in dealing with Christian reading – J. Fodor, 'Re-Capturing Religious Reading: Prospects and Challenges' (unpublished, 2002). See also Griffiths's monumental work, *Religious Reading: The Place of Reading in the Practice of Religion* (Oxford University Press, 1999).
61. See Roberts, *Religion*, pp. 192–207.

# *Bibliography*

## ABBREVIATIONS

| | |
|---|---|
| CSEL | Corpus Scriptorum Ecclesiasticorum Latinorum |
| DDS | Dictionnaire de Spiritualité |
| KSTS | Kashmir Series of Texts and Studies |
| PG | Patrologiæ cursus completus series græca |
| PL | Patrologiæ cursus completus series latina |
| PTS | Pali Text Society |

## REFERENCES


Abhinavagupta *Paramārthasāra with the Vivṛti of Yogarāja*, ed. J. C. Chatterjee. Srinagar: KSTS 7, 1916.

*Tantrasāra*, ed. Mukund Ram Shastri. Srinagar: KSTS 27, 1918.

*Tantrāloka with the Viveka by Jayaratha*, ed. M. S. Kaul (vols. II–XII) and M. R. Sastri (vol. I). Srinagar: KSTS, 12 vols. 1938.

*Parātriṁśikalaghuvṛtti*, ed. J. Zadoo. Srinagar: KSTS 68, 1947.

Adidevānanda, Svāmī *Śrī Rāmānuja Gītābhāṣya*. Madras: Sri Ramakrishna Math 1991.

Alper, H. P. (ed.) *Understanding Mantras*. Albany: SUNY Press, 1989.

Alter, J. S. *The Wrestler's Body: Identity and Ideology in North India*. Berkeley: University of California Press, 1992.

Amélineau, E. (ed.) *Histoire des Monastères de la Basse Egypte*, pp. 157–58, *Annales du Musée Guimet*, vol. XXV, pp. 118–202.

Āpaṭe, Hari Nārāyaṇa (ed.) *Pātañjalayogasūtrāṇi*. Benares: Ānandāśrama, 1908.

Āraṇya, Swāmi Hariharānanda *Yoga Philosophy of Patañjali*, trs. P. N. Mukerji. Albany: SUNY Press, 1988 (1963).

Asad, Talal *Genealogies of Religion: Discipline and Reasons of Power in Christianity and Islam*. Baltimore: The Johns Hopkins University Press, 1993.

Auroux, Sylvain (general ed.) *Encyclopédie Philosophie Universelle: Les Nations Philosophiques Dictionnaire* vol. II. Paris: Presses Universitaires de France, 1990.

Bakhtin, M. 'Discourse in the Novel' in T. Holquist (ed.), *The Dialogic Imagination: Four Essays*. Austin: University of Texas Press, 1981.

*Problems of Dostoyevsky's Poetics.* Minneapolis: University of Minnesota Press, 1984.

*Speech Genres and Other Late Essays*, trs. Vern W. McGee. Austin: University of Texas Press, 1986.

*Art and Answerability: Early Essays by M. M. Bakhtin.* Austin: University of Texas Press, 1990.

*Towards a Philosophy of the Act*, trs. Vadim Liapunov. Austin: University of Texas Press, 1993.

Barnes, Michael *Theology and the Dialogue of Religions.* Cambridge University Press, 2002.

Bayly, S. *The New Cambridge History of India*, vol. 4.3 *Caste, Society and Politics in India from the Eighteenth Century to the Modern Age.* Cambridge University Press, 1999.

Bechert, H. 'The Date of the Buddha Reconsidered', *Indologica Taurinensia* vol. 10, 1982, pp. 26–36.

'A Remark on the Problem of the Date of Mahavira', *Indologica Taurinensia* vol. 11, 1983, pp. 287–90.

'Remarks on the Date of the Historical Buddha', *Buddhist Studies* vol. 17, 1988, pp. 97–117.

(ed.) *The Dating of the Historical Buddha* part 2. Göttingen: Vandenhoeck and Ruprecht, 1992.

Behr, John 'Shifting Sands: Foucault, Brown and the Framework of Christian Asceticism', *The Heythrop Journal* vol. 34, 1993, pp. 1–21.

*Asceticism and Anthropology in Irenaeus and Clement.* Oxford University Press, 2000.

Bell, C. *Ritual: Perspectives and Dimensions.* New York: Oxford University Press, 1997.

Bell, R. H. (ed.) *Simone Weil's Philosophy of Culture: Readings Towards a Divine Humanity.* Cambridge University Press, 1993.

Bertram, J. *The Monastic Institutes, Consisting of On the Training of a Monk and The Eight Deadly Sins.* London: Saint Austin Press. 1999.

Bigg, C. *The Christian Platonists of Alexandria.* 2nd ed. Oxford: Clarendon Press, 1913.

Blackburn, S. H. *Singing of Birth and Death: Texts in Performance.* Philadelphia: University of Pennsylvania Press, 1988.

Blacking, J. (ed.) *The Anthropology of the Body.* New York, London: Academic Press, 1977.

Blowers, Paul M. *Exegesis and Spiritual Pedagogy in Maximus the Confessor: An Investigation of the* Questiones ad Thalassium. Notre Dame: University of Notre Dame Press, 1991.

Blum, Owen J. *St. Peter Damian: His Teaching on the Spiritual Life.* Washington: The Catholic University of America Press, 1947.

Blum, Owen J. (trs.) *Peter Damian Letters 61–90*. Washington: The Catholic University of America Press, 1992.
Blumenberg, H. *The Legitimacy of the Modern Age*, trs. R. W. Wallace. Massachusetts Institute of Technology, 1983 (1966).
Bolshakoff, S. *Russian Mystics*. Kalamazoo: Cistercian Publications, 1976.
Bourdieu, P. *Language and Symbolic Power*, trs. Matthew Adamson. Cambridge: Polity Press, 1991.
*Outline of a Theory of Practice*, trs. Richard Nice. Cambridge University Press, 1977.
Bowie, A. *From Romanticism to Critical Theory: The Philosophy of German Literary Theory*. London and New York: Routledge, 1997.
Bowker, John *The Religious Imagination and the Sense of God*. Clarendon Press: Oxford, 1978.
*God: A Brief History*. London: Dorling Kindersly Publishing, 2002.
Brock, Sebastian *The Syriac Fathers on Prayer and the Spiritual Life*. Kalamazoo: Cistercian Publications, 1987.
Brock, Sebastian and Susan Ashbrooke *Holy Women of the Syrian Orient*. Berkeley: University of California Press, 1998 (1987).
Brodbeck, Simon *Asakta Karman in the Bhagavadgita*. Ph.D. SOAS, 2002.
Bronkhorst, J. *The Two Traditions of Meditation in Ancient India*. Delhi: Motilal, 1993.
'Asceticism, Religion and Biological Evolution', *Method and Theory in the Study of Religion* vol. 13, no. 4, 2001, pp. 374–417.
Brown, Peter *The Cult of the Saints: Its Rise and Function in Latin Christianity*. Chicago University Press, 1981.
*The Body and Society: Men, Women and Sexual Renunciation in Early Christianity*. London and Boston: Faber and Faber, 1989.
Bruce, S. *God is Dead: Secularization in the West*. Oxford: Blackwell, 1992.
Brunner, Hélène 'Le Sādaka, Personnage Oublié de l'Inde du Sud', *Journal Asiatique* vol. 263, 1975, pp. 411–43.
Buddhaghosa, *The Path of Purity*, trs. Pe Maung Tin. London: PTS, 1975.
Burghart, R. 'Renunciation in the Religious Traditions of South Asia', *Man*, vol. 18, 1983, pp. 635–53.
Buy, J.-C. *Les Apophtègmes des Pères du Desert, Série Alphabétique*. Textes de Spiritualité Orientale 1; Begrolles, 1968.
Bychkov, V. *The Aesthetic Face of Being: Art in the Theology of Pavel Florensky*. Crestwood: SVS Press, 1993.
Bynum, Caroline Walker *Holy Feast Holy Fast: Studies in the Spirituality of the Higher Middle Ages*. Berkeley: University of California Press, 1982.
*The Resurrection of the Body in Western Christianity*. New York: Columbia University Press, 1995.
Cabezon, J. I. (ed.) *Buddhism, Sexuality and Gender*. Albany: SUNY Press, 1992.

Carrette, Jeremy (ed.) *Religion and Culture by Michel Foucault.* Manchester University Press, 1999.

*Foucault and Religion: Spiritual Corporality and Political Spirituality.* London and New York: Routledge, 2000.

Carrithers, M. *The Forest Monks of Sri Lanka: An Anthropological and Historical Study*. Delhi: Oxford University Press, 1983.

Carrithers, Mary *The Book of Memory: A Study of Memory in Medieval Culture.* Cambridge University Press, 1990.

*The Craft of Thought: Meditation, Rhetoric, and the Making of Images 400–1200.* Cambridge University Press, 1998.

Carruthers, Mary, Steven Collins and Steven Lukes (eds.) *The Category of the Person.* Cambridge University Press, 1985.

Cassian, John PL 49. See Ramsey, Boniface (trs.).

Castoriadis, C. *The World in Fragments: Writings on Politics, Society, Psychoanalysis, and the Imagination*, trs. David Ames Curtis. Stanford University Press, 1997.

de Certeau, Michel *Culture in the Plural.* Minneapolis, London: University of Minnesota Press, 1997.

*The Writing of History*, trs. Tom Conley. New York: Columbia University Press, 1998.

Chadwick, H. *John Cassian: A Study in Primitive Monasticism.* Cambridge University Press, 1950.

*Christianity and the Classical Tradition.* Oxford: Clarendon Press, 1966.

Chadwick, Owen *John Cassian*. 2nd ed. Cambridge University Press, 1968.

Clark, Elizabeth A. *The Origenist Controversy: The Cultural Construction of an Early Christian Debate.* Princeton University Press, 1992.

*Reading Renunciation: Asceticism and Scripture in Early Christianity.* Princeton University Press, 1999.

Clayton, John 'Thomas Jefferson and the Study of Religion'. Inaugural Lecture, University of Lancaster, 1992.

Clooney, Francis X. *Hindu God, Christian God: How Reason Helps Break Down the Boundaries Between Religions.* Oxford University Press, 2001.

Cockburn, David *Other Times.* Cambridge University Press, 1997.

Coles, R. *Simone Weil: A Modern Pilgrimage.* Reading: Addison-Wesley, 1987.

Colledge, Edmund, J. C. Marler, and Judith Grant: Margaret Porete, *The Mirror of Simple Souls.* University of Notre Dame Press, 1999.

Collins, Steven *Selfless Persons: Imagery and Thought in Theravada Buddhism.* Cambridge University Press, 1982.

*Nirvana and Other Buddhist Felicities.* Cambridge University Press, 1999.

Constable, Giles *Three Studies in Medieval Religious and Social Thought.* Cambridge University Press, 1995.

Cooper, Adam G. 'Maximus the Confessor on the Structural Dynamics of Revelation', *Vigilae Christianae: A Review of Early Christian Life and Language* vol. 55, no. 2, 2001, pp. 161–86.

d'Costa, Gavin *Theology and Religious Pluralism.* Oxford: Blackwell, 1986.

Cousins, Lance 'Buddhist *jhāna*: Its Nature and Attainment According to the Pali Sources', *Religion* vol. 3, 1973, pp. 115–31.

'Samatha-yāna and Vipassanā-yāna' in G. Dhammapala et al. (eds.), *Buddhist Studies in Honour of Hammalava Saddhatissa.* Nugegoda: University of Jayewardenepura, 1984, pp. 56–68.

'Vitakka/Vitarka and Vicāra Stages of samādhi in Buddhism and Yoga', *Indo-Iranian Journal* vol. 35, 1992.

Creel, Austin B. and Vasudha Narayanan (eds.) *Monastic Life in the Christian and Hindu Traditions: A Comparative Study.* Lewiston, Queenston, Lampeter: Edwin Mellen Press, 1990.

Critchley, S. *Very Little, Almost Nothing: Death, Philosophy and Literature.* London and New York: Routledge, 1997.

Crouzel, Henri *Origen*, trs. A. S. Worrall. Edinburgh: T & T Clark, 1989.

Dallmayr, F. *Beyond Orientalism: Essays on Cross-Cultural Encounter.* Albany: SUNY Press, 1996.

Damian, Peter PL 145. See under Blum; McNulty; Payer.

Daniélou, J. 'Origène comme Exégète de la Bible', *Studia Patristica* vol. 1, 1957, pp. 280–90.

Das, V. *Structure and Cognition.* Delhi: Oxford University Press, 1982.

*Critical Events: An Anthropological Perspective on Contemporary India.* Delhi: Oxford University Press, 1995.

Davies, Oliver *Meister Eckhart Mystical Theologian.* London: SPCK, 1991.

*A Theology of Compassion: Metaphysics of Difference and the Renewal of Tradition.* London: SCM, 2001.

Davies, Richard *Śiva in an Oscillating Universe.* Princeton University Press, 1991.

Doniger, W. *The Laws of Manu.* Harmondsworth: Penguin, 1991.

Dostoyevsky, F. *The Brothers Karamazov*, vol. II, trs. David Magarshack. Harmondsworth: Penguin, 1958.

Driscoll, J. *The* Ad Monachos *of Evagrius Ponticus: Its Structure and a Select Commentary.* Rome: Studia Anselmiana, 1991.

'Spousal Images in Evagrius Ponticus', *Studia Mystica* vol. 38, 1996, pp. 243–56, especially p. 246.

Dronke, P. *Women Writers of the Middle Ages.* Cambridge University Press, 1984.

Dumont, L. *Homo Hierarchicus: The Caste System and its Implications.* University of Chicago Press, 1980 (1966).

Dundas, P. *The Jains.* London: Routledge, 1992.

Dunn, Marilyn *The Emergence of Monasticism: From the Desert Fathers to the Early Middle Ages.* Oxford: Blackwell, 2000.

Dupré, Wilhelm *Patterns in Meaning: Reflections on Meaning and Truth in Cultural Reality, Religious Traditions, and Dialogical Encounters.* Kampen: Pharos, 1994.

Dviveda, V. (ed.) *Netra-tantra with Udyota by Kṣemarāja.* Delhi: Parimala Publications, 1985.

Dyczkowski, M. *The Canon of the Śaivāgama and the Kubjikā Tantras of the Western Kaula Tradition.* Albany: SUNY Press, 1988.

Eck, Diana L. *Darshan: Seeing the Divine in India.* Chambersburg: Anima Books, 1985.

Edgerton, F. 'The Meaning of Samkhya and Yoga', *American Journal of Philology* vol. 45, 1924, pp. 1–46.

Eliade, M. *The Quest.* University of Chicago Press, 1969.

*Yoga: Immortality and Freedom*, trs. Willard R. Trask. Princeton University Press, 1970.

Elias, N. *The Civilizing Process: The History of Manners and State Formation and Civilization.* Oxford: Blackwell, 1994 [1939].

Elm, J. *'Virgins of God': The Making of Asceticism in Late Antiquity.* Oxford: Clarendon Press, 1994.

Elsthain, Jean Bethke *Power Trips and Other Journeys: Essays in Feminism as Civil Discourse.* Madison: University of Wisconsin Press, 1990.

Evagrius. PG 40. See under Guillaumont, A.

*Les Vertus de Notre Père, le Juste et Grand Abba Macaire* in E. Amélineau (ed.), *Histoire des Monastères de la Basse Egypte, Annales du Musée Guimet,* vol. XXV. Paris: Editions du Cerf, 1894.

Evdokimov, P. *The Art of the Icon: A Theology of Beauty.* Oakwood: Redondo Beach, 1990 [1972].

Farrell, Frank B. *Subjectivity, Realism and Postmodernism: The Recovery of the World in Recent Philosophy.* Cambridge University Press, 1994.

Faure, B. *The Rhetoric of Immediacy: A Cultural Critique of Chan/Zen.* Princeton University Press, 1991.

*The Red Thread: Buddhist Approaches to Sexuality.* Princeton University Press, 1998.

Feher, Michel (ed.) *Fragments for a History of the Human Body*. 3 vols. New York: Zone, 1989.

Feuerstein, G. *The Essence of Yoga: Contribution to the Psychohistory of Indian Civilization.* London: Rider, 1974.

*The Philosophy of Classical Yoga*, New York: St. Martin's Press, 1980.

Fitzgerald, Tim *The Ideology of Religious Studies.* Oxford University Press, 1999.

Flood, Gavin *Beyond Phenomenology: Rethinking the Study of Religion.* London and New York: Cassell, 1999.

'The Purification of the Body in Tantric Ritual Representation', *Indo-Iranian Journal* vol. 45, no. 1, 2002, pp. 25–43.

Flood, Gavin (ed.) *The Blackwell Companion to Hinduism.* Oxford: Blackwell, 2003.

Fodor, J. 'Re-Capturing Religious Reading: Prospects and Challenges' (unpublished, 2002).

Ford, David *Self and Salvation: Being Transformed.* Cambridge University Press, 1999.

*Theology, A Very Short Introduction.* Oxford University Press, 1999.

Foucault, M. *The Order of Things: An Archaeology of the Human Sciences.* New York: Pantheon, 1970.

*The History of Sexuality*, vol. II: *The Use of Pleasure*, trs. Robert Hurley. London: Penguin, 1992 [1984].

Franco, Eli and Karin Preisendanz (eds.) *Beyond Orientalism: The Work of Wilhelm Halbfass and Its Impact on Indian and Cross-Cultural Studies.* Rodopi: Atlanta, 1997.

Frankenberg, W. *Euagrius Pontikus.* Abhandlungen der Königlichen Gesellschaft der Wissenschaften zu Göttingen, Philologisch-Historische Klasse, Neue Folge, Band XIII, 2. Berlin, 1912.

Freeman, R. 'Formalised Possession among the Tantris and Teyyams of Malabar', *South Asian Research* vol. 18, 1998, pp. 73–98.

'Dynamics of the Person in the Worship and Sorcery of Malabar' in J. Assayag and G. Tarabout (eds.), *Possession in South Asia: Speech, Body, Territory*, special edition of *Puruṣārtha*. Paris: Ecole des Hautes Etudes en Sciences Sociales, 1999, pp. 149–81.

Freud, S. *Civilization and its Discontents*, trs. J. Strachey. New York: Norton, 1961.

*The Future of an Illusion*, trs. J. Strachey. New York: Norton, 1961.

Freund, Stephan *Studien zur literarischen Wirksamkeit des Petrus Damiani.* Hanover: Hahnsche Buchhandlung, 1995.

Fricker, Miranda and Jennifer Hornsby (eds.) *The Cambridge Companion to Feminism in Philosophy.* Cambridge University Press, 2000.

Gadamer, H. G. *Truth and Method*, trs. Joel Weinsheimer and Donald G. Marshall. London: Sheed and Ward, 1989.

Garrigues, Juan Miguel *Maxime le Confesseur: La Charité Avenir Divin de l'Homme.* Paris: Beauchesne, 1976.

Gerth, H. H. and C. Wright Mills *From Max Weber: Essays in Sociology.* London: Routledge, 1991.

Gethin, R. *The Buddhist Path to Awakening: A Study of the Bodhipakkhyadhamma.* Leiden: Brill, 1992.

*Foundations of Buddhism.* Oxford University Press, 1996.

'Cosmology and Meditation from the Aggañña-sutta to the Mahāyāna', *History of Religions* vol. XXXVI, 1997, pp. 183–217.

Geuss, R. *Morality, Culture and History: Essays on German Philosophy.* Cambridge University Press, 1999.

Gibson, E. C. S. *The Works of John Cassian.* Nicene and Post-Nicene Fathers Series, vol. XI. Oxford: James Parker and Co., 1894.

Giddens, A. *The Consequences of Modernity.* Cambridge: Polity, 1990.

Glucklich, Ariel *Sacred Pain: Hurting the Body for the Sake of the Soul.* New York: Oxford University Press, 2001.

Gobry, J. *Les Moines en Occident*, 3 vols. Paris: Fayard, 1985–87.

Godelier, Maurice and Michel Panoff (eds.) *La Production du corps. Approches Anthropologiques et Historiques.* Amsterdam: Editions des Archives Contemporaines, 1998.

*Le Corps Humain: Supplicié, Possédé, Cannibalisé.* Amsterdam: Editions des Archives Contemporaines, 1998.

Goleman, D. 'The Buddha on Meditation and Higher States of Consciousness', *The Wheel Publication*, nos. 189/190. Kandy: Buddhist Publication Society, 1973, pp. 1–60.

Gombrich, R. *Theravada Buddhism: A Social History from Ancient Benares to Modern Columbo.* London and New York: Routledge and Kegan Paul, 1988.

'The Date of the Buddha: A Red Herring Revealed' in Heinz Bechert (ed.), *The Dating of the Historical Buddha* part 2. Göttingen: Vandenhoeck and Ruprecht, 1992.

'The Buddha and the Jains: A Reply to Professor Bronkhorst', *Etudes Asiatiques* vol. 48, 1994, pp. 1069–96.

*How Buddhism Began: The Conditioned Genesis of the Early Teachings.* London: Athlone Press, 1996.

Gombrich R. and S. Gupta 'Kings, Power and the Goddess', *South Asian Research* vol. 6, no. 2, 1986, pp. 123–38.

Goodall, D. *Bhaṭṭa Rāmakaṇṭha's Commentary on the Kiraṇatantra*, vol. I. Pondicherry: Institut Français de Pondichéry, 1998.

Goudriaan, T. *Māyā Divine and Human.* Delhi: Motilal, 1978.

Goudriaan, T. and J. A. Schoterman (eds.) *Kubjikāmata-tantra.* Leiden: Brill, 1988.

Gracia, Jorge J. E. *Texts: Ontological Status, Identity, Author, Audience.* Albany: SUNY Press, 1996.

*Can We Know What God Means? The Interpretation of Revelation.* New York and Basingstoke: Palgrave, 2001.

Gray, Francine du Plessix *Simone Weil.* London: Weidenfeld and Nicolson, 2002.

Gregg, R. C. and introduction by W. Clebsch *The Life of Anthony and the Letter to Marcellinus.* Classics of Western Spirituality. New York: Paulist Press, 1980.

Griffiths, Morwenna and Margaret Whitford (eds.) *Feminist Perspectives in Philosophy.* London: Macmillan, 1988.

Griffiths, Paul *Religious Reading: The Place of Reading in the Practice of Religion.* Oxford University Press, 1999.

Guha, R. and G. Spivak (eds.) *Selected Subaltern Studies.* Oxford University Press, 1988.

Guillaumont *Les Six Centuries des 'Kephalaia Gnostica' d'Evagre le Pontique.* Edition critique de la version syriaque commune et édition d'une novelle version syriaque, intégrale, avec une double traduction française. Patrologie Orientalis vol. XXVIII, fasc. 1. Paris: Frimin Didot, 1958.

*Les 'Kephalaia Gnostica' d'Evagre le Pontique et l'Histoire de l'Origénisme chez les Grecs et chez les Syriens.* Patristica Sorbonensia 5. Paris: Editions du Seuil, 1962.

Gumperz, John J. and Stephen C. Levinson (eds.) *Rethinking Linguistic Relativity.* Cambridge University Press, 1992.

Gusie, T. W. 'Patristic Hermeneutics and the Meaning of Tradition', *Theological Studies* vol. 32, 1971, pp. 647–58.

Gutting, Gary (ed.) *The Cambridge Companion to Foucault.* Cambridge University Press, 1994.

Hadot, P. 'Un Dialogue Interrompu avec Michel Foucault: Convergences et Divergences' in *Exercices Spirituels et Philosophie Antique* (Paris: Etudes Augustiniennes, 1987), pp. 229–33.
Halbfass, Wilhelm *India and Europe: An Essay in Understanding.* Albany: SUNY Press, 1988.
Halbfass, Wilhelm (ed.) *Philology and Confrontation: Paul Hacker on Traditional and Modern Vedanta.* Albany: SUNY Press, 1995.
Halperin, David M. *Saint Foucault: Towards a Gay Hagiography.* New York and Oxford: Oxford University Press, 1995.
Hamilton, Paul *Historicism.* London and New York: Routledge, 1996.
Hanson, R. P. C. *Allegory and Event: A Study of the Sources and Significance of Origen's Interpretation of Scripture.* London: SCM, 1959.
Haraway, Donna J. 'The Cyborg Manifesto', in *Simians, Cyborgs, and Women: the Reinvention of Nature.* London: Free Association Books, 1991.
Hardy, D. W., Peter Ochs, David F. Ford with Basit Koshul (eds.) 'The Tent of Meeting' (unpublished, version 4, 2003).
Hare, E. M. (trs.) *The Book of Gradual Sayings* vols. III, IV. Oxford: PTS (1973), 1995.
Harl, M. 'Origène et les Interprétations Patristiques Grecques de l'Obscurité Biblique', *Vigiliae Christianae* vol. 36, 1982, pp. 334–71.
Harpham, Geoffrey G. *The Ascetic Imperative in Culture and Criticism.* University of Chicago Press, 1987.
Harrey, Susan A. *Asceticism and Society in Crisis: John of Ephesus and the Lives of the Eastern Saints.* Berkeley: University of California Press, 1990.
Hauerwas, S. *The Hauerwas Reader*, ed. John Berkman and M. Cartwright. Durham: Duke University Press, 2001.
Hecht, F. X. 'Geisselung', *Lexikon für Theologie und Kirche*, vol. IV, 1932, p. 344.
Heelas, Paul, Scott Lash, and Paul Morris (eds.) *Detraditionalization.* Oxford: Blackwell, 1996.
Heelas, Paul and Andy Locke (eds.) *Indigenous Psychologies: The Anthropology of the Self.* London: Academic Press, 1981.
Heesterman, J. *The Inner Conflict of Tradition: Essays on Indian Ritual, Kingship and Society.* University of Chicago Press, 1985.
Heinzer F. and C. von Schönborn (eds.) *Maximus Confessor, Actes du Symposium sur Maxime le Confesseur.* Fribourg, Switzerland: Editions Universitaires, 1982.
Hervieu-Léger, D. *Religion as a Chain of Memory*, trs. Simon Lee. New Brunswick: Rutgers University Press, 2000 (1993).
Hiltebeitel, Alf *The Cult of Draupadi* vols. I and II. University of Chicago Press, (1988), 1991.
Hollywood, Amy *The Soul as Virgin Wife: Mechtild of Magdeburg, Marguerite Porete, and Meister Eckhart.* Notre Dame and London: University of Notre Dame Press, 1995.
Hopkins, Gerard Manley *Poems and Prose*, ed. W. H. Gardner. Harmondsworth: Penguin, 1970.

Horner, I. B. (trs.) *The Book of Discipline.* London: PTS, 1951.
*Milinda's Questions* 2 vols. London: PTS, 1964.
*The Middle Length Sayings*, vols. I, II. London: PTS, 1967, 1970.
Husserl, E. *The Crisis of European Sciences and Transcendental Phenomenology: An Introduction to Phenomenological Philosophy*, trs. D. Carr. Evanson: Northwestern University Press, 1970.
Inden, R. *Imagining India.* Oxford and Cambridge, MA: Blackwell, 1990.
Irigaray, Luce *Amante Marine de Friedrich Nietzsche.* Paris: Les Editions de Minuit, 1980.
*Je, Tu, Nous: Pour une Culture de la Différence.* Paris: Bernard Grasset, 1990.
Irwin, Kevin W. 'Lectio Divina' in W. M. Johnston (ed.), *Encyclopedia of Monasticism.* Chicago and London: Fitzroy Dearborn, 2000, vol. I, pp. 751–52.
Isayeva, Natalia *Śaṅkara and Indian Philosophy.* Albany: SUNY Press, 1993.
Ishwaran, K. (ed.) *Ascetic Culture: Renunciation and Worldly Engagement.* Leiden: Brill, 1999.
Jaimini *Pūrva Mīmāṁsā Sūtra*, trs. G. Jha, vol. I. Baroda: Gaekwad Oriental Series, 66, 1973.
Janzen, Grace M. *Power, Gender and Christian Mysticism.* Cambridge University Press, 1995.
*Becoming Divine: Towards a Feminist Philosophy of Religion.* Manchester University Press, 1998.
Jayatilleke, K. N. *Early Buddhist Theory of Knowledge.* London: George Allen and Unwin, 1963.
Jolly, J. (ed.) *Mānava Dharma-Śāstra: The Code of Manu.* London: Trübner, 1887.
Jordan, William C. et al. (eds.) *Order and Innovation in the Middle Ages: Essays in Honour of Joseph R. Strayer.* Princeton University Press, 1976.
Kaelber, Lutz *Schools of Asceticism: Ideology and Organization in Medieval Religious Communities.* Philadelphia: University of Pennsylvania Press, 1998.
Kahrs, Eivind *Indian Semantic Analysis: The 'Nirvacana' Tradition.* Cambridge University Press, 1998.
Kangle, R. P. (ed. and trs.) *The Kauṭilya Arthaśāstra in Three Parts.* University of Bombay, 1960–65.
Kapferer, Bruce (ed.) *Transaction and Meaning: Directions in the Anthropology of Exchange and Symbolic Behaviour.* Philadelphia: Institute for the Study of Human Issues, 1976.
Katz, N. *Buddhist Images of Human Perfection.* Delhi: MLBD, 1982.
Kaul, M. S. (ed.) *Mālinīvijayotara Tantra.* Srinagar: KSTS, vol. I, 1921.
Kierkegaard, S. *Concluding Unscientific Postscript to Philosophical Fragments* vol. I, ed. and trs. H. V. and E. H. Hong. Princeton University Press, 1992.
King, Peter *Western Monasticism: A History of the Monastic Movement in the Latin Church.* Cistercian Studies 185. Kalamazoo: Cistercian Publications, 1999.
King, Richard *Orientalism and Religion: Postcolonial Theory and 'The Mystic East'.* London: Routledge, 1999.
Kornfield, Jack 'Questions and Answers with Achaan Chah.' Hemel Hempstead: Amaravati Buddhist Centre, 1986.

Krishnamacharya, E. (ed.) *Jayakha Samhita*. Baroda: Gaekwad's Oriental Series, 1931, reprinted 1967.
Kristeva, Julia 'Word, Dialogue, and the Novel' in *Desire in Language: A Semiotic Approach to Literature and Art*. Oxford: Blackwell, 1980.
Krueger, Derek 'Writing and the Liturgy of Memory in Gregory of Nyssa's *Life of Macrina*', *Journal of Eastern Christian Studies* vol. 8, no. 4, 2000, pp. 483–510.
Kṣemarāja *Pratyabhijñā dhṛdaya*, ed. J. C. Chatterji. Srinagar: KSTS, 1911.
*Śivasūtravimarśinī*, ed. J. C. Chatterji. Srinagar: KSTS, vol. 1, 1911.
Laidlaw, J. *Riches and Renunciation: Religion, Economy and Society Among the Jains*. Oxford: Clarendon Press, 1995.
Laidlaw, J. and C. Humphreys *The Archetypal Actions of Ritual*. Oxford: Clarendon Press, 1994.
Lampe, G. W. H. (ed.) *A Patristic Greek Lexicon*. Oxford: Clarendon Press, 1961.
Larchet, J.-C. *Maxime le Confesseur, Médiateur Entre l'Orient et l'Occident*. Paris: Editions du Cerf, 1998.
Larson, G. 'The Aesthetic (*rasāsvāda*) and the Religious (*brahmasvāda*) in Abhinavagupta's Kashmir Śaivism', *Philosophy East and West*, vol. 26, 1976, pp. 371–87.
Le Goff, J. *La Naissance Purgatoire*. Paris: Gallimard, 1981.
*History and Memory*, trs. Steven Rendall and Elizabeth Claman. New York: Columbia University Press, 1992.
Le Goff, J., R. Chartier and J. Revel (eds.) *La Nouvelle Histoire*. Paris: Retz, 1978.
Lee, Benjamin and Greg Urban (eds.) *Semiotics, Self and Society*. Berlin and New York: Mouton de Gruyter, 1989.
Lerner, R. E. *The Heresy of the Free Spirit in the Late Middle Ages*. Berkeley: University of California Press, 1972.
Levin, D. M. *The Body's Recollection of Being*. London: Routledge and Kegan Paul, 1985.
Levine, D. *Visions of the Sociological Tradition*. University of Chicago Press, 1995.
Lipner, Julius (ed.) *The Fruits of Our Desiring*. Calgary: Bayeux Publications, 1997.
Little, J. P. *Simone Weil, Bibliography*. London: Grant and Cutler, 1973.
Lot-Borodine, M. 'La Doctrine de la Déification dans l'Eglise Grecque jusqu'au XIe Siècle', *Revue d'Histoire des Religions* vol. 106, 1932, pp. 524–74, and vol. 107, 1933, pp. 8–35.
Louth, Andrew *Maximus the Confessor*. London and New York: Routledge, 1996.
Lubac, H. de *Histoire et Esprit: L'intelligence et l'Ecriture d'après Origène*. Paris: Aubier, 1950.
Lucy, John *Language Diversity and Thought*. Cambridge University Press, 1992.
Luibheid, Colm (trs.) *John Cassian: Conferences*. Classics of Western Spirituality. New York, Mahwah: Paulist Press, 1985.
Luibheid, Colm and Norman Russell (trs.) *The Ladder of Divine Ascent*. Classics of Western Spirituality. New York: Paulist Press, 1982.
Lutgendorf, Philip *The Life of a Text: Performing the Ramacaritmanas of Tulsidas*. University of California Press, 1991.

Malone, Edward E. *The Monk and the Martyr: The Monk as the Successor of the Martyr.* Washington: The Catholic University of America Press, 1950.

Masson, J. and M. V. Patwardhan *Śāntarasa and Abhinavagupta's Philosophy of Aesthetics.* Poona: Deccan College, 1969.

Maximus the Confessor PG 91. See under Sherwood.

McCann, Justin (trs.) *The Rules of St Benedict.* London: Sheed and Ward, 1970 (1952).

McCutcheon, Russell T. *Manufacturing Religion.* Oxford University Press, 1997.

MacDermot, Violet *The Cult of the Seer in the Ancient Middle East: A Contribution to Current Research on Hallucinations Drawn from Coptic and Other Texts.* Berkeley: University of California Press, 1971.

McGinn, B. *The Foundations of Christian Mysticism.* New York: Crossroads, 1995.

*The Growth of Mysticism: Gregory the Great through the 12th Century.* New York: Crossroads, 1996.

*The Flowering of Mysticism: Men and Women in the New Mysticism 1200–1350.* New York: Crossroads, 1998.

McGinn, B. (ed.) *Meister Eckhart and the Beguine Mystics.* New York: Continuum, 1994.

McLellan, David *Simone Weil: Utopian Pessimist.* London: Macmillan, 1989.

McNay, Lois *Gender and Agency: Reconfiguring the Subject in Feminist and Social Theory.* Cambridge: Polity Press, 2000.

McNulty, Patricia *St. Peter Damian: Selected Writings on the Spiritual Life, translated with an Introduction.* London: Faber and Faber, 1959.

Mellor, P. and C. Shilling *Re-Forming the Body: Religion, Community and Modernity.* London: Sage, 1997.

Merleau Ponty, M. *The Phenomenology of Perception*, trs. Colin Smith. London: Routledge and Kegan Paul, 1962.

*Signs*, trs. R. C. McCleary. Evanson: Northwestern University Press, 1964.

Meyer, Robert T. *Palladius: The Lausiac History.* London: Longmans, Green and Co., 1965.

Moulakis, A. *Simone Weil and the Politics of Self-Denial*, trs. Ruth Hein. Columbia and London: University of Missouri Press, 1998.

Müller, Max *Introduction to the Science of Religion: Four Lectures* (1893). Bharata Manishia: Varanasi, 1972.

Murdock, Brian 'The Origins of Penance: Reflections of Adamic Apocrypha and of the *Vita Adamae* in Western Europe' in *Annals of the Archive of 'Ferran Valls I Taberner's Library'* nos. 9–10, 1991, pp. 205–27.

Nāṅamoli, Bhikku and Bhikkhu Bodhi (trs.) *The Middle Length Discourses of the Buddha.* London: PTS, 1995.

Neuhouser, F. *Fichte's Theory of Subjectivity.* Cambridge University Press, 1990.

Nietzsche, F. *The Genealogy of Morality*, trs. Carol Diethe. Cambridge University Press, 1994.

Norman, K. R. (trs.) *The Group of Discourses* (with alternative translations by I. B. Horner and Walpola Rahula). London: PTS, 1984.

Nowotny, Helga *Time: The Modern and Postmodern Experience*, trs. Neville Plaice. Cambridge: Polity Press, 1994.

Nyanasampanno, Phra Acharn Maha Boowa *The Venerable Phra Acharn Mun Bhuridatta Thera*, trs. Siri Buddhasukh. Wat Pa Barn Tard: private printing, 1982.

Ochs, Peter (ed.) *The Return to Scripture in Judaism and Christianity.* New York, Mahwah: Paulist Press, 1993.

*Peirce, Pragmatism, and the Logic of Scripture.* Cambridge University Press, 1998.

Oikonomou, E. B. 'Hermeneutical Logotypes: The Basic Elements of Patristic Hermeneutics', *Theologia* vol. 53, 1982, pp. 627–71.

Oldenberg, Hermann (ed.) *Vinaya Pitaka* vol. V. London: PTS, 1964.

Olivelle, P. *Vāsudevāśrama, Yatidharmaprakāśa* vol. II. Vienna: University of Vienna Institute for Indology, 1977.

*Renunciation in Hinduism: A Medieval Debate*, 2 vols. Vienna: De Nobili Research Library, 1986 and 1987.

*Saṁnyāsa Upaniṣads: Hindu Scriptures on Asceticism and Renunciation.* Oxford University Press, 1992.

*The Āśrama System: The History and Hermeneutics of a Religious Institution.* Oxford University Press, 1993.

*Rules and Regulations of Brahmanical Asceticism.* Delhi: Sri Satguru, 1997 (1995).

*The Early Upaniṣads: Annotated Text and Translation.* Oxford University Press, 1998.

O'Loughlin, T. 'Martyrs: Western Christian' in William M. Johnston (ed.), *Encyclopedia of Monasticism*, vol. II. Chicago and London: Fitzroy Dearborn, 2000.

Owen, David *Maturity and Modernity: Nietzsche, Weber, Foucault and the Ambivalence of Reason.* London and New York: Routledge, 1994.

Padoux, A. *Vāc: The Concept of the Word in Selected Hindu Tantras.* Albany: SUNY Press, 1990.

Palladius *Historia Lausica*, ed. C. Butler. Texts and Studies Series, vol. II, 1989.

Palmer, G. E. H., Philip Sherrard and Kalistos Ware (eds. and trs.) *The Philokalia* vol. I. London and Boston: Faber and Faber, 1979.

Pandey, R. *Hindu Samskaras: Socio-Religious Study of the Hindu Sacraments.* 2nd ed. Delhi: MLBD, 1969.

Pasnau, Robert *Theories of Cognition in the Later Middle Ages.* Cambridge University Press, 1997.

Pattison, George *Anxious Angels: A Retrospective View of Religious Existentialism.* London: Macmillan, 1999.

Patton, Kimberley C. and Benjamin C. Ray (eds.) *A Magic Still Dwells: Comparative Religion in the Postmodern Age.* Berkeley and Los Angeles: University of California Press, 2000.

Payer, Pierre J. *Book of Gomorrah: An Eleventh-Century Treatise Against Clerical Homosexual Practices.* Ontario: Wilfred Laurier University Press, 1982.

Pelikan, Jaroslav *The Spirit of Eastern Christendom (600–1700).* University of Chicago Press, 1974.
*The Vindication of Tradition.* New Haven and London: Yale University Press, 1984.
*Jesus through the Centuries: His Place in the History of Culture.* New Haven and London: Yale University Press, 1985.
Perrin, Joseph-Marie *Mon Dialogue avec Simone Weil.* Paris: Nouvelle Cité, 1984.
Perrin, J. M. and Gustave Thibon *Simone Weil as We Knew Her*, trs. Emma Craufurd. London: Routledge and Kegan Paul, 1953.
Pétremont, Simone *La Vie de Simone Weil*, 2 vols. Paris: Fayard, 1973.
Petschenig, Michael (ed.) *Iohannis Cassiani Opera.* Vindabonae: CSEL, vols. XIII, XVII, 1886, 1888.
Porete, Marguerite *Le Mirouer des Simples Ames*, ed. Romana Guarnieri. With Latin text ed. Paul Verdeyen. Corpus Christianorum 69. Turnholt: Typographi Brepol Editores Pontificii, 1986.
Prebish, C. S. *Monastic Discipline: The Sanskrit Prātimokṣa Sūtras of the Mahāsāṁgikas and Mūlasarvāstivādins.* Philadelphia: University of Pennsylvania Press, 1975.
Rabinow, Paul (ed.) *The Foucault Reader.* Harmondsworth: Penguin, 1984.
Rader, Rosemary *Breaking Boundaries: Male/Female Friendships in Early Christianity.* New York: Paulist Press, 1983.
Rājānaka Rāmakaṇṭha *The Bhagavadgītā with the Commentary Called Sarvatobhadra, Shāstrī*, Pandit M. K. Shāstrī (ed.). KSTS 64. Srinagar: Research Dept. Jammu and Kashmir, 1943.
Ramsey, Boniface (trs.) *John Cassian: The Conferences.* New York: Paulist Press, 1997.
*John Cassian: The Institutes.* New York: Newman Press, 2000.
Rappaport, R. A. *Ecology, Meaning and Religion.* Berkeley: North Atlantic Books, 1979.
*Ritual and Religion in the Making of Humanity.* Cambridge University Press, 1999.
Rhys Davids, Caroline A. *The Book of Kindred Sayings.* 2 parts. London: PTS, 1971, 1972.
Rhys Davids, T. W. and William Stede (eds.) *The Pali Text Society's Pali–English Dictionary.* London, Henley and Boston: PTS, 1921–1925.
Ricoeur, P. *Oneself as Another.* Chicago University Press, 1990.
Rist, J. M. *Eros and Psyche: Studies in Plato, Plotinus, and Origen.* University of Toronto Press, 1964.
*Augustine.* Cambridge University Press, 1994.
Roberts, R. *Religion, Theology and the Human Sciences.* Cambridge University Press, 2002.
Rogers, Eugene F. *Sexuality and the Christian Body.* Oxford: Blackwell, 1999.
Rose, Gillian *Love's Work.* London: Vintage, 1997.
Rosenthal, Raymond *Simone Weil: A Life.* New York: Pantheon, 1976.

Rousse, Jacques 'Lectio Divina et Lecture Spirituelle', DDS, 1976 vol. IX, pp. 470–87.
Rousseau, Philip *Ascetics, Authority and the Church.* Oxford University Press, 1978.
Rubin, Miri *Corpus Christi: The Eucharist in Late Medieval Culture.* Cambridge University Press, 1991.
Ryan, J. Joseph *Saint Peter Damiani and his Canonical Sources.* Toronto: Pontifical Institute of Mediaeval Studies, 1956.
Sadhale, Shastri Gajanana Shambu *The Bhagavadgītā with Eleven Commentaries* vols. I, III. Bombay: Gujarati Printing Press, 1935.
Said, E. *Orientalism.* New York: Pantheon, 1978.
Sanderson, A. 'Purity and Power Among the Brahmans of Kashmir' in M. Carruthers et al. (eds.), *The Category of the Person.* Cambridge University Press, 1985, pp. 190–216.
'Mandala and Agamic Identity in the Trika of Kashmir' in A. Padoux (ed.), *Mantras et Diagrammes Rituels dans l'Hindouisme*. Paris: CNRS, 1986, pp. 175–207.
'Śaivism and the Tantric Traditions' in Sutherland et al. (eds.), *The World's Religions*. London: Routledge, 1988, pp. 660–704.
Sargeant, W. *The Bhagavad-Gītā*. Revised ed. Albany: SUNY Press, 1994.
Sastri, A. Mahadeva *The Bhagavad-Gītā with the Commentary of Sri Sankaracharya.* Mysore: GTA Printing Works, 1901.
Śāstri, M. R. (ed.) *Vijñānabhairava with Commentaries of Kṣemarāja and Śivopaddhyāya.* Srinagar: KSTS, vol. 8 1918.
Sawan Singh *Philosophy of the Masters* vol. I. Beas: Radha Soami Satsang, 1963.
Schechner Richard and Willa Appel (eds.) *By Means of Performance: Intercultural Studies of Theatre and Ritual.* Cambridge University Press, 1990.
Schmalz, Matthew N. 'Tradition and Transgression in the Comparative Theology of Francis X. Clooney, S. J.' *Religious Studies Review* vol. 29, no. 2, April 2003, pp. 131–36.
Schopen, G. *Bones, Stones and Buddhist Monks.* Honolulu: University of Hawaii Press, 1997.
Settar, S. *Inviting Death: Indian Attitudes Towards Ritual Death.* Leiden: Brill, 1997.
Sharpe, E. *Comparative Religion: A History.* London: Duckworth, 1975.
Sherwood, Polycarp *St. Maximus the Confessor: The Ascetic Life and the Four Centuries on Charity.* London and Westminster, Maryland: The Newman Press and Longmans, Green and Co., 1955.
*The Earlier Ambigua of St. Maximus the Confessor.* Rome: Studia Anselmiana, 1955.
Shilling, C. *The Body and Social Theory.* 2nd ed. London: Sage, 2003.
Shils, Edward *Tradition.* London: Faber and Faber, 1981.
Silbur, Ilana F. *Virtuosity, Charisma and the Social Order: A Comparative Sociological Study of Monasticism in Theravada Buddhism and Medieval Christianity.* Cambridge University Press, 1995.
Silburn, Lilian *Kuṇḍalinī: Energy of the Depths*, trs. Jacques Gontier. Albany: SUNY Press, 1988.

Silburn, L. and A. Padoux (trs.) *Abhinavagupta – La Lumière sur les Tantras, Chapitres 1 à 5 du Tantrāloka.* Paris: Collège de France, Publications de l'Institut de Civilization Indienne, 1998.

Silverstein, M. and G. Urban (eds.) *Natural Histories of Discourse.* University of Chicago Press, 1996.

Sinkewicz, Robert E. *Evagrius of Pontus: The Greek Ascetic Corpus.* Oxford University Press, 2003.

Skudlarek, W. (ed.) *The Continuing Quest for God, Monastic Spirituality in Tradition and Transition.* Collegeville, MN: Liturgical Press, 1982.

Sobo, Elisa J. and Sandra Bell (eds.) *Celibacy, Culture and Society: The Anthropology of Sexual Abstinence.* Madison: University of Wisconsin Press, 2001.

Solignac, Aimé 'Péchés Capitaux', DDS, vol. XII part I, pp. 853–62.

Sontheimer, G.-D. and H. Kulke *Hinduism Reconsidered.* 2nd ed. Delhi: Manohar, 1997.

Sophrony, Archimandrite *St Silouan the Athonite,* trs. Rosemary Edmonds. New York: St Vladimir's Seminary Press, 1999.

Spiro, M. *Buddhism and Society: The Great Tradition and its Burmese Vicissitudes.* London: George Allen and Unwin, 1971.

Staal, Frits 'The Twelve Ritual Chants of the Nambudiri Agniṣṭoma' in J. C. Heesterman et al. (eds.), *Pratidānam Indian, Iranian and Indo-European Studies Presented to Franciscus Bernardus Jacobus Kuiper on his Sixtieth Birthday.* The Hague: Mouton, 1968, pp. 409–29.

'The Independence of Rationality from Literacy', *European Journal of Sociology* vol. 30, 1989, pp. 301–310.

*Rules Without Meaning: Ritual, Mantra and the Human Sciences.* New York: Peter Lang, 1989.

Stewart, C. *Cassian the Monk.* Oxford: Oxford University Press, 1998.

Stramara, Daniel F. 'Double Monasticism in the Greek East, Fourth through Eighth Centuries', *Journal of Early Christian Studies* vol. 6, no. 2, 1998, pp. 269–312.

Sutherland, Stewart, Leslie Houlden, Peter Clarke, and Friedhelm Hardy (eds.) *The World's Religions.* London, Routledge, 1988.

Tambiah, S. *The Buddhist Saints of the Forest and the Cult of Amulets: A Study of Charisma, Hagiography, Sectarianism, and Millennial Buddhism.* Cambridge University Press, 1984.

Taylor, Charles *The Sources of the Self: The Making of the Modern Identity.* Cambridge University Press, 1989.

Thompson, John B. 'Editor's Introduction' in P. Bourdieu, *Language and Symbolic Power,* trs. Matthew Adamson. Cambridge: Polity Press, 1991.

Thunburg, Lars *Microcosm and Mediator: The Theological Anthropology of Maximus the Confessor.* Alta Seminarii Neotestamentii Upsaliensis. Boktryckeri: Lund, 1965.

*Man and Cosmos: The Vision of St Maximus the Confessor.* New York: St Vladimir's Seminary Press, 1985.

Tiyavanich, Kamala *Forest Recollections: Wandering Monks in Twentieth-Century Thailand.* Honolulu: University of Hawaii Press, 1997.

Trainor, K. *Relics, Ritual, and Representation in Buddhism: Rematerializing the Sri Lankan Theravada Tradition.* Cambridge University Press, 1997.

Trenckner, V. (ed.) *The Milindapañho: Being Dialogues Between King Milinda and the Buddhist Sage Nāgasena.* London: PTS, 1962.

Turner, Denys *The Darkness of God: Negativity in Christian Mysticism.* Cambridge University Press, 1995.

Urban, Greg 'The "I" of Discourse' in Benjamin Lee and Greg Urban (eds.), *Semiotics, Self and Society.* Berlin, New York: Mouton de Gruyter, 1989, pp. 27–51.

*A Discourse-Centred Approach to Culture: Native South American Myths and Rituals.* Austin: University of Texas Press, 1991.

Vaage, Leif E. and Vincent L. Wimbush (eds.) *Asceticism and the New Testament.* New York and London: Routledge, 1999.

Valantasis, R. 'Constructions of Power in Asceticism', *Journal of the American Academy of Religion* vol. 63, 1995, pp. 775–821.

'Is the Gospel of Thomas Ascetical? Revisiting an Old Problem with New Theory', *Journal of Early Christian Studies* vol. 7, 1999, pp. 55–81.

Van Deun, Peter (ed.) *Liber Asceticus.* Corpus Christianorum Series Graeca 40. Leuven University Press, 2000.

Vāsudevāśrama, *Yatidharmaprakāśa*, vol. II. Vienna: University of Vienna Institute for Indology, 1977.

Vasugupta *Spanda-kārikā with the Vṛtti by Kallaṭabhaṭṭa*, ed. J. C. Chatterji. Srinagar: KSTS, vol. 5, 1916.

Vetö, Miklos *The Religious Metaphysics of Simone Weil*, trs. Joan Dargan. Albany: SUNY Press, 1994.

Viller, M. 'Aux Sources de la Spiritualité de S. Maxime. Les Oeuvres d'Evagre le Pontique', *Revue d'Ascetique et de Mystique* vol. 11, 1930, pp. 156–84, 239–68, 331–36.

Vitestam, Gösta 'Seconde Partie du Traité, qui Passe sous le Nom "La grande lettre d'Evagre le Pontique à Mélanie l'Ancienne". Publiée et Traduite d'après le Manuscrit du British Museum Add. 17 192.' *Scripta Minora.* Lund: Regiae Societatis Humaniorum Litterarum, vol. III, 1963–1964, pp. 3–29.

Vogüé, A. de *Histoire Littéraire du Mouvement Monastique dans l'Antiquité*, part I. Paris: Les Editions du Cerf, 1991.

von Balthasar, Hans Urs *Kosmische Liturgie.* French trs. Lhaumet, L. and H.-A. Prentout, *Liturgie Cosmique.* Paris: Aubier, 1947.

Vööbus, Arthur *History of Asceticism in the Syrian Orient: A Contribution to the History of Culture in the Near East* vol. II *Early Monasticism in Mesopotamia and Syria.* 3 vols. Louvain: Corpus Scriptorum Christianorum Orientalium, 184, 197, 500, 1958, 1960, 1988.

Ward, Benedicta *Sayings of the Desert Fathers: The Alphabetical Collection.* Kalamazoo: Cistercian Publications, 1975.

Warren, Henry Clark (ed.) *The Visuddhimagga of Buddhaghosacariya.* Cambridge, MA: Harvard University Press, 1950.

Weil, Simone *Waiting for God*, trs. Emma Craufurd. London: Routledge and Kegan Paul, 1951.

*The Need for Roots*, trs. Arthur C. Wills. London and Boston: Routledge and Kegan Paul, 1978 (1952).

*Gravity and Grace*, trs. Emma Craufurd. London: Routledge and Kegan Paul, 1952.

*The Notebooks of Simone Weil*, trs. A. Wills. 2 vols. London: Routledge and Kegan Paul, 1956.

*Oppression and Liberty*, trs. Arthur Wills and John Petrie. London: Routledge, 1958.

*First and Last Notebooks*, trs. Richard Rees. Oxford University Press, 1970.

*Formative Writings 1924–1941*, ed. and trs. Dorothy Tuck McFarland and Wilhemina van Hess. London: Routledge and Kegan Paul, 1987.

*Oeuvres Complètes*, ed. André A. Devaux and Florence de Lussy. 6 vols. Paris: Gallimard, 1994.

White, D. G. *The Alchemical Body: Siddha Traditions in Medieval India*. University of Chicago Press, 1996.

(ed.) *Tantra in Practice*. Princeton University Press, 2001.

*The Kiss of the Yoginī: Tantric Sex in its South Asian Contexts*. University of Chicago Press, 2003.

Wiethaus, Ulrike (ed.) *Maps of Flesh and Light: The Religious Experience of Medieval Women Mystics*. Syracuse University Press, 1993.

Wijayaratna, Mohan *Buddhist Monastic Life According to the Texts of the Theravāda Tradition*. Cambridge University Press, 1990.

Wimbush, V. C. and R. Valantasis (eds.) *Asceticism*. Oxford University Press, 1995.

Winch, Peter *Simone Weil: The Just Balance*. Cambridge University Press, 1989.

Woodward, J. F. L. (trs.) *The Book of Kindred Sayings*, part IV, vol. V. London: PTS, 1972.

Wyschogrod, Edith *Saints and Postmodernism: Revisioning Moral Philosophy*. University of Chicago Press, 1990.

Young, Katherine K. (ed.) *Hermeneutical Paths to the Sacred Worlds of India*. Atlanta: Scholars Press, 1996.

Zaner, R. *The Problem of Embodiment*. The Hague: Nijhof, 1971.

# Index